Samuel Woolcock Christophers

Hymn-Writers and their Hymns

Samuel Woolcock Christophers

Hymn-Writers and their Hymns

ISBN/EAN: 9783744780926

Printed in Europe, USA, Canada, Australia, Japan

Cover: Foto ©Lupo / pixelio.de

More available books at **www.hansebooks.com**

HYMN-WRITERS

AND

THEIR HYMNS.

BY

THE REV. S. W. CHRISTOPHERS.

"There are, it may be, so many kinds of voices in the world, and none of them are without signification...... What is it then? I will sing with the spirit, and I will sing with the understanding also."—1 COR. xiv. 10, 15.

SECOND EDITION.

ANSON D. F. RANDOLPH & CO.,
770 BROADWAY, COR. 9TH ST.,
NEW YORK.

TO THE DAUGHTER OF A HOME ONCE RICH IN THE

MUSIC OF HYMNS AND PSALMS;

TO

EMMA,

THE WIFE AND MOTHER,

WHOSE VOICE AND SMILE STILL AWAKEN DAILY SONGS

IN THE HOUSE OF MY PILGRIMAGE,

These pages are Dedicated,

WITH MOST TENDER AND HALLOWED AFFECTION,

BY HER HUSBAND,

S. W. CHRISTOPHERS.

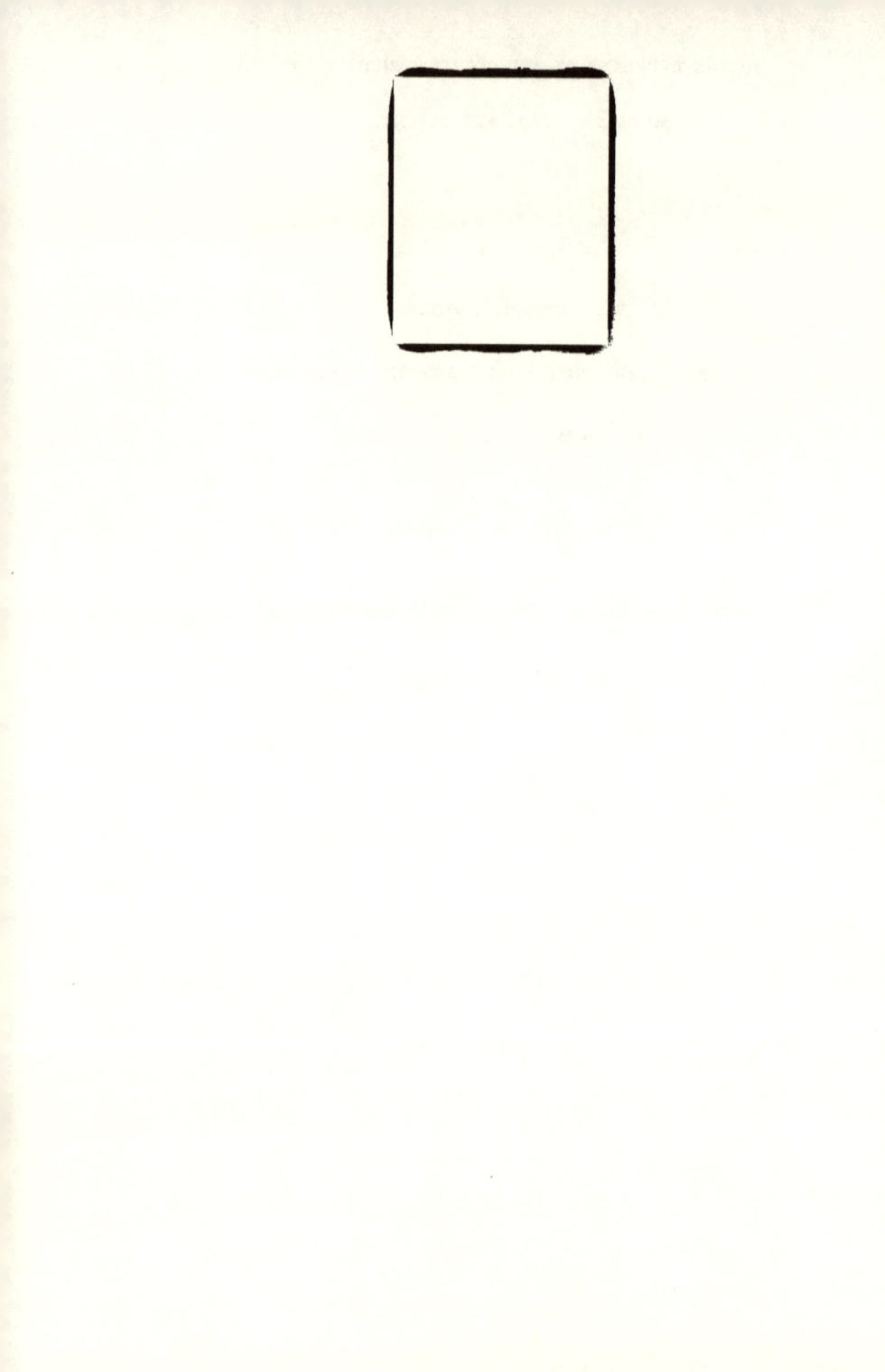

CONTENTS.

	PAGE
TO THE READER	ix

CHAPTER I.

INTRODUCTORY CHAPTER 1

CHAPTER II.

THE FIRST HYMN-BOOK 14

CHAPTER III.

HYMNS OF THE LATTER DAY MORNING 29

CHAPTER IV.

HYMNS OF THE FATHERS 44

CHAPTER V.

MORE HYMNS OF THE FATHERS 57

CHAPTER VI.

HYMNS OF OLD ENGLAND'S CHRISTIAN BIRTH-TIME . . . 71

CHAPTER VII.

HYMNS FROM OLD CLOISTERS 86

CHAPTER VIII.

SONGS IN HIGH PLACES 100

CHAPTER IX.

SONGS IN PRISON 116

CHAPTER X.

PSALMS IN ENGLISH METRE 132

CHAPTER XI.

HYMN-MENDERS 148

CHAPTER XII.

HYMNS OF CREATION 164

CHAPTER XIII.

HYMNS ABOUT THE BOOK 180

CHAPTER XIV.

HYMNS OF THE SABBATH 195

CHAPTER XV.

HYMNS BY THE WAY 211

CHAPTER XVI.

HYMNS ON THE WATERS 227

CONTENTS. vii

CHAPTER XVII.

PAGE
SONGS OF THE MORNING 243

CHAPTER XVIII.

SONGS IN THE NIGHT 257

CHAPTER XIX.

MARRIAGE SONGS AND BIRTH-DAY HYMNS 272

CHAPTER XX.

HYMNS FROM BENEATH THE CLOUD 290

CHAPTER XXI.

HYMNS OF GETHESEMANE AND THE CROSS 306

CHAPTER XXII.

FUNERAL HYMNS 322

CHAPTER XXIII.

JUDGMENT HYMNS 335

CHAPTER XXIV.

SONGS OF GLORY 349

TO THE READER.

"What! another hymn-book? Why surely the world has hymn-books enough." Well, that may be, and yet here is something like another. It is something like another, as there are hymns in it; and yet it is rather unlike any other, in that it has the hymns interwoven with what may be called gossip, innocent, and, it is hoped, not unpleasant gossip, about the hymns and those who wrote them. Who does not like to know the why, the when, and the wherefore of men and things? Who does not love a chat about the people and the affairs which interest him? Here, then, is chat about hymns, their birth and parentage, their circumstances, their character and their influence. These pages make no pretensions to learning—that is left to the doctors. Nor do they aim at criticism, that belongs to those who go up the Rhine. Neither do they affect the style of history—that has been well done in other volumes. It will be enough if the lover of sacred music should snatch up the book now and then, after a good practice in psalmody, and opening it anywhere, find a chapter containing some story about a dear old hymn which makes that hymn still dearer to his heart. Or, if those who like to have some fresh stanzas always on their merry lips, should catch new strains from the voices which mingle in these chapters of chat; or, if those who turn over the leaves should find an hour's pleasant communion with the spirit of Christian hymns, or with the mind and hearts of those who wrote them; or, if a chapter, perchance, arrest the soul of any reader, and teach him the secret of a happy, cheerful, and tuneful life, a life of inward hymn and song,—the book will answer its purpose, and fill its place. Whatever may be thought of the setting, the gems with which these pages are enriched, the psalms and hymns which illuminate the text, need no commendation but their own transparent richness and beauty.

Many of these hymns are from living authors, and grateful acknowledgments are due for permission to reprint them. Mrs. Julius Collins's fine rendering of the hymn from the Synagogue Morning Service has been inserted by the kind consent of Dr. Benisch. Mrs. Charles has freely sanctioned the use of several of her translations of ancient hymns. The following are hers:—Hymn from Ephrem Syrus "On the Children in Paradise;" St. Ambrose's "Advent Hymn;" Bede's hymn "On the Ascension;" portions of St. Bernard's hymn, "To Christ on the Cross;"

the "Veni, Sancte Spiritus," by King Robert II. of France; and the "Dies Iræ." These are all taken from her beautiful and instructive "Voice of Christian Life in Song." Five hymns translated by Miss Winkworth are reprinted from her "Lyra Germanica," by permission of Messrs. Longman, Green, and Co.—"Gustavus Adolphus' Battle Song," "Queen Maria of Hungary's Song," "Jesus my Redeemer Lives," by Louisa Henrietta, Electress of Brandenburg; "Leave all to God," by Anton Ulrich, Duke of Brunswick; and Notker's hymn by Luther, "In the Midst of Life, Behold." All the other renderings of ancient hymns, without a name in the volume, are new. Among the modern hymns selected, those by the Rev. John S. B. Monsell are from his "Parish Musings," and are given by the gifted author's permission. The Rev. John Keble, author of the "Christian Year," very kindly sanctions the use of those hymns, which are inserted as from his pen. Most of the other hymns in the volume come from hymnists who are now above our thanks; but "the memory of the just is blessed."

Yes, it may be repeated, "the memory of the just is blessed;" for scarcely had the above record of John Keble's Christian kindness found its way to the press, before he too had joined the hymnists who are "now above our thanks." It was but the other evening that one looked at him as his bending form moved gently over the sands along the beautiful shore of Mount's Bay, in

Cornwall; and as his peaceful face was now and then turned upwards to the star-lighted heavens, it seemed as if he were inwardly singing his own deeply spiritual hymn for "the Fourth Sunday after Easter;" but those who kept him company little thought that he would so soon realize the consoling prophecy of his own verse :—

>Then, fainting soul, arise and sing;
>Mount, but be sober on the wing;
>Mount up, for heaven is won by prayer,
>Be sober, for thou art not there;
>Till death the weary spirit free,
>Thy God hath said, 'Tis good for thee
>To walk by faith and not by sight:
> Take it on trust a little while;
>Soon shalt thou read the mystery right
> In the full sunshine of His smile.

S. W. C.

CROYDON, *May*, 1866.
  (*First Edition.*)

HYMN-WRITERS AND THEIR HYMNS.

INTRODUCTORY CHAPTER.

PSALMS of praise were the first-fruits of creation. Hymns were the earliest utterances of human nature in the morning light of the world—man's first responses to the voice of his Creator—the earth's first echoes to the music of the heavens, when "the morning stars sang together, and all the sons of God shouted for joy." This world's first love was told in hymns. Music first broke forth in psalms. The earliest recorded essays of human language are in spiritual song. Spiritual songs were the delight of the world in the days of her youth; they have been her solace during her advance towards maturity; and they will brighten the eventide and close of her life. The antediluvian age seems to have had its darling household songs. In patriarchal times the father's blessing was sometimes poured forth in lofty hymnic measures. In the youth-tide of her national life Israel gave out her joys of deliverance in sea-side hymns. She was once shut up between the mountains, the sea, and her infuriated enemies. In her distress God divided the waters before her, and the tribes went safely through the depths. Their foes, essaying to follow them, were overwhelmed in the flood; and while chariotcer and horseman were struggling with the waves, and the sea was uttering a loud requiem over the sinking hosts, the redeemed multitude confidently stood on the

A

shore, and mingled their hymn of triumph with the sound of the waters.

> Sing unto the Lord,
> For He hath triumphed gloriously!
> The horse and his rider
> He hath cast into the sea!
> The Lord is my strength and song,
> And He is become my salvation.
>
> . . . . . .
>
> Who is like unto Thee,
> O Lord, among the gods?
> Who is like Thee—
> Glorious in holiness,
> Fearful in praises,
> Doing wonders?
>
> . . . . . .
>
> The Lord shall reign for ever and ever!

The song which thus first rose "o'er Egypt's dark sea" rose again, ever and anon, along the desert and in the land of promise. Israel kept up the circlings of her religious dances to the song of Moses and the music of Miriam. In the fulness of her meridian strength, her psalms were her delights as she went up to the house of the Lord, and plaintive hymns have been the solace of her faithful children all through the weary periods of her decline. The primitive and purer literature of even those false or corrupted systems of religion which sprung up against the early claims of the true Messiah take the hymnic form, as if that form must be the most natural, the most sacred, and the most happy mode of religious utterance. The foundations of the Christian Church, too, were laid amidst the hymnings of her first converts. She owes the preservation of her spiritual life, and the continued purity of her belief, in a large measure, to the service of song; and how many of her generations have left hymns as the only living memorials of their character and works. "Psalms and hymns and spiritual songs" form the native language of Christianity. The religion of the new covenant is the happy religion. It calls its people to "rejoice evermore, and in everything to give thanks." When it is allowed to exert its proper and full influence on the human character, it regulates the affections, without destroying man's capacity for delight; it composes and cheers the soul; it banishes mere levity, and checking all vicious and boisterous mirth, it fills the mind with serene joy, and gives a tone of cheerfulness to the manners and to the voice. But how many have mistaken the Christian's calling! The Christianity of some has been seemingly made up of depressing recollections of the past, gloomy views of the present, and dark apprehensions of the future. And if an inward joy is ever felt, such people think it their duty to repress it, or at least not to give it expression, but rather to keep up an aspect in unbroken accordance with the gravity of their notions. They are not of this world, they say, and therefore they have no smiles for those around them, no songs for themselves. Theirs are melancholy manners, austere looks, and voiceless lives—a religion which threatens to extinguish all gladness, to dark the face of nature, and to destroy the very relish of life. But does not the Saviour call His people to open a cheerful face upon the world, and to cheer it with grateful hymns? "Let your light so shine before men," says He, "that they may see your beautiful works, and glorify your Father which is in heaven." "Who is she that looketh forth as the morning, fair as the moon, and clear as the sun?" Is it not the Messiah's spouse, the Saviour's Church? And who should be as cheerful as the sunlight, if Christ's people are not? "Truly the light is sweet, and a pleasant thing it is to behold the sun; which is as a bridegroom coming out of his chamber, and rejoiceth as a strong man to run a race." All nature is glad when the day-spring opens. The sparkling sea, the lucid rivulet, the fluttering leaf, the colours and the tones of creation, all tell how the sunbeams cheer the world. All see the light, and all bless the light-bearer. And what is so cheerful in its character and influence as the Christian religion? "Light is sown for the righteous, and gladness for the upright in heart." Revelation opens around the Christian solemnities holy enough to chasten his spirit, but it throws a light upon God's character and will which inspires the believer with sacred cheerfulness. All the principles and all the feelings which now command him dispose the Christian to form the habit of turning the bright side of things towards himself—the habit of keeping Divine goodness in sight, of marking the blessings of every moment as it passes, and of communing with a happy future, until he learns to speak to himself "in psalms and hymns and spiritual songs, singing, and making melody in his heart unto the Lord." And when praise thus lives in the heart, it will express itself in pleasant music and lively measures. The peaceful conscience and merry heart will have songs for the outside world. And when all Christians breathe this happy spirit of their religion, the Christian Church will be the beautiful embodiment of a happy godliness, and will be ceaseless in its service of song.

But as the rise and advance and decline of the human race, or of human empires, or of religious systems, may somewhat answer to the stages of an individual life—or as the history of a single life may picture the course of the world, or the career of a people—so those favourite modes of utterance which the world or any one of its communities have used, as distinctive of the different stages of its course have their answering types in the most-loved forms of individual expression. Childhood loves to lisp its joys in a hymn. Manhood, in its times of purest and most exalted feeling, speaks to itself in hymns. Hymns, too, most naturally weave themselves into the language of declining life, and often supply the departing soul with its most happy words.

There is scarcely anything that retains a more permanent influence over human thought and feeling in the present life than the hymns and songs which the soul drinks in during our childhood. The simplicity of children makes them capable of being swayed through life by the earliest lessons. The little one's mind is so retentive that first impressions are most lasting and powerful. The first supplies of knowledge find the deepest and most secure lodgment in the soul; and especially when the knowledge comes in an agreeable form, as in the rhythm and rhyme of simple hymns. These are entertained for life, and often live to make themselves felt in spite of all the changes and distracting circumstances of the later course. There has been many, many an instance like those which, a few years ago, were recorded in a pastoral address to a Christian Church. The minister was guarding his flock against the danger of betrayal into hardness and bitter feeling by those trials which spring out of the seeming unequal distribution of good and evil in the world. "I am free to tell you," said he, "that sometimes in the course of my life, I have been powerfully tempted to hardness when the thought has been insinuated, that my share in life has been wearisome toil and frequent depression, while others have been lapped in ease and plenty, though apparently not a whit more deserving than myself; and I confess that now and then the temptation has been so timed that my soul has gone too far through the process of transformation into something like cold iron or steel. But one gentle corrective has always prevented the hardening process from being complete. When I have been all but shut up to the curse of a stony heart, some stanza from one of the simple hymns or 'divine songs,' which used to touch and soften me in childhood, has come up from its home in my memory, and like a divine charm has soothed and melted me into childlike tenderness, simplicity, and love. Verses that seemed to have been lost for years have suddenly sprung into life again, and brought so many good recollections in their train, that my rugged nature has yielded at once, and all within and all without have responded to the music of the hymn, as the face of nature answers to the genial sunbeams of spring. And I have met in the course of my life with many others whose experience might be taken as a reflection of my own. One remarkable instance, however, somewhat varies from the rest; inasmuch as it shows how the well-timed recurrence of verses once fondly cherished by the young memory and heart, may give the deciding touch to the wandering soul, and convert a prodigal from 'the error of his way.' A good man in declining life told me that the first book in which, as a child, he took an interest, was a small edition of Watts's 'Hymns and Divine Songs' for children. Each hymn was headed by a woodcut, and one especially was his favourite. It represented a little boy, something like himself, as he thought, leaning at an open window, looking with a calm happy face on the setting sun, which was throwing his parting light upon a quiet country scene. Many of the hymns, and that one in particular, had been read often, until they lived in his soul. But as he grew up, the impressions were worn off by more exciting and less pure thoughts and pursuits. He fell into a course of dissipation and vice, and seemed for a time to be given up to sin, and devoted to ruin. Worn down at last, and threatened with consumption, he was ordered into the country for change of air ; and after some time spent in quietness and retirement, far away from the scenes of old temptations, he wandered out one evening about sunset, and hanging pensively over a gate, he watched the sun as it sunk behind the copse, and was throwing its last beams upon the silent and peaceful hill-side. There was a hush upon his spirits, and suddenly, as if sketched by an unseen hand before his inward eye, the little picture which used to interest his boyish mind lived again, and the hymn which it illustrated seemed to be spoken sweetly to his heart—

> And now another day is gone,
> I'll sing my Maker's praise.

The tear started. He had seen many of his days go, but as yet his Maker had never heard an even-song from his lips or from his heart. What an ungrateful life his had been! The 'remembrance was grievous.' But his heart was broken, and there and then the softened man made his vows of return to God, and offered the prayer which was answered in blessings which filled both the mornings and evenings of his mature life with hymns and songs of thanksgiving and praise."

And how important, and holy, and happy is the office of psalms and hymns in the service of human nature amidst the struggles and toils, the conflicts and victories, the sorrows and joys of mature life. Their mission has been to the multitude as well as the individual heart. How often has the popular use of a few songs swayed the thoughts and feelings of a nation, or quickened, united, directed, and ruled the energies of a people, or permanently given a distinct character to an entire race. Facts would sustain the philosophy of the man who said, "Let me furnish a nation with its songs, and I will govern it." Psalms and hymns, too, have many times afforded the secret of union, and harmony, and strength, and consolation to persecuted households, down-trodden tribes, and oppressed populations. They have been as food to the famine-stricken crowd, and as waters in the wilderness to fugitive churches. How often have they cheered the souls of congregated confessors in Roman catacombs, in the recesses of Eastern deserts, in the fastnesses of Swiss mountains, and in the Highland glens and moorland hollows of Scotland. The psalm and choral chant have sometimes nerved the host for battle on behalf of home, and conscience, and truth. The Divine Spirit Himself has recorded an exemplar "hallelujah victory." Jehoshaphat's appeal for Divine help against the enemies of goodness and faith was answered by a revelation of God's order of battle. "And when he had consulted with the people, he appointed singers unto the Lord, and that should praise the beauty of holiness as they went out before the army, and to say, Praise the Lord, for His mercy endureth for ever. And when they began to sing and to praise, the Lord set ambushments against the children of Ammon, Moab, and Mount Seir, which were come against Judah, and they were smitten." The singers were victorious; the spoil was gathered to the music of psalms. "And on the fourth day they assembled themselves in the valley of Berachah, for there they blessed the Lord; therefore the name of the same place was called the valley of Berachah unto this day. Then they returned every man of Judah and Jerusalem, and Jehoshaphat in the forefront of them, to go again to Jerusalem with joy, for the Lord had made them to rejoice over their enemies." Yes, and since then many a Christian army has kept up the strain, and have made prayerful hymns and hymns of praise their battle songs. Nor has Jehoshaphat's victory been the only "hallelujah victory." It was probably repeated once on the Welsh border, and has had its antitypes in the history of Protestant struggles for freedom on many a storied field of Europe.

And how much of their youthful freshness, and manly courage, and constitutional vigour, and public spirit, nations owe to the habitual use of their national anthems, who can tell? How France has glowed at the sound of a popular hymn! how Scotland kindles at an old psalm or song which embalms the name of her hero! and how Englishmen's hearts swell and come together when they sing
Rule Britannia!
or when they uncover and unite in the grand old strain,
God save our gracious Queen!

It is most pleasant to the Christian, however, to trace

the influence of devout psalmody in the shaping of a people's happily distinct character. Among the most blessed results of faithfully-administered truth to a teachable and obedient people, is their perpetuated fondness for "psalms, and hymns, and spiritual songs." Nor can there be any richer or more agreeable fruits of the Holy Spirit's work upon human masses than a popular love for psalmody, the culture of sacred music in the people's homes, and the habitual enjoyment of favourite hymns continued from parents to children, and renewing its freshness among children's children. Will the old Scotch version of the psalms ever cease to be music to those who owe so much to the covenanting fathers who first sang them? Will the spiritual songs of the first Reformers ever die out from the mind and heart of Germany? The cheerful character and influence of the primitive churches left memorials for many generations among the hymn-singing populations of many spots in Europe. Richard Baxter's labours at Kidderminster were crowned with many a holy song. He toiled and prayed until from every house within his pastorate there was daily the all but ceaseless voice of psalms and hymns. He was literally "compassed about with songs of deliverance." Vital piety makes people cheerful, and their cheerfulness naturally expresses itself in devout and merry rhyme and metre.

Perhaps no district in England has a population so deeply and widely imbued with religious thought and feeling as the county of Cornwall. As a whole, the Cornish folk may be called a religious people, and their great love for sacred music, and especially hymn singing, may be at once a cause and effect of their sustained religious life. Nowhere has the gospel of Christ wrought more happy changes; nowhere has it left a more permanently cheerful impress; nowhere could an entire population so generally illustrate obedience to the apostolic rule, "Is any merry? let him sing psalms." No one who has seen them can forget the lines and knots of merry creatures who preserve a kind of elegant appearance amidst their rough work, in open sheds, and among heaps of tin and copper ore on the surface of the Cornish mines. Who could forget these girls' standard and style of beauty? and who that has heard them will ever forget the music of their hymns, as they sing in concert, while they ply their hammers, that music at once so reverent, so earnest, and so lovely? They seem to have hymns appropriate for all times and seasons, and sometimes their stanzas have been beautifully timed. A few of the more gay and thoughtless of a large group had been indulging a laugh at one good Christian girl, whom they charged with inconsistent conformity to the world because she wore a pair of tasteful ear-rings. The jeers were meekly borne for a while, but at length the persecuted girl lifted up her voice in song, and quietly taking the jewels from her ears, she placed them on the block before her, and demolished them with a stroke of her hammer, singing as she did it a stanza from a favourite hymn—

> Neither passion nor pride Thy cross can abide,
> But melt in the fountain that streams from Thy side.

Her persecutors were silenced, and blushed as she sang out her hymn of submissive but triumphant faith. The same spirit of holy song is breathed by the men, who cheer the deep caverns in which they toil with heartfelt psalmody. The road-side and the cottage hearth, the engine-house, the stream-works, the moorland, and the barren carn, the unpretending chapel, and the quiet grave-yard, are all hallowed in turn by the melodies and harmonies of this hymn and anthem-loving race. Seldom have the hearts and voices of a race been more graciously blended in the service of Him who said, by the spirit of prophecy, "In the midst of the church will I sing praise unto Thee."

The claims of Christianity as the religion of universal man, and its adaptation to all races and people, circumstances and times, are beautifully illustrated by the fact, that those happy features of character which it impressed upon the Cornish families are the same with those which distinguish the Christianized tribes of Southern Africa. On the testimony of a venerable misssionary, who was the first to open the gospel to the Little Namacquas, that popular love of sacred song which is so peculiar to the Keltic masses in Western England, became the habitual feeling and distinctive pleasure of the converted African tribes. Hymn singing in both cases seemed to be the natural action of public religious life. Spiritual songs, says the African evangelist, were soon interwoven with their daily existence; all their movements seemed to be made to the music of hymns; and how many a time I have listened to their voices of an evening, as they walked homeward from the field or the bush singing some favourite hymn, as a kind of spiritual march. I remember having my heart deeply touched once as I hearkened to the happy bands psalming it, and responding to one another while approaching the village. I caught the strain of an old Dutch hymn—

> Faith loves the Saviour, and beholds
> His sufferings, death, and pain;
> And this shall ne'er grow old nor cold,
> Till we with Him shall reign.

It was the song of Southern Africa's first love. The first-fruits of Ethiopia's praise to God; the tuneful earnest of what an ancient hymn foretold. "Princes shall come out of Egypt, Ethiopia shall soon stretch out her hands unto God. Sing unto God, ye kingdoms of the earth; O sing praises unto the Lord; Selah!"

But what Christian psalmody has done for nations, and races, and tribes, it does for many an individual man and woman. What hymns have been to the multitude they have been to many a solitary Christian soul. To the gentle and to the simple, to the great and to the small, to the bond and to the free, to the strong and to the weak, to the cultured and to the rude, divine songs have served to brighten and bless the different stages and turns of personal history. Many of the ruling spirits of the world, men whose names will be always landmarks in history, have had tender fondness for psalmody and holy song. There have been royal psalmists, imperial songsters, and courtly hymnists. Many a great leader of his generation, while he has been guiding the world's mind and heart amidst the dangers of revolution, and through the deep and broad processes of moral and religious renewal, has cheered his own soul with favourite hymns. Hymns have been his chosen expressions of joy in success. Hymns have been his solace in moments of darkness and depression. Luther and his companions, with all their bold readiness for danger and death in the cause of truth, had times when their feelings were akin to those of a divine singer who said, "Why art thou cast down, O my soul?" But in such hours the unflinching Reformer would cheerily say to his friend Melancthon, "Come, Philip, let us sing the forty-sixth Psalm;" and they could sing it in Luther's own characteristic version—

> A sure stronghold our God is He,
> A timely shield and weapon;
> Our help He'll be, and set us free
> From every ill can happen.
>
> . . . . .
>
> And were the world with devils fill'd,
> All eager to devour us,
> Our souls to fear shall little yield,
> They cannot overpower us.

Later Reformers in our own land have been equally remarkable for their love of sacred music, and their aptness at using it for the encouragement of the multitude, and their own secret comfort amidst their sufferings and toils.

Some of the noblest intellects, too, the most cultured and refined of their race—men whose thoughts and feelings are embalmed in an undying literature, have had each his own cherished psalm or tenderly-loved hymn. And the psalm or hymn has been called up in every time of need; as if it had a comforting power which no other voice could bring. The great Niebuhr was lovingly attached to von Lowenstern's hymn—

> Christ, Thou the champion of that war-worn host.

And might be heard now and then refreshing his own soul amidst its intense labours and researches by murmuring the metrical prayer—

> And give us peace; peace in the church and school,
> Peace to the powers who o'er our country rule,
> Peace to the conscience, peace within the heart,
> Do Thou impart.
>
> So shall Thy goodness here be still adored,
> Thou Guardian of Thy little flock, dear Lord;
> And heaven and earth through all eternity
> Shall worship Thee!

And what was the solace of Niebuhr has been the consolation of many a commanding and highly cultured mind.

The hymn of joy and the hymn of plaintive appeal have ministered strength and peace, in sweet alternation, through all the scenes of mental action.

And how often has the master mind, the truly great soul finished its brilliant and successful course with a closing hymn! Saintly and useful men like Rowland Hill have died on consecrated ground with the music of a hymn in their souls. But minds of another class also have ended their course with songs. Walter Scott's last utterances were stanzas of favourite ancient hymns. It is stated that Cobden departed repeating that grand old strain, rendered from the German by John Wesley—

> Thee will I love, my joy, my crown,
>   Thee will I love, my Lord, my God:
> Thee will I love, beneath Thy frown,
>   Or smile—Thy sceptre or Thy rod:
> What though my flesh and heart decay,
> Thee shall I love in endless day!

And our own Prince Albert "the good," breathed as his last song, while his spirit mounted—

> Rock of Ages, cleft for me,
> Let me hide myself in Thee!

And how many thousands after thousands in the more retired and obscure scenes of life have had psalms and hymns of victory on their dying lips.

Indeed, the holiest and best of people, those who have done most to make the world happy, have hallowed every stage of life, every turn in their history, every relation which they have sustained, and every time and season of their mortal pilgrimage with "thanksgiving and the voice of melody." Their record is above; but neither they nor their hymns can be forgotten below. Many of their names are recorded in the following pages; and some of their hymns are interwoven with the outlines of their character and the memorials of their history.

And perhaps the lover of sacred melody will learn to love hymn-writers and their hymns more deeply, and to sing with more spiritual joy, while he spends an hour, now and then, over chapters about the first hymn-book; and hymns of the latter day morning, hymns of the fathers, and hymns of old England's Christian birth-time; hymns from old cloisters, songs in high places, and songs in prison. From these he may pass to chapters about psalms in English metre, hymn menders, and songs of creation. Then come hymns about the book, songs of the Sabbath, hymns by the way, hymns on the waters, hymns of the morning, and songs in the night. Nor will the world ever lose its interest in chapters on marriage songs and birthday hymns, or hymns from beneath the cloud, hymns of Gethsemane and the cross, funeral hymns, judgment hymns, and songs of glory.

To catch the spirit, and to be enriched with the music of the first hymn-book, is to be prepared for daily " speaking to ourselves in psalms, and hymns, and spiritual songs, singing and making melody in our hearts to the Lord; giving thanks always for all things unto God and the Father, in the name of our Lord Jesus Christ;" and a life thus spent will certainly issue in songs of glory.

CHAPTER II.

THE FIRST HYMN-BOOK.

"Thy statutes have been my songs in the house of my pilgrimage."

SPEAK to yourselves in psalms, and hymns, and spiritual songs, singing and making melody in your heart to the Lord. Happy advice from a happy man! If ever man had his life on earth enriched and brightened by the psalmody of heaven, St. Paul was that man. He seems now and then to be an impersonation of the jubilant religion which he preached. Here and there he uses a threefold form of speech, as if the notion of a Trinity were ever in his mind, and as if the Triune form gave the completest possible expression to his feeling as to that full harmony of fixed belief, triumphant principle, and exultant feeling, to which he called the Christian Church. He challenged the generations of the future to an unbroken service of song, and the family lines of God's children have ever since been singing and chanting in response. Paul had heard the chant of the Temple service, and had so often joined in the songs and hymns of the synagogue, that, like his fellow apostles of the circumcision, he enjoyed ample means of expression for all the joys of the Holy Spirit's dispensation. The church of his fathers had treasured the forms of praise which now furnish the kingdom of Christ with hymns and songs for all ages of its militant and triumphant course. Nor is the harmony of inspired truth ever felt to be more impressive than in the use which the blessed Spirit makes of Old Testament psalmody in his work on the souls of New Testament saints. The three inspired songs which graced the manifestation of Immanuel: the rich gush of Mary's devotional joy, the prophetic strain of Zacharias, and the holy song of Simeon, all show the influence of Old Testament style and spirit. "The Word of Christ," as once issued in the law of "Moses, and in the Prophets, and in the Psalms," had dwelt in Mary's heart so "richly" as to give its own character to her rapturous utterances. The lips of Zacharias were touched with fire from the very altar before which the Messianic seers had kindled into ecstasy. And Simeon had chanted the hymns of his rapt ancestry until his own inspired sentences breathed in unison with voices from "holy men of old." Mary, and Hannah, and Deborah drank into one another's spirit; and their tones have that likeness and unlikeness which belong to daughters of the same family. The celebration of Old Testament victories and the joy of gospel salvation melt into oneness and harmony in "the song of Moses and the Lamb." And when will earth or heaven cease to echo to the psalms of ancient Zion? Judah's holy song book, "the Book of Psalms, hath exercised the hearts and lips of all saints, and is replenished with the types of all possible spiritual feelings, and suggests the forms of all God-ward emotions, and furnishes the choice expressions of all true worship, the utterances of all divine praise, the expressions of all spiritual humility, with the raptures of all spiritual joy." This well-spring in the desert has never failed to refresh the pilgrim church from age to age. Israelite and Samaritan, "Greek and Jew, circumcision and uncircumcision, barbarian, Scythian, bond and free," east and west, the old world and the new—all confess the sacred power and sweetness of David's voice; all kindle into songs under his leadership. That ever-living sympathy with the most cherished interests of God's children, that spirituality which so deeply touches the believer's inner man; and that expression which so engages all conditions of men, and adapts itself to all circumstances of humanity; indeed, all the immortal sweetness, grandeur, and power which distinguish the Old Testament Psalms, are found living still, and renewing their freshness in the inspired hymns and songs of those who went up to the Temple in "the last days," and spoke "in other tongues the wonderful works of God, as the Spirit gave them utterance." How much like a psalm of ancient Israel is that early song of the primitive Christians which the Spirit has left on record. The little persecuted community sang in the style of their fathers, when they "lift up their voices to God with one accord and said,"

> Lord, Thou art God,
> Which hast made heaven and earth,
> And the sea,
> And all that in them is:
> Who by the mouth of David
> Thy servant, hath said,
> Why did the heathen rage
> And the people imagine vain things?
> The kings of the earth stood up,
> And the rulers were gathered together
> Against the Lord,
> And against His Christ.
> For of a truth,
> Against Thy Holy Child Jesus,
> Whom Thou hast anointed,
> Both Herod and Pontius Pilate,
> With the Gentiles,
> And the people of Israel,
> Are gathered together;
> For to do whatever Thy hand
> And Thy counsel
> Determined before to be done.
> And now, Lord!
> Behold their threatenings!
> And grant unto Thy servants,
> That with all boldness
> They may speak Thy word,
> By stretching forth Thy hand to heal;
> And that signs and wonders
> May be done
> By the name
> Of Thy Holy Child Jesus.

Nearest akin to these odes of highest inspiration are the songs of the synagogue service. The family features, and much in the distinctive manner, sometimes deeply touch the soul. In their simple grandeur, lofty vigour, solemn measure, and glow of holy feeling, they are felt to be close allies of the anthems of revelation; though not bearing the divine honours of those holier forms into which the Spirit of God once "breathed the breath of life." Would you realize the grand simplicity of primitive hymns? Then go to the synagogue and hear the lineal descendants of

God's ancient people sing in their Sabbath morning service—

> Praised be Thy name for ever, O our King!
> Thou Sovereign God!
> The Great and the Holy in heaven and in earth:
> For unto Thee, Jehovah, our God,
> And the God of our fathers,
> Belong song and praise;
> Hymn and psalm;
> Strength and dominion;
> Victory, greatness, and power;
> Adoration and glory;
> Holiness and majesty;
> Blessings and thanksgivings;
> From this time forth and for ever!
> Blessed art Thou, Jehovah!
> Sovereign God!
> Great in praises;
> The God of thanksgivings;
> The Lord of wonders;
> The Chooser of song and psalmody;
> King Eternal! Ever-living God!

Sometimes the utterance of the synagogue is as the voice of one longing soul; now jubilant, now melting into warm, tender, spiritual feeling, and now swelling again into lofty celebrations of Divine Majesty; as if the devout heart breathed by turns the spirit of the Psalms, the Canticles, and the Prophets. So it is in "the Hymns of Glory."

> Sweet hymns I attune,
> And songs I weave,
> For my soul panteth after Thee!
> My soul longeth in the shadow of Thy hand
> All Thy secret of secrets to know!
> Whilst my words speak Thy glory,
> My heart is yearning for Thy love.
> Therefore in Thee I speak of Thy glorious things;
> And with songs of love I honour Thy name:
> I will tell of Thy glory
> Though I saw Thee not;
> And though I knew Thee not,
> I arrange my similitudes of Thee.
> By the hand of Thy prophets,
> By Thy trusty servants,
> Thou hast symbolized the glorious honour of Thy majesty.
> Thy greatness and Thy might
> They named after the powers of Thy creation.

B

> They compared Thee,
> But not as Thou art;
> And they likened Thee,
> According to Thy works,
> They represented Thee in multiplied visions:
> Yet behold, Thou art one in all semblances!
>
> . . . .
>
> The Head, Thy Word, is the Truth,
> Proclaiming from the beginning,
> From generation to generation,
> Thy people are ever seeking Thee!
> Array thyself in the multitude of my psalms,
> And let my singing come near to Thee!
> Let my praise be a crown to Thy head,
> And my hymns acceptable incense.
> Let the song of the poor be precious to Thee,
> As the anthems over the gifts of the altar.
> Let my blessing ascend to the Almighty Head,
> The Beginning, the Lifegiver, the Righteous Mighty One!
> And when I bless, let Thy Head be inclined to me,
> And take it to Thyself as chief perfumes;
> Let it be pleasant to Thee,
> For my soul panteth unto Thee!

The daughters of Israel have not yet lost the spirit of ancient psalmody. There are Hebrew women now who can emulate the mothers of Hebrew song, who have spiritual warmth enough to revive the service of praise in both synagogue and household; and whose heart, intellect, taste, and culture are sufficient to prove that the hymns of their fathers may be happily rendered in English metre and rhyme. Mrs. Hester Rothschild has inserted the opening hymn of the Sabbath morning service in her volume of "Prayers and Meditations," and acknowledges her obligation to the talented pen of Mrs. Julius Collins for this beautiful version:—

> Before Thy heavenly Word revealed the wonders of Thy will;
> Before the earth and heavens came forth from chaos, deep and still;
> E'en then Thou reignedst Lord supreme! as Thou wilt ever reign,
> And moved Thy Holy Spirit o'er the dark unfathomed main;
>
> But when through all the empty space Thy mighty voice was heard,
> Then darkness fled, and heavenly light came beaming at Thy word;
> All nature then proclaimed the king, most blessed and adored!
> The great Creator! God alone!—the Universal Lord!

And when this vast created world returns to endless night,
When heaven and earth shall fade away at Thy dread word of
  might;
Still Thou in Majesty wilt rule, Almighty One alone,
Great God, with mercy infinite, on thy exalted throne.

Immortal power! Eternal One! with Thee what can compare,
Thy glory shines in heaven and earth, and fills the ambient air;
All time, all space, by Thee illumed, grows bright and brighter still,
Obedient to Thy high behest, and to Thy heavenly will.

To Thee dominion sole belongs, and 'tis to Thee alone,
My Father! Saviour! living God! I make my sorrows known;
Thy love celestial and divine descends upon my heart,
Inspiring courage, hope, and joy, and bidding grief depart.

Protected by Thy boundless love, my body sinks to rest;
My soul, within Thy heavenly arm reposes, calm and blest.
Lord of my life! in darkest night I sleep and have no fear,
And in the early dawn of day I wake and find Thee near.

As the official honours and powers which have their united seat in Him who is Head over all things to the Church, are by His Spirit divided and distributed among His people, so the "lights and perfections" which are all harmoniously embodied in the psalmody of Holy Writ, are scattered and variously apportioned among the later children of song. With one is the grandeur, with another the beauty; here the sweetness, there the power; this voice is plaintive, that triumphant. Now we have harmony, now gracefulness; now deep contemplative life, and now a full and holy unction. There are different ministrations. Nor has the gift of coming most agreeably near to the standard of highest hymnic inspiration always fallen on those to whom the Church would soonest look for aid. That God, who perfectly knows every man's mental and moral constitution, and sees at a glance all the fitnesses of human agency for the fulfilment of His own purposes, may sometimes tax the gifts of even a Balaam, and, wrapping him in awful visions, constrain him to give out utterances with which his own will and disposition are somewhat in discord, and which become immortalized as at once witnesses for God, and memorials of the faithless prophet's unconsecrated talents. A Rousseau may dream of heavenly music, and wake to jot down the melody which has helped many Christians to give touching expression to their purest and sweetest hymns. And who would expect a combination of features so near akin to those of old prophetic psalmody as are now associated in a few productions of Byron, Scott, and Olivers? What a trio! a sensuous scorner, and idolized novelist, and a Methodist preacher! And were all these among the prophets? If to write hymns like prophets' hymns is to have the shadow of a prophet's claim, let them share the honour of being in the train of prophetic hymnists. The three men wrote three remarkable hymns, each of which is instinct with some virtue of Hebrew psalmody. Byron has happily caught the spirit of the 137th Psalm, and in his plaintive but spirited melody gives the soul pleasant yet mournful touches, after the manner of the original ode, "By the rivers of Babylon," etc.—

> We sat down and wept by the waters
>   Of Babel, and thought of the day
> When our foe, in the hue of his slaughters,
>   Made Salem's high places his prey;
> And ye, oh her desolate daughters!
>   Were scatter'd all weeping away.
>
> While sadly we gazed on the river
>   Which rolled on in freedom below,
> They demanded the song; but, oh never
>   That triumph the stranger shall know!
> May this right hand be wither'd for ever,
>   Ere it string our high harp for the foe.
>
> On the willow that harp is suspended—
>   Oh Salem! its sound should be free;
> And the hour when thy glories were ended,
>   But left me that token of thee:
> And ne'er shall its soft tones be blended
>   With the voice of the spoiler by me!

He who could breathe so deeply in unison with the harp of captive Judah cannot, with all his sins and errors, be shut out from among the children of sacred minstrelsy. It may still be a wonder how such a hand as his could string its harp to melody like this; but there must have been something in the poet, both in his heart and intellect, which was capable of occasional sympathy with the sublime mysteries of the Old Testament, the grand march of its history, and the deep variations of its prophetic songs. It was this occasional sympathy which expressed itself in the awful dramas, "Cain" and "Heaven and Earth," and which sometimes showed itself in more pleasing beauty and power in his "Hebrew Melodies." Will the religious world ever forget his musical verses on Sennacherib?

> The Assyrian came down like a wolf on the fold;

but where and when had the touch been given which ever after acted now and then like a charm, and hushed his dark tempestuous soul into communion with the scenes, and the men, and the music of the Bible? Minds and hearts like his are not left by God without Divine visitation from above. Truth speaks at intervals with commanding power. A loving voice sometimes whispers, "My salvation is near;" and to Byron such a voice came in his earlier course.

"Lord Byron and I met once," said an old man to a friend, as they sat in the window of a quiet little parlour looking out upon Falmouth harbour. "It was one evening in the year 1809. I had been sitting here thinking how Providence and the Holy Ghost work together in promoting the salvation of man, when the servant girl, who had gone out on an errand, came rushing back in a great hurry, and ran upstairs. She was closely followed by a gentleman, who, when he saw me, apologized in a jaunty way for his intrusion, but at the same time walked in, took a seat, and seemed at perfect ease. He was a noble, handsome young man. I shall never forget the bright glance of his light eyes as they playfully lightened from under his very dark eyebrows. There sparkles of fire seemed to float on the surface of a thoughtful depth.

"'Was that your girl, old gentleman?' said he.

"'Yes, sir; pray what is the matter?'

"'Oh, nothing; but I wanted to make her acquaintance on the terrace yonder. She gave me a spirited reception, and provoked me to the chase; so here I am. I admire that girl of yours for her virtuous energy. But now, letting her alone in her retreat, turn out your cards, and let us have some play.'

"'We keep no cards here, sir,' said I, looking at him gravely.

"'No cards! Perhaps you have a novel or two one could look over?'

"'No, sir; such things are never found in this house.'

"'What have you got then, eh?'

"'I have a book here that might interest you,' I replied, 'and one that I am sure will not only refine your taste, but do your heart good.' I opened the Bible before him. He started. The gay life passed away from his countenance, and he was silent and thoughtful, while I gave him some lessons on the Bible and from the Bible. 'I have not the pleasure of knowing your name, sir,' said I, as he rose to depart, 'but I pray God to bless you.'

"'Thank you,' was his parting reply, 'my name is George, Lord Byron. Good-bye!'"

It was the future poet on his way to Lisbon, and who knows how far the quiet old Methodist's lesson "on the Bible and from the Bible" influenced his after thought and feeling, as the author of "Hebrew Melodies;" and was it the echo of that good little man's touching appeal that sometimes in after days, and in other climes, made him "silent and sombre," as when he said in the presence of his friend Shelley, "Here is a little book which somebody has sent me about Christianity, that has made me very uncomfortable; the reasoning seems to me very strong, the proofs are very staggering. I don't think you can answer it, Shelley, at least, I am sure I can't, and what is more, I don't wish it." Poor Byron! his heart cherished some early lessons "on the Bible and from the Bible;" and sometimes, as in his correspondence with Mr. Shepherd, prompted him to express his feelings of concern about his own spiritual condition, by nobly saying, "I can assure you that all the fame which ever cheated humanity into higher notions of its importance would never weigh in my mind against the pure and pious interest which a virtuous being may be pleased to take in my welfare." But whatever he owed to the words and prayers of the old man in the quiet parlour at Falmouth, he owed something, and, perhaps, much, to another, who seems to have been the only man who was kind, and faithful, and Christian enough to warn him against evil, and recommend him to the good, in the midst of his successes, and in the height of his poetic glory. That man was Sir Walter Scott.

"Would you have me turn Methodist?" said Byron, in reply to his friend's advice.

"No," was the reply, "I cannot conceive of your being a Methodist, but you might be a Catholic Christian."

His heart seems never to have lost the impression of that affectionate touch, and he recorded it by saying, "I have known Sir Walter Scott long and well, and in occasional situations which call forth the real character; and I can assure you that his character is worthy of admiration. I say that Walter Scott is as nearly a good man as man can be, because I know it by experience to be the case." Scott had shown himself to be Byron's true friend; but he proved too that he was akin to him in sympathy with the Hebrew psalmist. His higher moral standing, however, gave him the advantage, and his immortal hymn is more full in its conformity to the ancient and holy standard. Byron had the pathos and the tone of wailing Israel, but Scott, equal in all this, entered into the spirit of Hebrew worship, and rises into the grandeur of devout submission and holy trust.

> When Israel of the Lord beloved,
>   Out of the land of bondage came;
> Her father's God before her moved,
>   An awful guide in smoke and flame.
> By day along the astonished lands
>   The cloudy pillar glided slow;
> By night, Arabia's crimsoned sands
>   Returned the fiery column's glow.
>
> There rose the choral hymn of praise,
>   And trump and timbrel answered keen:
> And Zion's daughters poured their lays,
>   With priest's and warrior's voice between.
> No portents now our foes amaze,
>   Forsaken Israel wanders lone;
> Our fathers would not know Thy ways,
>   And Thou hast left them to their own.
>
> But present still, though now unseen,
>   When brightly shines the prosperous day;
> Be thoughts of Thee a cloudy screen
>   To temper the deceitful ray.
> And oh, when stoops on Judah's path,
>   In shade and storm the frequent night;
> Be Thou long-suffering, slow to wrath,
>   A burning and a shining light.

> Our harps we left by Babel's streams,
>   The tyrant's pest, the Gentile's scorn:
> No censer round our altar beams,
>   And mute are timbrel, trump, and horn.
> But Thou hast said the blood of goat,
>   The flesh of rams I will not prize;
> A contrite heart, a humble thought,
>   Are mine accepted sacrifice.

But it remained for the Methodist preacher to show the modern hymn in its stronger family likeness to those old spiritual songs in which all beautiful, grand, and devout thoughts, expressions, and feelings are so richly combined. He has done more than this. He has brought the spirit of the old covenant into harmony with that of the new; and in one hymn has finely blended the voices of all Abraham's spiritual children, whether "Greek or Jew, barbarian, Scythian, bond or free." His hymn takes position above those of Byron and Scott. The hymns of this remarkable trio are like a "psalm of degrees." They move in an upward gradation, raising the swell of Christian song until it rivals the music of Hebrew fathers. Under Byron's hand, the distinctive form of beauty began to breathe and unfold its tender charms. At Scott's touch it expands into more majestic proportions, and puts forth more of its inner life. But at Olivers' command, it manifests its maturity of soul, and gives full and harmonious expression to all its heavenliness of thought and affection. In the course of conversation a few years ago, the son of an old minister said, " I remember my father telling me that he was once standing in the aisle of City-road Chapel, during a Conference in Wesley's time, and Thomas Olivers, one of the preachers, came down to him, and unfolding a manuscript, said, 'Look at this, I have rendered it from the Hebrew, giving it as far as I could a Christian character, and I have called on Leoni, the Jew, who has given me a synagogue melody to suit it; here is the tune, and it is to be called Leoni.' I read the composition, and it was that now well-known, grand imitation of ancient Israel's hymns—

> The God of Abraham praise,
>   Who reigns enthroned above,
> Ancient of everlasting days,
>   And God of love;

Jehovah! Great I am!
　By earth and heaven confest;
I bow and bless the sacred name
　　For ever blest!

The God of Abraham praise!
　At whose supreme command
From earth I rise and seek the joys
　　At His right hand:
　I all on earth forsake,
　Its wisdom, fame, and power,
And Him my only portion make,
　　My shield and tower.

The God of Abraham praise!
　Whose all-sufficient grace
Shall guide me all my happy days
　　In all my ways:
　He by Himself hath sworn,
　I on His oath depend;
I shall, on eagle's wings upborne,
　　To heaven ascend;
　I shall behold His face,
　I shall His power adore,
And sing the wonders of His grace
　　For evermore.

Though nature's strength decay,
　And earth and hell withstand,
To Canaan's bounds I urge my way
　　At His command:
　The watery deep I pass
　With Jesus in my view,
And through the howling wilderness
　　My way pursue.

The goodly land I see,
　With peace and plenty blest,
A land of sacred liberty,
　　And endless rest:
　There milk and honey flow,
　And oil and wine abound,
And trees of life for ever grow,
　　With mercy crown'd.

There dwells the Lord our King,
　The Lord our Righteousness,
Triumphant o'er the world and sin,
　　The Prince of Peace!
　On Zion's sacred height
　His kingdom still maintains,
And glorious with His saints in light,
　　For ever reigns!

He keeps His own secure;
He guards them by His side;
Arrays in garments white and pure
　　His spotless bride;
With streams of sacred bliss,
With groves of living joys,
With all the fruits of Paradise,
　　He still supplies.

Before the great Three-One
They all exulting stand,
And tell the wonders He hath done,
　　Through all their land;
The listening spheres attend
And swell the growing fame,
And sing in songs which never end,
　　The wondrous name!

The God who reigns on high,
The great archangels sing,
And "Holy, Holy, Holy," cry,
　　"Almighty king!
Who was and is the same,
And evermore shall be!
Jehovah! Father! great I Am!
　　We worship Thee!"

Before the Saviour's face
The ransom'd nations bow,
Overwhelm'd at His almighty grace,
　　For ever new:
He shows His prints of love;
They kindle to a flame,
And sound, through all the worlds above,
　　The slaughter'd Lamb!

The whole triumphant host
Give thanks to God on high;
"Hail! Father, Son, and Holy Ghost!"
　　They ever cry:
Hail! Abraham's God and mine!
I join the heavenly lays;
All might and majesty are Thine,
　　And endless praise!

How little Byron knew, when he shrank from what he thought to be Scott's recommendation of Methodism, that a Methodist preacher would be honoured as more than his equal in true "Hebrew melodies." And how little Scott thought, when he found himself arrested by Wesley's preaching in Kelso churchyard, that the name of one of Wesley's itinerant companions would stand in the lists of immortality above his own, in the line of Israelitish hymnists. It is interesting, too, to see posterity balancing the relative claims of Olivers and his bitter theological antagonist Toplady. Wesley employed Olivers as his "corrector of the press." But he was more. He sometimes took part in the doctrinal strife which was raging then between the Arminians and the Calvinists. Olivers, though once a cobbler, had a great deal of native logic, and could use a syllogism with all the effect which he was once apt to give to his awl. He knew how to stitch up collegians like Toplady; and poor Toplady was now and then irritated under the process, until bitter and even vulgar outcries were his only mode of defence. "Mr. Wesley," cries he, "has taken refuge under a cobbler's apron!" Alas! for the gentleman when the theological polemic rises. Human nature is a strange complexity, even in its most hallowed condition, especially when its religious taste and temper take the form of controversy. He who grins about a cobbler's apron to-day, sings to-morrow,

> Rock of Ages, cleft for me,
> Let me hide myself in Thee!

and has thus rendered it difficult to say whether he or his cobbler foe was the greater benefactor to the Christian world when they exercised their higher and diviner calling as Christian hymnists. Toplady's name will ever be balmy to those whose tremulous spirits feel the need of the cross; while those who can rise into the jubilant assurance of pilgrims on the very banks of Jordan will bless the memory of the man whose memorial is thus recorded by his companions in travel with characteristic brevity and force. "Thomas Olivers died advanced in years. In his younger days he was a zealous, able, and useful travelling preacher; but for a long period of his life he was employed by Mr. Wesley as the corrector of his press. His talents were very considerable: and his attachment to Mr. Wesley and Methodism was fully evidenced by several masterly publications." He proved himself to be no mean writer, logician, poet, and musical composer. With all this he was a good man; and long ago he fully realized the blessedness which his last stanza anticipated—

>Hail! Abraham's God and mine!
>I join the heavenly lays;
>All might and majesty are Thine,
>   And endless praise!

CHAPTER III.

HYMNS OF THE LATTER DAY MORNING.

"But who the melodies of morn can tell."

THE morning light of the Christian Church fell upon Pliny the younger; and in that light he saw the martyr spirit of our first century. He had seen the Christians of his time suffer, and knew that their sufferings never broke their joy. Their morning hymns had never, perhaps, touched his ear; but he has bequeathed a precious testimony to the cheerful devotion of the people who could be charged with no crime but that of meeting on "a stated day before it was light, to sing hymns to Christ as God," and to renew their mutual pledges of truthfulness, purity, and love. Blessed souls! "The word of Christ dwelt in them so richly" that they must needs "prevent the dawning of the day" with their songs. The apostolic spirit was still alive in them. They were rejoicing in the dawn of the latter day. They were in jeopardy every hour; every little group was "baptized for the dead;" but they ate their "meat with gladness," cheering their meat-time with joyful psalmody; their love-feasts were brightened with chant and chorus, and their homes were vocal with simple melodies and favourite hymns. What hymns must they have been which were pure overflowings of hearts full of divine influence? What songs, when every singer gave out the form of old anthems newly instinct with Christian life, or extemporized in melody and rhythm according to his own distinctive spiritual gift? What was their style of hymn? How did they sing? Their psalmody must have been at once a reiteration of the past and an embodiment of exemplar songs for the future. Echoes from that morning of church music come to our ears and hearts even now in some hymns which still breathe the perfume of an apostolic age. The warm and jubilant spirit, and the triumphant heavenliness of tone which distinguish those ancient songs, give life to our modern liturgies, and are so like the worship of prophets, apostles, and martyrs, that in singing them we may enjoy a feeling of unison with choirs of the first Christian converts. When we join "with angels and archangels" in the "thrice holy," or lift up our hearts with the "*gloria in excelsis*," or help to swell the anthem peal of the *Te Deum*, are we not using fragments from that early collection of hymns in which the praises of the old covenant saints were taken up and poured onward in richer Christian harmony through the first ages of Messiah's kingdom? In them we have the first Christian responses to the songs of patriarchal and prophetic days. The first song in which the people join at the Holy Communion "with angels and archangels," etc., is one of the first echoes of the Christian Church to those voices of seraphims which the prophet heard in the temple, and which were answered and repeated from Patmos in the hearing of a rapt apostle:—

> Holy, holy, holy,
> Jehovah Sabaoth,
> The whole earth is full
> Of His glory.

The anthem of "Glory to God in the Highest," sang by the multitude of "heavenly hosts," was first responded to by the happy shepherds as they "returned glorifying and praising God for all the things they had heard and seen;" and then both angels and shepherds were answered by the martyr church in the glorious old Greek hymn which in our English Liturgy the communicants are called to chant at the close of the Sacramental Supper. And if, as the tradition goes, the *Te Deum* broke in alternate parts from the lips of Ambrose and Augustine during the solemnities of Augustine's baptism, it is probable that the holy singers merely caught the full-toned expression of an earlier time, the day-spring of the Church, when the company of believers gave forth utterances in which creeds, and praises, and thanksgivings, and intense prayer, and living hopes were interwoven and wrought up into one grand church hymn for all generations and all times. One incident in the history of Robert Hall serves to set forth the native majesty of the *Te Deum*, and its close conformity to the spirit and manner of inspired psalms. He had composed a sermon on a text which had touched his fine sense of grandeur and had deeply moved his heart. On completing his sermon, he turned to the concordance to find the text. It was not to be found. It was not in the Bible. It was a sentence from the *Te Deum*, "All the earth doth worship Thee, the Father everlasting." All ears are not fine enough to be charmed with the rhythm of these ancient hymns; and many sincere worshippers even lack the power of fairly appreciating their simple grandeur and glowing power. Translations necessarily dim their glory, lower their tone, and lessen their power. But now and then some hymnist of deep sympathy with the past, drinks inspiration from these ever-living springs of song, and casts the whole breathing measures into metrical form and rhyme, which at once suit the taste and command the hearts of wider multitudes and later times. How many who were never moved into fellowship with "all the company of heaven" by the liturgical translation of the *Ter Sanctus*, have risen into something like an approach to the old strain when singing Bishop Mant's more popular but beautiful verses—

> Bright the vision that delighted
>   Once the sight of Judah's seer,
> Sweet the countless tongues united
>   To entrance the prophet's ear.
> Round the Lord in glory seated,
>   Cherubim and seraphim
> Fill'd his temple, and repeated
>   Each to each th' alternate hymn.
>
> "Lord, thy glory fills the heaven,
>   Earth is with its fulness stored;
> Unto Thee be glory given,
>   Holy, holy, holy, Lord!"
> Heaven is still with glory ringing,
>   Earth takes up the angels' cry,
> "Holy, holy, holy," singing,
>   "Lord of hosts, the Lord most high!"
>
> Ever thus in God's high praises,
>   Brethren, let our tongues unite;

Chief the heart when duty raises
  God-ward at his mystic rite :
With His seraph train before Him,
  With His holy Church below,
Thus conspire we to adore Him,
  Bid we thus one anthem flow !

"Lord, Thy glory fills the heaven,
  Earth is with its fulness stored :
Unto Thee be glory given,
  Holy, holy, holy Lord !"
Thus Thy glorious name confessing,
  We adopt Thy angels' cry,
"Holy, holy, holy," blessing
  Thee, "the Lord of hosts most high !"

As rank after rank from "the noble army of martyrs" passed away during the morning tide of the Church, leaving no record, and without the least care about the preservation of their memory upon earth, so, many of the hymnists of early days were happy in expressing their joys in song while they lived, and then departed, bequeathing their hymns to following generations, without a single effort to secure for their own names the future honours of authorship. Some of their simple, tender, trustful, hymns, full of Christ and winged with heavenliness, still remain as nameless memorials of the generation whose purity inspired contemporary authorities with wonder. One hymn there is which seems to claim a place among those which Pliny says the Christians used to sing before the morning dawn. It is in the spirit of the Psalmist, who said, "My eyes prevent the night watches," and may be rendered thus :—

From our midnight sleep uprising,
  Thee, Gracious One, we will adore ;
Loud the angels' hymn uplifting
  To Thee, Almighty, evermore !
The holy, holy, holy Lord and God art Thou !
In mercy's name, have mercy on us now !

From the couch and death-like slumber
  Thou makest me, O Lord, to rise :
Thou my mind and heart enlighten,
  And free my lips from sinful ties,
So may I 'fore Thee, Triune God, with praises bow ;
For holy, holy, holy Lord and God art Thou !

With multitudes on multitudes,
　The coming Judge will soon be here;
And ev'ry deed of ev'ry man
　Will bare and open then appear.
We'll wait in filial fear, cheering our midnight now,
With holy, holy, holy Lord and God art Thou!

Many of the voices which were thus lifted up in the night watches of Pliny's time were contemporaries of the "beloved disciple;" and among the rhythmical fragments which survive there seem to be traces of the influence which the last of the apostles had shed upon the mind and heart of the youthful Church. Indications may be found here and there of familiarity with the last apostle's closing utterances, "Hereby know ye the Spirit of God: every spirit that confesseth that Jesus Christ is come in the flesh is of God, ... and we know that the Son of God is come, and hath given us an understanding, that we may know Him that is true, and we are in Him that is true, even in His Son Jesus Christ. This is the true God and eternal life. Little children, keep yourselves from idols." This closing admonition was sacredly observed by these "little children," while they kept their adoring eyes on John's last vision of "the Lamb in the midst of the throne," and continued to admonish one another "in psalms, and hymns, and spiritual songs" about the incarnate Saviour, their reigning Lord. One of their strains is so like John, and so befitting his "little children" in its pure simplicity, its joyful earnestness, and reverent friendship with a present Saviour, that it must ever have a charm for all who have spiritual sympathy with the apostle of "perfect love." It loses much, of course, by translation into English rhyme, but in that form it is most likely to touch the present generation:—

We adore Thy pure image,
　O good Lord, imploring Thee!
Pardon all our sins and failures,
　Christ, our gracious Deity.
Thou didst come in Thy good-will,
　Taking flesh with all its woe,
Thy own creatures to redeem
　From the bondage of the foe.
Therefore cry we thankfully,
　Fulness of delight, to Thee,
Our Saviour, once appearing,
　Purging earth's iniquity.

Some of the hymns of early dawn must have mingled with the joy of angels over penitent hearts. Human nature was sinful then as it is now. The contrite heart and broken spirit had its psalm then as it ever will. Apostle churches were never lacking in—

> The godly grief, the pleasing smart,
> The meltings of a broken heart;
> The tear that tells the son's forgiven,
> The sighs that waft the soul to heaven.
>
> The guiltless shame, the sweet distress,
> The unutterable tenderness,
> The genuine meek humility,
> The wonder, "why such love to me!"

One of these plaintive psalms of primitive repentance seems to sob and moan with gentle sorrow, and to palpitate with mystic penitential joy and tender longings for Christ:—

> Long-suff'ring Jesus, precious Jesus!
> Heal, oh, heal my wounded soul!
> Oh, sweeten Thou my heart, my Jesus!
> Save, I pray Thee, make me whole!
>   That saved by Thee, my Saviour, I
>   May Thy great mercy magnify.
>
> Lover of man, oh, hear me, Saviour!
> Thine afflicted servant cries:
> Oh, deliver me from judgment;
> Bid the sentenced culprit rise!
>   Thou merciful, long-suffering Son,
>   Oh, most sweet Jesus, only One!
>
> Do let Thy servant come, my Saviour!
> Sinking 'fore Thee now with tears;
> Save me, Jesus! me repenting!
> Save from hell, and hellish fears!
>   O Master! my deep wounds I feel!
>   Now heal me! blessed Saviour, heal!
>
> With Thy strong hand, my Saviour, rescue
> From that Spirit-murd'rer fell;
> In compassion snatch from Satan;
> Though I've sinn'd and merit hell:
>   Merciful, long-suff'ring One, I flee
>   To Thy defence! to Thee! to Thee!
>
> Oh, meeten me to Thy blest kingdom,
> Jesus, be my inward light!
> To my lost soul Thou art salvation;
> From hell redeeming by Thy might.
>   Here, weeping like a helpless child,
>   Save me, O Christ! O Jesus mild!

Such meltings, bemoanings, struggles of thought, regrets, half-plaintive, half-joyful, now desponding, and now hopeful appeals, are felt to be his own by every prodigal sinner in every age, and all the world over. Repentance never changes its character. Its language, though varied in metre, is essentially one. The old eastern penitential psalm falls naturally from the lips of a penitent transgressor in our modern western world, and any genuine living hymn from a truly softened English heart, appealing to its Saviour, would be chanted amidst tears by penitent worshippers in an Eastern basilica. A good man from the far West, not many years ago, during his pilgrimage in the East, found his way into an Armenian church at Constantinople. The people were singing. The language of their hymn was foreign; but it was evident that the singers were in earnest, and that there was deep feeling in the words of their song. The music was a simple melody. All sang with closed eyes, but as the strain continued, tears were starting, and trickling down many, many a cheek. Dr. Pomeroy would fain have joined in the plaintive, tender, yet glowing hymn. What were they singing? The stanzas were translated, and as they fell on his ear, his heart responded to the precious, well-known verses—

> Rock of Ages, cleft for me,
> Let me hide myself in Thee;
> Let the water and the blood,
> From Thy wounded side which flowed,
> Be of sin the double cure,
> Cleanse me from its guilt and power.
>
> Not the labours of my hands
> Can fulfil Thy law's demands,
> Could my zeal no respite know,
> Could my tears for ever flow,
> All for sin could not atone;
> Thou must save, and Thou alone.
>
> Nothing in my hand I bring,
> Simply to Thy cross I cling;
> Naked, come to Thee for dress;
> Helpless, look to Thee for grace;
> Foul, I to the Fountain fly:
> Wash me, Saviour, or I die!
>
> While I draw this fleeting breath,
> When my eye-strings break in death,

> When I soar through tracts unknown,
> See Thee on Thy judgment-throne:
> Rock of Ages, cleft for me,
> Let me hide myself in Thee!

Who would not like to have heard and seen the author of this hymn? He might have been found once in a sequestered village in the eastern corner of Devon. There, amidst the beautiful hills which are overlooked by the western slopes of the Black Down range, the quiet parish church of Broad Hembury stands silently inviting the folks of the hamlet to "seek the living among the dead." Within those walls on any Sunday about the year 1770 the vicar might be found, during church hours, fervently leading the devotions of his flock, and then dispensing saving truth from the pulpit in a style and spirit not to be enjoyed everywhere, especially in those times. The preacher is described as having an "ethereal countenance, and light, immortal form. His voice was music. His vivacity would have caught the listener's eye, and his soul-filled looks and movements would have interpreted his language, had there not been such commanding solemnity in his tones as made apathy impossible, and such simplicity in his words that to hear was to understand. From easy explanations he advanced to rapid and conclusive arguments, and warmed into importunate exhortations, till conscience began to burn and feelings to take fire from his own kindled spirit, and himself and his hearers were together drowned in sympathetic tears." The preacher was Augustus Montague Toplady. He was the son of Major Toplady, who died at the siege of Carthagina in 1740, leaving his infant Augustus to the care of a tender but judicious mother, under whose oversight the gentle and affectionate character of the future hymnist was happily developed and matured. He owed much to his mother; and his heart was always ready for returns of filial love and duty. The genuine and decided nature of his conversion, however, was the deeper secret of his distinctive character as a divine, a preacher, and a hymnist. "When he was but sixteen, during a visit to Ireland with his mother, he found his way into a barn at Codymain," where an uncultivated but warm-hearted layman was preaching from Eph. ii. 13. The human instrument was unpolished, but the divine word was effectual; and looking back, after some years, on the happy change which passed over his heart during that hour in the barn, and speaking of the gracious sentence which so deeply touched him, he says, "It was from that passage that Mr. Morris preached on the memorable evening of my effectual call by the grace of God. Under the ministry of that dear messenger, and under that sermon, I was, I trust, 'brought nigh by the blood of Christ,' in August, 1756. Strange that I, who had so long sat under the means of grace in England, should be brought nigh unto God in an obscure part of Ireland, amidst a handful of God's people met together in a barn, and under the ministry of one who could hardly spell his name. Surely it is the Lord's doing, and it is marvellous. The excellency of such power must be of God, and cannot be of man."

He was ordained in June, 1762. The circumstances and mode of his conversion seem to have disposed him to a strong and ruling conviction of the Calvinistic sense of the articles to which he subscribed, and to which, as he said, he subscribed because he believed them. He entered on his rural charge at Broad Hembury in 1768. And there his finely-tempered soul regaled itself now and then amidst the delicious retreats on the banks of the Otter stream, by celebrating the grace of his Redeemer in the immortal hymns and spiritual songs from which so many penitent and believing hearts continue to gather saving balm. Strange that harsh and bitter words should have been uttered in controversy with such kindred hymnists as Wesley and Olivers! When these poetic spirits sang, they were in perfect harmony; but when they dogmatized, there was intemperate discord. Toplady's strong conviction and warm zeal for those dogmas whose exclusive claims he thought to be demonstrated by his own conversion, sometimes mastered his native gentleness and Christian feeling, and led him astray into a false position. His example cautions the lover of truth against allowing himself to be provoked into controversy. Better let the truth work its own way. His polemic essays may repose on the theological shelf, but his hymns will for ever wreathe his name with holy light in the memory and heart of the Christian Church.

How beautiful was the closing scene of his life; "Sickness is no affliction," said the saintly pilgrim, "pain no curse, death itself no dissolution." To one who inquired whether his consolations always abounded, it was replied, "I cannot say there are no intermissions; for if there were not, my consolations would be more and greater than I could possibly bear; but when they abate they leave such an abiding sense of God's goodness, and of the certainty of my being fixed upon the eternal rock Christ Jesus, that my soul is still filled with peace and joy." Happy hymnist! He now realized the full meaning of his own

> Rock of Ages, cleft for me.

Like many others, he had mistaken Wesley on one point, and, with strange perversity of error, condemned him for teaching the doctrine of "absolute perfection," as the Christian's privilege. It was in his zeal against this illusion that he entitled his "Rock of Ages," "A living and dying PRAYER for the HOLIEST BELIEVER in the world." But Wesley was as innocent of this alleged heresy as was Toplady himself; and no believer in the world would sing Toplady's hymnic prayer with more reverent feeling than John Wesley. Indeed, the last utterances of the two men were graciously akin. Wesley breathed the spirit of Toplady's hymn when in departing he sang—

> I the chief of sinners am,
> But Jesus died for me.

Blessed spirits! They have met in clearer light, and now see "eye to eye."

Hallowed genius continues to consecrate itself to that holy "name whereby we must be saved." Nor does it fail to furnish the succession of believing penitents with happy, suitable forms of tuneful expression in their appeals to Jesus. What the old Greek hymnists did for those who were coming to Christ in their day, and what Toplady did for later generations, both in east and west, has been done for the hearts that the Lord opens by still later voices of equal sweetness and power. Some of these are the voices of "devout women." A woman took the lead in holy song at the dawning of the "latter day." Women were most ready to weep with Him who wept for us, and to rejoice in His joy. The voices of women swelled the joy of the resurrection, mingled in the strains which cheered the simple tables around which the first disciples "ate their meat with gladness," and filled up the harmonies of those gatherings whose cheerful worship and happy expression gave them "favour with all the people." Many of the hymns preserved to us from the Syrian and Greek hymnists were, doubtless, from the hearts and pens of sons of holy mothers; or, it may be, some of the simple rhythmical celebrations of the birth and glory of the "Child Jesus" were utterances of widow-confessors, or mothers of consecrated "little ones." No name, however, has come down to us. No fragment can be verified as a woman's hymn. It has remained for more modern days to hear songs from "devout women" which equal the tenderest and most happy of all tender and happy melodies adapted to the softened hearts which long for a Saviour. One of these comes from Devon, from its southern coast. If anybody wishes to enjoy, within the limits of a few days' ramble, one of the richest interminglings of balmy air and bright blue sea, of hill and dale, copsy knoll and ferny hollow, villa-crowned heights and cottages in dells, noble cliffs and terraced gardens, mountain-paths and quiet sparkling beaches, weedy rocks and whispering caverns, ever-varying, ever-harmonizing scenes, amidst which, above, beneath, around, and everywhere, grandeur is melting into beauty—he must be a quiet sojourner for a little while in the neighbourhood of Torquay. Of those who seek and find enjoyment in that delicious retreat, one lady has happily brightened the scenes already bright by the charm of a pious example, the quiet but diligent diffusion of truth, and the gracious exercise of her Christian charity. A lover of nature, a lover of souls, a lover of Christ, her talents and zeal have shed their best and most lasting blessing on the Christian world by the issue of those hymns which promise ever to reflect blessing on her name. Thousands who never saw Torquay, thousands who merely know the name of Charlotte Elliott, will find themselves nearer to the blessed Jesus while they sing her justly popular hymn—

> Just as I am, without one plea
> But that Thy blood was shed for me,
> And that Thou bidst me come to Thee,
> O Lamb of God, I come!

Just as I am, and waiting not
To rid my soul of one dark blot,
To Thee, whose blood can cleanse each spot,
    O Lamb of God, I come!

Just as I am, though toss'd about
With many a conflict, many a doubt,
Fightings and fears within, without,
    O Lamb of God, I come!

Just as I am, poor, wretched, blind,
Sight, riches, healing of the mind,
Yea, all I need, in Thee I find,
    O Lamb of God, I come!

Just as I am, Thou wilt receive,
Wilt welcome, pardon, cleanse, relieve!
Because Thy promise I believe,
    O Lamb of God, I come!

Just as I am (thy love unknown
Has broken every barrier down),
Now to be Thine, yea, Thine alone,
    O Lamb of God, I come!

Just as I am, of that free love
The breadth, length, depth, and height to prove,
Here for a season, then above,
    O Lamb of God, I come!

This sounds like repeated and still repeated echoes of some sweet music; and indeed the verses may be listened to as if they were the echoes of the coast-hills of Devon answering to the voice of spiritual songs which a century before arose from a quiet garden on the borders of the Hampshire downs. That, too, was a woman's voice; and that voice, too, was the voice of tender, melting desire for the Saviour—the voice of a penitent believer answering to the Divine call, "Come unto Me, and I will give you rest." It was the voice of one chosen "in the furnace of affliction;" but the tones were sweet and clear, with that gentle ring which thrills the devotional heart as if something of pure heavenliness had touched it. So where it was when this song was uttered—

    Thou lovely Source of true delight,
      Whom I unseen adore,
    Unveil Thy beauties to my sight,
      That I may love Thee more.

> Thy glory o'er creation shines,
>   But in Thy sacred word
> I read, in fairer, brighter lines,
>   My bleeding, dying Lord.
>
> 'Tis here, whene'er my comforts droop,
>   And sins and sorrows rise,
> Thy love, with cheerful beams of hope,
>   My fainting heart supplies.
>
> But ah, too soon the pleasing scene
>   Is clouded o'er with pain;
> My gloomy fears rise dark between,
>   And I again complain.
>
> Jesus, my Lord, my life, my light,
>   Oh come with blissful ray,
> Break radiant through the shades of night,
>   And chase my fears away.
>
> Then shall my soul with rapture trace
>   The wonders of Thy love;
> But the full glories of Thy face
>   Are only known above.

This hymn, with many others, had a deep interest in the heart of a venerable Nonconformist minister, who, in 1757, had the pastoral charge of a congregation, meeting in the village of Broughton in Hampshire, on the spot where their fathers had worshipped from the time of the Commonwealth. The good pastor writes in his diary:— "1757, Nov. 29. This day Nanny sent a part of her composition to London to be printed. I entreat a gracious God, who enabled and stirred her up to such a work, to direct in it, and bless it for the good and comfort of many." And again:—" Oct. 1759. Her brother brought with him her poetry, not yet bound. I earnestly desire the blessing of God upon that work, that it may be made very useful. I can admire the gifts that others are blessed with, and praise God for His distinguishing favours to our family. I have now been reading our daughter's printed books, which I have earnestly desired might be accompanied with the Divine Spirit in the perusing." And yet again:— "Nov. 27. Mr. W—— spoke very highly in commendation of her book. I pray God to make it useful, and keep her humble." Which is most beautiful in all this, the simple naturalness of the father's feeling, or the devout spirit of the Christian parent? The good man's prayers were richly answered in his daughter's character and life, and in the hearts of all who read her pious, pure, and finely-toned hymns. One song alone of hers forbids a doubt of this—

> Jesus, my Lord, in Thy dear name unite,
>   All things my heart calls great, or good, or sweet;
> Divinest springs of wonder and delight,
>   In Thee, Thou fairest of ten thousand, meet.
>
> Do I not love Thee? ah, my conscious heart
>   Nor boldly dares affirm, nor can deny;
> Oh, bid these clouds of gloomy fear depart,
>   With one bright ray from Thy propitious eye!
>
> Do I not love Thee? can I then allow
>   Within my breast pretenders to Thy throne?
> Oh, take my homage, at Thy feet I bow!
>   No other Lord my heart desires to own.
>
> Take, take my passions in Thy sovereign hand,
>   Refine and mould them with Almighty skill;
> Then shall I love the voice of Thy command,
>   And all my powers rejoice to do Thy will.
>
> Thy love inspires the active sons of light,
>   With swift-wing'd zeal they wait upon Thy word;
> Oh, let that love, in these abodes of night,
>   Bid my heart glow to serve my dearest Lord.
>
> Come, love Divine, my languid wishes raise!
>   With heavenly zeal this faint cold heart inflame,
> To join with angels in my Saviour's praise,
>   Like them obey His will, adore His name.
>
> But can the mind, with heavy clay opprest,
>   To emulate seraphic ardour rise?
> While sin pollutes her joys, forbids her rest,
>   How can she join the worship of the skies?
>
> Yet He commands to love and to obey,
>   Whose hand sustains those happy spirits there;
> In Him, my soul, who is thy Guide, thy Stay,
>   In Him confide, to Him commit thy care.
>
> Jesus, my Lord, oh give me strength divine!
>   Then shall my powers in glad obedience move;
> Receive the heart that wishes to be Thine,
>   And teach, oh teach me to obey and love!

This is one of the hymns from the volume on which the fond father invoked a blessing—a volume of hymns and poems by "Theodosia." And who and what Theodosia was is happily revealed in one of her letters to her "honoured father:"—"As many of these verses have been favoured with your approbation, I have now at your desire collected them into a little book, which I beg leave to present to you as a humble acknowledgment of my grateful sense of your parental affection, and the benefit I have received from your instructions. If you should survive me, it will, I doubt not, be preserved by you (however inconsiderable its real value) as a mournfully pleasing remembrance of a departed child who once shared your tender regard. If you think they are capable of affording pleasure or profit, you may, if you please, communicate any of them to friends or fellow-Christians. They may, perhaps, find seasons when the thoughts of the unworthy writer may suit their own, and the resemblance produce delight. If while I am sleeping in the silent grave my thoughts are of any real benefit to the meanest of the servants of my God, be the praise ascribed to the Almighty Giver of all grace. May the blessed hope of eternal life cheer my soul amidst the pangs of dissolution! May the blissful smiles of my Redeemer illuminate the gloomy shades of death, and point out my passage to the mansions of eternal day; that I may be able to say, in the full evidence of faith and hope, I am going to 'be ever with the Lord.' Then shall my God be glorified, and my dear relatives comforted in my death. May the Almighty long preserve your valuable life, and continue to make you a blessing to your family, a useful instructor to the people under your care, and an ornament to religion, is the ardent wish and prayer of, dear and honoured father, your ever dutiful and grateful daughter, "ANNE STEELE."

CHAPTER IV.

HYMNS OF THE FATHERS.

"Our holy and beautiful house, where our fathers praised Thee."

WHO, in his dreams of the past, has not sometimes found himself floating across the Mediterranean down to ancient Egypt, and there moving, as none but spirits can move, along the face of those venerable and mysterious deposits of the Delta over which Egyptian, Ethiopian, Assyrian, Persian, Roman, and Saracen, in successive generations, have passed before him? and whose imagination has not wandered up the Nile in quiet visionary fashion, now under the shadow of African palms, and now through lily banks by the side of gliding pelicans, and within sight of the giraffe and the gazelle freely rambling on the desert sands? Who has not in his dreams looked at the calcareous cliffs from which the generations of the Old World dug their lime? or at the sandstone quarries which supplied slabs and blocks for the temples that had fallen into ruin long before England began her course? or at the awful granite piles from whence came the materials for those gigantic sculptures which still overawe mankind? or at the wilderness of ruins and sepulchres which, with their myriads of mummy forms, give to our hearts such lessons on human life? Who has not wandered there thinking of Abraham and Sarah, Joseph and his brethren, Jacob worshipping on his staff, his embalmment, and his funeral; and then of another Joseph and Mary, and the Holy Child; and then of the first Christian disciples, and their first flight to the desert? Our dreamy flights have sometimes led us from Egypt across the Red Sea to the base of Mount Colzim, just where its bend looks out through the desert pass of Mount Kallil towards the plain of Baccarah, there to look at a few palms, sustained by three brackish springs, with a little garden of potherbs, onions, and dourah; and to find a human form seated at the entrance of a recess, dressed in wash-leather, with a sallow face expressive of quiet earnestness and high purpose, the lustrous depth of his upturned eye revealing the joy of his communion with heaven; the man who might be called the father of that recluse life which, though springing from perverted Christian principle, yet for so many ages swayed the movements of the Christian world, and gave out the precious streams of hymns and songs which helped to preserve the spiritual life of a cloistered church. Then, have there not been visions of old Alexandria? visions which, like dissolving views, have changed from brilliant palaces to libraries and lecture-halls, from close retired streets to old basilicas, from students' cells to crowded places filled with multitudes struggling and heaving amidst the processes of transition from old heathenism to a half-formed Christianity; and then our visionary path has been crossed by the shadows of such men as Clement, and Origen, and Didymus, and their trains of disciples who peopled the first Christian schools of Alexandria. One would like to arrest the shade of Clement, and ask him to give us a few more hymns, or to sing to us some of the fragments that we have caught up from the ruins of his music-school, and to sing them as he and his scholars used to sing them both at home and in the church. It is difficult to catch even a dreamy outline of Clement's person and life; he has left a few touches of his own character. At the end of the second century, Alexandria was like a great centre of telegraphic communication, mysteriously linking itself with all the outstanding points in the world of thought. In and around that centre many were running to and fro asking and answering questions, and voices from all nations were mingling in deep-toned inquiries after the supreme good. There, in the midst, was Clement, anxiously looking hither and thither, always intensely hungering and thirsting after truth. Now, he took lessons from the retreats of Lebanon, now from Assyria, and now from the Hebrew school of Tiberias. It was a weary search; but perfect sincerity is always honoured from above, and is sure of its goal. His heart found rest at last; where his heart rested, there the wants of his intellect were supplied. He says enough about himself and Christianity to prove that he had found the secret of Christian life, and that he had been "transformed by the renewing of his mind." Still, his long in and out and round-about search for truth, and the hard processes through which his mind and heart had passed in the course of his religious pursuit, gave a peculiar shaping to his mental and spiritual character as a Christian. Some of his peculiar views, his views of Christian perfection, caught the attention of Wesley, who, stigmatized as a perfectionist himself, though coming very much nearer to the truth than the Alexandrian father, has ingeniously given a versified exposition of Clement's mistaken notion, and has embodied it in his collection of hymns and sacred poems. It seems fitting that one of the earliest hymnists among the Fathers should have his distinctive views thrown into a hymnic form by a modern Father of spiritual hymns and songs. Wesley sings "on Clement Alexandrinus's description of a perfect Christian:"—

> Here from afar the finish'd height
>   Of holiness is seen;
> But oh what heavy tracts of toil,
>   What deserts lie between!
>
> Man for the simple life divine
>   What will it cost to break,
> Ere pleasure soft and wily pride
>   No more within him speak?
>
> What ling'ring anguish must corrode
>   The root of nature's joy?
> What secret shame and dire defeats
>   The pride of heart destroy?
>
> Learn thou the whole of mortal state
>   In stillness to sustain;
> Nor soothe with false delights of earth,
>   Whom God hath doomed to pain.
>
> Thy mind no multitude of thoughts,
>   Nor stupor shall distress;
> The venom of each latent vice
>   Wild images impress.

> Yet darkly safe with God thy soul
>   His arm still onward bears,
> Till through each tempest on her face
>   A peace beneath appears.
>
> 'Tis in that peace we see and act
>   By instincts from above,
> With finer taste of wisdom fraught,
>   And mystic powers of love.
>
> Yet ask not in mere ease and pomp
>   Of ghostly gifts to shine,
> Till death, the lownesses of man,
>   And pitying griefs are thine.

As an exposition of Clement's doctrine of Christian perfection, this is sufficiently clear to guard those whose service of song the author intended to regulate; while it is aptly made to fall off into that kind of haziness which indicates the uncertain theology of the Alexandrine Father. But whatsoever peculiar turn of thought Clement's mind might take on some theological points, Christianity had simplified his heart and kindled his poetic powers into hallowed devotion to his beloved Redeemer. The artless child seems to brighten into the praiseful seraph in his hymn "of the Saviour Christ." An English rendering, somewhat in imitation of the original metre, may help us to sing with Clement:—

> Lead, Holy One, lead!
> The little ones need
> The voice of their King.
> The footprints of Jesus
> Are shining before us,
> His children to lead,
> On the heavenly way their footsteps to bring.
>
> O Age Infinite!
> Original Light!
> Divine Living Word!
> The Fountain of mercy!
> Creator of beauty!
> Sustainer of might
> To all happy spirits; Christ Jesus our Lord!
>
> By milk from above
> For babes of Thy love,
> Thy wisdom's sweet store,
> Their tender lips nourished,

Refreshed, and replenished;
They sing o'er and o'er
Their own artless hymns, as tow'rds Thee they move.

O Christ our King,
Together we sing;
Our hymns never cease.
Of rewards from the Holy;
To the child ever mighty,
Our chorus shall sing,
Till thy kindred see the God of all peace.

The history of Christian hymnology affords here and there an interesting illustration of the truth, "Surely the wrath of man shall praise Thee." When the apostate Julian ascended the throne, he turned his legislation against Christ, and prohibited all Christians from learning or teaching the classic literature of the Gentile world. He thought to extinguish Christianity by shutting up Christians to barren ignorance. His policy, however, worked against his own purpose. The poetic power and taste of Christian leaders were now called forth to supply purer elements of education than the popular classic poets could yield; and driven from heathen measures, Christians were supplied with hymns and songs, which at once formed literary lessons and means of chaste excitement for the heart. Among several who took the lead in opening these fresh supplies of poetic food for youthful Christianity, there was one who had been a schoolfellow and companion of Julian himself. The interior of Asia Minor, now so little known, was open during the third century to the genial influence of the Christian religion. To us the richly diversified landscapes are all but forbidden ground; but once the mountain ranges and romantic glens, the fruitful plains and garden-like valleys, the charming dales and upland forests of pine and beach and odorous cedar, the perfumed flower-beds broadly sheltered by the plane-tree, and the river banks adorned with the verdure of mastic and tamarind groves, combined to form a scene in which the Christian Church trained some of her noblest sons. Several of these were the sons of holy women: one was Basil the Great; and another was his schoolfellow and life-long friend, Gregory of Nazianzen, whose father lived to see his son associated with him in the bishopric of his native township, and whose saintly mother, Nonna, had her last days cheered by the hymns and spiritual songs of the boy in whose holy character and life she saw the answer to her prayers. Basil's letters to his friend, from his own religious retreat, throw some light upon Gregory's character as a Christian poet; and from one to whose love for nature and fine taste the cultivated Basil could make such affectionate and charming appeals, we might expect such hymnic contributions as even now assist our service of song. Gregory might be said to have spent his useful life—

> 'Twixt the mount and multitude;
> Doing or receiving good.

With the multitude he sang of Christ; and he instructed his flock in their creed, while he taught them to sing—

> Hear us now, O King eternal;
> Give us power to hymn Thy praise;
> Thou, our Lord; and Thou our Master;
> By Thee alone our songs we raise.
>   By Thee the choirs of angels glow;
>   By Thee the ceaseless ages flow.
> By Thee the sun appears in glory;
> The moon in brightness keeps her pace;
> Stars shine forth in smiling beauty!
> And reason marks the human race.
>   Man breathed that light from Thee alone,
>   That all Thy other works outshone.
> Thou art of all things the Creator;
> Life springs where'er Thy voice is heard;
> All is ordered by Thy wisdom;
> All is finished by Thy word:
>   Thy Holy Word, Thy only Son
>   With Thee in might and glory one.
> As Lord of all we Him confess;
> With Him the Holy Ghost we bless;
> Pervading and inspiring all,
> O Triune God; on Thee we call!

But the junior bishop had to psalm it in "troublous times." He was sometimes touched by circumstances so like those of ancient psalmists, that his feelings seemed to be reflections of theirs; and his metrical expression is sweetly attuned to their measures. Things around him, both in Church and State, were heaving and breaking up, threatening indeed a return of chaotic confusion. "Men's hearts were failing them for fear, and for looking after those things which were coming on the earth"—Ecclesiastical tremor, social corruption, storms from "high places," and faithlessness among the masses, all pressed hardly upon the spirits of Gregory. His heart was overwhelmed at times, and like another sweet singer, he was ready to cry, "Oh, that I had wings like a dove! for then would I fly away, and be at rest. Lo, then would I wander far off, and remain in the wilderness. I would hasten my escape from the windy storm and tempest." One of his plaintive songs has reached us from his religious retreat—

> My fatherland alone to me remains,
> The floods of faction o'er my country sweep;
> For my uncertain feet, the land retains
> No resting-place; no friend to weep;
> No child to soothe the homeless poor forlorn;
> I wander day by day with trembling limbs and torn.
>
> What lot awaits me? What my mortal doom?
> Where shall this jaded body find its rest?
> Shall this poor trembling flesh e'er find a tomb?
> By whom shall these dim eyes in death be blest?
> Will any watch? Will any pity me?
> Will they be Christian watchers? Or, shall sinners see?
>
> Or shall no grave enclose this mortal frame?
> When laid a heavy breathless corpse of clay?
> Cast on the rock uncovered and in shame;
> Or tossed in scorn to birds and beasts of prey?
> Or burnt to ashes, given to the air?
> Or thrown into the weedy deep to perish there?
>
> Thy will be done, O Lord! That day shall spring,
> When at Thy word, this clay shall reappear!
> No death I dread, but that which sin will bring;
> No fire or flood without Thy wrath I fear;
> For Thou, O Christ, my Lord, art fatherland to me!
> My wealth, and might, and rest; my all I find in Thee!

There is something in the calm light and devout stillness of the evening hour which touchingly answers to the solemn peacefulness of the Christian's last moments on earth. This has been felt in all ages by Christian genius. And the feeling has found expression in a line of evening hymns, hymns which served to hush the spirits of God's children from generation to generation; and from age to age to hallow the mysterious advances of nightly repose.

Gregory is among the leaders in evening song; and how his music lulls us—

> Christ, my God, I come to praise Thee,
>   As the day dims into night;
> Thou who art from everlasting—
>   Light of ever living light.
>
> Thou didst melt orig'nal darkness,
> Give to light its first unfolding,
>   That all things might live in light.
> Settling the unsettled chaos
> Into forms of beauteous order,
>   As we see them fair and bright.
>
> Reason's light to man Thou gavest,
> 'Bove the speechless creature's dight,
> That on light in Thy light gazing,
>   He himself might be all light.
>
> Thou hast deck'd the heavens with radiance;
> With Thy clust'ring lamps of glory,
>   Hanging the expanse above;
> Calling day and night to service,
> Like a happy brotherhood, by turns
>   Obedient to the law of love.
>
> Thou by night, from tears and toiling,
>   Giv'st our wearied nature rest,
> Waking us as day arises,
>   To the works Thou lovest best.

While the last stanza lingers on our ears, who does not think of Bishop Ken? who is not ready to sing that immortal "even-song" of his, which for a century and a half has been naturally rising to the lips of English Christians—

> Soon as the evening shades prevail?

How alike were Bishop Gregory of Nazianzen and Bishop Ken in some of the closing circumstances of their career! and how alike was their mode of uttering the quiet joys of their life in retreat. Gregory had mastered the swellings of heresy, and had weathered the storm of imperial hate; but just as he saw the dawn of favour from "high places," and there was the promise of some reward for his faithfulness on earth, unforeseen difficulties beset his way to ecclesiastical preferment; and shrinking from strife for mere position, he turned aside from the public scenes of action, and, as a lone man, spent his last few years in attuning his heart to the melodies of heaven. So, good Bishop Ken, having stood a faithful witness for Christian purity in two courts, under William of Orange in Holland, and then as chaplain to Charles II. of England, securing in both cases the esteem of those whom he consistently reproved; and having shared imprisonment with his six episcopal brethren, for resisting the irregular measures of James II., his conscience found difficulty in accepting the continuance of ecclesiastical honour under William, and he retired into private life, to solace himself with hymns and songs while waiting for his divine Master's coming. His spirit shrank from the strife of party. He would take no part in the vain contention. "No, no!" said he, in his own style,

> I gladly wars ecclesiastic fly,
> Where'er contentious spirits I descry;
> Eas'd of my sacred load, I live content,
> In hymns, not in disputes, my passions vent.

And had his meek and tuneful spirit found no other vent than in his blessed evening hymn, his memory would never lose its freshness, interwoven as it is with the evening devotion of so many English homes. Have you, as a lover of contemplative goodness, ever lingered of an evening among the peaceful homes of Berkhampstead, in Hertfordshire, Ken's birthplace? or did you ever sit in the summer gloaming on the old bench in Winchester School, where he took his early lessons, and try to call up the presence of the poetic boy? or have you joined at even song, in the noble old church at Bath, where the pious bishop used to compose prayers as well as hymns for his flock? or have you watched the sunset from amidst the quiet beauties of Longleat, in Wiltshire, where the venerable pilgrim closed his life-journey, saying, "I die in the communion of the Church of England, as it stands distinguished from all Papal and Puritan innovations, and as it adheres to the doctrine of the Cross"? Have you? Then the evening hymn will always have music for your heart; and like one who had caught the spirit of the gentle-minded hymnist, you will learn at every night-fall to pass devoutly into sleep singing within your soul—

All praise to Thee, my God, this night,
For all the blessings of the light,
Keep me, oh, keep me, King of kings,
Beneath Thine own Almighty wings!

Forgive me, Lord, for Thy dear Son,
The ill that I this day have done;
That with the world, myself, and Thee,
I, ere I sleep, at peace may be.

Teach me to live that I may dread
The grave as little as my bed!
To die, that this vile body may
Rise glorious at the awful day!

Oh, may my soul on Thee repose,
And may sweet sleep mine eyelids close;
Sleep, that may me more vig'rous make,
To serve my God when I awake!

When in the night I sleepless lie,
My soul with heavenly thoughts supply!
Let no ill dreams disturb my rest,
No powers of darkness me molest!

Dull sleep, of sense me to deprive!
I am but half my time alive;
Thy faithful lovers, Lord, are grieved
To lie so long of Thee bereav'd.

But though sleep o'er my frailty reigns,
Let it not hold me long in chains;
And now and then let loose my heart,
Till it an hallelujah dart!

The faster sleep the senses binds,
The more unfettered are our minds;
Oh, may my soul from matter free,
Thy loveliness unclouded see!

Oh, when shall I in endless day,
For ever chase dark sleep away,
And hymns with the supernal choir
Incessant sing, and never tire?

Oh, may my Guardian while I sleep,
Close to my bed his vigils keep;
His love angelical instil;
Stop all the avenues of ill:

May he celestial joy rehearse,
And thought to thought with me converse;
Or in my stead, all the night long,
Sing to my God a grateful song!

> Praise God, from whom all blessings flow,
> Praise Him, all creatures here below!
> Praise Him above, ye heavenly host!
> Praise Father, Son, and Holy Ghost!

Gregory of Nazianzen and Bishop Ken have long since met, and sung together where evening shadows never fall; and there, too, are the kindred spirits whose evening hymns form the links between the times of Gregory and Ken. There, among the rest, is Hilary of Arles, once bishop, popular preacher, theologian, and poet. And there is Ambrose of Milan, whose morning and evening melodies gave form of devotional expression to the softened heart of the great Augustine, who "alone upon his bed" remembered the verses of his friend—

> Maker of all, the Lord
>   And ruler of the height,
> Who, robing day in light, has poured
>   Soft slumbers o'er the night,
> That to our limbs the power
>   Of toil may be renew'd,
> And hearts be rais'd that sink and cower,
>   And sorrows be subdu'd.

From one of these hymnists we have one touching strain, one of the living links in the Church's line of evening hymns—

> Christ our day, our brightest light,
> With Thy face illume the night;
> Very Light of light art Thou,
> Most blessed light imparting now.
>
> Oh most holy Lord, we pray;
> Mighty Guardian, with us stay;
> With quiet blest these hours be;
> All calm, while we have rest in Thee.
>
> Let not heavy sleep oppress;
> Let no deadly foe distress;
> Nor our flesh through him beguile,
> And in Thy sight our souls defile.
>
> Though sleep fasten on our eyes,
> Keep our hearts in wakeful guise;
> With Thine own right hand defend
> Thy servants who on Thee depend.

> Servants purchased with Thy blood,
> Bearing still their mortal load,
> Lord, remember! meet us here,
> Thou soul defender, now be near!

How beautiful are the oneness and the harmony of the evening voices that thus come to us from the different periods of Christian history. And no one can catch the tones of evening worship from far-off ages without feeling that they sweetly melt into that tender melody of John Keble's, to which so many hearts of our own times respond, in singing the evening hymn founded on St. Luke xxiv. 29, "Abide with us: for it is toward evening, and the day is far spent"—

> 'Tis gone, that bright and orbed blaze,
> Fast fading from our wistful gaze;
> Yon mantling cloud has hid from sight
> The last faint pulse of quivering light.
>
> In darkness and in weariness
> The traveller on his way must press,
> No gleam to watch on tree or tower,
> Whiling away the lonesome hour.
>
> Sun of my soul! Thou Saviour dear,
> It is not night if Thou be near;
> Oh may no earth-born cloud arise
> To hide Thee from Thy servant's eyes.
>
> When round Thy wondrous works below,
> My searching rapturous glance I throw;
> Tracing out Wisdom, Power, and Love,
> In earth or sky, in stream or grove;—
>
> Or by the light Thy words disclose,
> Watch Time's full river as it flows;
> Scanning Thy gracious providence,
> Where not too deep for mortal sense;—
>
> When with dear friends sweet talks I hold,
> And all the flowers of life unfold;
> Let not my heart within me burn,
> Except in all I Thee discern.
>
> When the soft dews of kindly sleep
> My wearied eyelids gently steep;
> Be my last thought, how sweet to rest
> For ever on my Saviour's breast.
>
> Abide with me from morn till eve,
> For without Thee I cannot live:
> Abide with me when night is nigh,
> For without Thee I dare not die.

Thou Framer of the light and dark,
Steer through the tempest Thine own ark;
Amid the howling wintry sea
We are in port if we have Thee.

The rulers of this Christian land,
'Twixt Thee and us ordained to stand;
Guide Thou their course, O Lord, aright.
Let all do all as in Thy sight.

Oh, by Thine own sad burthen, borne
So meekly up the hill of scorn,
Teach thou Thy priests their daily cross
To bear as Thine, nor count it loss!

If some poor wandering child of Thine
Have spurn'd to-day the voice divine;
Now, Lord, the gracious work begin;
Let him no more lie down in sin.

Watch by the sick: enrich the poor
With blessings from Thy boundless store:
Be every mourner's sleep to-night
Like infant's slumbers, pure and light.

Come near and bless us when we wake,
Ere through the world our way we take;
Till in the ocean of Thy love
We lose ourselves in heaven above.

CHAPTER V.

MORE HYMNS OF THE FATHERS.

"Showing to the generations to come the praises of the Lord."

PRIMITIVE Christianity soon found its way to the old seats of patriarchal life. Some of its first songs came from across the land which has "neither mountain, valley, or even plain—the whole being an unequal surface like the high and long waves of a deep sea when subsiding from a tempest into a calm;" with verdant hollows here and there, but with no "tree anywhere in sight to relieve the monotony of the scene." Along this mysterious reach, this Mesopotamia, Abraham came, refreshing himself now and then on a grassy plot, on his way to Canaan. He came out of "Ur of the Chaldees" to be the Father of the faithful; and from the same place one, at least, of the Christian fathers came. He, too, was faithful; and by his Christian hymns he made faithfulness pleasant to his own generation and to many following ages. Ephrem Syrus was born by the crystal waters which refresh the city of Orfah, once Edessa, and which form the lake known to those who enjoy the mulberry groves which overshadow its banks as "Abraham the beloved, or the Friend of God." Ephrem, like all who aimed at high spirituality in the fourth century, became a devoted monk; and on some aspects of his character there still remain shadows of the asceticism which was peculiar to a time of reaction from social licentiousness and decay. But with all Ephrem's asceticism, his hymns testify that he had learnt the lesson which the Saviour so gracefully taught his disciples; that, though in some cases religious celibacy might be in keeping with the spirit and principles of His kingdom—hardness and severity were in no case consistent with Christian piety; that the hardness which the law of Moses admitted, and which showed itself in those stern rebukes which were cast on the women who brought their infants to Jesus, must yield to that gentle love which looked with utmost tenderness upon the little ones whose humility, simplicity, and submissiveness typify the highest style of the Christian character. The venerable Mesopotamian hymnist, however severe in his treatment of self, was like his divine Master in his feelings towards children. He must have laid his hands on them lovingly. His smile must have been full of blessing. How sweetly he attunes his music to the voices of his "little flock," while he teaches them to sing in unison with the children in paradise—

> To Thee, O God, be praises
> From lips of babes and sucklings,
> As in the heavenly meadows
>   Like spotless lambs they feed.
>
> 'Mid leafy trees they pasture,
> Thus saith the Blessed Spirit;
> And Gabriel, prince of angels,
>   That happy flock doth lead.
>
> The messengers of heaven,
> With sons of light united,
> In purest regions dwelling,
>   No curse or woe they see.
>
> And at the resurrection,
> With joy arise their bodies;
> Their spirits knew no bondage,
>   Their bodies now are free.
>
> Brief here below their sojourn,
> Their dwelling is in Eden,
> And one bright day their parents
>   Hope yet with them to be.

The heart that is gentle enough to be childlike among children must always have deep sympathy with parents, especially under the sorrows of bereavement. And many a lover of little children, though never himself really touched by the unspeakable pang of seeing his own babe breathe its last, has shown himself capable of entering very deeply into the feeling of the desolated parent, almost as if that feeling were his own. A few touching verses from a living author afford an example of such inspirations of sympathizing genius. The author of "Records of the Western Shore," had no child of his own when he issued his first volume but he utters the grief of a Cornish mother thus:—

> They say 'tis a sin to sorrow,
>   That what God doth is best,
> But 'tis only a month to-morrow
>   I buried it from my breast!
>
> I know it should be a pleasure
>   Your child to God to send,
> But mine was a precious treasure
>   To me and to my poor Friend!
>
> I thought it would call me mother
>   The very first words it said;
> Oh! I never can love another,
>   Like the blessed babe that's dead!
>
> I shall make my best endeavour
>   That my sins may be forgiven;
> I will serve God more than ever
>   To meet my child in heaven!
>
> I will check this foolish sorrow,
>   For what God doth is best;
> But oh! 'tis a month to-morrow,
>   I buried it from my breast!

Ephrem Syrus, too, monk as he was, could deeply sympathize with a bereaved heart; and he shows how truly he made another's sorrows his own when he personates the Christian father lamenting the death of his boy. He becomes as natural in his utterance of parental feeling as he is happy in the expression of living faith:—

> Babe, the gift of God's sweet mercy
>   To thy mother's heart and mine,
> To this world of sorrow coming,
>   Beautiful by Grace Divine;
> Fair as some sweet summer flower:
>   Till that hand of deathly shade
> Scathed the beauty of my blossom,
>   Made the lovely petals fade.
> Yet I will not grieve nor murmur,
>   For the King of kings is thine;
> To his marriage chamber taken,
>   Bridal joys are ever thine.

> Nature would have me repining,
>   Love would hold a mournful sway:
> But I tell them heav'n has call'd thee
>   To its scenes of endless day.
> And I fear that by lamenting,
>   Breathing tearfully thy name,
> I might in the Royal presence
>   For my sorrow merit blame;
> By my tears of bitter anguish
>   Desecrate the home of joy;
> Therefore will I, meekly bending,
>   Give thee up to God, my boy.
>
> Still thy voice, thy infant music
>   Dwells for ever in my ears;
> And fond mem'ry, while I listen,
>   Sheds forth many natural tears.
> Of thy pretty prattle thinking,
>   And the lispings of thy love,
> I should soon begin to murmur,
>   Were I not to look above;
> But the songs of blessed spirits
>   Make me wonder, love, and long:—
> Oh those endless sweet hosannas;
>   Angels sing thy bridal song.

Hymns like these come down to us as pleasant records of that Christian simplicity with which some of the fathers showed forth the spirit and meaning of their Saviour's words, "Whosoever therefore shall humble himself as this little child, the same is greatest in the kingdom of heaven." One of the finest examples of this Christian greatness, this beautiful association of mental dignity and spiritual power with childlike simplicity and pure humbleness and submissiveness, is seen in the justly-celebrated and sainted Augustine. He has not, like Ephrem, embalmed his gentle spirit in hymns for little ones; but he has immortalized those who, like himself, were "converted and became as little children," and who, amidst the joys of their first love, consecrated their genius to the work of providing both the elders and the children of the Church with hymns and spiritual songs. "I remember," says he, in his holy converse with God—"I remember the tears I shed at the psalmody of Thy Church, in the beginning of my recovered faith. . . . . How did I weep through Thy hymns and canticles, touched to the quick by the voices of Thy sweet attuned Church. The voices sank into mine ears, and the truth distilled into mine heart; whence the affections of my devotions overflowed, tears ran down, and happy was I therein. . . . . And how at this time I was moved, not with the singing, but with the things sung. When they are sung with a clear voice and modulation most suitable, I acknowledge the great use of this institution." His account of the first hymn-service in the church at Milan, the place of his first love, is touching and instructive. "It was a year, or not much more, that Justina, mother to the Emperor Valentinian, then a child, persecuted Thy servant Ambrose in favour of her heresy, to which she was seduced by the Arians. The devout people kept watch in the church, ready to die with their bishop, Thy servant. There my mother, Thy handmaid, bearing a chief part in those anxieties and watchings, lived for prayer. We, yet unwarmed by the heat of Thy Spirit, still were stirred up by the sight of the amazed and disquieted city. Then it was instituted that, after the manner of the Eastern Churches, hymns and psalms should be sung, lest the people should wax faint through the tediousness of sorrow, and from that day to this the custom is retained." The Christian flock which thus kept up their chant and song in "troublous times," were supplied with many of their favourite hymns by their diligent, faithful, and gifted bishop, Ambrose, Augustine's beloved friend. Some of his songs are favourites still, and have been sung from age to age, becoming fresher and fresher until our own times, and are now giving the promise of renewed life. It is interesting to see that the man who, under the prejudices of his times, utters libels upon matrimony, melts into childlike tenderness when he sings of Jesus, and feels that his Saviour became an infant that He might save infants, and hallow human nature in all its relations. This more pure and gentle Christian feeling may be traced in the "Advent Hymn," so well known as one of the flowers which wreathe his memory—

> Redeemer of the nations, come;
> Pure offspring of the Virgin's womb,
> Seed of the woman promised long,
> Let ages swell Thine advent song.
>
> Once from the Father came He forth,
> Home to the Father rose from earth;

> The depths of hell the Saviour trod,
> Now seated on the throne of God.
>
> To God the Father equal, Word,
> Thy mortal vesture on Thee gird;
> The weakness of our flesh at length
> Sustaining by Thy changeless strength.
>
> Thy cradle shine the darkness through,
> Illuming night with lustre new,
> Which never night shall hide again,
> But faith in ceaseless light retain.

Nor has hallowed genius lost its tender affection for the "Holy Child Jesus." Ephrem Syrus has long since left his Eastern retreat, and the cloisters of the West no longer echo to the voices of Ambrose and his companions; but spirits of equal simplicity, and voices of even more than equal sweetness continue to supply God's children with hymns and spiritual songs. One of Ambrose's last strains seems to have some gentle relation to the hymn of a modern bishop, whose amiable soul breathes its music from an Eastern mission Church. Ephrem, and Ambrose, and Heber were kindred spirits. They might be thought to emulate each other in songs on "the childhood of Christ." The pure and delicate beauty of Heber's hymn would have charmed the ancient hymnists, as it insinuates its affectionate devotion into every "new-born babe" in Christ who has learnt to sing it—

> By cool Siloam's shady rill
> How sweet the lily grows;
> How sweet the breath beneath the hill
> Of Sharon's dewy rose!
>
> Lo, such the child, whose early feet
> The paths of peace have trod;
> Whose secret heart, with influence sweet,
> Is upward drawn to God!
>
> By cool Siloam's shady rill
> The lily must decay;
> The rose that blooms beneath the hill
> Must shortly fade away.
>
> And soon, too soon, the wintry hour
> Of man's maturer age,
> Will shake the soul with sorrow's power,
> And stormy passions rage!

O Thou whose infant feet were found
  Within Thy Father's shrine!
Whose years, with changeless virtue crowned,
  Were all alike divine.

Dependent on Thy bounteous breath,
  We seek Thy grace alone,
In childhood, manhood, age, and death,
  To keep us still Thine own!

We can never sing thus about the childhood of Christ without having our pleasures deepened by the assurance that our children have a sacred interest in "the Holy Child." Yes, Jesus smiles to see the cradled infant hushed by a Christian lullaby. Each little one is sacred to Him who was once swaddled in the manger. It was this thought that used at once to melt and brighten the sturdy German Reformer as he hung over his sleeping darling, and sang—

> Sleep well, my dear; sleep safe and free;
> The holy angels are with thee,
> Who always see thy Father's face,
> And never slumber nights nor days.
>
> Thou liest in down, soft every way;
> Thy Saviour lay in straw and hay;
> Thy cradle is far better drest
> Than the hard crib where He did rest.
>
> None dare disturb thy present ease;
> He had a thousand enemies;
> Thou liv'st in great security;
> But He was punished, and for thee!
>
> God make thy mother's health increase,
> To see thee grow in strength and grace,
> In wisdom and humility,
> As infant Jesus did for thee!
>
> God fill thee with His heavenly light
> To steer thy Christian course aright;
> Make thee a tree of blessed root,
> That ever bends with godly fruit!
>
> Sleep now, my dear, and take thy rest;
> And if with riper years thou'rt blest,
> Increase in wisdom, day and night,
> Till thou attain'st th' eternal light!

And who that knows George Wither's "rocking hymn" is not thankful to providence that it has outlived the storms that beset its author's later life, and is still adapted to its original purpose? "Nurses," says he, quaintly, "usually sing their children asleep, and, throught want of pertinent matter, they oft make use of unprofitable, if not worse songs; this was therefore prepared, that it might help acquaint them and their nurse children with the loving care and kindness of their heavenly Father."

> Sweet baby, sleep; what ails my dear;
> What ails my darling thus to cry?
> Be still, my child, and lend thine ear,
> To hear me sing thy lullaby.
>   My pretty lamb, forbear to weep;
>   Be still, my dear; sweet baby, sleep.
>
> Thou blessed soul, what can'st thou fear?
> What thing to thee can mischief do?
> Thy God is now thy Father dear,
> His holy spouse thy mother too.
>   Sweet baby, then, forbear to weep;
>   Be still, my babe; sweet baby, sleep.
>
> Whilst thus thy lullaby I sing,
> For thee great blessings ripening be;
> Thine eldest brother is a king,
> And hath a kingdom bought for thee.
>   Sweet baby, then, forbear to weep;
>   Be still, my babe; sweet baby, sleep.
>
> Sweet baby, sleep, and nothing fear,
> For whosoever thee offends,
> By thy protector threaten'd are,
> And God and angels are thy friends.
>   Sweet baby, then, forbear to weep;
>   Be still, my babe; sweet baby, sleep.
>
> When God with us was dwelling here,
> In little babes He took delight;
> Such innocents as thou, my dear!
> Are ever precious in His sight.
>   Sweet baby, then, forbear to weep;
>   Be still, my babe; sweet baby, sleep.
>
> A little infant once was He,
> And strength in weakness then was laid
> Upon his virgin mother's knee,
> That power to thee might be conveyed.
>   Sweet baby, then, forbear to weep;
>   Be still, my babe; sweet baby sleep.

In this thy frailty and thy need,
He friends and helpers doth prepare,
Which thee shall cherish, clothe, and feed;
For of thy weal they tender are.
    Sweet baby, then, forbear to weep;
    Be still, my babe; sweet baby, sleep.

The King of kings, when He was born,
Had not so much for outward ease;
By him such dressings were not worn,
Nor such like swaddling clothes as these.
    Sweet baby, then, forbear to weep;
    Be still, my babe; sweet baby, sleep.

Within a manger lodged thy Lord!
Where oxen lay, and asses fed;
Warm rooms we do to thee afford,
An easy cradle or a bed.
    Sweet baby, then, forbear to weep;
    Be still, my babe; sweet baby, sleep.

The wants that He did then sustain
Have purchased wealth, my babe, for thee;
And by His torments and His pain
Thy rest and ease secured be.
    My baby, then, forbear to weep;
    Be still, my babe; sweet baby, sleep.

Thou hast yet more to perfect this,
A promise and an earnest got,
Of gaining everlasting bliss,
Though thou, my babe, perceiv'st it not.
    Sweet baby, then, forbear to weep;
    Be still, my babe; sweet baby, sleep.

The author of this pattern Christian lullaby was born June 11, 1588. His portrait has come down to us surrounded by the quaint motto, "I grow and wither both together;" but neither the portrait nor the motto gives us so deep and clear an insight into his character as the poems of his earlier life. His genius shone brightest while he was a Royalist; and his "Rocking Hymn" was probably written before his tenderness had given way to the more bitter spirit of satire, which he sometimes vented after he had sided with Cromwell, and had tasted the bitter fruits of change in the loss of both power and fortune. Who is not sorry to see the man whose early hymns gave forth "the finest bursts of sunshine," struggling for popularity under the thick cloud which gathered at last over his party and his character, by sending out squibs under the title of "abuses whipt and stript?" Nevertheless, peace to his memory. He has taught many a Christian mother and nurse to hush her baby into rest by singing of its happy relation to Jesus: and perhaps Watts had seen his verses, and caught from them the notion of his own "Cradle Hymn." At all events, we naturally think of Watts as we sing the "Rocking Hymn" over the cradle. Nobody can sing about children, or teach children to sing, without grateful thoughts of Isaac Watts. He, too, had felt deeply that the "Holy child Jesus" had procured for our children the joy of taking a part in "Hosannas to the Son of David;" that the voice of "little ones" is divine music in the ears of Jesus; and that to Him the songs of infancy are as the incense of the morning. "During my stay by the sea-side, at one time," said a lady whose appearance was always graceful, though she never seemed to follow the fashion, "I used to be charmed every morning by the voices of the children in the nursery, singing as they dressed, under the guidance of the nurse, the inimitable little song by Watts, 'against pride in clothes.' The music seemed to be the voice of innocence itself. I used to think of Him who taught us how to be clothed with humility; and my soul felt now and then as if He must be listening with pleasure to the dear little creatures singing their morning lesson about the 'blest apparel.' The lesson was hallowed to me. The exquisite little song was never to leave me, and I am all the better for the habit which those darling children taught me of humming to myself, now and then—

> Why should our garments, made to hide
> Our parents' shame, provoke our pride?
> The act of dress did ne'er begin
> Till Eve our mother learnt to sin.
>
> When first she put the covering on,
> Her robe of innocence was gone;
> And yet her children vainly boast
> In the sad marks of glory lost.
>
> How proud we are, how fond to show
> Our clothes, and call them rich and new;
> When the poor sheep and silkworm wore
> That very clothing long before.

The tulip and the butterfly
Appear in gayer clothes than I :
Let me be drest fine as I will,
Flies, worms, and flowers exceed me still.

Then will I set my heart to find
Inward adornings of the mind ;
Knowledge and virtue, truth and grace,
These are the robes of richest dress.

No more shall worms with me compare,
This is the raiment angels wear ;
The Son of God, when here below,
Put on this blest apparel too.

It never fades, it ne'er grows old,
Nor fears the rain, nor moth, nor mold ;
It takes no spot, but still refines,
The more 'tis worn, the more it shines.

In this on earth would I appear,
Then go to heaven, and wear it there ;
God will approve it in His sight,
'Tis His own work, and His delight."

Would that the childish multitude were learning to "murmur" this beautiful lesson, and to practise it, in these days of growing strife and vicious rage for mere appearances. "Watts" should be a household name among all English children. He is always at home with little ones. He is heart to heart with them, and therefore always makes them understand; and never fails to sway their feeling. He is the child's hymnist. As such, none have surpassed him ; few are his equals. He never lowers the manliness of his simplicity when he sings with children, though he not unfrequently becomes puerile when he provides hymns for men. In this respect Charles Wesley has the advantage over him. Wesley never, like Watts, brings a mature congregation plump down from grandeur into childishness. When leading the devotions of adults, his vigour never fails, though his music may now and then falter. He never has to make so curious an apology for namby-pamby verses as Watts puts forth in excuse for occasional trips into tameness. "If," says Watts, "the verses appear so gentle and flowing as to incur the censure of feebleness, I may honestly affirm that sometimes it cost me labour to make it so. Some of the beauties of poesy are neglected, and some wilfully defaced, lest a more exalted turn of thought or language should darken or disturb the devotions of the weakest souls." Who can wonder that such an apologist should sometimes flatter the devotions of adult worshippers by forcing on them a sense of the ridiculous? Wesley never does that; at the same time, as a child's hymnist, he is never below the standard of Watts; never being out of tune with the voices, thoughts, or hearts of little ones. Some of his hymns for children have been issued, on some occasions, with Watts's name attached, comparative ignorance of hymnology favouring the notion that all merit in juvenile psalmody must necessarily belong to the author of "Divine and Moral Songs." So it has happened with one of the best known of Wesley's "Hymns for the Youngest."

> Gentle Jesus, meek and mild,
> Look upon a little child;
> Pity my simplicity,
> Suffer me to come to Thee.
>
> Fain I would to Thee be brought,
> Dearest God, forbid it not;
> Give me, dearest God, a place
> In the kingdom of Thy grace.
>
> Put Thy hands upon my head,
> Let me in Thy arms be stay'd,
> Let me lean upon Thy breast,
> Lull me, lull me, Lord, to rest.
>
> Hold me fast in Thy embrace,
> Let me see Thy smiling face,
> Give me, Lord, Thy blessing give,
> Pray for me, and I shall live:
>
> I shall live the simple life,
> Free from sin's uneasy strife,
> Sweetly ignorant of ill,
> Innocent and happy still.
>
> O that I may never know
> What the wicked people do!
> Sin is contrary to Thee,
> Sin is the forbidden tree.
>
> Keep me from the great offence,
> Guard my helpless innocence,
> Hide me, from all evil hide,
> Self, and stubbornness, and pride.

The second part of this favourite hymn is of surpassing beauty. It wins its way into the soul of every child who lisps it; gently opening the heart to let the infant Saviour in:—

> Lamb of God, I look to Thee,
> Thou shalt my example be;
> Thou art gentle, meek, and mild;
> Thou was't once a little child.
>
> Fain I would be as Thou art,
> Give me Thy obedient heart;
> Thou art pitiful and kind,
> Let me have Thy loving mind.
>
> Meek and lowly may I be,
> Thou art all humility;
> Let me to my betters bow,
> Subject to Thy parents Thou.
>
> Let me above all fulfil
> God my heavenly Father's will,
> Never His good Spirit grieve,
> Only to His glory live.
>
> Thou did'st live to God alone,
> Thou did'st never seek Thine own,
> Thou thyself did'st never please,
> God was all Thy happiness.
>
> Loving Jesus, gentle Lamb,
> In Thy gracious hands I am,
> Make me, Saviour, what Thou art,
> Live Thyself within my heart.
>
> I shall then show forth Thy praise,
> Serve Thee all my happy days,
> Then the world shall always see
> Christ, the holy Child, in me.

James Montgomery has followed Watts and Wesley, not to rival their fame, or to eclipse it; but to claim a share in the joy of teaching childhood to honour and love the Divine lover of little children. Nor does he claim an equal place in vain. His voice, his taste, his manner, and his heart are all worthy of a position in the leading choir of children's hymnists; and one of his tender expressions of youthful devotion may be gracefully associated with the most pure and touching hymns of the fathers about the childhood of Jesus.

When Jesus left His Father's throne,
  He chose an humble birth;
Like us, unhonoured and unknown,
  He came to dwell on earth.

Like Him, may we be found below
  In wisdom's paths of peace;
Like Him, in grace and knowledge grow,
  As years and strength increase.

Jesus pass'd by the rich and great
  For men of low degree;
He sanctified our parents' state,
  For poor, like them, was He.

Sweet were His words, and kind His look,
  When mothers round Him press'd;
Their infants in His arms He took,
  And on His bosom bless'd.

Safe from the world's alluring harms,
  Beneath His watchful eye,
Thus in the circle of His arms
  May we for ever lie!

When Jesus into Salem rode,
  The children sang around;
For joy they pluck'd the palms, and strew'd
  Their garments on the ground.

Hosanna our glad voices raise,
  Hosanna to our King!
Should we forget our Saviour's praise,
  The stones themselves would sing!

CHAPTER VI.

HYMNS OF OLD ENGLAND'S CHRISTIAN BIRTH-TIME.

"And the people that shall be created shall praise the Lord."

"When I lived at Lichfield," said a lady to a clerical friend, "I used, now and then, to attend the ordination service; and I learnt one thing at least."

"What was that?"

"Why, that there are some hymns which, though they are known to be mere human compositions, are scarcely ever sung without touching the soul in a manner very like that of inspired truth."

"Pray, what impressed you with that thought?"

"Well, I observed that there were always some among the candidates for ordination who seemed disposed to go through the service without seriousness, if not in a style approaching to levity, even during the time allowed for silent prayer; but that as soon as the hymn '*Veni Creator Spiritus*' was begun, a solemn hush and reverent feeling appeared to rest on each and all."

"Which of the hymns do you refer to? There are two in the ordination service."

"The first. And now let me read it. And if I can read so as to give you the feeling with which it always impresses me, I think you will believe as I do, that the Holy Ghost honours the hymn by which He is honoured, and breathes a holy power into its gracious lines. Let me read."

Come, Holy Ghost, our souls inspire,
And lighten with celestial fire.

Thou the anointing Spirit art,
Who dost Thy seven-fold gifts impart.

Thy blessed unction from above
Is comfort, life, and fire of love.

Enable with perpetual light
The dulness of our blinded sight.

Anoint and cheer our soiled face
With the abundance of Thy grace.

Keep far our foes, give peace at home:
Where Thou art guide no ill can come.

Teach us to know the Father, Son,
And Thee of both to be but one;

That through the ages all along,
This may be our endless song;

> Praise to Thine eternal merit,
> Father, Son, and Holy Spirit.

The lady was right; and her clerical friend confessed to the feeling in which many, many have shared, a sense of the spiritual unction which attends this as well as several other hymns of like primitive simplicity and power. And he was reminded, he said, of Keble's Ordination Hymn, in which this feeling is so sweetly expressed. The hymn is founded on that passage in the rubric in the "Office for Ordering Priests," "After this the congregation shall be desired, secretly in their prayers to make their humble supplication to God for all these things; for the which prayers there shall be silence kept for a space. After which shall be sung or said by the bishop (the persons to be ordained priests all kneeling) '*Veni Creator Spiritus.*'"

'Twas silence in Thy temple, Lord,
  When slowly through the hallowed air,
The spreading cloud of incense soared,
  Charged with the breath of Israel's prayer.

'Twas silence round Thy throne on high,
  When the last wondrous seal unclos'd;
And in the portals of the sky
  Thine armies awfully repos'd.

And this deep pause, that o'er us now
  Is hovering—comes it not of Thee?
Is it not like a mother's vow,
  When with her darling on her knee,

> She weighs and numbers o'er and o'er
>   Love's treasures hid in her fond breast;
> To cull from that exhaustless store
>   The dearest blessing and the best?
>
> And where shall mother's bosom find,
>   With all its deep love-learned skill,
> A prayer so sweetly to her mind,
>   As, in this sacred hour and still,
>
> Is wafted from the white-rob'd choir,
>   Ere yet the pure high-breathed lay,
> "Come, Holy Ghost, our souls inspire,"
>   Rise floating on its dove-like way?
>
> And when it comes, so deep and clear
>   The strain, so soft the melting fall,
> It seems not to the entranced ear
>   Less than Thine own heart-cheering call.
>
> Spirit of Christ—Thine earnest given
>   That these our prayers are heard; and they
> Who grasp, this hour, the sword of heaven
>   Shall feel Thee on their weary way.

The "*Veni Creator Spiritus*" was introduced into the ritual of the Western Church about the end of the eleventh century; and with beautiful consistency, as an utterance, probably, from the lips of one whose name marks an era in the history of church music; and it was gracefully retained in the service of the English Church as a contribution from the man to whom England owes her first lesson in Christianity. This was Gregory the Great, a man whose name is one of the landmarks of history, and whose character, in grand outline, will ever remain as the most distinguished honour of his generation. He was a man for his times. Shut up in Rome, with savage hordes at the gates, and pestilence, famine, and flood within; with heresy in the provinces, and the care of every department weighing heavily upon him at home, he never "bated jot of heart or hope," but met every demand in turn; always ready, always prompt, always decided, and generally successful. He was modest and simple in his dress, plain in his household, severe to himself, but ceaselessly kind to others. He was at once the domestic economist, the vigilant landowner, the municipal overseer. Now, he is the watchful diplomatist; then the soldier, superintending his own commissariat, planning his own defences, and directing his troops. Now in the pulpit, passionately rousing his flock to spiritual life and action; in the cloisters, keeping his monks to their discipline; or in his closet, writing "morals" on the Book of Job, or keeping up a wide correspondence with kings and queens, ecclesiastics and scholars. Then, in the choir, reforming the church service, and giving that musical impulse to the Christian world which will be felt as long as the "Gregorian Chant" continues to charm a human soul. Indeed he was everything which his church and his times required. If to us he seems over-credulous, he was only conformed to the fashion of his day; and it is a remarkable fact that the same reproach, if reproach it be, has been cast upon almost every man who has been a leader of his generation. In his time the Teutonic tribes had cut out their "marks" in this island, and had fairly taken possession of the soil. They were as yet heathen, but they were the chosen instruments of heaven in renovating and reorganizing the western world, and in preparing Christendom for her benevolent mission

"to the farthest verge
Of the green earth."

But who first ministered to them the truth which touched, and purified, and consecrated their minds and hearts to the nobler service of Him by whose providence they had so far been trained? It was Gregory the Great. Let no Protestant be alarmed; his religion is not in danger. Protestantism must never be blind to truth, nor do its interests ever require us to be unfair. The scattered remnants of the unfaithful British Church had proved themselves unable or unwilling to evangelize the rude Teutons, and the first Christian mission to these Teutons was from Gregory. The sight of some young Saxon slaves in the Roman markets probably touched his heart, and suggested the first thought of a mission to England. He would fain have entered on the mission himself, but he was too valuable a man for Rome to lose. When raised to the Papal chair, amidst all his labours and cares, his favourite scheme was not forgotten. His first purpose was to procure young natives from the slave market, and have them trained as evangelists to their countrymen. This process, however, was too slow for his impatient zeal. He fell back on his monks, selected a missionary band of nearly forty, and in the year 596 sent them, with many exhortations and blessings, to the coast of Kent. England still reaps the fruit of his success, and, it may be, records her early sense of obligation to Gregory in her national legend of "St. George (or St. Gregory) and the Dragon." Paganism (the "Dragon") in England fell before the cross; and the ultimate result of Augustine's mission was the establishment of a Saxon Church, which, for many generations, exemplified the purity and power of the Christian faith. Like the primitive churches, it had its "psalms, and hymns, and spiritual songs," some of them borrowed from the land to which it owed its spiritual birth, and others, in native Saxon rhythm, springing from the warm and simple hearts of English converts. A few precious fragments of native hymnology remain, and a translation from the *Codex Exoniensis* may afford some notion of the simple heartiness and quaint music of a Saxon hymn "to the Holy Trinity."

> Holy art Thou, holy,
> Lord of archangels,
> True Lord of triumph,
> Ever Thou art holy,
> Lord of lords.
> Thy power for ever lasteth
> Earthly with men,
> In every time
> Widely revered;
> Thou art God of hosts,
> For Thou hast filled
> Earth and heavens—
> Safeguard of warriors!
> With Thy glory,
> Patron of all beings!
> Be to Thee in the highest
> Eternal health,
> And on earth praise,
> Bright with men.
> Live Thou blessed,
> Who, in the Lord's name,
> With power comest,
> In comfort to the humble:
> To Thee in the heavens be,
> Ever without end,
> Eternal praise.

But the Saxon Church was not left to its own resources merely for supplies to its "service of song." Many a choral chant and many a grand old Latin hymn came floating across the Channel from the churches of Italy and Gaul. England had its schools of church music, and diligently enriched its public devotion with the compositions of Continental hymnists. Venantius Fortunatus was in his prime during Gregory's early life. A monk, too, in his later days, he exemplified the possibility of harmonizing literary freedom and cheerful or even light-hearted contentment with monastic vows. He could enjoy many a quiet laugh in his correspondence with saintly ladies, and yet furnish them with grand hymns to grace their church processions. One of these immortal productions was composed for a special service, in which Gregory of Tours and the author's lady friend St. Radigund took a leading part. It would be sung as a kind of spiritual march, "a song of degrees," as they moved with devout steps towards the church which was to be consecrated. The strain is not quite so simple and unpretending as some hymns of an earlier time, but it has a solemn swell and a subduing pathos:—

> The royal ensigns onward go;
>   The cross in mystic glory beams,
> Where He who made us bears our woe,
>   Our curse removes, our soul redeems.
>
> Where gushing life flows from His side,
>   To wash our hearts—a precious flood;
> Where deeply once the spear was dy'd,
>   And mingling water came with blood.
>
> Fulfill'd is David's song of old,
>   How David's Son and Lord is He
> Who rules the nations, as foretold;
>   The God who triumphs from the tree.*
>
> In royal purple richly drest,
>   O cross of light! O tree of grace!
> Chosen was Thy triumphal breast,
>   For holy limbs, a resting-place!

---

* An allusion to Psalm xcvi. 10, which, in the Italic version, is rendered, "Tell it among the heathen that the Lord reigneth from the tree."

> So widely Thy dear arms were spread,
>   The ransom of the world to bear—
> To pay the price in sinners' stead,
>   And spoils from our fell spoiler tear.
>
> From all thy boughs, O fragrant tree,
>   Sweetest of nectar sweets distil,
> And praises richly bloom on thee,
>   And fruits of peace thy branches fill.
>
> Hail, holy victim! Hail, O life!
>   Who death for sinners once endured;
> Victorious from Thy passion's strife,
>   Thy death hath life for man procured!

We can never think of England's Christian birth-time without thinking of one of her first and holiest Christian children—one whose memory is now honoured under the title of the "Venerable Bede." Nor can this name ever cease to be associated with Christian psalmody. Born, about the year 672, near the spot on which the good Benedict Biscop soon afterwards founded the Abbey of Wearmouth, he became a pupil under Biscop when seven years old, and remained a devout brother of the monastery of Wearmouth until death. His earlier years were spent in the study of the Scriptures, and in the practice of psalmody, which formed a prominent part in the daily services of the church. His taste for psalms and hymns and holy music was cultivated under the care of John the arch-chanter, who had accompanied Biscop from Rome. In his nineteenth year he was made deacon, and at thirty was ordained a priest. His life was spent in tranquil study, earnest prayer, and cheerful praise. His disciple and friend Cuthbert, who witnessed his end, gives us the following beautiful and touching story:—"He had been labouring under a severe attack of difficulty of breathing, yet without pain, for nearly two weeks before the day of our Lord's resurrection; and in this state he continued, cheerful and rejoicing, and giving thanks to Almighty God, both day and night, even every hour, until ascension day. He daily instructed us his disciples, and spent the remainder of the day in the singing of psalms, and continued on also during the night in joy and thanksgiving, except when interrupted by a moderate sleep. On awaking, he returned to his accustomed occupation, and with outstretched hands ceased not to give thanks to God. He was in truth a blessed man. He chanted the passage from St. Paul, 'It is a fearful thing to fall into the hands of the living God;' and many other passages of Holy Writ, in which he admonished us to rise from the sleep of the soul by anticipating the last hour. And being skilled in our poetry, he thus spoke in the Saxon language of the awful departure of the soul from the body:—

> Before the need-fare
> No man becometh
> Of thought more prudent
> Than is needful to him
> To consider
> Before his departure
> What, to his spirit,
> Of good or evil
> After his death-day
> Will be adjudged.

He also sang anthems, as well for our consolation as his own, one of which was the following:—

> O King of glory,
> God of might,
> Who didst ascend to-day,
> In triumph above all heavens,
> Leave us not orphans,
> But send upon us
> The promise of the Father,
> The Spirit of truth.
>   Hallelujah!

And when he came to the words, 'Leave us not orphans,' he burst into tears, and wept much; and, after the space of an hour, he resumed the repetition of what he had begun. As we heard, we wept along with him; one while we read, another while we wept; and our reading was always mingled with tears. In such kind of joy as this we passed the days between Easter, and up to the day which I have mentioned; and he rejoiced exceedingly, and thanked God, who had thought him worthy of suffering.... In addition to the lessons we received from him, and the singing of psalms, he strove all this time to finish two very important works—the Gospel of St. John, which he was translating into Saxon for the use of the Church, and certain extracts from the books of the Rotæ of St. Isidore. 'Learn quickly,' he would say, 'for I know not how long I may abide, nor how soon He who created me may take me away.' One of us remained with him one day, and said, 'Dearly beloved master, one chapter is still wanting; and it appears to be painful to you that I should ask any further questions.' But he said, 'It does not trouble me; take your pen, and be attentive, and write quickly.' At the ninth hour he expressed a wish to see all the presbyters, that he might admonish them, and distribute a few gifts among them. They all mourned or wept, chiefly because he told them that they should no longer see his face in the world; but they rejoiced when he said, 'It is time that I returned to Him who made me, who created me, and formed me out of nothing. I have had a long life upon the earth; the merciful Judge has also been pleased to ordain for me a happy life. The time of my departure is at hand, for I have a desire to depart, and to be with Christ.' And with many such like remarks he passed the day until eventide; then the boy whom we have already mentioned said to him, 'Still one sentence, dear master, remains unwritten.' He replied, 'Write quickly!' After a little while the boy said, 'Now the sentence is finished.' He answered, 'You have spoken the truth; it is indeed finished. Raise my head in your hands, for it pleases me much to recline opposite to that holy place of mine in which I used to pray, so that, while resting there, I may call upon God my Father.' And being placed upon the pavement of his cell, he said, 'Glory be to the Father, and to the Son, and to the Holy Ghost!' and as soon as he had named the name of the Holy Ghost, he breathe out his own spirit, and so departed to the kingdom of heaven." Blessed man! he has followed

> The Saviour's pathway to his home above.

And while we linger around the scene of his departure, we catch the music of that divine "Ascension hymn" of his, in which he used to express the longing of his soul in its upward gaze after the ascending Lord:—

> A hymn of glory let us sing;
> New hymns throughout the world shall ring;

> By a new way none ever trod,
> Christ mounteth to the throne of God.
>
> The apostles on the mountain stand—
> The mystic mount in Holy Land;
> They, with the Virgin Mother, see
> Jesus ascend in majesty.
>
> The angels say to the eleven,
> "Why stand ye gazing into heaven?
> This is the Saviour—this is He!
> Jesus hath triumph'd gloriously!"
>
> They said the Lord should come again,
> As these beheld Him rising then,
> Calm soaring through the radiant sky,
> Mounting its dazzling summits high.
>
> May our affections thither tend,
> And thither constantly ascend,
> When, seated on the Father's throne,
> Thee, reigning in the heavens, we own!
>
> Be Thou our present joy, O Lord,
> Who wilt be ever our reward;
> And as the countless ages flee,
> May all our glory be in Thee!

In this hymn, as well as in the other fragments which have come to us from the venerable Bede, there is the holy familiarity with the historical parts of the New Testament, and the same simple and devout pleasure in them which distinguish most of the earlier hymns of the Christian Church. Bede, too, keeps up that fixed adoring gaze upon the divine objects of faith, and that deeply reverent yet jubilant feeling of devotion which give the songs of Christianity's first love the secret of their beauty and life. In him, also, there is sometimes that tender sympathy with infancy and youth which is so often associated with pure heavenliness of spirit in the truly primitive Christian Fathers. This feeling breathes sweetly in his hymn "for the Holy Innocents:"—

> Raise the conquering martyr's song;
> Song of the Victor Innocents;
> Outcasts from th' unholy throng,
> Number'd now with heaven's saints;
> Those whose angels see God's face,
> Pour unceasing shouts along;
> While they ever hymn His grace,
> Raise the conquering martyr's song!

By that cursed ruler slain;
By their loving Maker crowned;
Sorrowless with Him to reign,
Where beauty, light, and peace abound.
There He gives them mansions all;
They have changed their loss for gain;
In their heavenly Father's hall,
By that cursed ruler slain.

A wailing voice in Ramah rose,
From weeping mothers all forlorn;
Sad Rachel mourned her children's woes,
Her victim babes, for murder born.
Now their triumph is complete;
Unconquered by tormenting foes;
Though once from homes, and fields, and street,
A wailing voice in Ramah rose.

Blest little flock, no longer fear
The lion that prey'd on your life,
For now your heav'nly Shepherd dear
Gives pastures never scath'd by strife:
On Sion's hill now dwelling safe,
The footprints of the Lamb are clear;
No tyrant there your souls will chafe,
Blest little flock, no longer fear.

The tear is wiped from every eye
By His, your tender Father's, hand;
No harm of death is ever nigh,
Where life breathes o'er the happy land.
Who sow in tears, in joy shall reap;
Their harvest-home is found on high;
The light of heav'n sees no one weep;
The tear is wiped from every eye.

A city blest through all the earth,
With martyrs' triumphs, martyrs' love;
Thy boast is in thy Saviour's birth,
Which gives thee greatness far above
All cities that would count thee small,
Or rival thee in pride or mirth;
Thy holy claim surpasses all.
O city blest through all the earth!

That venerable hymnist, who thus supplied the choir with appropriate means of celebrating the day of "Holy Innocents," quotes from other hymnists here and there—hymnists whose names, it may be, we shall never know in this world, but whose hymns seem to have been familiar to Bede, and were probably used in the English Church in that its Christian birth-time. Of these, one is a fine old judgment hymn, which, as Dr. Neale observes, manifestly contains the germ of the *Dies Iræ*, to which, however inferior in lyric fervour and effect, it scarcely yields in devotion and simple realization of its subject:—

> That great day of wrath is coming,
>   Day of doom and final woe;
> Like a midnight robber breaking
>   On the sons of men below;
> When the world's proud life is over,
>   All her pomp of ages pass'd,
> And her children stand in anguish,
>   That the end is come at last;
> And the blast of that loud trumpet,
>   Through earth's quarters pealing dread,
> Louder and yet louder waxing,
>   Calls together quick and dead;
> And the glorious King appearing
>   On His throne so high and white,
> And His holy bands of angels
>   Wait within His circling light;
> And the sun, like sackcloth darkling,
>   And the moon a bloody red,
> And the stars from heaven falling,
>   As untimely figs are shed;
> Tempests, fires, and desolation
>   'Fore the Judge's footsteps go;
> Earth and sea, all life's abysses,
>   Shall his final sentence know.
>
> . . . . . .
>
> Wherefore man, while judgment lingers,
>   Fly the dragon's charm of sin;
> And with bread supply the needy,
>   If thou would'st thy heaven win;
> Gird thy loins, be up and ready,
>   Heart all pure, and conscience right;
> Let the Bridegroom, when He cometh,
>   Find thy lamp-flame clear and bright.

Who does not wish to realize oneness with those who used to sing such hymns? In many respects mere translations are defective, but in this case they may be so far in the spirit and manner of the originals as to show us that the early English Christians really learnt to "admonish one another in psalms, and hymns, and spiritual songs."

England, however, may be said to have had a second Christian birth-time, when she was saved from the darkness and corruption which for many centuries, in her later history, had been enclosing and oppressing her Christian life, when in all her sanctuaries she might have sung one of her own bishop's hymns:—

> Hence in Thy truth Thy Church delights,
>   From all corruptions freed;
> Unblemish'd worship, spotless rites,
>   And unadulterate creed:
> Hence Thy pure words her children lead
>   To speak the united prayer,
> Their Saviour's name alone to plead,
>   His cup of blessing share.
>
> O God, whose love, our country's guides,
>   Once nerved with courage strong,
> And still o'er us, their sons, presides,
>   Accept our grateful song.
> And oh, the truth, revived among
>   Our sires from times of old,
> Do Thou to future times prolong,
>   And grant our sons to hold!

The process of England's Christian renewal was somewhat slow; beginning amidst the changes under Henry VIII., and unfolding its first definite results as the claims of the Stuart dynasty yielded to the rights of conscience and of law. The seventeenth century may be called the age of England's renovation, and the period was marked by a quickening in every department of public life. Every sphere of science, literature, arts, and religion was adorned with the most illustrious talent, learning and genius. Nor was the age wanting in poets whose hallowed powers were given to Him whose grace had inspired the new Christian life. Psalms and hymns broke forth then, as well as in the earlier times of deliverance. The hymns were not perhaps so simple, so childlike; their manner and style had more of the artificial; and, like the times which gave them birth, they had too many elaborated conceits, and quaint turns of thought and expression; still, they had their distinctive beauty, and were quite equal in spirituality, and cheerfulness, and warmth. Among other hymnists of the age there was Francis Quarles. Who can forget him? He was "the darling of our plebeian judgments," as Milton's nephew, Phillips, called him, with a kind of prophetic insight into the unfailing popularity of "Quarles' Divine Emblems," in the cottage homes of his country. Born in Essex in 1592, Quarles was by and by known among the Cambridge scholars, then respected as a student in Lincoln's Inn; and then, by turns, he acted as cupbearer to a royal hymnist, Elizabeth of Bohemia, as secretary to Archbishop Usher, and as chronologer to the City of London. Amidst all the activities of his busy and public life his poetic genius was kept in full play; ever and anon giving to the world either a "Job Militant," or a "Feast of Worms," or "Sion's Elegies," or the fruits of "the Morning Muse." The good man, however, like many of his fellows, suffered so much from the strife of parties that he fell a victim to sorrow at the age of fifty-two. His "Emblems" have enriched the thoughts of many a peasant; but peasant and prince alike may enjoy his noble hymn on "Delight in God Only."

I love (and have some cause to love) the earth:
She is my Maker's creature; therefore good:
She is my mother, for she gave me birth;
She is my tender nurse—she gives me food;
 But what's a creature, Lord, compared with Thee?
 Or what's my mother, or my nurse to me?

I love the air: her daily sweets refresh
My drooping soul, and to new sweets invite me;
Her shrill-mouth'd quire sustains me with their flesh,
And with their polyphonian notes delight me;
 But what's the air, or all the sweets that she
 Can bless my soul withal, compared to Thee?

I love the sea: she is my fellow creature,
My careful purveyor; she provides me store;
She walls me round; she makes my diet greater;
She wafts my treasure from a foreign shore:
 But, Lord of oceans, when compared with Thee,
 What is the ocean, or her wealth to me?

To heaven's high city I direct my journey,
Whose spangled suburbs entertain my eye,
Mine eye, by contemplations great attorney,
Transcends the crystal pavement of the sky:
 But what is heaven, great God, compared to Thee?
 Without Thy presence heaven's no heaven to me.

Without Thy presence earth gives no refection;
Without Thy presence sea affords no treasure;

Without Thy presence air's a rank infection;
Without Thy presence heaven itself no pleasure;
    If not possess'd, if not enjoy'd in Thee,
    What's earth, or sea, or air, or heaven to me?

The highest honours that the world can boast,
Are subjects far too low for my desire;
The brightest beams of glory are (at most)
But dying sparkles of Thy living fire:
    The loudest flames that earth can kindle, be
    But mighty glow-worms, if compared to Thee.

Without Thy presence wealth is bags of cares;
Wisdom but folly; joy disquiet sadness:
Friendship is treason, and delights are snares;
Pleasures but pain, and mirth but pleasing madness;
    Without Thee, Lord, things be not what they be,
    Nor have they being when compared with Thee.

In having all things, and not Thee, what have I?
Not having Thee, what have my labours got?
Let me enjoy but Thee, what further crave I?
And having Thee alone, what have I not?
    I wish nor sea nor land; nor would I be,
    Possess'd of heaven, heaven unpossess'd of Thee.

CHAPTER VII.

HYMNS FROM OLD CLOISTERS.

"The wilderness and the solitary place shall be glad for them; and the desert shall rejoice and blossom as the rose. It shall blossom abundantly, and rejoice even with joy and singing."

HAVE you learned to bless the name of Jesus from the depth of a loving heart? Then, at times, you have been sweetly touched or strangely warmed, while trying to realize communion with all that is holy in the past, as you caught the music of a hymn coming, now but faintly, and now in swelling fervent tones from successive generations of the faithful. Listen! Do you know the gracious heart-felt verses?

> Jesus, the only thought of Thee,
>   With sweetness fills my breast;
> But sweeter far it is to see,
>   And on Thy beauty feast.
>
> No sound, no harmony so gay,
>   Can art, or music frame:
> No thought can reach, no words can say,
>   The sweets of Thy bless'd name.
>
> Jesus, our hope, when we repent,
>   Sweet source of all our grace;
> Sole comfort in our banishment;
>   O! what when face to face!
>
> Jesus! that name inspires my mind
>   With springs of life and light,
> More than I ask in Thee I find,
>   And lavish in delight.

Nor art or eloquence of man
    Can tell the joys of love;
Only the saints can understand,
    What they in *Jesus* prove.

Thee, then I'll seek, retired apart
    From world and business free;
When these shall knock, I'll shut my heart,
    And keep it all for Thee.

Before the morning light I'll come,
    With Magdalen to find,
In sighs and tears, my Jesus' tomb,
    And there refresh my mind.

My tears upon His grave shall flow,
    My sighs the garden fill;
Then at His feet myself I'll throw,
    And there I'll seek His will.

Jesus, in Thy bless'd steps I'll tread,
    And walk in all Thy ways;
I'll never cease to weep and plead,
    Till I'm restored to grace.

O King of love, Thy blessed fire,
    Does such sweet flames excite,
That first it raises the desire,
    Then fills it with delight.

Thy lovely presence shines so clear
    Thro' every sense and way,
That souls which once have seen Thee near,
    See all things else decay.

Come then, dear Lord, possess my heart,
    Chase thence the shades of night;
Bid all but perfect love depart,
    Before Thy shining light.

Thy name I then will ever sing,
    And with Thy saints rejoice;
My heart shall own Thee as its king,
    Midst never-ending joys.

From whence did this song arise? Who first sang it? Let us seek its birthplace in a many-storied land. In one of the eastern departments of France, not far from the source of the Seine, and on the banks of the tranquil Saone, we should be far away from commercial bustle and mechanical strife, in a region where a simple and quiet husbandry is content, without the aid of science; where the multiplied subdivisions of the fruitful soil, wild and neglected tracts, and a population of unaspiring cultivators would scarcely seem to witness of an illustrious past. Nevertheless, we should find ourselves surrounded by monuments of former splendour. There are ancient tokens of lordly pride and martial power, footprints of bright intellect, hallowed learning, religious mystery, saintly thought, and heavenly devotion. There are remnants of old cities, and castles, and abbeys, with garden grounds, and vine-covered slopes, and verdant hills; indeed, enough in nature, and still enough of art to show that old Burgundy was "a land of corn and wine," in appearance, and resources, and fruitfulness, verily the "golden land." There, in a forest valley, within a recess adorned with interwoven flowers, and overshadowed by primitive oaks and beeches, somewhat more than seven centuries ago, heaven first heard the music of our hymn to "the sweet memory of Jesus." It arose from the sanctified heart and lips of Bernard, deservedly honoured as St. Bernard, the "mellifluous doctor." He was a monk; but, though a monk, he was never what one prejudiced biographer supposed that, as a monk, he must necessarily be, "a turbulent and hot-headed fanatic." No; Bernard was a saintly man. He was not "above his Master." It was enough for him that "the disciple be as his Master"; and there had been those who said of his Master, "He hath a devil and is mad." But who could sing of Jesus as Bernard did, unless he was ruled by "the love of Christ"? The monastery in Bernard's day was the only home for such high-toned piety as his. He had scarcely passed into mature manhood when he was elected as the leader of twelve recluses, who, with himself, were devoted to the work of founding a new religious community in the desert. Their chief design was to save themselves and the souls of the people among whom they exercised their itinerant ministry; but they were also bent upon toiling until "the land that was desolate was become like the Garden of Eden." They were among the first "model farmers" of Europe. And though they may not be classed with the "genial fraternities" whose names still mark the most distinguished vineyards of modern times, they share the honour of those labourers who first broke the soil of our western wastes, and taught it to unfold its resources so as to meet the advancing claims of modern civilization. Bernard found a spot within a pathless forest, haunted by robbers, and dreaded as the "valley of wormwood"; and there he and his companions began their task with cheerful courage, and worked, now in a devotional silence, and now, with chant and psalmody, literally speaking to themselves and answering one another, "in psalms, and hymns, and spiritual songs," till "the valley of wormwood" became *Clairvaux*, "the bright valley"; and the fruitful little church in the desert might rejoice in the fulfilment of the promise, "I will give her her vineyards from thence, and the valley of Achor for a door of hope; and she shall sing there as in the days of her youth, and as in the day when she came up out of the land of Egypt." It was amidst the toils and songs, the prayers and chants of that valley that the character of Bernard attained its maturity of Christian manliness. There his character seemed to perfect its balance, and to show how unearthliness and tender humanity, the contemplative and the practical, the severe and the gentle, the strict and the free, the frugal and the generous, the truthful, the wise, and the loving, could all harmonize in blessing the existing generation, and in shedding balmy lessons on the minds and hearts of following ages. How much Bernard owed to his mother! and how often when his name occurs do we think of Hannah and the child of her many prayers. Hannah's inspired joy as a mother gave holy song to the "church throughout all the world"; and the prayers of the Lady Aletta for her boy who first saw the light in A.D. 1091, under the vine slopes of Côte d'Or, had their full answer in the jubilant piety and songful life of her converted Bernard. She prayed that he might be a monk; believing that such a life was best for his soul; and what she prayed for, her well-trained child was brought to enjoy. Like Hannah, she had "lent him to the Lord," and like Hannah's son he found the joy of his life in the "Beauty of Holiness." His mother's death-chamber was to him the birthplace of a new life. Aletta wished to depart with the chant of a litany on her ears. She lived to catch the touching appeal, "By thy cross and passion," and her last words were the response, "Good Lord deliver us!" She was gone to her rest; her works of piety and charity follow her; but her boy was left to record the hour of her departure as the turning point of his own life. He had lost his mother, but Jesus her Saviour was now his own; and with the hallowed memory of Aletta's final hour still touching his soul, he breathed his hymn of appeal to Christ—

> When my dying hour must be,
> Be not absent then from me;
> In that dreadful hour, I pray,
> Jesus, come without delay,
>   See and set me free!
> When Thou biddest me depart,
> Whom I cleave to with my heart,
> Lover of my soul be near,
> With Thy saving cross appear,
>   Show Thyself to me!

The character of Bernard was a faithful mirror of his times. The crusade against the "infidel," and the rescue of his own countrymen's souls from sin, both engaged his burning zeal and effective eloquence and prayers. He advocated a high spiritual standard of Romanism. He entered the controversial lists against sceptical Churchmen and fashionable heresies; but whatever he did, he did it "to the Lord," and did it with all his heart. It is most pleasant, however, to commune with him as the expositor of evangelical truth, and the tender, ardent, and spiritual hymnologist of the universal Church. We love him for his warm and spirited, but reverent, testimony for Christ, especially in his atoning work; but how all our powers and feelings harmonize in choral service, when his theme of Christian controversy glows and kindles into song! Where is the Christian heart that is not ready to sing with him?—

> Fix, oh, fix each crimson wound,
> And those nail-prints so profound,
> In my heart engrave them fully,
> That I may grow like Thee wholly,
>   Jesus, Saviour, sweet!
> Pitying God, to Thee I cry,
> Guilty at Thy feet I lie;
> Oh! be merciful to me,
> Nor bid me, unworthy, flee
>   From Thy sacred feet!

> Prostrate, see Thy cross I grasp,
> And Thy pierced feet I clasp;
> Gracious Jesus, spurn me not;
> On me, with compassion fraught,
>   Let Thy glances fall.
> From Thy cross of agony,
> My beloved, look on me;
> Turn me wholly unto Thee;
> "Be thou whole," say openly;
>   "I forgive thee all."

Of all the men of his time, he seems to have had the deepest insight into St. Paul's spirit and views; and he richly exemplified the connexion between right views of the cross and genuine zeal for the Church and the salvation of the world. His recorded views of the atonement show that he kept his acute intellect attuned to his subdued will and high-toned affections, while they afford us an insight into the secret of his deep feeling and power as a leader in psalms, and hymns, and chants in praise of Christ. "We cannot fathom the mystery of the Divine will," says he; "yet we can feel the effect of the (atoning) work, we can be sensible of the benefit. Why did He accomplish that by His blood which He might have accomplished by a word? Ask Himself? It is vouchsafed to me to know that the fact is so, but not the *wherefore*. . . . It was not the *death* of Christ in itself, but the will of Him who freely offered Himself, that was acceptable to God; and because this precious death, procuring the downfall of sin, could only be brought about by sin, so God had no pleasure in the sin, but used it for good. God did not only require the death of His Son, but accepted it when offered. He did not thirst for man's blood, but for man's salvation. . . . . Three things here meet together—the humility of self-renunciation; the manifestation of love, even to the death of the cross; the mystery of redemption, whereby He overcame death. The two former facts are nothing without the third. The examples of humility and love are something great, but have no firm foundation without the redemption." . Some of Bernard's first converts were his own father, and brothers, and personal friends. Like Andrew, "he first found his *own*, and brought them to Jesus." He closed his father's eyes in peace and hope, and then he saw his best-beloved brother, Gerard, take his flight into eternal life. What a touching memorial he has bequeathed to us of the last scene! It is like a plaintive parting hymn, having all poetic beauty and pathos in the form of prose. "Who could ever have loved me as he did? He was a brother by blood, but far more by religion. . . . God grant, Gerard, I may not have lost thee, but that thou hast preceded me; for of a surety thou hast joined those whom, in thy last night below, thou didst invite to praise God, when suddenly, to the great surprise of all, thou, with a serene countenance and a cheerful voice, didst commence chanting, 'Praise ye the Lord from the heaven; praise Him, all ye angels!' At that moment, O my brother, the day dawned on thee, though it was night to us; the night to thee was all brightness. . . . Just as I reached his side, I heard him utter aloud those words of Christ, 'Father, into Thine hands I commend my spirit!' Then repeating the verse over again, and resting on the word 'Father!' 'Father!' he turned to me, and, smiling, said, 'Oh, how gracious of God to be the Father of men, and what an honour for men to be His children!' And then, very distinctly, 'If children, then heirs.' And so he died; and so dying, he well nigh changed my grief into rejoicing, so completely did the sight of his happiness overpower the recollection of my own misery. . . . O Lord, Thou hast but called for Thine own. Thou hast but taken what belonged to Thee! And now my tears put an end to my words, I pray thee teach me to put an end to my tears!" By and by Bernard's own call was come. He had lived as a witness for the truth. He had taught his neighbours to be industrious, and holy, and happy. He had preached Christ as the life and soul of the "Song of songs." He had helped to brighten and enrich the aspect of his native land. He had gathered many a family of spiritual children, had led his own household to the Saviour, and now, having spent his little remaining strength in the work of a "peace-maker," he found his reward, and passed into the "kingdom of heaven." He departed exhorting his weeping friends to "abound more and more in every good work," and murmuring, as his last sentence on earth, "I am in a strait betwixt two, having a desire to depart and to be with

Christ, which is far better!" Happy Bernard! His Redeemer had given the full response to his hymn—

> Let me true communion know
> With Thee in Thy sacred woe,
> Counting all beside but dross,
> Dying with Thee on Thy cross;—
>   'Neath it will I die!
> Thanks to Thee, with every breath,
> Jesus, for Thy bitter death;
> Grant Thy guilty one this prayer,
> When my dying hour is near,
>   Gracious God, be nigh!

Old Burgundy was verily the "golden land;" for it found a cloistered home for a second Bernard—a monk likewise, and contemporary with the saint; one who, from the fulness of his gifted and consecrated soul, gave birth to that "thing of beauty," the hymn now so widely known as "Jerusalem the Golden." Two such hymnists, in the same province, in the same time, and of the same name, and saints both, may well be confounded, as they have sometimes been, by people who are more equal to the joy of singing their hymns than to the pains of exploring the old cloisters in which they wrote them. Bernard of Morlaix never found a place in the saints' calendar; but his glorious verses have now secured a home for him in the best hearts of Christendom. Of English parentage, and a child of old Brittany, he found his way into the cloisters of the celebrated Cluny, and spent his devoted life in praying and singing of judgment and of heaven, under the fatherly direction of Peter the venerable abbot, himself a master of spiritual song, and then at the summit of his reputation. Bernard's home was supreme in monastic fame. Surrounded by a host of brethren, worshipping in the grandest old church in France, and daily joining in the most full and impressive ritual of his times, there would seem to be no way open for unpleasant intrusion on his contemplative life. But, alas! no cloisters, however richly furnished, or however strictly guarded, are at all times inviolable retreats from the gathering woes and sorrows of a sinful world. Bernard felt the heaving outside. He saw the darkness thickening on society, he heard the voices of woe foretelling dissolution, change, and judgment. To him the judge was at the door, and he tried to keep himself in the posture of readiness by singing hymns of admonition. How plaintive is his voice, yet how it thrills!—

> The world is old and sinful,
>   Its passing hour is near;
> Keep watch, be hushed, and sober,
>   The Judge's knock to hear.
> The Judge in mercy coming,
>   The Judge enthroned in might,
> All evil things to banish,
>   All good to crown with light.
> That Monarch just and gentle
>   The dead from thrall shall free.
> Let trembling seize the guilty,
>   For God and man is He!
> Rise, Christian, rise to meet Him,
>   Let wrong give way to right,
> Let tears of godly sorrow
>   Melt into songs of light—
> The light that has no setting,
>   Too new for moon or sun.
> So crystal-like and golden,
>   So like its Maker, one.
> And when the Son shall render
>   The kingdom up once more,
> And God the Father's glory
>   Shall brighten evermore,
> Then light, as yet unfolded,
>   Shall open on the blest,
> All mysteries revealing
>   Of holy, endless rest.

The note struck in the last stanza opened a transition movement, and Bernard's soul caught an insight into the clear jasper light and balmy atmosphere of his own "sweet and happy region." What a happy proof of the harmonizing power of heavenliness is shown in the fact that the hymn of this heavenly-minded monk has found its way into the hearts of all classes of Christians, and into the choirs and public services of all Christian Churches. The sweet accordance of this hymn with the spirit of the New Jerusalem, and with the mind of its Divine Lord, is shown, too, in the response which it has from the most hallowed depths of the consecrated heart, and in its sacred charm over the spirit of those of whom Jesus said, "Whosoever, therefore, shall humble himself as this little child, the same is greatest in the kingdom of heaven." The hymn has sometimes brought heaven still nearer, even when the departing spirit has felt itself on the threshold of its home. So it was with the dear little sufferer mentioned by Dr. Neale in his notes on Bernard. Almost unequalled agony attended the upward passage of the child, but the youthful sufferer was hushed by the music of this hymn, and would lie without a murmur while they repeated it—

>Jerusalem, the golden,
>Where milk and honey flow,
>Both heart and voice sink fainting
>Beneath thy crystal glow.
>
>I know not, oh, I know not
>What joys of home are there,
>What bright unfolding glory,
>What bliss beyond compare!
>
>They stand, those courts of Zion,
>All glad with holy song,
>And radiant with the angels,
>And all the martyr throng;
>
>The Prince abides within them,
>Amid serenest light,
>And all the blest ones' pastures
>In glorious sheen are dight.
>
>There is the throne of David,
>And there, all free from care,
>Are conquerors in triumph;
>And feast and song are there.
>
>And they who with their Captain
>Have overcome in fight,
>For ever and for ever
>Are robed with Him in white!
>
>. . . . . .
>
>O sacred, peaceful harp-notes!
>O never-ending hymn!
>O hallow'd, sweet refreshment,
>And peace of seraphim!
>
>O ceaseless, ardent thirsting,
>With ever full content!
>O real matchless vision
>Of God omnipotent!

There are the many mansions
For many a saintly heir,
And various compensations
For divers claimants there;

As 'midst the starry clusters
That deck our lower sky
One star excels another,
So will it be on high!

Jerusalem, the glorious,
The pride of the elect,
Dear vision of the future,
That longing hearts expect.

By faith I now behold thee,
Thy walls I here discern;
My thoughts are kindling for thee,
And strive, and pant, and yearn!

Jerusalem, in oneness,
That dost our lowness see,
Thou, thou art all my boasting;
All shame belongs to me!

. . . . .

Jerusalem, triumphant,
On that safe, happy shore,
I hope, I long, I sing thee,
And love thee more and more!

I do not plead my merit,
I seek not such a plea;
My merit is perdition
Abiding upon me;

And yet I venture, trusting,
And hoping on my way,
For those rewards immortal
To labour night and day.

My Father, best and dearest,
Who made and saved His child,
Bore with me in my weakness,
And washed me when defiled.

When in His strength contending,
For joy my spirits leap;
When quailing in the conflict,
I weep, or fain would weep.

And grace, sweet heavenly unction,
Shall all its virtue prove,
And David's royal fountain
Shall every stain remove.

O Sion, mine, the golden,
More lovely far than gold;
With bands of laurell'd bright ones
For ever there enrolled!

O sweet and happy region,
Wilt thou ever bless my eyes?
O sweet and happy region,
Wilt thou ever be my prize?

I *have* the inward earnest,
The hope to cheer and bless,
Shall I ever gain the land itself?
Tell me, O tell me, yes!

Rejoice, O dust and ashes!
The Lord shall be thine own!
And thou art His for ever!
His now, and His alone!

For many generations such winged thoughts as these about the new Jerusalem continued, at times, to rise acceptably to heaven from the monastic cells of Europe. The song of the Monk of Cluny is so akin to the strain of another monk, a Dutch brother of "The Common Life," that to sing the one is to be carried in imagination to the cloisters where the other first came gushing from the soul of its devout author. About the middle of the fifteenth century, in one of the retreats of his order, an eminently pious recluse, as he used to walk with his brethren in the cloisters or in the garden, would sometimes stop and say, "Dear brethren, I must go; there is some one waiting for me in my cell." That "some one" was the object of his supreme affection, the chosen companion of his soul, his Redeemer and Lord. Those who heard him knew with whom he wished to commune, and have told us that what he said to the Lord, and what the Lord said to him at such times, is left for our instruction in his tract on the inward discourse of Christ to the faithful soul. This tract forms the first part of that book which "came forward as an answer to the sighing of Christian Europe for light from heaven, and which contained so many rivulets of truth silently stealing away unto light from that interdicted fountain," the Bible, that its wide-spread "diffusion over Christendom, anticipated in 1453 the diffusion of the Bible itself in 1853." In that "one remarkable book," as Dean

G

Milman says, "was gathered and concentrated all that was elevating, passionate, profoundly pious, in all the older mystics. Gerson, Rysbroek, Tauler, all who addressed the heart in later times, were summed up and brought into one circle of light and heat, in this single small volume. That this book supplied some imperious want in the Christianity of mankind, that it supplied it with fulness and felicity, which left nothing, at this period of Christianity, to be desired, its boundless popularity is the one unanswerable testimony. . . . The size of the book, the manner, the style, the arrangement, as well as its profound sympathy with all the religious feelings, wants, and passions; its vivid and natural expressions, to monastic Christianity what the Hebrew psalms are to our common religion, to our common Christianity; its contagious piety; —all conspired to its universal dissemination. Its manner, its short quivering sentences, which went at once to the heart, and laid hold of and clung tenaciously to the memory with the compression and completeness of proverbs; its axioms, each of which suggested endless thought; its imagery, scriptural and simple, were alike original, unique. . . . No book has been so often reprinted, no book has been so often translated, or into so many languages, as 'The Imitation of Christ.'" Who does not bless the memory of its author; who does not enjoy the sentences of the man who wrote as the Saviour was speaking to his heart? who does not love the name of Thomas à Kempis? He who instructed the world on the "Imitation of Christ," could sing too of the heaven where he hoped to see his beloved Master. He was a hymnist, and the joys above formed his chosen theme. Let those who would, like him, find Christ after waiting for them in their cell, be, like him, ever ready for devotion, and breathing more and more deeply his heavenly spirit from day to day, they will find a daily joy in singing with him—

> High the angel choirs are raising
> Heart and voice in harmony;
> The Creator King still praising,
> Whom in beauty there they see.
>
> Sweetest strains, from soft harps stealing;
> Trumpets, notes of triumph pealing;
> Radiant wings and white stoles gleaming,
> Up the steps of glory streaming;

When the heavenly bells are ringing,
Holy, holy, holy, singing
  To the mighty Trinity;
Holy, holy, holy! crying;
For all earthly care and sighing
  In that city cease to be!

Every voice is there harmonious,
Praising God in hymns symphonious;
Love each heart with light enfolding,
As they stand in peace beholding
  There the Triune Deity!
Whom adore the seraphim,
Are with love eternal burning;
  Venerate the cherubim.
    To their want of honour turning;
    Whilst angelic thrones adoring
    Gaze upon His majesty.

Oh, how beautiful that region,
And how fair that heavenly region,
  Where thus men and angels blend;
Glorious will that city be,
Full of deep tranquillity,
  Light and peace from end to end!
All the happy dwellers there
  Shine in robes of purity,
  Keep the law of charity,
  Bound in fervent unity;
Labour finds them not, nor care.
  Ignorance can ne'er perplex,
  Nothing tempt them, nothing vex;
Joy and health their fadeless blessing,
Always all things good possessing.

CHAPTER VIII.

SONGS IN HIGH PLACES.

"Praise Him in the heights. Kings of the earth, and all people, princes, and all judges of the earth, let them praise the name of the Lord."

THE great dramatist gives us no mere fancy sketch when he makes an inheritor of royalty say of himself:—

> The government I cast upon my brother,
> And to my state grew stranger, being transported
> And rapt in secret studies.
>
> . . . .
>
> I pray thee mark me.
> I thus neglecting worldly ends, all dedicated
> To closeness and the bettering of my mind
> With that which, but by being so retired,
> O'er prized all popular rate, in my false brother
> Awaked an evil nature.

Such princes have lived, and studied, and prayed, and suffered, to the edification of a few, and to the sorrow of many. Hugh Capet, the father of the third line of French kings, showed himself quite equal to his position, and held the reins so as to keep his rude and kicking subjects within the traces. He knew how to preserve quietness within his own border, and how to make a sufficiently awful impression outside. He was a ruler at home and a terror abroad; and in those days both were desirable virtues in men of his calling. He prospered, and finished his royal career in 996. But like does not always beget like. His son Robert came to the throne, bringing to it all his father's softer virtues, without those sterner qualities for government which are necessary to keep the balance of state. He wanted to be good, and was good. But he was too willing to cast the affairs of government upon some brother, and false brothers are not lacking. If not to be found in France, Italy could furnish one. Gregory the Fifth could do the politics for him, and the fighting too, and manage at the same time to lord it over King Robert's conscience. The king was not fit for kingship; he was more disposed to the cloisters. Anybody might rule for him. He might have had rule in Italy; yes, and the imperial crown might have been on his brow. But no, not he: "Let me alone," he seemed to say, "my joy is in secret; give me my psalter, my service-book, my psalm, my hymn, and I am happy." And so he was. He took his choice. The outside world might wag its way as it pleased; he would be a royal monk, and his palace should be his cell. And so he lived, and prayed, and chanted, and sung; and whether France or the world were ever the better for his rule or not, Christendom is the better for one hymn at least, which he left as the fruit of his devotion, and in which his reverent, tender, and peaceful spirit is graciously embalmed. As a king, his memory might have melted into oblivion; but as a hymnist his name will be dear to every following generation of those who breathe the feeling and sustain the music of his *Veni Sancte Spiritus*.

> Holy Spirit come, we pray,
> Come from heaven and shed the ray
>   Of Thy light divine.
>
> Come, thou Father of the poor,
> Giver from a boundless store,
>   Light of hearts, O shine!
>
> Matchless comforter in woe,
> Sweetest guest the soul can know,
>   Living waters blest.
>
> When we weep our solace sweet,
> Coolest shade in summer heat,
>   In our labour rest.
>
> Holy and most blessed light,
> Make our inmost spirits bright,
>   With Thy radiance mild;
>
> For without Thy sacred powers,
> Nothing can we own of ours,
>   Nothing undefiled.
>
> What is arid, fresh bedew,
> What is sordid, cleanse anew,
>   Balm on the wounded pour.

What is rigid, gently bend,
On what is cold Thy fervour send;
What has strayed, restore.

To Thine own in every place
Give the sacred, seven-fold grace,
Give Thy faithful this.

Give to virtue its reward,
Safe and peaceful end afford,
Give eternal bliss.

By bequeathing this hymn to us King Robert has left the world better than he found it. Nevertheless, it is a mercy for the world that Providence makes heroes as well as monks. Monkish monarchs have been blessings in their way. But both men and things need leaders now and then of harder make. Human nature being as it is, the master heart may be called for, the mighty arm, and the sceptre of steel. And there have been men starting up, at some junctures, above the strife and rage of human opposition to the good and the true, who have exemplified the possibility of being valiant for truth in the field as well as in the closet and the choir. And if these have not been hymnists, they have never lacked a hymn to cheer them in the day of battle, in the day of victory, in the day of death. Gustavus Adolphus of Sweden had the spirit of a king, the powers of a hero, and the heart of a Christian; all this he proved in his chivalrous advance to the succour of the German Protestants in their long and terrible struggle for liberty of conscience and worship. He landed on the coast of Pomerania with thirty thousand men on the 24th of June, 1630, and in unison with his German allies marched to successive victories, and, as it proved, to victorious death. He was cheered onward by those who hailed him as their deliverer; but he needed more. His heart looked to the source of might; and who can tell how richly and mightily that heart received responses of power by means of one hymn? If he could not, like Robert of France, write hymns for his own use, God could supply the lack. Out of the ranks of battling Protestants the hymnist rose whose words were to nerve the arm and strengthen the heart of the hero and his bands. In 1631 Altenburg issued that hymn, now so widely known and loved by so many hearts. He called it "a heart-cheering song of comfort, or the watchword of the evangelical army in the battle of Leipsic, September 7, 1631, 'God with us.'" This became the battle song of Gustavus. The conqueror often sung it with his troops. He sang it for the last time when entering the field of Lützen against the famous Wallenstein—his last field, the scene of his last victory, and to him the field of triumphant death. The hero's parting song has cheered many a Christian soldier since then. Let it cheer us now.

> Fear not, O little flock, the foe
> Who madly seeks your overthrow,
>   Dread not his rage and power;
> What though your courage sometimes faints,
> His seeming triumph o'er God's saints
>   Lasts but a little hour.
>
> Be of good cheer, your cause belongs
> To Him who can avenge your wrongs,
>   Leave it to Him our Lord.
> Though hidden yet from all our eyes,
> He sees the Gideon who shall rise
>   To save us and His word.
>
> As true as God's own word is true,
> Nor earth nor hell with all their crew
>   Against us shall prevail.
> A jest and by-word are they grown;
> God is with us, we are His own,
>   Our victory cannot fail.
>
> Amen, Lord Jesus, grant our prayer!
> Great Captain, now Thine arm make bare;
>   Fight for us once again!
> So shall Thy saints and martyrs raise
> A mighty chorus to Thy praise,
>   World without end. Amen.

Songs in high places have not been always "songs of deliverance," or hymns of victory. No high places on earth are so high as to be beyond the swell of human sorrow. The floods will arise in days of darkness, and occasionally desolate the homes and hearts of royal life. So it was in the court of Hungary in 1526. The Turkish hordes had swept down upon the Christian borders, and the king, who had armed himself for the defence of his throne, had been cut down with the flower of his nobility, leaving Maria, his queen, a defenceless widow, open not only to Turkish violence, but what was more dreadful to her, an invasion of her Christian rights of conscience on the part of those who bore the hallowed name of the Saviour, whom she loved. Her attachment to the reformed doctrine rendered her desolated home unsafe; and for her religion's sake she fled from Buda, trusting alone to Him, who is the husband of the widow, and the "present help" and reward of those who suffer for His name's sake. Nothing is grander than the sight of a human soul cut off from all visible help, casting itself with all its interests in time and eternity upon the power and goodness of God alone. Such sublime action is recorded in the song of this bereaved, persecuted, and fugitive queen.

> Can I my fate no more withstand,
>   Nor 'scape the hand
>   That for faith would grieve me;
> This is my strength, that well I know
>   In weal or woe,
>   God's love the world must leave me.
> God is not far, though hidden now,
> He soon shall rise and make them bow,
>   Who of His Word bereave me.
>
> Judge as ye will my cause this hour,
>   Yours is the power,
>   God bids me strive no longer;
> I know what mightiest seems to-day
>   Shall pass away,
>   Time than your rule is stronger.
> The eternal God I rather choose,
> And fearless all for this I lose,
>   God help me thus to conquer!
>
> All has its day, the proverb saith;
>   This is my faith,
>   Thou, Christ, wilt be beside me,
> And look on all this pain of mine
>   As were it Thine,
>   When sharpest woe betide me;
> Must I then tread this path—I yield;
> World, as thou wilt, God is my shield,
>   And He will rightly guide me!

We have no record of the divine response to the widow's act of trust, but the "record is on high." Trust in God is never long without its answering hush from above. God arranges His times and instruments of blessing so as most happily to aid the sufferer and most fully to glorify Himself, and how often does the blessing come by means of a comfortable hymn? From time to time the hymn of plaintive appeal is replied to by the hymn of consolation. In many an individual history it is so; and it is always so in the history of the Church. Now God's children are supplied with hymns expressive of reliance; and now with forms of "joy in tribulation." Thus, "one generation shall praise His works to another." Nor can it be otherwise than instructive and cheering to listen to the voices of song from the "high places" of Germany, as they come in successive responses through the periods of her suffering, joy answering to sorrow, and triumph to depression. Though a century passes between, it is not difficult to recognise something like an inspiration responsive to Queen Maria's trustful hymn in the song which in 1653 rose from the full heart of Louisa Henrietta, Electress of Brandenburgh. How the music lulls the tremulous sufferer!

> Jesus, my Redeemer, lives,
>   Christ, my trust, is dead no more;
> In the strength this knowledge gives,
>   Shall not all my fears be o'er,
> Though the night of death be fraught
> Still with many an anxious thought?
>
> Jesus, my Redeemer, lives,
>   And His life I once shall see;
> Bright the hope this promise gives,
>   Where He is I too shall be.
> Shall I fear, then? Can the Head
> Rise and leave the members dead?
>
> Close to Him my soul is bound,
>   In the bonds of hope enclasp'd;
> Faith's strong hand this hold hath found,
>   And the Rock hath firmly grasp'd;
> And no care of death can part
> From our Lord the trusting heart.
>
> I shall see Him with these eyes,
>   Him whom I shall surely know;
> Not another shall I rise,
>   With His love this heart shall glow;
> Only there shall disappear
> Weakness in and round me here.

Ye who suffer, sigh, and moan,
　Fresh and glorious there shall reign;
Earthly here the seed is sown,
　Heavenly it shall rise again;
Natural here the death we die,
Spiritual our life on high.

Body, be thou of good cheer,
　In thy Saviour's care rejoice;
Give not place to gloom and fear,
　Dead thou yet shalt know His voice,
When the final trump is heard,
And the deaf cold grave is stirr'd.

Laugh to scorn, then, death and hell;
　Laugh to scorn the gloomy grave:
Caught into the air to dwell
　With the Lord, who comes to save,
We shall trample o'er our foes,
Mortal weakness, fear, and woes.

Only see ye that your heart
　Rise betimes from earthly lust:
Would ye there with Him have part,
　Here obey your Lord and trust,
Fix your hearts beyond the skies,
Whither ye yourselves would rise.

Another short interval, and the soothing response to the widow's hymn is repeated by a masculine voice, in fine harmony with the utterance of the Brandenburgh Princess. The voice comes this time from an ancient and princely house, the name of which is dear to every English heart, loyal and reverent enough to acknowledge the Providence which associated that name with the happiest period of English royalty. Who does not thank God for the line of Brunswick? Even losing sight of the blessings which have come to us in our national relation to that illustrious line, there will always be Christian hearts, which, while the German or the English language lives, will gather strength and joy from one, at least, who graced that Brunswick pedigree. In the noble family succession from Henry the Lion to the honoured and beloved lady who now sways the sceptre of Great Britain, there have been names distinguished by many family virtues and courtly actions; but one has left a longer-lived memorial in a few sweet and touching hymns. One of these is a song for the soul in bereavement and sorrow. It comes upon the burdened heart with a soothing music, like that which touched the lonely spirit of the bereaved widow at Nain, when Jesus "had compassion on her, and said unto her, Weep not!"

> Leave all to God,
> Forsaken one, and stay thy tears;
> For the Highest knows thy pain,
> Sees thy sufferings and thy fears;
> Thou shalt not wait His help in vain,
> Leave all to God.
>
> Be still and trust!
> For His strokes are strokes of love,
> Thou must for thy profit bear;
> He thy filial fear would move,
> Trust thy Father's loving care,
> Be still and trust!
>
> Know, God is near!
> Though thou think Him far away,
> Though His mercy long have slept,
> He will come and not delay,
> When His child enough hath wept,
> For God is near!
>
> Oh, teach Him not
> When and how to hear thy prayers;
> Never doth our God forget,
> He the cross who longest bears
> Finds his sorrows' bounds are set,
> Then teach Him not.
>
> If thou love Him,
> Walking truly in His ways,
> Then no trouble, cross, or death
> E'er shall silence faith and praise;
> All things serve thee here beneath,
> If thou love God!

This was the hymn of Anthony Ulric, Duke of Brunswick Wolfenbuttel. He gave it to the Christian world in 1667, and it will ever live as the precious utterance of a noble heart in its purest and most hallowed state of feeling. There is, however, another hymn whose birth and history claim a page in the chronicles of the House of Brunswick. How finely wrought are some of the most important links of things in human history; how minute and delicate the points on which the most weighty consequences turn; how slight a touch, at certain junctures, would have turned the mightiest current of human affairs! About the middle of the sixteenth century, the seven sons of William of Brunswick cast lots to determine which of them should marry. Poor young princes! the patrimony was probably not rich enough to bless them all with matrimonial rights! The lot fell upon George, the sixth son. After four of his brothers had reigned, of course without issue, the government came to Christian Lewis, his son; then to George William, another son, who left as his heiress Sophia Dorothea, who married her cousin, George Lewis, of Hanover, afterwards George I. of England. George Lewis was, on his mother's side, the grandson of Elizabeth, Queen of Bohemia, daughter of James I. of England. The houses of Stuart and Brunswick were thus at one, and the results, as happily developed in the history of modern England, may, perhaps, illustrate the divine proverb, "The lot is cast into the lap, but the whole disposing thereof is of the Lord." This remarkable linking of Stuart and Brunswick has a peculiar interest for the lover of spiritual hymns and songs. There was a hymnist among the Brunswickers, and one, too, among the Stuarts. Elizabeth, the grandmother of George 1., used to solace herself with hymns; and one of these has come down to us among the evidences of her piety and talents. Its music is not flowing throughout; it has some of the quaintness of its time, but it is pleasant in its simplicity; it breathes a vigorous spirit, and has a rich and cheerful tone of Christian feeling. The hymnist was the daughter of James I. The morning-tide of her life was bright; she had been brought from Scotland an infant when her father came to the throne of the United Kingdom; and her first English residence was Combe Abbey, in Warwickshire, where, amidst scenes of quiet rural beauty, she spent some of the happiest days of her life. She soon gave promise of those charms of person, mind, and manners which afterwards secured for her the title of "Queen of Hearts." She must have had an inspiring presence to bring from Ben Jonson that remarkable poetic combination of compliment and prophecy which he addressed to the King and Queen when their eldest son was created Prince of Wales:—

> Nor shall less joy your royal hopes pursue
> In that most princely maid, whose form might call
> The world to war, and make it hazard all
> Its valour for her beauty; she shall be
> Mother of nations, and her princes see
> Rivals almost to these.

Could Ben Jonson have foreseen that she would be the mother of that illustrious line now represented by our beloved Queen Victoria? A foreign prince, who saw Elizabeth in 1608, says that she was "handsome, and of a noble expression of countenance;" and one of her own countrymen, who knew her, tells us that she was " a princess of lovely beauty, in whom at the first glance, majesty shines out, though hidden by courtesy. Although she has not yet passed her twelfth year, yet all behold in her lively proofs of most excellent and noble dispositions. Her wit is acute, her memory tenacious, her judgment discerning, beyond her years. In piety and knowledge of languages she excels. She also diligently cultivates music, and is a great proficient in the art; for this tranquil liberal science most fittingly accords with the temper of the most placid and illustrious maiden. Added to this, her manners are most gentle; and she shows no common skill in those liberal exercises of mind and body which become a royal maiden. In fine, whatever was excellent or lofty in Queen Elizabeth is all compressed into the tender age of this virgin princess, and if God spare her to us, will be found there accumulated." She and her brother, Henry, Prince of Wales, loved one another very tenderly. The one could scarcely be happy in the other's absence. Nor was the tender bond at all loosened by the attachment which now sprang up between Elizabeth and her husband elect, Frederic V., Count Palatine of the Rhine. Just, however, as all were preparing themselves for mutual congratulations on Elizabeth's marriage, Henry was seized with fever. His affectionate sister, distressed at being forbidden to see him, stole away from St. James's more than once in disguise, and made vain attempts to gain admittance to his chamber. She never saw him again. He died, saying, "Where is my dear sister?" A dark shadow fell on the soul of the tender-hearted princess. This was her first pang of bereavement; and, alas! it proved to be the foreshadowing of future sorrows, the earnest of a long succession of clouds upon her eventful life. It was while this early tribulation pressed upon her heart that she gave expression to her feelings in the hymn so remarkable for its beauty and pathos :—

This is joy, this is true pleasure,
If we best things make our treasure,
And enjoy them at full leisure,
Evermore in richest treasure.

God is only excellent,
Let up to Him our love be sent;
Whose desires are set or bent
On aught else, shall much repent.

Theirs is a most wretched case
Who themselves so far disgrace,
That they their affections place
Upon things named vile and base.

Let us love of heaven receive,
These are joys our hearts will heave
Higher than we can conceive,
And shall us not fail nor leave.

Earthly things do fade, decay,
Constant to us not one day;
Suddenly they pass away,
And we cannot make them stay.

All the vast world doth contain,
To content man's heart, are vain,
That still justly will complain,
And unsatisfied remain.

God most holy, high, and great,
Our delight doth make complete;
When in us He takes His seat,
Only then we are replete.

Why should vain joys us transport,
Earthly pleasures are but short,
And are mingled in such sort,
Griefs are greater than the sport.

. . . . . .

O my God! for Christ His sake,
Quite from me this dulness take;
Cause me earth's love to forsake,
And of heaven my realm to make.

If early thanks I render Thee,
That Thou hast enlightened me
With such knowledge that I see
What things most behoveful be;

That I hereon meditate,
That desire I find (tho' late)
To prize heaven at higher rate,
And these pleasures vain to hate;

O enlighten more my sight,
And dispel my darksome night,
Good Lord, by Thy heavenly light,
And Thy beams most pure and bright.

Since in me such thoughts are scant,
Of Thy grace repair my want,
Often meditations grant,
And in me more deeply plant.

Work of wisdom more desire,
Grant I may, with holy ire,
Slight the world, and me inspire
With Thy love to be on fire.

What care I for lofty place,
If the Lord grant me His grace;
Showing me His pleasant face,
And with joy I end my race.

This is only my desire,
This doth set my heart on fire,
That I may receive my hire,
With the saints and angels' quire.

O my soul, of heavenly birth,
Do thou scorn this basest earth;
Place not here thy joy and mirth,
Where of bliss is greatest dearth.

From below thy mind remove,
And affect the things above;
Set thy heart and fix thy love
Where thou truest joy shalt prove.

If I do love things on high,
Doubtless them enjoy shall I;
Earthly pleasures if I try,
They pursued faster fly.

O Lord, glorious, yet most kind,
Thou hast these thoughts put in my mind;
Let me grace increasing find,
Me to Thee more firmly bind.

To God glory, thanks, and praise,
I will render all my days;
Who hath blest me many ways,
Shedding on me gracious rays.

To me grace, O Father, send,
On Thee wholly to depend;
That all may to Thy glory tend—
So let me live, so let me end.

Now to the true Eternal King,
Not seen with human eye,
Th' immortal, only wise, true God,
Be praise perpetually!

Ill-fated hymnist! How many, many a time after she penned this first hymn, and gave it into the hand of her friend and tutor, Lord Harrington, was she called to test the faithfulness of her God in hours of trouble. She went a happy bride to her husband's hereditary palace at Heidelberg, became a happy mother at eighteen, saw her husband placed on the throne of Bohemia, and realized the dream of her own youthful ambition—a crown. But scarcely had she shown her queenly presence in Bohemia, before her husband was driven from his royalty. She fled for her life, and entered on the dark succession of misfortunes which crowded on her all through the "thirty years' war." Hers was indeed a life of royal suffering. Widowed at last, beggared, tortured by her father's crooked policy, living to hear of her brother Charles's death on the scaffold, parting with her children for lack of means to support them, treated with cold neglect by the only son who could help her, having her sound Protestant heart smitten at the perversion of others of her children to Romanism; yet her hopeful and buoyant heart kept up until, after forty sorrowful years of exile, and thirty years of desolate widowhood, she returned, at the age of sixty-five, to finish her eventful career in the land of her infancy. She died in Leicester House, Leicester Square, leaving the relics of her royal furniture to be preserved in that same Combe Abbey which had witnessed the pleasures of her youth, and the beginnings of that piety which sustained her in sorrow, and gave peace to her last hour. Of her surviving daughters, it was said that Elizabeth, Abbess of Hervarden, was the most learned woman, that Louise was the greatest artist, and that Sophia, her youngest, was the most accomplished woman in Europe. Elizabeth's memory as a hymnist is remarkably associated with the names of some of the most distinguished hymnists of her time. Dr. John Donne wrote her epithalamium on her marriage-day. George Wither presented complimentary stanzas on her betrothal, and her music master was no other than John Bull, the reputed author of that national hymn in which all British hearts now offer their prayer for the illustrious living descendant of her youngest daughter—

> God save our gracious Queen,
> Long live our noble Queen,
>   God save the Queen!
> Send her victorious,
> Happy and glorious,
> Long to reign over us,
>   God save the Queen!
>
> O Lord our God, arise,
> Scatter her enemies,
>   And make them fall.
> Frustrate their knavish tricks,
> Confound their politics;
> On her our hearts we fix:
>   God save the Queen!
>
> Thy richest gifts in store,
> On her be pleased to pour;
>   Long may she reign!
> May she defend our laws,
> And ever give us cause
> To sing with heart and voice,
>   God save the Queen!

On the Sunday after the coronation of Victoria, "our most religious and gracious Queen," there was an interesting scene at Brixham in South Devon. A crowd of sailors and fishermen attended the church—the church that looks out upon Torbay, on whose waters so many of the hardy sons of that beautiful sea-board have been trained to man "the wooden walls of Old England." The parson of the parish was in the pulpit, the gifted and gentle-spirited Henry F. Lyte, beloved by all who knew him, and still talked of with reverence and affection by the children of those whom he taught in sea-songs to remember God upon the mighty waters. He had intended to preach from another text that day; but seeing the character of his congregation, he changed his theme, and addressed them from the Lord's words to the fishermen of Galilee, "Cast the net on the right side of the ship, and ye shall find." He showed his hearers that "it is the religious man that is always, and in every relation of life, the best member of society, the most useful to others, and the most happy in himself," and that no man ever "casts the net on the right side of the ship, none ever catches anything worth his finding, who does not seek and find the favour of God through Christ." Then referring to the circumstances under which they were met—those of the coronation week —he said, "The manner in which our fishermen have conducted themselves through all this week cannot have failed to gratify all who have witnessed it. The people of Brixham may well be proud of a body of men who have so practically proved that they can command themselves. . . . . But if the opening of your proceedings was praiseworthy, the close of them is not less so. To meet you here, my brethren, in the house of God, to witness your orderly conduct, your devotional manner, is, indeed, most pleasing and encouraging. . . . . It seems to me to intimate that you have a proper sense of the religious nature of the great ceremony we have just been celebrating in these realms; that you view it, as indeed it is, as a solemn national transaction, carried on in the sight of God, in one of His holy temples, between His vicegerent on earth and the people He has committed to her charge; and that you are aware that God must be appealed to, in order that she may prove a blessing to us, or that we may be enabled to discharge our duties to her. My dear friends, nothing is really great in which God and religion have not a place. Deprive the coronation of these, strip the pageant of its heavenly halo, and how poor and insignificant does it become! It is, as connecting itself with God, with His will, His sanctuary, His appointment, and His blessing, that the ceremony becomes truly impressive. In this light I trust that your presence here to-day shows that you view it. It is, I trust, as if you said, We have but half discharged our duty on this occasion till we have gone to the house of God, and asked His blessing on our youthful sovereign—asked the King of kings and the Lord of lords to supply the deficiencies of our services towards her. The prayers in which we have all joined here to-day afford a striking compendium both to monarch and subject of their respective duties to each other; and I trust that we shall all make a point of studying their contents, and of pouring them forth earnestly every Sabbath at the throne of grace. Then may our loyalty be expected to be, not like the vows and garlands that adorned the festal hour, and then faded away, but like the jewels of the royal crown, that have come down, precious and untarnished, through successive generations. Oh, let the loyalty of British hearts once thus vent itself in fervent, persevering prayer for their sovereign, and who shall say what benefits may thus descend upon her head, and, through her, upon her people?" The preacher's address was closed, and all rose and sang a hymn, a beautifully condensed and accommodated paraphrase of the 21st Psalm, composed for the occasion by the pastor himself:—

> Lord, Thy best blessings shed
> On our Queen's youthful head;
>   Round her abide.
> Teach her Thy holy will,
> Shield her from every ill,
> Guard, guide, and speed her still
>   Safe to Thy side.
>
> Grant her, O Lord, to be
> Wise, just, and good like Thee,
>   Blessing and blest.
> With every virtue crowned,
> Honoured by nations round,
> Midst earthly monarchs found
>   Greatest and best.
>
> Long let her people share
> Here her maternal care;
>   Long 'neath her smile
> May every good increase,
> May every evil cease,
> And freedom, health and peace
>   Dance round our isle.
>
> Under Thy mighty wings
> Keep her, O King of kings!
>   Answer her prayer:
> Till she shall hence remove
> Up to Thy courts above,
> To dwell in light and love
>   Evermore there.

CHAPTER IX.

SONGS IN PRISON.

"From the freed spirit every shackle falls,
Earth's gloom is lost in heaven's glorious light."

WHO would not like to have heard that midnight song of Paul and Silas in the prison at Philippi? With bodies lacerated by the executioner's whip, and cast upon the bare floor of the dungeon under the torturing burden of the Roman stocks, parched and weary after a day's labour, excitement, and abuse, whither should they look for help and comfort? They knew their refuge, and, "having prayed, they sang a hymn to God, and the prisoners heard them." They sang heartily, "with the spirit and with the understanding also." Their hymn is not recorded; but we may be sure that Jesus was its leading theme, that they uttered their theme distinctly enough for the prisoners to know what they were singing about, and that the spirit of their hymn and its rhythm, its manner and its music, were such as accorded most fully with the simple, childlike devotion of the unselfish and heavenly-minded prisoners. Had their strain come down to our ears with sufficient clearness and certainty to allow us to render it into English metre or rhyme, it might have appeared somewhat similar to an ancient hymn which broke forth from the bars of a prison a few centuries later. It was on a Palm Sunday, about seven hundred and fifty years after Paul's song in the prison. The Emperor Louis, the Debonnaire, and his Court, were on their way to the cathedral at Mentz in full procession, and, when passing a dungeon, the following hymn issued from an open window, and was taken up by the choristers:—

Glory, and honour, and praise,
  To Thee, our Redeemer and King;
To whom little children sang lays,
  To whom our hosannas we bring.

David's own heir to the throne
  Of Israel's royal domain;
Thou Blessed One, come to Thine own,
  Thy kingdom for ever maintain!

Angelical choirs above
  Sing glory to Thee from on high;
And mortals and all things that move
  Give anthems and songs in reply.

Those Hebrew people of old
  Went singing before Thee with psalms;
With prayers and praises untold,
  We, too, will be waving our palms!

While hastening on to Thy death,
  They loudly uplifted their voice;
But we with our every breath,
  In Thy exaltation rejoice.

Fragrant to Thee was their praise,
  Oh smile on the offering we bring;
Thy joy is in all pleasant lays,
  Thou Blessed and All-gracious King!

This was the prison song of Theodulph of Orleans, afterwards named in the calendar as a "saint"; and not without some reason, for he was a saintly man. Like many other saintly men, he had incurred the ill-will of those on whom his goodness reflected reproof, and suffered imprisonment on the testimony of false accusers. His hymn from the prison, however, touched the heart of Charlemagne's imperial son, and the persecuted bishop, like Paul and Silas, found the joy of deliverance coming after his song. Those who have Christian cheerfulness enough to begin their hymns in the straits of tribulation will often find themselves swelling the chorus "in a large place."

Songs in prison! who can think of them without some thought about the "beloved disciple," the last of his order, the apostle of love, in his banishment, his narrow sea-girt prison. Shut up "for the word of God, and for the testimony of Jesus Christ," he had songs nevertheless. His Patmos was "compassed about with songs of deliverance"; songs from the New Jerusalem; songs that for ever filled his heart with responsive music. How his soul must have repeated the hymns which he had caught in his vision of the Holy City! His record of the vision is a lofty hymn, whose music lives for ever. "And I John saw the holy city, New Jerusalem, coming down from God out of heaven, prepared as a bride adorned for her husband. And I heard a great voice out of heaven saying, Behold, the tabernacle of God is with men, and He will dwell with them, and they shall be His people; and God Himself shall be with them, and be their God. And God shall wipe away all tears from their eyes; and there shall be no death, neither sorrow nor crying, neither shall there be any more pain: for the former things are passed away." How many suffering Christians, from generation to generation since "the Lord's-day" of the apostle's vision, have caught the light of the city from the narrow windows of their prison-house in the flesh. Into how many a deep cell has his ever-living vision shed its cheering radiance! Some fragments of one "prisoner's song" have come to our ears, witnessing to the power of Christian hope in giving the soul a refreshing sense of its heavenly freedom, even while the body is pining in bondage. The prisoner solaced himself in his loneliness by writing and singing of the New Jerusalem. Happy man! his cell became his little heaven, while he was preparing for a "better inheritance." Some cell in that storied old "Tower" on the banks of the Thames was often illumed by a light from the distant home, towards which the imprisoned citizen of heaven was daily and nightly turning his longing eyes. It was there, probably, towards the end of Elizabeth's reign, that a long prison song was written by F. B. P., alias Francis Baker. His hymn found a home in the British Museum. It is too long to be sung every hour, but it had too much life to stay, all of it, in its Museum cell. Precious bits have slipped out into tuneful liberty, and have found their way into thousands of hearts, north and south, in the Old World and in the New. How many a prisoner of hope has been heard singing—

> Jerusalem, my happy home,
>   When shall I come to thee?
> When shall my sorrows have an end,
>   Thy joys when shall I see?

Oh happy harbour of the saints!
　Oh sweet and pleasant soil!
In Thee no sorrow may be found,
　No grief, no care, no toil.

There lust and lucre cannot dwell,
　There envy bears no sway;
There is no hunger, heat, nor cold,
　But pleasure every way.

Thy walls are made of precious stones,
　Thy bulwarks diamonds square;
Thy gates are of right orient pearl,
　Exceeding rich and rare.

Thy turrets and thy pinnacles
　With carbuncles do shine;
Thy very streets are paved with gold,
　Surpassing clear and fine.

Oh, my sweet home, Jerusalem,
　Would God I were in thee!
Would God my woes were at an end,
　Thy joys that I might see!

Thy saints are crown'd with glory great;
　They see God face to face;
They triumph still, they still rejoice,
　Most happy in their case.

We that are here in banishment
　Continually do moan,
We sigh, and sob, we weep, and wail,
　Perpetually we groan.

Our sweet is mix'd with bitter gall,
　Our pleasure is but pain,
Our joys scarce last the looking on,
　Our sorrows still remain.

But there they live in such delight,
　Such pleasure and such play;
As that to them a thousand years
　Doth seem as yesterday.

Thy gardens and thy gallant walks
　Continually are green,
There grow such sweet and pleasant flowers
　As nowhere else are seen.

Quite through the street with silver sound
　The flood of life doth flow;
Upon whose banks on every side,
　The wood of life doth grow.

> There trees for evermore bear fruit
>   And evermore do spring;
> There evermore the angels sit,
>   And evermore do sing.
>
> Jerusalem, my happy home,
>   Would God I were in thee!
> Would God my woes were at an end,
>   Thy joys that I might see!

Many versions of this "prisoner's hymn" have found their way into different parts of Europe; and many a home and many a prison, it may be, have been made the happier by its simple soothing tones, and its tuneful alternations of plaintiveness and triumph. Snatches of it used to be heard among the hills and glens of Scotland. They lived in the memory and heart of many a Scotch mother; and seem to have been sung as devout and cheering accompaniments to the daily duties of cottage life. Nor was this without good fruit even in distant lands—fruit that sprang up far away from the spot where the seed first fell. A young Scotchman who was on his death-bed at New Orleans, says the American biographer of Whitefield, was visited by a Presbyterian minister, but continued for a time to shut himself up against all the good man's efforts to reach his heart. Somewhat discouraged, at last the visitor turned away, and scarcely knowing why, unless it was for his own comfort, began to sing, "Jerusalem, my happy home." That was enough, a tender chord was touched. The young patient's heart was broken; and with bursting tears he said, "My dear mother used to sing that hymn." His softened spirit was now open to his Redeemer. Jesus gave the penitent peace; and hope threw light upon his passage to the city which is now for ever the " happy home " of his mother and her son. The prisoner, too, whose song went out from the Tower to fulfil such heavenly missions, now enjoys the city of his desire; and many have gathered around him there, whose way thither had been brightened by the music of his hymn. And there he has met with others, once psalmists like himself in prison, but now at large to commune amidst the joys of immortal freedom, and to watch the accumulating fruit of their prison psalmody. Among the rest is one rapt spirit, the spirit of a sainted lady who now realizes the truth of her Saviour's words,

"Blessed are ye when men shall revile you and persecute you, and shall say all manner of evil against you falsely, for my sake. Rejoice, and be exceeding glad: for great is your reward in heaven."

Jane Marie Bouviers de la Mathe Guion was a sufferer for Christ; and was in one sense a martyr for the honour of the Blessed Spirit. "In the time of the ancient law," as she herself remarks, "there were several of the Lord's martyrs, who suffered for asserting and trusting in the one true God. In the primitive Church of Christ, the martyrs shed their blood for maintaining the truth of Jesus Christ crucified; but now there are martyrs of the Holy Spirit, who suffer for their dependence on Him, for maintaining His reign in souls, and for being subject to the Divine will. . . . The devil now directly attacks the dominion of the Holy Spirit, opposing His celestial unction in souls, and discharging his hatred on the bodies of those whose minds he cannot hurt." Like many others whose spirituality has been too high and full for a carnal world and a worldly Church, she was called to suffer from human efforts to repress and shut up the overflowings of "perfect love." She was imprisoned for her spiritual-mindedness and her uncontrollable zeal for a religion of inward spirit and power. Born on Easter Eve, April 13, 1648, at Montargis, about 50 miles south of Paris, of gentle blood, tender and delicate constitution, and trained in a style which prepared her for intercourse with frequenters at court, while it made her familiar with the sorrows of ill-tempered government at home; this distinguished woman entered on her remarkable course of suffering, discipline, and activity, in her sixteenth year, when, as a tall, beautiful girl, she was made the victim of convenience, by marriage with an elderly gentleman, who in conjunction with his mother ruled her as a pupil if not a slave. Her decided conversion to vital Christianity, however, very soon laid the foundation of that exemplary piety, charity, and devotion, which she sustained for so many years as a wife, a mother, a widow, and a consecrated evangelist for Christ. The instrument of her conversion was a modest but devoted religious recluse, who quietly dropped a passing word to her on the subject of inward godliness. It was "a word in season." She had been groping after truth, feeling after God; but those few "good words" opened the blessed to her heart. "They were unto me," she says, "like the stroke of a dart, which pierced my heart asunder. I felt at the instant a wound very deep, smitten with the love of God; a wound so delightful that I desired it never to be cured. These words brought into my heart what I had been seeking so many years. . . . O infinite goodness! O Beauty ancient and new! why have I known Thee so late? Alas! I sought Thee where Thou wast not, and did not seek Thee where Thou wast. It was for want of understanding these words of Thy gospel, 'The kingdom of God cometh not with observation; neither shall they say, lo here, or lo there; for behold the kingdom of God is within you.' This I now experienced, since Thou became my King, and my heart Thy kingdom, where Thou didst reign as sovereign, and didst all Thy will. This fell out on Magdalen's Day, 1668." On Magdalen's Eve, 1676, her husband died, and on the following morning she renewed what she called her marriage-contract with the Lord Jesus Christ. "I renewed it every year," she writes, "on Magdalen's Day." She proved herself equal to all the business of settling her husband's affairs; and then, she gave herself as a "widow indeed" to the work of proclaiming the salvation which she had found, and of gathering souls for her Divine Lord. Full of spiritual power and love, she went everywhere, wherever her way was open, in France and in Italy; and under great bodily suffering, "in perils of waters, in perils of robbers, in perils by her own countrymen, in perils of the city, in perils of the wilderness, in perils among false brethren," and false sisters, "in weariness and painfulness, in watchings often, and in fastings often," she prayed, and exhorted, and taught, and persuaded, until in convents, in monasteries, in homes, by the way, wherever she came indeed, the fruit of her labours multiplied in many souls saved from sin, and brought to love Christ with all their heart, and to commune with the Father and the Son in the Holy Ghost. Her writings were voluminous, and these brought upon her, at last, the ecclesiastical authorities of the day. Her soul-converting power excited the wrath of many; but her writings, not in all points accurate, and never to be understood by those who were most forward to judge, afforded seeming reason for that continued persecution which resulted, at length, in her consignment to prison by order of the king. She was at first consigned to a convent, under the cruel oversight of a severe nun; her child was torn from her, and all comforts were withdrawn; but she had "an interior joy at her new humiliation." By and by, however, after various examinations by church dignitaries, she was thrown into the prison at Vincennes. "There," she tells us, "I passed my time in great peace, content to pass the rest of my life there, if such were the will of God. I sang songs of joy, which the maid who served me learned by heart, as fast as I made them; and we together sang Thy praises, O my God! The stones of my prison looked in my eyes like rubies. I esteemed them more than all the gaudy brilliancies of the world. My heart was full of that joy. Thou givest to them that love Thee in the midst of their greatest crosses." The free music of her hymn, and her warm and flowing devotion, move us even now as she and her maid sing—

> Great God, here at ease,
> Thee singly to please,
>   I sing all the length of the day;
> Shut up in a cage,
> Yet sheltered from rage,
>   Oh listen and smile on the lay!
>
> From sorrow released,
> With solace increased,
>   The bars of my prison I love;
> All toil here untried,
> All wants well supplied,
>   I am blest and enriched from above.
>
> What if aliens are prone
> To despise, as unknown,
>   A language in heaven understood?
> 'Tis a feast to the taste
> Of the soul that is chaste,
>   As it flows from the fountain of good.
>
> Tho' my foes have combined,
> And my body confined,
>   Yet my soul is with liberty blest;
> I am humbly content
> With whatever is sent,
>   For I know that Thy pleasure is best.

Oh pleasure divine,
All excellence Thine,
  And Thee will I love and adore;
The more piercing my pain,
The more freedom I gain,
  And of every choice blessing the more.

Accept then, I pray,
The tribute I pay,
  I sing, as a bird full of joy;
Vivacious, exposed,
In a cage when enclosed,
  His warbling effusions employ.

Grant my hymns uttered here,
Melodious to cheer,
  Tho' tend'rer and softer than fine;
And the strength ever deign
Of my life to sustain,
  Of that durable life which is Thine.

Thy wondrous defence
Makes a cell seem immense—
  It sheds so peculiar a grace;
Such a pleasure abounds,
Such a glory surrounds,
  And the joys of Thy kingdom embrace.

All my foes I behold,
All the stout and the bold,
  Perplexing their hearts with their pain;
Confounded, I see,
While happily free,
  How they vent all their furies in vain!

With a spirit thus unsubdued, and a soul thus joyfully communing with the heaven which the storms of persecution never disturb, she found her enemies still unwearied with the efforts of their false zeal. They kept her in prison several years in a sick and suffering condition. Her keepers in every case learnt to respect and love her; and then, to avert the danger of such attachments, she was moved from prison to prison. Now at Vincennes, then at Vaugirard, and from Vaugirard to the Bastile. Still her truthfulness was clear, her purity was transparent, and her unsullied character as a Christian convinced even the gainsayers. Her songs, too, were unfailing. Nor was the notorious Bastile left unsanctified by a hymn. There she sang—

My dearest Protector, see how they detain
My life in a dungeon! Yet let me remain
While such is Thy pleasure: for better no doubt
In a *prison* with Thee than a *palace* without!

No thought in my heart dares to lift up its head,
But the thought which to love, and to serve Thee, is led.

I wish'd to be Thine from my tenderest age:
No lovers beside have I sought to engage;
No slender supports of the loftiest reeds;
No trust in their words, and no hope of their deeds.

In every probation, to Thee the recourse
Of my soul, in Thy grace is its only resource.
What else can I do, so surrounded with foes,
But fly to Thy goodness which heals all my woes?

When my hair shall grow white, and infirmities shake
This old shatter'd fabric, Thou wilt not forsake.

I was formerly pain'd when I saw night and day,
What innocence suffered in walking her way;
But since I have learn'd, we are summon'd to prove
By the weight of our suffering the weight of our love.

Love perfect and pure goes farther than thought;
None knows, till he proves it, how dear 'twill be bought;
Yet 'tis well worth its price, and a thousand times more,
Since it brings us to heaven when our labours are o'er.

The imprisoned sufferer was happy in the will of God; but she felt herself called ceaselessly to demand a fair trial, that her crime, if there were any, might be openly specified and proved. The only response to her appeals seems to have been an inquisitorial process of inquiry for some evidence to damage her case. All, however, was vain; her character was stainless. She was dismissed from prison; but because of the alleged doubtfulness of her doctrines, they banished her to Blois, where for nearly twelve years her example shed the calm and pure light of a Christian eventide, and in the end left bright memorials of its holiness in the hearts of all who knew her. She died in peace amidst a few of her best friends. Some of Madame Guion's teachings would have seemed less doubtful, it may be, had her terminology been fully understood; or had her mode of expression been less symbolical and dreamy. Her experience as a Christian was not far different from that of many other highly spiritual Christians who have never been accused of an approach to error. "Perfect love," in all ages, bears the same Divine impress. Some of Madame Guion's last sayings must ever secure a hallowed memory for her name. "Nothing," says she, "is greater than God, nothing less than myself. He is rich, I am poor; and yet I want nothing. Life or death is equal to me; God is love. I want nothing but God and His glory." The leading notion of her theology, if she may be said to teach theology, is given in her "Spiritual Torrents." "As soon as a soul is touched of God in such a manner as to return to Him in all sincerity, after the first purgation, or cleansing, which confession and contrition have made, God gives it a certain instinct for turning to Him in a more perfect manner, to be united to Him; as it then clearly sees that it was not created for the amusements and trifles of the world, but that it has a centre, to which it must strive to return, and out of which it can never find true repose." That her holiness was truly Christian is seen in her last words to her many spiritual children: "Oh, my dear children, open your eyes to the light of truth. 'Holy Father, sanctify them through Thy truth.' Thy Divine Word has spoken to them through my mouth. Christ alone is the Truth. He said of His apostles, 'For their sakes I sanctify myself, that they also may be sanctified through the truth.' Oh, say the same thing to my children. Sanctify Thyself in them and for them. It is being truly sanctified in all holiness, to have none of our own, but only the holiness of Jesus Christ. Let Him alone be all in all in us, and for us, that the work of sanctification may be carried on through the experimental knowledge of the Divine truth. . . . . My children, receive the instruction from your mother, and it will procure you life. Receive it through her, not as for her, but as of and for God. Amen. Lord Jesus Christ." Amen!

> Give glory to Jesus, our Head,
>   With all that encompass His throne;
> A widow, a widow indeed,
>   A mother in Israel is gone!
>
> . . . .
>
> Rejoice for a sister deceased,
>   Our loss is her infinite gain;
> A soul out of prison released,
>   And free from its bodily chain.

> With song let us follow her flight,
> And mount with her spirit above,
> Escaped to the mansions of light,
> And lodged in the Eden of love.

It is pleasant to read the songs of a prisoner who has learned to be happy in prison; and the pleasure is greater when the hymns come from a "prisoner of Jesus Christ"— one who suffers bondage purely for Christ's sake. But even that pleasure is equalled, if not surpassed, by the joy with which we joy over that goodness of heart, that overflowing charity which constrains a man to task his genius in providing appropriate, instructive, and cheery prison hymns for those who have neither heart nor genius to compose hymns for themselves, or in teaching those who have merited imprisonment so to sing as to beguile their hours of confinement, to make legal penalties contribute to their heart's welfare, and to prepare themselves while in bondage for the privileges and duties of freedom. Such is the joy which must bless those who tune themselves for companionship with the man under whose striking old portrait the lover of quaint but well-strung psalmody may read—

> So this is he whose infant muse began
> To brave the world before years styled him man;
> Though praise be slight, and scorns to make his rhymes
> Beg favours or opinion of the times,
> Yet few by good men have been more approved
> None so unseen, so generally loved.

A very good character, especially for a man whose sympathy with prisoners was strengthened by his own experience as a prisoner, having been in "durance vile" three successive times—once for writing a little too freely, as some people thought, about public abuses; a second time because he chose to be a "roundhead," while some of his more powerful neighbours lorded it as cavaliers; and once more because it was thought impertinent for him to remonstrate against being stripped of the spoils which he had picked up while he happened to stand on the winning side of the game. His second period of bondage might have been fatal but for the plea of a fellow-poet, Denham, who wore royalist colours. "Let him live," was the plea, "for while he lives I shall not be thought the worst poet." It was a good joke, for it saved a good life; and George Wither lived to show his tuneful sympathy with poor prisoners. "Men in affliction," says he, very kindly, "are somewhat easier when they can find words whereby to express their sufferings; to help them who want expression of their endurance in imprisonment, and to remember prisoners of such meditations as are pertinent to their condition, is the intent of this hymn:"—

> I whom of late
>   No thraldom did molest,
> Of that estate
>   Am wholly dispossess'd:
> My feet once free,
>   Are strictly now confined,
> Which breeds in me
>   A discontented mind.
>
> Those prospects fair
>   Which I was wont to have,
> That wholesome air
>   Which fields and meadows gave,
> Are changed now
>   For close, unpleasant cells,
> Where secret woe
>   And open sorrow dwells.
>
> Instead of strains
>   Delightful to mine ear,
> Gyves, bolts, and chains
>   Are all my music here;
> And ere I get
>   Those things for which I pray,
> I must entreat
>   With patience in delay.
>
> To feed or sleep,
>   To work or take mine ease,
> I now must keep
>   Such hours as others please:
> To make me sad,
>   Complaints are likewise heard,
> And often made
>   Of wrongs without regard.
>
> Lord! as I ought
>   My freedom had I used,
> Of this, no doubt,
>   I might have been excused:

But I confess
    The merit of my sin
Deserves no less
    Than hath inflicted been.

Let me, O God!
    My sin Thine anger move;
But let this rod
    Correct my faults in love:
With patient mind
    Let me Thy stripes endure,
And freedom find
    When they have wrought their cure.

Whilst here I 'bide
    Though I unworthy be,
Do Thou provide
    All needful things for me:
And though friends grow
    Unkind in my distress,
Yet leave not Thou
    Thy servant comfortless.

So though in thrall
    My body must remain,
In mind I shall
    Some freedom still retain;
And wiser made
    By this restraint shall be,
Than if I had
    Until my death been free.

Tender-hearted Wither! This hymn, which in his gentleness he offers to the lips and heart of a prisoner as a devout mode of beguiling his solitary hours, was doubtless the very song of his own soul, under the rigours of his unalleviated confinement, and in the damp and gloomy atmosphere of his comfortless dungeon. His were hard times; and those who got the upper hand sometimes forgot their own sufferings in their turn. It was not easy, however, to clip or singe the wings of Wither's muse. Some of his best verses were made in the Marshalsea; and we cannot but pay honourable tribute to the memory of the man who, while he helped those who had less genius and fewer resources than himself to sing with him, cheered on his own muse in a style like this—

    If thy verse do bravely tower,
    As she makes wing she gets power;

Yet the higher she doth soar,
She's affronted still the more;
Till she to the high'st hath past,
Then she rests with fame at last:
Let naught, therefore, thee affright,
But make forward in thy flight;
For, if I could match thy rhyme,
To the very stars I'd climb;
There begin again, and fly
Till I reached eternity.
But alas! my muse is slow;
For thy page she flags too low:
Yea, the more's her hapless fate,
Her short wings were clipt of late;
And poor I, her fortune rueing,
Am myself put up a-mewing;
But if I my cage can rid,
I'll fly where I never did;
And though for her sake I'm crost,
Though my best hopes I have lost,
And knew she would make me trouble
Ten times more than ten times double:
I should love and keep her too,
Spite of all the world could do.
For, though banish'd from my flocks,
And confin'd within these rocks,
Here I waste away the light,
And consume the sullen night,
She doth for my comfort stay,
And keeps many cares away.

. . . . . .

She doth tell me where to borrow
Comfort in the midst of sorrow;
Makes the desolatest place
To her presence be a grace;
And the blackest discontents
Be her fairest ornaments.
In my former days of bliss,
Her divine skill taught me this,
That, from everything I saw,
I could some invention draw;
And raise pleasure to her height,
Through the meanest object's sight:
By the murmur of a spring,
Or the least bough's rustleing;
By a daisy, whose leaves spread,
Shut when Titan goes to bed;
Or a shady bush or tree,
She could more infuse in me,
Than all Nature's beauties can
In some other wiser man.

By her help I also now
Make this churlish place allow
Some things that may sweeten gladness,
In the very gall of sadness.
The dull loneness, the black shade,
That these hanging vaults have made;
The strange music of the waves,
Beating in these hollow caves;
This black den which rocks emboss,
Overgrown with eldest moss;
The rude portals that give light
More to terror than delight;
This my chamber of neglect,
Walled about with disrespect;—
From all these and this dull air,
A fit object for despair,
She hath taught me by her might
To draw comfort and delight.
Therefore, thou best earthly bliss,
I will cherish thee for this.

Well sung, Wither! He has broken his prison; he has reached the home of freedom, and now drinks at its very source the inspiration which still gives life to his best hymns. Let his name be wreathed with peace!

CHAPTER X.

PSALMS IN ENGLISH METRE.

> " As through Thy temple now the deep strains peal,
> And choral minstrelsy is heard to swell,
> Devotion wakes within us, and we feel·
> All that the Psalmist hath expressed so well."

How few among the legion of modern versifiers have ever caught either the spirit or the manner of the sacred old hymns, which they have tried to throw into English metre. With few exceptions, those who have aimed at a literal version of the Psalms in metre are tame, and have lost the soul of the original; while many of the paraphrasers are lacking in dignity, and excite any feeling but that of devotion, by calling their neighbours to sing their psalms "done into metre." Sternhold and Hopkins must be venerated as we revere antiquity even in its dotage. Brady and Tate are always associated with our early impressions of old Church psalmody, when the parish-clerk used to act as head singer, and give the key-note on a doleful instrument that they called a pitch-pipe. As to the music of the Scotch version, it is enough that it is admired most by those who abominate the organ, while they are agreeably moved by the notes of a Highland piper. It would be better to let the old English Psalter alone. Many a weary poet would have been spared his pains, and many psalm-singers would have escaped bewilderment amidst wildernesses of dreary verse, had due and wide attention been given to a few verses from one whose happily expressed opinion is of some value. An author who inherited poetic taste from a gifted father, who shared poetic power with two brothers still more gifted, who had passed twenty years of classical discipline in Westminster

School, and who lived to catch the spirit of Hebrew melodies, and enjoy communion with holy psalmists among the inspiring beauties of Devonian valleys and hills, has a right to have his opinion respected on the question of metrical psalmody. Who that has sought out the loveliest retreats of our native island can ever forget the valley of the Exe, as it winds down from the borders of Exmoor to the old-storied town of Tiverton, overlooking from its southern slopes the ancient fords of the Exe and the Leman, lapped amidst orchards and gardens, and its streets and houses refreshed and beautified by the clear bright stream which flows down through it from the upper springs? Two pilgrims of nature once found their way to this old Two-ford-town. One of them lives to remember that, having lingered about the remains of the castle, and having mused and talked over the fortunes of the pensive daughter of Edward IV., who spent the days of her widowhood in its delicious retirement, and having talked about those who for many ages had lived, and sung, and fought, and died in and around the sturdy fortress, they found their way, by an avenue of venerable trees, into the famous grammar-school, founded in 1599, by the will of Peter Blundell; and there, after sundry speculations over the ponderous antique oaken desks and benches, with their multitudinous records of penknife work, they found themselves standing in silence before a remarkable portrait. It represented one of the former masters of the school, nor could its distinctive family features be mistaken. "Look at that," said the one to the other, "does not the face seem instinct with life? It looks as if it knew what we have been saying, in our way down the valley, about the various efforts of people to produce a metrical version of the Psalms. Surely those lips are moving, as if they would re-utter what they expressed so long ago."

"What was that?"

"What? Why, just listen, and hear with what quiet ease keen polished satire may be made to pass into warm and beautiful hymnic devotion"—

>Has David *Christ to come* foreshow'd?
>Can Christians then aspire
>To mend the harmony that flow'd
>From his prophetic lyre?

How curious are their wits, and vain,
  Their erring zeal how bold,
Who durst with meaner dross profane
  His purity of gold!

His Psalms unchanged the saints employ,
  Unchanged our God applies;
They suit th' apostles in their joy,
  The Saviour when He dies.

Let David's pure unaltered lays
  Transmit through ages down
To Thee, O David's Lord, our praise!
  To Thee, O David's Son!

Till judgment calls the seraph throng
  To join the human choir,
And God, who gave the ancient song,
  The new one shall inspire.

So thought and so sang Samuel Wesley; thereby somewhat condemning, not only Watts, against whom chiefly these lines had been directed, but his brother Charles also—yea, his own father, and even himself; for each of them had tried his powers in translating or paraphrasing Hebrew psalms into English rhyme. Nor had Samuel Wesley, the father, failed in every case. His version of Psalm cxiv. may be sung with unbroken pleasure—

When ransom'd Israel came
  From faithless Egypt's bands,
The house of Jacob's name
  From foreign hostile lands,
    Judah alone
    God's holy place,
    And Israel's grace
      Was His bright throne.

Amazed old ocean saw,
  And to its chambers fled;
While Jordan's streams withdraw
  To seek their distant head.
    Tall mountains bound
    Like jocund rams,
    The hills like lambs
      Skipp'd lightly round.

What ail'd thee, O thou sea,
  To leave thine ancient bed?
Why did old Jordan flee,
  And seek its distant head?
    Ye mountains, why
    Leap'd ye like rams,
    While hills like lambs
      Skipp'd lightly by?

> All nature's utmost bound
> The God of Jacob's own,
> Where sea or land is found,
> Fall trembling at His throne;
> At whose command
> Hard rocks distil
> A crystal rill
> And drench the sand.

The tasteful old rector shows himself alive to the grand simplicity, the condensed power, elegant conciseness, and noble imagery of this seeming fragment of a sublime ode; and he will be thought to have approached nearer to the original than his own son Charles, who has rendered the same psalm more freely, and in more pompous measure. The mind and pen which gave its distinctive character to the "Spectator" would naturally feel the inspiration of a psalm like this; and Addison has remarked that "its author has written so as deeply to impress the mind of his readers by pointing out miraculous effects without mentioning an agent, till at last, when the sea is seen rapidly retiring from the shore, Jordan retreating to its source, and the mountains and hills running away like a flock of affrighted sheep, that the passage of the Israelites might be every way uninterrupted; then the cause of all is suddenly introduced, and the presence of God in His grandeur solves every difficulty." Literature was Addison's calling. Like many others who have been tempted into positions unsuited to their character, or to which their powers have not proved equal, Addison found that marriage into high life afforded "no addition to his happiness," and that elevation to official state entailed burdens from which an easy and happy relief is not always possible. Retreat alone gave him the promise of peace at the last. Pensioned and in retirement, he sought for solace in preparing a "defence of the Christian religion," and in planning a new poetical version of the Psalms. Neither plan was completed. And perhaps it is better for his reputation, as a psalmist, that he left mere specimen fragments of his intended version.

What he wrote will always live. Nor is there in what he wrote anything, either in spirit or tone, which favours in the least degree the suspicion which some have cast upon his Christian sincerity. His memory will not be damaged by the unworthy insinuations of Pope, neither will lovers of charity think the worse of him because the unsympathizing and unloving Tonson "always thought him a priest in his heart." As an undying minister of instruction and pleasure to English minds and hearts, his memory will not take the tarnish of contemporary slander. All lovers of well-applied genius will love him, were it only for his version of Psalm xix. It has been thought that the pure love for "silently living nature" which gives such a devotional charm to his verses, and which he so sweetly expresses on introducing his psalm to the readers of the "Spectator," must have breathed its first and deepest inspiration into his soul amidst some of the quiet scenes of his boyhood. One of these was the cathedral close at Lichfield. It was evening when for the first time we entered that reverend enclosure. The sun had gone down, and it was our time of preparation for the Sabbath. Where could such an hour be more solemnly kept than amidst the associations which, seen and unseen, gathered beneath the shadows of so venerable a sanctuary? The outer world was growing dim, but everything that was visible offered an agreeable introduction to the invisible. Among the whisperings which came to the ear of fancy, as we paced up and down that noble avenue on the north side of the church, known as "the Dean's walk," there came many remarkable names, which, as they touched us in succession, called up some deep thinkings about the present life and action of those who once enjoyed the shade of these same trees, and figured familiarly in these same sequestered dwellings. On this scene the last century had witnessed some curious interlacings of character. The sober and the frolicsome, the comic and the tragic, the sacred and the profane, had strangely mingled and manœuvred here at times. Many a day had seen Addison, as a school-boy, passing to and fro through the deanery garden. There the wit and imagination of Farquhar were stimulated to immortalize the dishonours of his licentious age; there the Bishop's Registrar, Gilbert Walmsley, saved his own name from oblivion by acting the patron to David Garrick. At the end of the walk, the eye could wander over the parapet of the close, and command the beautiful valley where Samuel Johnson used to wander in early life. The mysteries of nightfall were beginning to shroud it here and there; but Stow Hill was standing in clear outline against the sky, in affectionate watchfulness over its still waters. There, at the foot of the hill, was the old tower of St. Chad's church, where, tradition says, "Ovin heard the angels sing at St. Chad's obit." We lingered long, watching the brightening reflections of the stars in Stow-Pool, and musing on the possibility of angels taking a part in the anthem at a saint's burial, until our ear caught a sweet, thrilling harmony coming up seemingly from the recesses of the cathedral crypt, and floating tremulously along the dark aisles above. Was it the music of angels? It might rather be the voice of choristers tuning themselves for the morrow's psalmody. But it touched one's very soul, and called up the voice of a psalm from within. Just then the rising moon threw up her light from the horizon, and gave the last inspiring touch. The spirit of Addison himself might be there joining us in his own inimitable psalm—

> The spacious firmament on high,
> With all the blue ethereal sky,
> And spangled heavens, a shining frame,
> Their great Original proclaim.
> The unwearied sun, from day to day,
> Does his Creator's power display,
> And publishes to every land
> The work of an Almighty hand.
>
> Soon as the evening shades prevail,
> The moon takes up the wondrous tale,
> And nightly to the listening earth
> Repeats the story of her birth;
> Whilst all the stars that round her burn,
> And all the planets in their turn,
> Confirm the tidings as they roll,
> And spread the truth from pole to pole.
>
> What, though in solemn silence all
> Move round the dark terrestrial ball;
> What, though no real voice or sound
> Amidst their radiant orbs be found;
> In reason's ear they all rejoice,
> And utter forth a glorious voice,
> For ever singing as they shine,
> "The hand that made us is Divine."

The author of this noble psalm in English metre may have been thrown back in imagination to quiet evenings under the elms in Lichfield Close, when, amidst the excitements of literary life, he issued his Saturday invitation to the pleasures of psalmody, and prepared his readers for them by saying, "Faith and devotion naturally grow in the mind of every reasonable man who sees the impressions of Divine power and wisdom in every object on which he casts his eye. The Supreme Being has made the best arguments for His own existence, in the formation of the heaven and the earth; and these are arguments which a man of sense cannot forbear attending to, who is out of the noise and hurry of human affairs." Peace to the memory of the man who thus taught his generation to enjoy the inspired utterance that "the heavens declare the glory of God, and the firmament showeth His handy-work." Nor can any one despise the reflections of Divine power and goodness which come upon us from suns, moons, and stars, without being in danger of debasing his own soul; at the same time, to confine ourselves to the lights of the visible creation, or even to the lessons of a more general providence, is to rest in a religion of sentiment rather than of life, and to be in danger of looking for satisfaction in a partial and comparatively powerless devotion. No, God must be sought chiefly in His revealed Word, and should be contemplated in the work of His Holy Spirit, and in the person and kingdom of His manifested Son. How the devotion of the inspired psalmist kindles and glows when he looks at God in the face of the reigning Messiah! Can anything be more sublime than Psalm lxxii? Could there be a more perfect harmony of the Divine and the human in prayer and praise? And who does not thank God for the man who threw that song into English metre, so happily as to give it all the charms of new music, so effectually as to naturalize it to the purest taste and to the warmest hearts of Christian England? James Montgomery did this when he taught us to sing—

> Hail to the Lord's Anointed,
>   Great David's greater Son!
> Hail, in the time appointed,
>   His reign on earth begun!
> He comes to break oppression,
>   To let the captive free,
> To take away transgression,
>   And rule in equity.

He comes with succour speedy,
　To those who suffer wrong;
To help the poor and needy,
　And bid the weak be strong;
To give them songs for sighing,
　Their darkness turn to light,
Whose souls, condemn'd and dying,
　Were precious in His sight.

He shall come down like showers
　Upon the fruitful earth,
And love, joy, hope, like flowers,
　Spring in His path to birth;
Before Him on the mountains,
　Shall peace, the herald, go;
And righteousness, in fountains,
　From hill to valley flow.

Arabia's desert ranger
　To Him shall bow the knee;
The Ethiopian stranger
　His glory come to see;
With offerings of devotion
　Ships from the isles shall meet,
To pour the wealth of ocean
　In tribute at His feet.

Kings shall fall down before Him,
　And gold and incense bring;
All nations shall adore Him,
　His praise all people sing;
For He shall have dominion
　O'er river, sea, and shore;
Far as the eagle's pinion
　Or dove's light wing can soar.

For Him shall prayer unceasing,
　And daily vows ascend,
His kingdom still increasing,
　A kingdom without end.
The mountain dews shall nourish
　A seed in weakness sown,
Whose fruit shall spread and flourish,
　And shake like Lebanon.

O'er every foe victorious,
　He on His throne shall rest,
From age to age more glorious,
　All blessing and all blest:
The tide of time shall never
　His covenant remove;
His name shall stand for ever,
　That name to us is Love.

But while a versifier here and there has given a psalm in rhyme without entirely degrading the holy strain of the inspired Psalmist; it may be said again, better, on the whole, to let the grand old English Psalter alone. Chant its measures, sing them, or murmur them in holy undertones, but let nobody try to make them all into a book of rhymes. Were we to judge from what Milton did in this line, even he would fail in the larger attempt; and, after his failure, we might expect as little as we get from Watts and Charles Wesley, and their modern followers in wholesale psalmody. Watts wrote too fast; Wesley was faster still. One of Wesley's zealous advocates amuses and instructs us by saying, "You may take all the poetry of Watts, and Cowper, and Pope, and the hymnic compositions of many others, who have a well-earned name as sacred poets, and they are all outnumbered by the single prolific pen of the poet of Methodism." The standard is quantity then! How much did he write? "*Seven thousand* 'psalms, and hymns, and spiritual songs'"! *Seven thousand* from one pen! and that the pen of a zealous, busy, evangelist and pastor! These thousands could not all be gems; nor, indeed, could multitudes of them have any claim even to the honour of paste jewellery. No man can write so many verses, and so fast, and always write well. Not that the voluminous pages of Wesley and Watts are left without adornment of rich gems set here and there. Amidst many dreary pages, Watts sometimes clothes a psalm in simple and unblemished beauty. Whose gratitude, and trust, and hope, have not kindled into quiet fervour while singing thus?

> My Shepherd will supply my need,
>   Jehovah is His name;
> In pastures fresh He makes me feed,
>   Beside the living stream.
>
> He brings my wandering spirit back,
>   When I forsake His ways;
> And leads me for His mercy's sake,
>   In paths of truth and grace.
>
> When I walk through the shades of death,
>   Thy presence is my stay;
> A word of Thy supporting breath
>   Drives all my fears away.

> Thy hand, in spite of all my foes,
>   Doth still my table spread;
> My cup with blessings overflows,
>   Thine oil anoints my head.
>
> The sure provisions of my God
>   Attend me all my days;
> O may Thy house be my abode,
>   And all my work be praise!
>
> There would I find a settled rest,
>   (While others go and come)
> No more a stranger or a guest,
>   But like a child at home.

Charles Wesley, however, is more equal throughout than Watts, and holds a more gracefully sustained flight. Where the rapt psalmist specially invites us to a celestial elevation, Watts sometimes

> Meets
> A vast vacuity: all unawares
> Fluttering his pennons vain, plump down he drops
> Ten thousand fathom deep.

Wesley's power in metrical psalmody is seen to the best advantage where most others are least successful. His version of Psalm cxix. is one of his best. What Manton required an awful folio to explain, Wesley sets forth, with charming fulness and transparency, in the light of twenty-four pages. He shows himself at once the expositor, the theologian, the Hebrew chorister, and the poet; nor is it too much to say that, in his version of this remarkable didactic ode, he has presented to us "an enchanting and well-sustained poem, which, without any approach to tautology, exhibits all the pleasing variety, warmth, and freshness of original verse, while it tenaciously adheres to the spirit of the inspired Psalmist." The world had well-nigh lost this pleasant morsel; the manuscript turned up to a friendly eye where it was not looked for. There are mysteries in the world of literature, and especially about the ins and outs of the literary market, which, in a way, answer to some of the curious secrets of nature. There have been precious germs of vegetable life unseen and unknown for years, treasured up far below the surface, until some modern road-makers effect their cutting through the hill-side, and then, at the very next spring season, up start, on the bare slope, many a plant and flower that had hitherto been thought foreign to the neighbourhood; or, as the warm summer sun opens on some sea-side garden of our inland coast, a tiny seed-vessel, borne on the ocean current or on the breeze, or by a winged carrier from across the water, opens its beauty on this strange soil, and excites a wonder how it should have come here. So, now and then, a freakish inroad on the deep accumulations of some venerable library makes way for some hidden treasures to show themselves; or, perhaps, a curious current of interest, or even a questionable side-wind, carries out a manuscript or two from their obscurity, and leaves them open to the daylight on some unpretending bookstall. How the wind blew, or from what point the stream came which dislodged Charles Wesley's manuscript from its college confinement, must still be a mystery. It is clear, however, that, with some of its library honours yet upon it, it was found by a book-hunter as he was scouring the book-market, possibly in one of the many indefinable stages of Bibliomania. Had there been nothing more in the volume than Wesley's rendering of Psalm cxix., it would have been worth finding. The seventh and eighth parts, answering to *Zain* and *Cheth* in the original, are fair specimens of the poet's embodiment of the Psalmist's spirit, in a kind of harmonized paraphrase and translation:—

Thee, O Lord, the good, the just,
  True and faithful I receive;
Keep Thy word, in which I trust,
  Thou who gav'st me to believe:
Hoping for Thy promised aid,
  Comfort in my grief I find;
This my fainting mind hath stay'd,
  Still it stays my fainting mind.

Me the proud have greatly scorn'd;
  Yet I still unshaken stood,
Never from Thy statutes turn'd,
  Never left the narrow road.
On Thine ancient works I thought,
  Look'd again the same to see;
Thou of old hast wonders wrought,
  Wonders Thou shalt work for me.

Fearless of the scorner's power,
  Fearful for their souls I was,

Saw hell open to devour
 All who break Thy righteous laws:
Lord, Thy laws my songs have been
 In my pilgrimage below,
Kept by them from woe and sin,
 In a world of sin and woe.

Thee I have remembered, Lord,
 Musing in the silent night,
Loved Thy name, and kept Thy word,
 Pure and permanent delight
I did in Thy precepts prove:
 Heaven on earth obedience is,
Perfect liberty and love,
 Perfect power and perfect peace.

Thou my portion art, O Lord!
 Long resolved through Thee I am
To fulfil Thine every word,
 Give me but the help I claim:
All my heart hath sought Thy face,
 Still Thy favour I implore;
Grant me now the promised grace,
 Bid me go and sin no more.

All my sins I call'd to mind,
 Own'd, and left them all for God;
Labour'd the right way to find,
 Thee with earnest zeal pursued;
Turn'd my feet without delay;
 Long'd Thine utmost will to prove,
Eager all Thy law to obey,
 Restless to retrieve Thy love.

Spoil'd and hated for Thy sake,
 Thee I never would forego,
Would not from Thy law turn back;
 Oh my Life, my Heaven below,
Thee I all day long will praise,
 Thee I will at midnight sing!
True and righteous are Thy ways,
 Glory to my God and King!

Join'd to all who fear the Lord,
 Them my dearest friends I own;
Them that keep Thy holy word,
 Saved by grace through faith alone.
Earth is full of love divine;
 Love divine for all is free;
Teach me, then, the law benign;
 Guide, and save, and perfect me.

Psalm xc. comes to us in a metrical English version of beautiful simplicity from one who has been called "the Shakespeare of Scotland." It is said of Robert Burns that he never failed in any poetic attempt, except in epigrams. He certainly did not fail in this essay at turning an old eastern ode into charming English verse. The man had indeed a versatile genius. He could sing in Scotch or English, or in a musical mixture of the two. He could be comic or serious, tender or lofty, each and all by turns. He engages our hearts in a "Cotter's" family devotion, laughs and jokes with "auld Nickie-ben," dances and rides with witches, mimics the voice of Bruce with effect, becomes an impersonation of passionate love for a "bonnie lassie," and melts into tenderness over a crushed daisy or a broken mouse's nest. With the prayerful he prays, with the toper he rants, and with the truly "merry" he can "sing psalms." Gifts that were distributed among many other penmen were happily combined in him. Would that we could always see Burns in the purer and generous light of his earlier days, in his youthful manliness and integrity. Would that we could always think of him as swayed by the better feelings of even his later life; when, for instance, those feelings prompted him to say in a letter to a lady, whose manners and principles reproved him at times, "I have some favourite flowers in spring, among which are the mountain daisy, the harebell, the foxglove, the wild-brier rose, the budding birch, and the hoary hawthorn, that I view and hang over with particular delight. I never hear the loud solitary whistle of the curlew on a summer noon, or the wild mixing cadence of a troop of grey plovers in an autumnal morning, without feeling an elevation of soul, like the enthusiasm of devotion or poetry. Tell me, my dear friend, to what can this be owing? Are we a piece of machinery, which, like the Æolian harp, passive, takes the impression of the passing accident? Or do these workings argue something within us above the trodden clod? I own myself partial to such proofs of those awful and important realities—a God that made all things—man's immaterial and immortal nature, and a world of weal or woe beyond death and the grave." It would be pleasant indeed ever to have the poet before us, warm with the feeling which moved him when he wrote—

But deep this truth impressed my mind,
  Through all His works abroad,
The heart benevolent and kind
  The most resembles God.

Or kindling into the still more devout spirit of his little gem of a psalm—

O Thou, the first, the greatest friend
  Of all the human race!
Whose strong right hand has ever been
  Their stay and dwelling-place.

Before the mountains heaved their heads
  Beneath Thy forming hand;
Before this ponderous globe itself
  Arose at Thy command,

That power which raised and still upholds
  This universal frame;
From countless unbeginning time
  Was ever still the same.

Those mighty periods of years,
  Which seem to us so vast,
Appear no more before Thy sight
  Than yesterday that's past.

Thou giv'st Thy word, Thy creature, man,
  Is to existence brought;
Again Thou sayest, "Ye sons of men,
  Return ye into nought."

Thou layest them, with all their cares,
  In everlasting sleep;
As with a flood Thou tak'st them off
  With overwhelming sweep.

They flourish like the morning flower,
  In beauty's pride arrayed;
But, long ere night, cut down it lies,
  All withered and decayed.

But shadows sometimes gather around the memory of this departed genius; shadows that even to this day dim the moral life of scenes in which that memory is cherished. It is not pleasant to doubt of any human life, whether the good it bequeathed is equal to the mischief it entails. But Burns is gone, as all the sons of genius must go, hallowed or unhallowed; gone with the "flood," as he himself psalmed it, or as Watts, with more sublimity, renders the same truth—

> The busy tribes of flesh and blood,
> With all their lives and cares,
> Are carried downwards by the flood,
> And lost in following years.
>
> Time, like an ever-rolling stream,
> Bears all its sons away;
> They fly, forgotten, as a dream
> Dies at the opening day.
>
> Like flow'ry fields the nations stand,
> Pleas'd with the morning light;
> The flow'rs, beneath the mower's hand,
> Lie with'ring ere 'tis night.

The fragment of this psalm which Burns has left is precious, were it only to show how a master of his own pure native English can succeed in imitating the crystal-like beauty and simple grandeur of an ancient Hebrew hymn, even though his own heart never realized full sympathy with the higher spiritual feeling of the original Psalmist. "The Spirit of the Psalms" has been more happily caught in later times by one whose own spirit had learnt deeply to converse with the author of holiest inspiration. Quietly toiling in a sea-side parish of South Devon, about thirty years ago, a devout and gentle-minded parson consecrated his poetic genius to the work of providing "an appropriate Manual of Psalmody" for the use of the Church. With characteristic modesty, he tells us that he "simply endeavoured to give the *spirit* of each psalm in such a compass as the public taste would tolerate, and to furnish, sometimes, when the length of the original would admit of it, an almost literal translation; sometimes, a kind of spiritual paraphrase; and at others, even a brief commentary on the whole psalm." He published his collection under the title of "The Spirit of the Psalms." What he wrote he taught his flock to sing, and beautiful was it to find Henry F. Lyte leading the psalmody of his congregation by singing with them his own metrical versions. One Sunday morning, in the summer of 1838, his church was crowded with seafaring men and their families. He took for his text the Saviour's words to the boatmen of

Galilee, "Cast the net on the right side of the ship, and ye shall find;" and he began by saying: "The affecting and interesting sight which presents itself here to-day induces me to select a subject directly suitable to our dear fishermen, whom I so rejoice to meet in the house of God this morning. There is surely not one person present who does not partake of the emotions which I feel in standing up among such a body of my parishioners, and who will not excuse me for addressing myself on this occasion almost exclusively to them." Then followed a faithful and touching appeal to those who saw God's "wonders in the deep," and then this beautiful and appropriate version of Psalm xlvi.:—

> The Lord is our refuge, the Lord is our guide;
> We smile upon danger, with Him at our side:
> The billows may blacken, the tempest increase,
> Though earth may be shaken, His saints shall have peace.
>
> A voice still and small by His people is heard,
> A whisper of peace from His life-giving word.
> A stream in the desert, a river of love,
> Flows down to their hearts from the Fountain above.
>
> Be near us, Redeemer, to shield us from ill;
> Speak Thou but the word, and the tempest is still.
> Thy presence to cheer us, Thy arm to defend,
> A worm grows almighty with Thee for a friend.
>
> The Lord is our helper; ye scorners, be awed!
> Ye earthlings, be still, and acknowledge your God.
> The proud He will humble, the lowly defend;
> O happy the people with God for a friend!

CHAPTER XI.

HYMN-MENDERS.

"For the ear trieth words as the mouth tasteth meat."

No man was ever more apt at writing an effective preface than John Wesley. Never did author more decidedly assert his own claims and powers, or more strikingly advertise the virtue of his own pages. Read the notice on the title-page of his remarkable "Pocket Dictionary:"—"N.B. The author assures you he thinks this is the best English Dictionary in the world!" And then, who does not enjoy the satirical humour and playful earnestness of his address to the reader, "as incredible as it may appear, I must avow that this dictionary is not published to get money, but to assist persons of common sense and no learning to understand the best *English* authors; and that with as little expense of time and money as the nature of the thing will allow. . . . . I should add no more, but that I have so often observed, the only way, according to the modern taste, for any author to procure commendation to his book is, vehemently to commend it himself. For want of this deference to the public, several excellent tracts lately printed, but left to commend themselves by their intrinsic worth, are utterly unknown or forgotten. Whereas if a writer of tolerable sense will but bestow a few violent encomiums on his own work, especially if they are skilfully ranged on the title-page, it will pass through six editions in a trice; the world being too complaisant to give a gentleman the lie, and taking it for granted he understands his own performance best. In compliance, therefore, with the taste of the age, I add, that this little dictionary is not only the shortest and the cheapest, but likewise by many degrees the most correct which is extant at this day. Many are the mistakes in all the other English dictionaries which I have yet seen. Whereas I can truly say, I know of none in this; and I conceive the reader will believe me; for if I had, I should not have left it there. Use then this help till you find a better." This is all anonymous, and some might doubt its authorship, but for its unmistakable claim to the same parentage with the preface to "A Collection of Hymns for the Use of the People called Methodists, by John Wesley, M.A." Who can doubt the identity of the self-reliance, firm decision, strong sense, straightforward sincerity, and transparent purity of purpose? "The hymn-book you have now before you," says the writer, "is not so large as to be either cumbersome or expensive; and it is large enough to contain such a variety of hymns, as will not soon be worn threadbare... As but a small part of these hymns is of my own composing, I do not think it inconsistent with modesty to declare that I am persuaded no such hymn-book as this has as yet been published in the English language. In what other publication of the kind have you so distinct and full an account of Scriptural Christianity? Such a declaration of the heights and depths of religion, speculative and practical? So strong cautions against the most plausible errors; particularly those that are now most prevalent? and so clear directions for making your calling and election sure; for perfecting holiness in the fear of God? May I be permitted to add a few words with regard to the *poetry?* Then I will speak to those who are judges thereof with all freedom and unreserve. To these I may say, without offence—1. In those hymns there is no doggerel; no blotches; nothing put in to patch up the rhyme; no feeble expletives. 2. Here is nothing turgid or bombast, on the one hand, or low and creeping on the other. 3. Here are no cant expressions; no words without meaning. Those who impute this to us know not what they say. We talk common sense, both in prose and verse, and use no word but in a fixed and determinate sense. 4. Here are, allow me to say, both the purity, the strength, and the elegance of the English language; and, at the same time, the utmost simplicity and plainness, suited to every capacity. Lastly, I desire men of taste to judge (these are the only competent judges) whether there be in some of the following hymns the true spirit of poetry, such as cannot be acquired by art and nature, but must be the gift of nature."

This is a fair challenge, and the majority of those to whom the appeal is made seem to have a growing conviction that Wesley's judgment was quite equal to his poetic taste and power; but now comes the assertion of other claims. "And here," continues the writer, "I beg leave to mention a thought which has been long upon my mind, and which I should long ago have inserted in the public papers, had I not been unwilling to stir up a nest of hornets. Many gentlemen have done my brother and me (though without naming us) the honour to reprint many of our hymns. Now, they are perfectly welcome so to do, provided they print them just as they are; but I desire they would not attempt to mend them, for they really are not able. None of them is able to mend either the sense or the verse. Therefore, I must beg of them one of these two favours—either to let them stand just as they are, to take them for better for worse; or to add the true reading in the margin, or at the bottom of the page, that we may no longer be accountable either for the nonsense or for the doggerel of other men." Who does not recognise here the voice of the humorous, trenchant, and self-possessed compiler of "the best English Dictionary in the world"? John Wesley feels himself equal alike to lexicography and hymnic composition. He might be called a prophet too. At all events, there is something in his preface like a forecasting of times, when the rage for compiling hymn-books would lead to all sorts of hymn-mending. Did he foresee this age of literary sacrilege? He seemed to deprecate the early attempts to improve his hymns, as foretokens of the days which have fallen upon us; days of adaptation hymn-books, when churches high and low, congregations great and small, communions close and open, connexions loose and tight, schools both wholesome and ragged, associations young and old, all sects, all parties, all shades and standards of doctrine and feeling, all and each must have a hymn-book; "yea, every one hath a psalm, hath a doctrine, hath a tongue, hath a revelation, hath an interpretation"? Poor Wesley! the reckless menders began while he was yet alive, and surely his critical sense must have been painfully touched when, among many other violations, the first verse of his brother's jubilant hymn on the name of Jesus was weakened into compliance with another creed. The original hymn sings—

> Let earth and heaven agree,
>   Angels and men be join'd,
> To celebrate with me
>   The Saviour of mankind;
> To adore the all-atoning Lamb,
> And bless the sound of Jesu's name.

But, instead of this closing couplet, the menders would make us sing—

> To fall before the atoning Lamb,
> And praise the blessed Jesu's name.

In another noble hymn "for the Jews," we are taught to pray—

> Come, then, Thou great Deliverer, come!
> The veil from Jacob's heart remove;
> Receive thy ancient people home!
> That, quickened by Thy dying love,
> The world may their reception find,
> Life from the dead for all mankind.

This, however, is too large a prayer for some, and, to suit their narrower views, the last lines are softened down to this—

> That, quickened by Thy dying love,
> The world may their reception view,
> And shout to God the glory due!

Of all that Charles Wesley ever wrote, nothing ought to have been held more sacred from the touch of mere senseless mutilators than the hymn which has hushed and cheered so many souls amidst the tempests of this mortal life. How many voices from both worlds pronounce it sacrilege to alter that hymn! One heart, at least, still beats by whom it is held as an invaluable treasure, nor is it for ever enshrined in that heart without good reason. About twenty years ago, on a winter's night, a heavy gale set in upon the precipitous rock-bound coast of one of our western counties. A tight, brave little coasting vessel struggled hard and long to reach some shelter in the Bristol Channel, but the struggle was vain; one dark fearful headland could not be weathered; the bark must go on shore, and what a shore it was the fated men well knew. Then came the last pull for life; the boat was swung off and manned; captain and crew united in one more brave effort, but their toiling at the oar was soon over, their boat was swamped. They seemed to have sunk together, "and in death they were not divided," for, when the morning dawned, they were found lying all but side by side under the shelter of a weedy rock. They might have been saved had they stayed in the ship, for she had been borne in upon a heavy sea close under the cliff, where she was jammed immovably between two rocks, and in the morning the ebb tide left her lying high and dry. There was no sign of life on deck, and below scarcely anything told of her late distress. One token of peace and salvation there was; it was the captain's hymn-book still lying on the locker, closed upon the pencil with which the good man had marked the last passages upon which his eye had rested before he left the ship to meet his fate. A leaf of the page was turned down, and there were pencil lines in the margin at several passages of Charles Wesley's precious hymn—

> Jesus, lover of my soul,
>   Let me to Thy bosom fly;
> While the nearer waters roll,
>   While the tempest still is high!
> Hide me, O my Saviour, hide,
>   Till the storm of life is past,
> Safe into the haven guide;
>   Oh receive my soul at last!
>
> Other refuge have I none;
>   Hangs my helpless soul on Thee;
> Leave, ah! leave me not alone,
>   Still support and comfort me:
> All my trust on Thee is stay'd,
>   All my help from Thee I bring:
> Cover my defenceless head
>   With the shadow of Thy wing!
>
> Wilt Thou not regard my call?
>   Wilt Thou not accept my prayer?
> Lo! I sink, I faint, I fall!
>   Lo! on Thee I cast my care!

> Reach me out Thy gracious hand!
>   While I of Thy strength receive,
> Hoping against hope I stand,
>   Dying, and behold I live!
>
> Thou, O Christ, art all I want;
>   More than all in Thee I find:
> Raise the fallen, cheer the faint,
>   Heal the sick, and lead the blind!
> Just and holy is Thy name;
>   I am all unrighteousness;
> False and full of sin I am,
>   Thou art full of truth and grace!
>
> Plenteous grace with Thee is found,
>   Grace to cover all my sin;
> Let the healing streams abound;
>   Make and keep me pure within!
> Thou of life the fountain art;
>   Freely let me take of Thee;
> Spring Thou up within my heart,
>   Rise to all eternity!

This was the pious captain's death-song. And who that loves his memory, or who that has mused by his green seaside grave, where his dust awaits the resurrection, or who that has learnt to sing his favourite verses, "with the spirit and with the understanding also," but must be painfully touched at finding any part of the hymn mangled and flattened, until its spirit and life are all but gone? Yet to such grief some of our hymn-manglers would subject the lovers of original poetic beauty and power. Alas! for the taste of the man who could blot out Charles Wesley's first four exquisite lines to substitute his own thus—

> Jesus, refuge of my soul,
>   Let me to thy mercy fly;
> While the raging billows roll,
>   While the tempest still is high!

But even this is nothing, compared with the stupid impertinence exemplified in some of the little spiritual song books which swarm from the press for the use of various parties professing to be the unsectarian representatives of spiritual revival. The two shores of St. George's Channel seem to strive for the mastery in doggerel. One manual gives a version of Wesley's glorious hymn—

> Oh love divine, how sweet thou art!
> When shall I find my willing heart
>   All taken up by Thee?
> I thirst, I faint, I die to prove
> The greatness of redeeming love,
>   The love of Christ to me!

The glowing climax of the last three lines, so finely expressive of the rising warmth of the soul in its longing for Christ, breaks down into flatness at the touch of the emendator's pen—

> Oh may I faint, and thirst to prove
> The greatness of redeeming love—
>   The love of Christ to me!

Wesley keeps up the swell of the soul's devotion in the following verse—

> God only knows the love of God:
> Oh that it now were shed abroad
>   In this poor stony heart!
> For love I sigh, for love I pine:
> This only portion, Lord, be mine,
>   Be mine the better part!

But our modern editor thinks the "poor stony heart" too cold, and makes it a "poor longing heart"; yet falls immediately into doubtfulness as to the reality of its present desires, and awkwardly changing both mood and tense, timidly promises, that if the love

> ——— were shed abroad
> In this poor longing heart,

he would sigh for it still, and pine for it still—

> For love I'*d* sigh, for love I'*d* pine!

The sublimest strain is not safe from the damaging touch of conceited hymn-menders. Evidence of this is found in the humiliating fact that the inimitable hymn founded on St. Paul's saying, "of whom the whole family in heaven and earth is named," has been published in a mutilated form. The first verse begins—

> Come let us join our friends above
>   That have obtained the prize,
> And on the eagle wings of love
>   To joys celestial rise.

Such eagle flights are beyond the power of some songsters, and they change it by singing—

> Come let us join our friends above
> Who have obtained the prize,
> And happy in the Saviour's love,
> To joys celestial rise.

Nor can that grand expression of realizing faith at the close of the hymn be allowed to remain, but instead of

> Our spirits too shall quickly join,
> Like theirs with glory crown'd!

The weaker and more wavering confidence says—

> The morning comes when all shall join,
> Alike with glory crown'd.

Another of Charles Wesley's joyful outbreaks of Christian assurance needs to be checked and qualified, as his censor thinks. The original hymnist shouts—

> Away with our sorrow and fear,
> We soon shall recover our home;
> The city of saints shall appear,
> The day of eternity come.
> From earth we shall quickly remove,
> And mount to our native abode!
> The house of our Father above,
> The palace of angels and God.

The second line is tamed down to

> We soon shall have enter'd our home.

And as if the good people were afraid to mount in Wesley's style, they sing—

> From earth we shall quickly remove,
> To dwell in our native abode,
> In mansions of glory above,
> Prepared by our Father and God.

And then follows a jumble of stanzas gathered from several hymns of the same metre, the heterogeneous mixture being introduced by a distinctive Irishism—

> Ah! who upon earth can conceive
> The bliss that in heaven *we'll* share?

The writer of course means the bliss that we *shall* share; but, like many of his incurable countrymen, he must have it *will*, expressive, doubtless, of his fixed determination to have his own share of hymning in the other world, as well as his own way of hymn-mending in this. But enough has been said to show that John Wesley had reason for shrinking from being "accountable for the nonsense or the doggerel of other men." It is not surprising, however, that the unskilful multitude should try their hands at hymn-mending, when masters in the art have set such examples. Critical inquiries into the history of hymnology open up some curious scenes. The Wesleys are seen mending Herbert and Watts, Toplady and Madan are found hashing and re-cooking Charles Wesley. Somebody else is trying to improve Toplady. Heber makes free with Jeremy Taylor. Montgomery is altering and altered. Keble, and Milman, and Alford are all pinched, and twisted, and re-dressed in turn. Among all these menders John Wesley was perhaps one of the best. He was positively sure that nobody could mend his own hymns; but he was not scrupulous in mending other people's. His critical power and poetic taste, however, were exercised chiefly on the productions of his brother Charles, and generally his emendations were improvements. And perhaps, too, it was happy for Charles that he had a brother so severe; for one who wrote so many verses and so fast, needed another eye and another hand to guard him from the consequences of voluminous rhyming. In dealing with other authors, whose hymns are brought to enrich his hymn-book, John Wesley's touches are, for the most part, delicate but effective. By the slightest stroke he sometimes turns weakness into strength, commonplaces into beauties, and irregularity into order. A transforming word or two from him, now and then, makes questionable things pure, and calls up grandeur from what was puerile or mean. Witness the transformation of some verses in Watts's hymn on "Heavenly joys on earth." The original first verse is—

> Come, we that love the Lord,
> And let our joys be known;
> Join in a song with sweet accord,
> And thus surround the throne.

Wesley takes away the sign of weakness by rendering it—

> Come, *ye* that love the Lord,
> And let *your* joys be known,
> E'en in a song with sweet accord,
> *While* ye surround *His* throne.

The rise from something akin to silliness into grandeur is still more strikingly seen in the change of the fourth verse from

> The God that rules on high,
> And thunders when He please,
> That rides upon the stormy sky,
> And manages the seas.

into

> The God that rules on high,
> That all the earth surveys,
> That rides upon the stormy sky,
> And calms the roaring seas.

The noble hymn is thus equalized, and saved from those occasional lapses into weaknesses which so sadly break the grand march of some of Watts's best productions. What additional dignity Wesley gives to Watts's version of the Psalm cxlvi. by a slight alteration of two lines, changing

> I'll praise my Maker *with* my breath,

into

> I'll praise my Maker *while I've* breath,

and rendering

> The Lord hath eyes to give the blind,

thus—

> The Lord pours eyesight on the blind.

Still more remarkable is the improvement in the hymn on "Christ dying, rising, and reigning." Watts's first verse begins too fondly, and then becomes puerile.

> He dies! The heavenly Lover dies!
> The tidings strike a doleful sound
> On my poor heart-strings. Deep He lies
> In the cold caverns of the ground.

Wesley's improvement opens with great beauty of thought and grandeur of imagery, consistently leading the mind into the noble strain of the following verses—

> He dies! The Friend of sinners dies!
> Lo! Salem's daughters weep around;
> A solemn darkness veils the skies,
> A sudden trembling shakes the ground.

The Christian Church will never cease to enjoy the grand swell of the Psalm c. as given by Watts; but thanks will ever be due to Wesley for making the first verses worthy of the last. Watts's verses begin without much promise:—

> Sing to the Lord with joyful voice;
> Let every land His name adore;
> The British isles shall send the noise
> Across the ocean to the shore.
>
> Nations attend before His throne
> With solemn fear, with sacred joy.

Wesley drops the first verse, and begins the second thus:—

> Before Jehovah's awful throne,
> Ye nations, bow with sacred joy;

giving a noble completeness to the hymn, opening it with a majesty suitable to its continued swell, and preparing us for that sublime close which leaves the devout multitude rapt before God in solemn joy.

> We'll crowd thy gates with thankful songs,
> High as the heavens our voices raise;
> And earth, with her ten thousand tongues,
> Shall fill Thy courts with sounding praise.
>
> Wide as the world is Thy command,
> Vast as eternity Thy love;
> Firm as a rock Thy truth shall stand,
> When rolling years shall cease to move.

The Wesleyan hymn-menders are not always as happy, in dealing with other hymnists, as in their emendations of Watts. For instance, when they alter that beautiful hymn by Berridge—

> Jesus, cast a look on me,

and place the altered form in their collection as beginning with

> Lord, that I may learn of Thee.

The original should have been held sacred. It is founded on Psalm cxxxi. 2, "My soul is even as a weaned child." Thus :—

> Jesus, cast a look on me,
> Give me sweet simplicity;
> Make me poor, and keep me low,
> Seeking only Thee to know.
>
> Weanèd from my lordly self,
> Weanèd from the miser's pelf,
> Weanèd from the scorner's ways,
> Weanèd from the lust of praise.
>
> All that feeds my busy pride,
> Cast it evermore aside;
> Bid my will to Thine submit,
> Lay me humbly at Thy feet.
>
> Make me like a little child,
> Of my strength and wisdom spoil'd;
> Seeing only in Thy light,
> Walking only in Thy might.
>
> Leaning on Thy loving breast,
> Where a weary soul may rest;
> Feeling well the peace of God,
> Flowing from Thy precious blood!
>
> In this pasture let me live,
> And hosannas daily give;
> In this temper let me die,
> And hosannas ever cry!

It must be said of John Wesley, that whether he worked as compiler, or critic, or hymn-writer, he evidently worked with a pure aim. His object was to provide for his people a hymn-book distinguished by completeness of rhyme, a large variety of metre, energy of thought and expression, sound argument, thorough evangelical orthodoxy, and pure and warm religious feeling. The great popularity and widening usefulness of his collection show the measure of his success. Many people would naturally ask what sort of hymns such a hymn-mender as he could write. He wrote but few. But these few fairly sustain his claims as a worthy member of a poetic family, and a leader among the hymnists of his day. One of his hymns is highly characteristic at once of his genius and his religious character, and marks some peculiar phases of his experience, as well as some points of his personal history. The hymn may be called "the Pilgrim's Hymn:"—

How happy is the pilgrim's lot!
How free from every anxious thought,
    From worldly hope and fear!
Confined to neither court nor cell,
His soul disdains on earth to dwell,
    His only sojourn's here.

His happiness in part is mine,
Already saved from low design,
    From every creature love;
Blest with the scorn of finite good,
My soul is lightened of its load,
    And seeks the things above.

The things eternal I pursue;
A happiness beyond the view
    Of those that basely pant
For things by nature felt and seen;
Their honours, wealth, and pleasures mean,
    I neither have nor want.

I have no babes to hold me here;
But children more securely dear,
    For mine I humbly claim;
Better than daughters or than sons,
Temples divine of living stones,
    Inscribed with Jesu's name.

No foot of land do I possess,
No cottage in this wilderness;
    A poor wayfaring man,
I lodge awhile in tents below,
Or gladly wander to and fro,
    Till I my Canaan gain.

Nothing on earth I call my own;
A stranger, to the world unknown,
    I all their goods despise;
I trample on their whole delight,
And seek a country out of sight,
    A country in the skies.

There is my house, my portion fair;
My treasure and my heart are there,
    And my abiding home;
For me my elder brethren stay,
And angels beckon me away,
    And Jesus bids me come.

> I come—Thy servant, Lord, replies—
> I come to meet Thee in the skies,
>   And claim my heavenly rest!
> Now let the pilgrim's journey end;
> Now, O my Saviour, Brother, Friend,
>   Receive me to Thy breast!

One stanza is now generally omitted. It was written probably while he was unmarried; and under the influence of views sometimes peculiar to unmarried life—

> I have no sharer of my heart,
> To rob my Saviour of a part,
>   And desecrate the whole :
> Only betrothed to Christ am I,
> And wait His coming from the sky,
>   To wed my happy soul.

There have been many Christian souls who, during some period of their life, would take up the language of this remarkable hymn, and sing it on their lonely way. It may be said of some one part of many a man's life-journey, "it was desert"; and that desert part he may have gone over single-handed, scripless and alone. How often, in such cases, has the music of this hymn risen on the silent air, as an acceptable sacrifice of holy confidence, gratitude, and joy. Of one singular character, at least, it may be said that he could adopt it, and use it from his first starting in Christian life to his final hour. To those who knew him, and many, many in the west of England were thankful to know him, it seemed as if the hymn were made for him. Nor was there a day through his somewhat lengthened life in which some stanza of it was not on his lips. "Foolish Dick," people called him, and not without some share of reason. In early life he was enough of an idiot to be unequal to any labour that required a tolerable amount of regulated thought or skill. But he proved to be one of those whose history strikingly shows the quickening, expanding, and regulating power of vital religion on the human intellect, even in its nearest approaches to hopeless idiocy. Dick was one morning on his way to the well for water, when an old Christian man who was leaning over the garden gate said, "So you are going to the well for water, Dick?"

"Yes, sir."

"Well, Dick; the woman of Samaria found Jesus Christ at the well."

"Did she, sir?"

"Yes, Dick."

That was enough. A quickening thought had struck into his half-awakened mind. The thought worked; and when he came to the well, he said, within himself, but loud enough to be heard by his Saviour, "Why should not I find Jesus Christ at the well? Oh that I could find Him! Will He come to *me?*" Yes, his prayer was heard; and Dick returned bearing his full pitcher; but bringing in his heart, too, the joy of which Jesus said, "It shall be in him a well of water, springing up into everlasting life." From that hour, Dick "left his watering-pot"; and gave himself up to the work of telling his neighbours the story of his conversion at the well, and indeed to the work of preaching Christ, in his way, in discourses marked by strong sense, warm feeling, and stirring appeals to the sinner's conscience and heart. Every faculty of his mind, and all the passions of his soul now seemed to unfold new powers and fresh life. He was verily born again. His memory soon showed marvellous power. To hear a chapter in the Bible, or a hymn read to him, was to know it, and to have power to reproduce it. His new gifts were used for Christ. He went forth as an itinerant evangelist; going without purse or scrip; and through a life-long pilgrimage round and round his native county, and sometimes over the Border, he went everywhere preaching Jesus. He never lacked food or raiment, and when he entered into rest, many, many happy spirits hailed him as the instrument of their salvation from sin and death. He was indeed a pilgrim preacher, rude and unpolished, as some thought, but certainly taught of Christ. The "Pilgrim's Hymn" was always in keeping from his lips. It was his favourite hymn, and every home that welcomed him had its hearth cheered by his music; for he would sit and wave too and fro, and sing, in a way that set forth the elegant simplicity of the lines—

> No foot of land do I possess,
> No cottage in this wilderness;
> A poor wayfaring man,
> I lodge awhile in tents below;
> Or gladly wander to and fro,
> Till I my Canaan gain.

This was his song all through the land of his pilgrimage. And not long ago, followed by the blessings of his generation, the weary old pilgrim departed, to realize the full answer to his last stanza—

> Now let the pilgrim's journey end;
> Now, O my Saviour, Brother, Friend,
> Receive me to Thy breast!

CHAPTER XII.

HYMNS OF CREATION.

"Thou art worthy, O Lord, to receive glory and honour and power: for Thou hast created all things, and for Thy pleasure they are and were created."

"I once joined a party for a day's pleasure trip in the west of England," says an old rambler; "our plan was to get to the top of the highest hill in the neighbourhood, and there for a time take our fill of joy from the grandeur and beauty of the scenes around and beneath us. Alas, for human pleasures! The morning opened with rain, and we were seemingly doomed to disappointment. At length, encouraged by some weather-wise folks, we resolved to accomplish our purpose, even at the risk of wet jackets by the way. We climbed the steeps in spite of wind and rain, and came by and by, on the highest peak, to some steps leading to the door of an old tower, which from time immemorial had withstood the rush of years and storms. As we mounted these steps, we found, to our wonderment and delight, that on looking out, our eyes glanced along the upper surface of the clouds; and when we had fairly reached the roof of the old tower, there was nothing of our native earth to be seen but the few square feet of stone-work on which we stood. Beneath us was an ocean of clouds; above us were the bright blue heavens. The sun had gone down just to the horizon, where the clear sky touched the cloud-billows. The faint-looking crescent of the new moon was peeping on us too from above the offing line of the cloudy deep. We could hear the carol of a lark, but otherwise the silence of nature was profound and solemn. We felt ourselves for once beyond the sight and sound of the world which gave us birth. One voice uttered the key-note, and then, as if we had but one soul, we sang—

> High in the heavens, Eternal God,
>   Thy goodness in full glory shines;
> Thy truth shall break through every cloud
>   That veils and darkens Thy designs.
>
> For ever firm Thy justice stands,
>   As mountains their foundations keep;
> Wise are the wonders of Thy hands;
>   Thy judgments are a mighty deep.

There was a charm in psalmody at that moment which I had never felt before, and it really seemed as if that charm were acknowledged by nature; for just at this moment there were movements in the cloud-world beneath us—the masses were rolling, heaving, and cleaving here and there. Now the top of a green hill appeared, like an island rising from the depths to court the sunlight; now a slope was seen opening from beneath the passing mist; now a spire rose above the surface; and now a village peeped on the hill-side, and the clustering roofs of a more distant town sparkled as the sunbeams touched them. The clouds resolved themselves at length into river-like courses, filling the valleys and leaving the uplands to show themselves. The rivers narrowed, became shallow streams, and at last, like silvery threads, they ran off towards the shore, until every filmy vapour was gone, even from the face of the sea, and the whole scene, with its glorious variety of hill and plain, valley and heath, woods and ocean, lay bright, calm, and beautiful beneath the setting sun. Fresh inspiration now came upon us, and we sang again—

> God is a name my soul adores,
>   Th' Almighty Three, th' eternal One,
> Nature and grace, with all their powers,
>   Confess the infinite Unknown.
>
> From Thy great self Thy being springs;
>   Thou art Thy own original,
> Made up of uncreated things,
>   And self-sufficience bears them all.
>
> Thy voice produced the seas and spheres,
>   Bid the waves roar and planets shine;
> But nothing like Thyself appears
>   Through all these spacious works of Thine.

Still restless nature dies and grows;
  From change to change the creatures run;
Thy being no succession knows,
  And all Thy vast designs are one.

A glance of Thine runs through the globes,
  Rules the bright world, and moves their frame:
Broad sheets of light compose Thy robes,
  Thy guards are formed of living flame.

Thrones and dominions round Thee fall,
  And worship in submissive forms;
Thy presence shakes this lower ball,
  This little dwelling-place of worms.

How shall affrighted mortals dare
  To sing Thy glory or Thy grace;
Beneath Thy feet we lie so far,
  And see but shadows of Thy face.

Who can behold the blazing light?
  Who can approach consuming flame?
None but Thy wisdom knows Thy might,
  None but Thy word can speak Thy name.

"'Well,' said one, as we came down from the tower, 'I never before felt the music and power of those fine old hymns so deeply. Watts does not always keep us up so steadily to the end of the strain. Dear old singer! he had times of deep sympathy with the natural world, and often helps one, as he helped us to-day, to catch the inspiring breath of natural grandeur and beauty, so as to feel as if we were one with all the works of our heavenly Father.'

"'Yes,' said somebody else; 'but we owe much of our enjoyment of Watts to association, to the lingering influence of our early impressions about his hymns; and a great deal, too, in his case, depends on the music to which his hymns are set. We enjoy his verses when they are sung more frequently than when we read them. I have a notion that it is with his hymns somewhat as it is with many of Thomas Moore's "Irish Melodies"; about which I am very willing to admit all that is said as to their graceful thought, their tender pathos, and bursts of heroic feeling. They have wonderful melody of words, too; but it strikes me that we have learnt to award to Moore's verses much that really belongs to the old tunes for which he provided the words. At all events, in reading many of them you but seldom find your soul arrested, while to hear them sung is to be mastered by the feeling which they create. Now, speaking of Tom Moore, I like him best when he gets away from amidst the rather wearisome gorgeousness of his Eastern imagery, and from the brilliant circles in which his genius and wit so brightly sparkle, and allows himself to be hushed into a devout feeling within the quietude of his cottage retreat. I like to find him in that little Wiltshire home, with its old-fashioned windows and trellised doorway, hung about with creepers and evergreens, and surrounded by such touching evidences of Divine goodness as melt the heart, and constrain the genius to express itself in hymns and spiritual songs. You say Watts had times of deep sympathy with the natural world—had not Moore? And had he not some reverent sympathy with the God of nature, too? And does he not help us to praise the source of life and beauty? Only listen to this:—

> Thou art, O God, the life and light
>   Of all this wondrous world we see;
> Its glow by day, its smile by night,
>   Are but reflections caught from Thee.
> Where'er we turn, Thy glories shine,
> And all things fair and bright are Thine.
>
> When day, with farewell beam, delays
>   Among the opening clouds of even,
> And we can almost think we gaze
>   Through golden vistas into heaven:
> Those hues that make the sun's decline
> So soft, so radiant, Lord, are Thine.
>
> When night, with wings of starry gloom,
>   O'ershadows all the earth and skies,
> Like some dark beauteous bird, whose plume
>   Is sparkling with unnumbered eyes:
> That sacred gloom, those fires divine,
> So grand, so countless, Lord, are Thine.
>
> When youthful spring around us breathes,
>   Thy Spirit warms her fragrant sigh;
> And every flower the summer wreathes,
>   Is born beneath that kindling eye.
> Where'er we turn, Thy glories shine,
> And all things bright and fair are Thine.

"'Yes,' said a pleasant-looking companion, as we all

flung ourselves down among the heath, as if we were all disposed to keep up the chat about hymns, 'yes, Moore is much to my taste in a few of his hymns; and I wish some severe people that I know would get a little more of his spirit. I know some who seem to have a notion that a knowledge and enjoyment of nature is so distinct from inward religion as to be opposed to it, that warm devotion to the one almost necessarily excludes any eminent success in the pursuit of the other. This notion leads them to set God's works in opposition to His Word, and to view what they call natural religion as altogether independent of revealed truth. But I think a deeper insight into the sacred volume convinces us that, as the harmony of the Divine character is absolutely perfect, so all the manifestations of that character to man are in sacred concord, whether they come as reflections from nature or revelations of the Spirit. While the mere intellect is cultivated to the neglect of the heart, or the will or affections are indulged at the expense of the understanding, the nature of man is out of course, and his character is so discordant in itself that he is incapable of discovering the invariable agreement of the natural and the spiritual, of religion and science. This Divine unison can be known and enjoyed by none but the harmonized soul. The human spirit must be attuned to the voice of God. The sanctified intellect must act in concert with the purified heart. The rectified will must fully accord with the Word of God. And then the visible universe and the region of mind, the creature, the Word, and the Spirit, the world without and the world within, all harmonize around the happy man, and lead him to his God. Now, you have spoken of Thomas Moore and his "Irish Melodies"; let me illustrate what I have said by a song from old Ireland. It comes from a quiet rectory in county Antrim, and shows that the truly harmonized Christian soul can exercise its hallowed genius in hymns to the God of nature, and teach us to live in the spirit of that hymnist who said, "All Thy works praise Thee, O Lord; and Thy saints bless Thee." Listen to John S. B. Monsell's song:—

> Oh, what a gloomy, cheerless scene,
> A world accursèd might have been,
> If He, who in His mercy hath
> Strew'd such delight along life's path,

Had changed each passing breath and sound
That floats in harmony around,
To discords, such as would destroy
Sensation's every pulse of joy!

But He who bids us seek His face
Makes Nature handmaiden to Grace;
And lest our souls—to earth too prone—
Should faint before they reach the throne,
The sea beneath, the sky above,
Hath form'd as mirrors of His love;
And ev'ry rock, and flow'r, and tree,
Made vocal for eternity.

Where'er we move or walk abroad,
We see, we feel a present God!
The very balm that scents the air
Breathes of a purer essence there;
The bubbling runnels, as they flow,
Chant sweetest anthems soft and low;
And every bird, from bush and brake,
To praise, the sylvan echoes wake.

Nature, with one harmonious voice,
Seems in her Maker to rejoice;
Earth's flowers reflect Him in their bloom,
And breathe His praise in rich perfume.
The sun by day, the moon by night,
The stars, those heavenly flow'rs of light,
All in one sweet accord, His name
Almighty! Wonderful! proclaim.

And oh, shall I, when flowers and trees,
Things soulless, senseless, such as these,
Live to His praise, as though they seemed
His own, His purchas'd, His redeem'd!
Shall I, for whom His blood was poured,
The blood of the Incarnate Lord,
Be silent, when this heart should raise
To its Redeemer hymns of praise?

Lord, when among the songs of earth,
Forgetful of my heavenly birth,
My harp hangs on the willow-tree,
And renders back no praise to Thee;
Let the sweet hymns of those who know
Not half the debt of love I owe,
If not for love, at least for shame,
Move this dull soul to praise Thy name.

" 'This is one of the tuneful "Parish Musings" which we owe to Mr. Monsell's hallowed taste and heart, open as they have been to the music of his Saviour's voice, and as, in companionship with the blessed Spirit, they have had suggestions from the "incidents or feelings of each passing day," as he tells us, "in storm or sunshine, by the way-side or on the hill-top, in the country meadow or the busy street, by day or by night, wherever duty called, and whenever the spirit caught from without or from within subject matter for serious conversation with heaven." I like the way in which he infuses the Christian element into his song of creation. Some professing Christians seem never to have either taste or heart for anything but what they term evangelical doctrine and experience; the outer world is never allowed to associate its happy influences with what they call their "inner life." But Christianity is love—love to God, and love for everything which bears His image, or is marked by Him as lovable. "We love Him," says an apostle, "because He first loved us." His love to us is shown first, and above all, in His only-begotten Son Jesus Christ. But as He "created all things by Jesus Christ," as Christ "upholds all things by the word of His power," and as, by virtue of the Redeemer's cross, all things are to be reconciled and harmonized, "whether they be things in earth or things in heaven," all who truly love God, and hold loving communion with "the Father and His Son Jesus Christ," will be affectionately ready to catch reflections of His love from everything that bears His impress, everything on which his mind and heart are set. The well-regulated Christian heart will turn pleasantly towards the tiniest thing for which God cares, or in which Jesus has shown an interest. All beauty, all grandeur, all light, all life, all melodies, harmonies, and fitnesses of things are His; He made them, He loves them, His sympathy with all is perfect. And so they are objects of admiration, sympathy, and love to human souls, just as these souls are "perfect as He, their heavenly Father, is perfect." The noblest minds, the greatest hearts, the most Christlike characters are those who, with the deepest spiritual intercourse with the heavenly and the unseen, have the most tender, gentle, childlike attachment to everything that God smiles upon in visible life. Now, I am disposed to class the author of the "Christian Year" with these; he is not always equal. In a few instances his verses lack vigour, are simply pretty; but when he hymns it in his best style, he gives us a sweet relish for that devotion which seems at once to hush and exalt the soul amidst the analogies of creation. How beautifully he interweaves nature and grace, the visible and the invisible, in his hymn for Septuagesima Sunday:—

> There is a book who runs may read,
>   Which heav'nly truth imparts;
> And all the love its scholars need,
>   Pure eyes and Christian hearts.
>
> The works of God above, below,
>   Within us and around,
> Are pages in that book to show
>   How God Himself is found.
>
> The glorious sky, embracing all,
>   Is like the Maker's love,
> Wherewith encompass'd, great and small,
>   In peace and order move.
>
> The moon above, the church below,
>   A wondrous race they run;
> But all their radiance, all their glow,
>   Each borrows of its sun.
>
> The Saviour lends the light and heat
>   That crowns His holy hill;
> The saints, like stars, around His seat,
>   Perform the courses still.
>
> The saints above are stars in heaven—
>   What are the saints on earth?
> Like trees they stand whom God has given,
>   Our Eden's happy birth.
>
> Faith is their fix'd, unswerving root,
>   Hope their unfading flower;
> Fair deeds of charity their fruit,
>   The glory of their bower.
>
> The dew of heaven is like Thy grace,
>   It steals in silence down;
> But where it lights, the favour'd place
>   By richest fruits is known.
>
> One name above all glorious names,
>   With its ten thousand tongues,
> The everlasting sea proclaims,
>   Echoing angelic songs.

> The raging fire, the roaring wind,
>   Thy boundless power display;
> But in the gentler breeze we find
>   Thy Spirit's viewless way.
>
> Two worlds are ours: 'tis only sin
>   Forbids us to descry
> The mystic heaven and earth within.
>   Plain as the sea and sky.
>
> Thou who hast given me eyes to see
>   And love this sight so fair,
> Give me a heart to find out Thee,
>   And read Thee everywhere.'

"'Thank you,' cried one of our most earnest young men—one whose full round bass voice I have often admired when coming into the chorus swell of a jubilant psalm or anthem, 'thank you. John Keble often succeeds, as he does in this case, in making us feel what he calls "that *soothing* tendency in the Prayer-Book"; and which, as he adds, "it is the chief purpose of" his hymns "to exhibit." But now, by way of a little variation, let us have that spirited and inspiriting psalm of George Wither's, which seems to bring up around one's expanding and rising heart all the voices and instruments that heaven and earth can muster, to swell the mighty chorus of creation before the throne of its Maker. Come!' said he starting up, and beckoning us into position, 'come let us chant it!'—

> Come, oh come! in pious lays
> Sound we God Almighty's praise;
> Hither bring in one consent,
> Heart and voice, and instrument.
> Music add, of ev'ry kind;
> Sound the trump, the cornet wind;
> Strike the viol, touch the lute;
> Let no tongue, nor string be mute;
>   Nor a creature dumb be found,
>   That hath either voice or sound.
>
> Let those things which do not live
> In still music praises give:
> Lowly pipe, ye worms that creep
> On the earth or in the deep:
> Loud aloft your voices strain,
> Beasts and monsters of the main:
> Birds, your warbling treble sing;
> Clouds, your peals of thunder ring:
>   Sun and moon, exalted higher,
>   And bright stars augment this choir.

Come, ye sons of human race,
In this chorus take a place,
And amid the mortal throng,
Be you masters of the song.
Angels, and supernal powers,
Be the noblest tenor yours;
Let in praise of God, the sound
Run a never-ending round:
   That our song of praise may be
   Everlasting as is He.

From earth's vast and hollow womb,
Music's deepest bass may come;
Seas and floods, from shore to shore,
Shall their counter-tenors roar.
To this consort when we sing,
Whistling winds, your descants bring;
That our song may over climb
All the bounds of place and time,
   And ascend from sphere to sphere,
   To the great Almighty's ear.

So from heaven, on earth He shall
Let His gracious blessings fall;
And this huge, wide orb we see,
Shall one choir, one temple be;
Where, in such a praise, full tone
We will sing what He hath done,
That the cursed fiends below
Shall thereat impatient grow.
   Then, oh come, in pious lays,
   Sound we God Almighty's praise.

"Our united chant seemed to awaken a kind of emulation in calling up favourite hymns. The scenes around us appeared to claim our homage to one theme. Our songs must all be songs of creation. It was suggested that a woman's voice had sometimes given forth sweet melodies; could any of us remember a hymn from among the daughters of holy song? Yes, of course; whose mind did not go off at once to that comfortable-looking old house in the village of Broughton in Hampshire, with its high roof and massive chimneys, its antique porch and rural garden palisades overshadowed by the trees which beautified Theodosia's village birthplace on the borders of the 'Downs'? Theodosia! 'The gift of God'; and 'eminently so in this world of ours'; and who would not think of that affectionate address to Theodosia's niece, by an old friend who loved her memory, and has helped us to love it too?—

> Still I am musing in your rustic bower,
> Under that moss-deck'd roof; and gaze in thought,
> Down the soft turfy vista, where, between
> Those aged pines (friends of your infancy),
> The fleeting sunshine and the broader shade
> Picture our path to heaven. I trace the walk,
> Where at this noontide hour, no foot perhaps
> Is seen: but thought hath peopled it. I see
> In fancy's telescopic mirror, forms
> Of some that were—that *are*, that *would* be there.
>
> I mark the forms that *were* there: those who walk'd
> With God, and spake to artless minds of Him;
> And, with them, one who pour'd a sylvan strain
> Of meek devotion in those quiet shades—
> Bequeathing thence her Christian heart and hope
> To other generations.

"Let the scene be immortalized; that terrace walk looking down on the shrubbery and garden, and the avenue of firs, where, about the middle of the last century, Anne Steele, with a body enfeebled by affliction, used to regale her tender and devout soul, and give forth those utterances of hallowed genius which so refresh all childlike spirits who long to sing of Him whom she supremely loved. 'I enjoy a calm evening on the terrace walk,' said that gentle voice, tremulous with holy feeling, 'and I wish, though in vain, for numbers sweet as the lovely prospect; and gentle as the vernal breeze, to describe the beauties of charming spring; but the reflection, how soon these blooming pleasures will vanish, spread a melancholy gloom, till the mind rises, by a delightful transition, to the celestial Eden—the scenes of undecaying pleasure and immutable perfection.' She did not wish for 'sweet numbers' entirely in vain. Her songs never rose to the higher strain which some have reached; but they never became unworthy of her theme. They are always read with as much pleasure as they are sung; always simple in thought and expression, always full of warm and tender feeling, and are always welcome to the peaceful heart when it wants a song to express its quiet joys. It was probably on her favourite terrace walk, or in the avenue where the zephyrs whispered music among the fir-trees, that she first sang her hymn 'On Creation and Providence'—

> Lord, when my raptured thought surveys
> Creation's beauties o'er,

All nature joins to teach Thy praise
   And bid my soul adore.

Where'er I turn my gazing eyes,
   Thy radiant footsteps shine;
Ten thousand pleasing wonders rise,
   And speak their source divine.

The living tribes of countless forms,
   In earth, and sea, and air;
The meanest flies, the smallest worms,
   Almighty power declare.

All rose to life at Thy command,
   And wait their daily food
From Thy paternal, bounteous hand,
   Exhaustless springs of good!

The meads array'd in smiling green,
   With wholesome herbage crown'd;
The fields with corn, a richer scene,
   Spread thy full bounties round.

The fruitful tree, the blooming flower,
   In varied charms appear;
Their varied charms display Thy power,
   Thy goodness all declare.

The sun's productive, quickening beams,
   The growing verdure spread;
Refreshing rains and cooling streams
   His gentle influence aid.

The moon and stars his absent light
   Supply with borrowed rays,
And deck the sable veil of night,
   And speak their Maker's praise.

Thy wisdom, power, and goodness, Lord,
   In all Thy works appear;
And oh, let man Thy praise record;
   Man, Thy distinguish'd care.

From Thee the breath of life he drew;
   That breath Thy power maintains;
Thy tender mercy ever new,
   His brittle frame sustains.

Let nobler favours claim his praise
   Of reason's light possess'd;
By revelation's brighter rays
   Still more divinely blest.

> Thy providence, his constant guard
> When threatening woes impend,
> Or will the impending dangers ward,
> Or timely succours lend.
>
> On me that providence has shone
> With gentle smiling rays;
> Oh let my lips and life make known
> Thy goodness and Thy praise.
>
> All bounteous Lord, Thy grace impart;
> Oh teach me to improve
> Thy gifts with ever grateful heart,
> And crown them with Thy love.

"Somebody inquired whether Anne Steele was not the daughter of a Dissenting minister. 'Yes,' was the reply, 'her father preached to the Baptist congregation in Broughton for sixty years, and he followed his uncle in the same pastorate, an uncle who was equally remarkable with her father for piety, amiable simplicity, and industrious attention to his flock. There is a story told of him which is rather instructive. He was so popular as a preacher in Broughton, his native village, that the parson reported at the Episcopal visitation that his parochial province was sadly invaded by the Dissenter. "How can I best oppose him?" was his query to the Bishop, the celebrated Gilbert Burnet. "Go home," said the wise Diocesan, "and preach better than Henry Steele, and the people will return;" a piece of good advice that might be happily followed in all other cases of parochial rivalry.'

"Anne Steele's connexion with Dissent naturally brought up the name of another lady hymnist, whose family relations belonged to the same religious school. Anna Letitia Barbauld issued her first lyrics during her residence with her father, Dr. Aiken, in a Dissenting academy at Warrington; continued her literary pursuits as the wife of a French Protestant minister, who acted in the double capacity of tutor and Dissenting pastor; while she cheered her widowhood with songs and hymns from her overflowing heart, and prolific and cultured genius. Her memory is fresh in many a family circle, in its association with the tales in 'Evenings at Home.' Her verses still speak of her extensive and varied reading, and show that she had vigour of intellect to balance her flowing imagination. Our conversation on the hill-side about songs of creation was closed with the rehearsal of her charming hymn, and one of her last:—

>Praise to God, immortal praise,
>For the love that crowns our days;
>Bounteous Source of every joy,
>Let Thy praise our tongues employ.
>
>For the blessings of the field,
>For the stores the gardens yield,
>For the vine's exalted juice,
>For the gen'rous olive's use.
>
>Flocks that whiten all the plain,
>Yellow sheaves of ripened grain;
>Clouds that drop their fattening dews,
>Suns that temperate warmth diffuse.
>
>All that spring, with bounteous hand,
>Scatters o'er the smiling land;
>All that liberal autumn pours
>From her rich o'erflowing stores.
>
>These to Thee, my God, we owe,
>Source whence all our blessings flow;
>And for these my soul shall raise
>Grateful vows and solemn praise.
>
>Yet, should rising whirlwinds rear
>From its stem the rip'ning ear;
>Should the fig-tree's blasted shoot
>Drop her green, untimely fruit;
>
>Should the vine put forth no more,
>Nor the olive yield her store;
>Though the sick'ning flocks should fall,
>And the herds desert the stall;
>
>Should Thine altered hand restrain
>The early and the latter rain,
>Blast each op'ning bud of joy,
>And the rising year destroy;
>
>Yet to Thee my soul shall raise
>Grateful vows and solemn praise;
>And when every blessing's flown,
>Love Thee for Thyself alone.

This agreeable and pious hymnist was a native of Kibworth, in Leicestershire, and ceased her psalmody on earth in March, 1825, aged fourscore years and two."

But no chapter of talk about Hymns of Creation should be ended without homage paid to the memory of one whose glorious hymn may always serve as the closing anthem peal to all such chapters. Scotland has given birth to many a genius, whose unfolding powers it has lacked either skill or disposition to cherish. Among the 'rest there was one who first saw the light at Ednam, in Roxburghshire, on the 11th of September, 1700; and there, amidst rich and varied scenery, in a land of wild romance, he gave the first promise of poetic wealth. But his sensuous and indolent, though guileless, generous, and glowing nature, must needs court the congenial influences of a more southern clime. Like many other young northern adventurers, however, his native powers were first put forth under the pressure of poverty. His pure, fresh, childlike "perfect love" of nature; his deep sympathy with all visible created things; his luxurious, enthusiastic affection for all living grandeurs, beauties, and harmonies, made their practice felt in the world of taste, when, in 1730, his "all-embracing genius" charmed the English public with his living pictures of "The Seasons." Thompson, "the fine fat fellow," was not without his errors; but he was a loving brother, a fast friend, a sharp and accurate observer of men and things, and gave hope, in his last hours, that he "died in the faith." Who can think of him without affection and gratitude as the author of that sublime hymn, with which his poem on the Seasons closes? It has been well said of that hymn "that in it the essential beauty of this poem is collected in a cloud of fragrance, and by the breath of devotion directed up to heaven." Who does not listen breathless to its opening music and its closing swell?

     Almighty Father!
       The rolling year
Is full of Thee. Forth in the pleasing spring
Thy beauty walks, Thy tenderness and love
Wide flush the fields; the softening air is balm;
Echo the mountains round; the forest smiles;
And every sense and every heart is joy.
Then comes Thy glory in the summer months,
With light and heat refulgent. Then Thy sun
Shoots full perfection through the swelling year;
And oft Thy voice in dreadful thunder speaks,

And oft at dawn, deep noon, or falling eve,
By brooks and groves, in hollow whispering gales;
Thy bounty shines in autumn unconfined,
And spreads a common feast for all that lives.
In winter, awful Thou! with clouds and storms
Around Thee thrown! on the whirlwind's wing
Riding sublime, Thou bidst the world adore,
And tremblest nature with Thy northern blast.

Should fate command me to the furthest verge
Of the green earth, to distant barbarous climes,
Rivers unknown to song, where first the sun
Gilds Indian mountains, or his setting beam
Flames on th' Atlantic isles, 'tis nought to me;
Since God is ever present, ever felt,
In the void waste, and in the city full!
And where He vital breathes there must be joy.
When e'en, at last, the solemn hour shall come,
And wing my mystic flight to future worlds,
I cheerful will obey; there with new powers,
With rising wonders, sing. I cannot go
Where universal love not shines around,
Sustaining all yon orbs, and all their suns,
From seeming evil still educing good,
And better them again, and better still,
In infinite progression. But I lose
Myself in Him, in light ineffable!
Come, then, expressive silence! muse His praise.

CHAPTER XIII.

HYMNS ABOUT THE BOOK.

"In God will I praise His word; in the Lord will I praise His word."

ENGLAND has her classic divinity; a theological creation affording everything to enlighten the minds, regulate the lives, and warm the hearts of the most cultivated Christians, as long as the English language lives. In the midst of this brilliant firmament of religious literature, like a central and imperishable sun, stands our Bible. This is the one Book of the Christian; that which affords enough to form his character, were all other volumes consumed with the dust of their authors. The great design of this Book is to regulate the affections of man, and to perfect his character for an immortal state. But it affords innumerable pleasures to the mind which it sways, and allures the soul toward religious maturity by gratifying its distinctive taste. Do we seek for beauty of composition? In the Bible we find the most natural simplicity and force, the most genuine strength and grandeur. Do we look for poetry? Here we may feast on the amazing sublimities of Isaiah, and read with pleasure the pastorals of Solomon; we are excited to heavenly feeling by the sound of David's lyre, are sometimes melted by the pathetic strains of Jeremiah, and at intervals overwhelmed by the awful grandeurs of the entranced Ezekiel. Does our taste lead us to inquire for the beauties of logic? In the Bible we have the most delicate distinctions, the most acute reasonings, and the most perfect developments of the human mind. Do we wish to gratify our taste for the science of numbers? Questions may be drawn from this Book, the solution of which may deeply engage the most profound calculators.

Are we astronomical in our propensity? Then we may follow the inspired penman, and ride upon the wings of the wind, fly above these lower elements, perform the circuit of the earth, consider the influences of the moon, mark the Pleiades, measure the bands of Orion, follow the "going forth" of Mazaroth, or commune with Arcturus and his sons. Are we in pursuit of geographical knowledge? Here are notices interesting, explanatory, and illustrative. Are we students in natural philosophy? Here the wide field of nature is open to us; and the philosophical writers of this Book direct us to particulars and universals. In the Bible the pious politician meets with the great principles of civil and ecclesiastical polity, and here is a system of moral philosophy which far transcends all that has been produced among men. And all these secondary lights are so placed in the sphere of truth, that their beams unite to glorify and render prominent the great Source of all good. Nor can we trace their rays without being led to contemplate the glorious character and righteous will of the Divine Being. The Book that thus gratifies our taste introduces the mind to God, and assimilates it to His image by calling it to enjoy the writings of the law, the oracles of the prophets, the doctrine of types, the experience of histories, the instruction of proverbs, the beauty of promises, and the music of psalms. There is no book which has such power to transform and perfect the character of the Christian; none which holds in such pleasurable servitude the intellect over which it has the entire sway. While the mind has a strong passion for books, and a relish for great variety prevails, it is difficult for the young Christian to give the Bible its proper place, to afford it its proper share of his time, attention, and heart. But to the self-denying student, who devotes himself to revealed truth, that Book opens its hitherto veiled beauties, and fixes and absorbs the wondering and ravished mind. Dr. Kennicott was occupied for thirty years on his edition of the Hebrew Bible. During that time it was Mrs. Kennicott's office, in their daily airings, to read to him those different portions to which his immediate attention was called. When preparing for their ride, the day after his great work was completed, upon her asking him what book she should now take, "Oh," exclaimed he, "let us begin the Bible again." So, then, the love of the sacred volume grows as our acquaintance with it deepens; and just as its various riches and powers open our hearts, we shall take up the simple but touching melody of Anne Steele's hymn on "the excellency of the Scriptures," and sing—

> Father of mercies, in Thy Word,
>   What endless glory shines!
> For ever be Thy name adored
>   For these celestial lines.
>
> Here mines of heavenly wealth disclose
>   Their bright unbounded store;
> The glittering gem no longer glows,
>   And India boasts no more.
>
> Here may the wretched sons of want
>   Exhaustless riches find;
> Riches above what earth can grant,
>   And lasting as the mind.
>
> Here the fair tree of knowledge grows,
>   And yields a free repast;
> Sublimer sweets than nature knows
>   Invite the longing taste.
>
> Here may the blind and hungry come,
>   And light and food receive;
> Here shall the meanest guest have room,
>   And taste, and see, and live.
>
> Amidst these gloomy wilds below,
>   When dark and sad we stray;
> Here beams of heaven relieve our woe,
>   And guide to endless day.
>
> Here springs of consolation rise,
>   To cheer the fainting mind;
> And thirsty souls receive supplies,
>   And sweet refreshment find.
>
> When guilt and terror, pain and grief,
>   United rend the heart,
> Here sinners meet divine relief,
>   And cool the raging smart.
>
> Here the Redeemer's welcome voice
>   Spreads heavenly peace around;
> And life, and everlasting joys,
>   Attend the blissful sound.

But when His painful sufferings rise
(Delightful, dreadful scene!)
Angels may read with wondering eyes
That Jesus died for men.

Oh, may these heavenly pages be
My ever dear delight,
And still new beauties may I see,
And still increasing light.

Divine instructor, gracious Lord,
Be Thou for ever near;
Teach me to love Thy sacred Word,
And view my Saviour there.

There is something, too, in this blessed Book which seems to infuse a kind of immortal vigour into the writings of those men who have made it their chief study. There are two authors whose writings breathe immortality, whose books will live, while myriads of subsequent productions pass into oblivion — John Milton and John Bunyan. Milton's masterpiece is his "Paradise Lost," and though every page of that poem shows the vast range of his reading, it would seem that we owe the life of its best parts to the poet's deep communion with the Hebrew Scriptures. Some of the most sublime passages of "Paradise Lost" are poetic translations and paraphrases of Hebrew words and sentences used by Moses and the prophets; in his daily intercourse with whom, Milton's soul gathered strength for a flight through the depths of chaos, and into the regions of the blessed. And where is the secret of that life which animates "Pilgrim's Progress"? that undying vigour and immortal beauty which enchant every successive generation of readers? Why, you have it in the fact that Bunyan was a man of *one* Book, and that Book was the *English* Bible. Bunyan and Milton, both imperishable authors, gather their life, the one from the Hebrew Scriptures, and the other from their incomparable *English* version.

To the same volume we may trace that power which formed those mature and influential characters who have left such gracious impressions on the Church and the world — Luther, Calvin, Wesley, and Whitefield. One of them has opened his heart to us, and has shown the source of that energy which distinguished his preaching, and which still lives in the volumes which he wrote. He says:—"To candid, reasonable men, I am not afraid to lay open what have been the inmost thoughts of my heart. I have thought I am a creature of a day, passing through life as an arrow through the air. I am a spirit come from God, and returning to God; just hovering over the great gulf, till, a few moments hence, I am no more seen; I drop into an unchangeable eternity! I want to know one thing—the way to heaven; how to land safe on that happy shore. God Himself has condescended to teach the way; for this very end He came from heaven. He hath written it down in a Book. Oh give me that Book! At any price, give me the Book of God! I have it. Here is knowledge enough for me. Let me be a man of one book. Here I am, far from the busy ways of men. I sit down alone; only God is here. In His presence I open, I read His Book; for this end I find the way to Heaven. Is there a doubt concerning the meaning of what I read? Does anything appear dark or intricate? I lift up my heart to the Father of lights:—Lord, is it not Thy word, 'If any man lack wisdom, let him ask of God'? Thou 'givest liberally and upbraidest not.' Thou hast said, 'If any man be willing to do Thy will, he shall know.' I am willing to do, let me know Thy will. I then search after and consider parallel passages of Scripture, 'comparing spiritual things with spiritual.' I meditate thereon with all the attention and earnestness of which my mind is capable. If any doubt still remains, I consult those who are experienced in the things of God; and then the writings, whereby being dead, they yet speak. And what I thus learn, that I teach." Thus speaks John Wesley in his preface to his sermons; and the spirit of the beautiful and striking passage has been happily caught by his brother Charles, and embodied in the form of a metrical paraphrase on Deut. vi. 6, 7—"And these words, that I command thee this day, shall be in thine heart; and thou shalt teach them diligently unto thy children, and shalt talk of them when thou sittest in thine house, and when thou walkest by the way, and when thou liest down, and when thou risest up."

> The table of my heart prepare
> (Such power belongs to Thee alone),

And write, O God, Thy precepts there,
  To show Thou still canst write in stone,
So shall my pure obedience prove
All things are possible to love.

Father, instruct my docile heart,
  Apt to instruct I then shall be,
I then shall all Thy words impart,
  And teach (as taught myself by Thee)
My children, in their earliest days,
To know and live the life of grace.

When quiet in my house I sit,
  Thy Book be my companion still,
My joy Thy sayings to repeat,
  Talk o'er the records of Thy will,
And search the oracles divine,
Till every heartfelt word is mine.

Oh, might the gracious words divine
  Subject of all my converse be,
So would the Lord His follower join,
  And walk and talk Himself with me;
So would my heart His presence prove,
And burn with everlasting love.

Oft as I lay me down to rest,
  Oh, may the reconciling Word
Sweetly compose my weary breast,
  While on the bosom of my Lord
I sink in blissful dreams away,
And visions of eternal day.

Rising to sing my Saviour's praise,
  Thee may I publish all day long,
And let Thy precious word of grace
  Flow from my heart and fill my tongue;
Fill all my life with purest love,
And join me to Thy Church above.

This hymn has become a sort of household joy to thousands who guide the daily devotions of their families; and its music promises to be happily familiar to a widening circle of devout Bible students whose homes are hallowed as scenes of daily communion with inspired truth. As a hymnist, however, Charles Wesley was never content merely to record his own or even his brother's experience in tuneful measures. He was not among the lyric poets who find full employment for their muse amidst the intricacies and subtle workings of their own inner world. He had a large share of that unselfishness which so eminently distinguished his more active brother, and longed, like an apostle, "to spend and be spent," rather in guiding, blessing, and saving others than in dwelling complacently or uneasily upon the throne of his own spiritual kingdom. Or if, like St. Paul, he sometimes threw his own experience into the form of an example, it was only that he might the more effectually teach the world, and assist the devotions of the Church. Thus, while in one hymn he takes the individual mode of expression, singing as a person, that every like-minded person may have a song about the Book; in another he pours the desire of his soul into a metrical prayer so adapted to the many, that ministers and people may sing together in "the great congregation."

> Inspirer of the ancient seers,
>   Who wrote from Thee the sacred page,
> The same through all succeeding years,
>   To us in our degenerate age,
> The spirit of Thy Word impart,
> And breathe the life into our heart.
>
> While now Thine oracles we read,
>   With earnest prayer and strong desire,
> O let Thy Spirit from Thee proceed,
>   Our souls to awaken and inspire;
> Our weakness help, our darkness chase,
> And guide us by the light of grace!
>
> Whene'er in error's paths we rove,
>   The living God through sin forsake,
> Our conscience by Thy Word reprove,
>   Convince and bring the wanderers back,
> Deep wounded by Thy Spirit's sword,
> And then by Gilead's balm restored.
>
> The sacred lessons of Thy grace,
>   Transmitted through Thy Word, repeat;
> And train us up in all Thy ways,
>   To make us in Thy will complete;
> Fulfil Thy love's redeeming plan,
> And bring us to a perfect man.
>
> Furnish'd out of Thy treasury,
>   Oh may we always ready stand
> To help the souls redeemed by Thee,
>   For what their various states demand;
> To teach, convince, correct, reprove,
> And build them up in holiest love!

There are but two hymns "on the Scriptures" in the Olney collection; and they stand side by side, as if to remind us of that bond of spiritual fellowship which once held their authors heart to heart. In some respects it was a strange association, that of Cowper and Newton. The one robust, trained to hardihood upon the high seas; the other frail, instinctively shrinking from both wave and wind. Unlike in birth and education, and, indeed, in all the circumstances of their earlier course, yet one in their love of truth, and united in their work of giving new songs to the Christian world. Many passages of the blessed Book, Cowper, in his morbid depression, would misinterpret against his own soul; as if he were unwilling that the fire of Divine wrath should ever glance on any but the one on whom they were to be concentrated—himself. Whether his friend Newton's spiritual direction was the best for him has been a question; but, however that may be, there were times when his enjoyment of the Sacred Volume was equal not only to his own support, but to the consolation of all lovers of truth, who have followed him, and have learnt his bright and hopeful little hymn, on "The Light and Glory of the Word:"—

> The Spirit breathes upon the Word,
>   And brings the truth to sight;
> Precepts and promises afford
>   A sanctifying light.
>
> A glory gilds the sacred page,
>   Majestic like the sun;
> It gives a light to ev'ry age,
>   It gives, and borrows none.
>
> The hand that gave it still supplies
>   The gracious light and heat;
> His truths upon the nations rise,
>   They rise but never set.
>
> Let everlasting thanks be Thine,
>   For such a bright display,
> As makes a world of darkness shine
>   With beams of heavenly day.
>
> My soul rejoices to pursue
>   The steps of Him I love;
> Till glory breaks upon my view
>   In brighter worlds above.

Then comes Newton's happy song on "The Word more Precious than Gold." How like a man of his temper is this hymn? How expressive from the lips of one who had passed through the remarkable experiences of his life. How differently Cowper and he had been dealt with by Divine mercy. But as it was in both cases the same providence and the same spirit, so they were brought to the same goal. Newton himself has put this in his own style. "Imagine to yourself a number of vessels, at different times, and from different places, bound to the same port, there are some things in which all these would agree—the compass steered by, the port in view, the general rule of navigation, both as to the management of the vessel and determining their astronomical observations, would be the same in all. In other respects they would differ; perhaps no two of them would meet with the same distribution of wind and weather. Some we see set out with a prosperous gale; and when they almost think their passage secured, they are checked by adverse blasts; and after enduring much hardship and danger, and frequent expectations of shipwreck, they just escape, and reach the desired haven. Others meet the greatest difficulties at first; they put forth in a storm, and are often beaten back; at length their voyage proves favourable, and they enter the port with a 'rich and abundant entrance.' Some are hard beset with cruisers and enemies, and obliged to fight their way through; others meet with little remarkable in their passage. Is it not so in the spiritual life? All true believers 'walk by the same rule,' and mind the same things; the Word of God is their compass; Jesus is their polar star. . . . . Yet their experience, formed upon these common principles, is far from being uniform. The Lord, in His first call, and His following dispensations, has a regard to the situation, temper, talents of each, and to the particular sorrows or trials He has appointed them for. Though all are exercised at times, yet some pass through the voyage of life much more smoothly than others."

With all the varieties of their personal histories, both Cowper and Newton had learnt to love the Bible; and both hearts found an inexhaustible treasure in that "one Book." Newton's mother had taught him to read the Bible, and to store his memory with its chapters, when he was but four years old, and, as he says, "though in process of time I sinned away all the advantages of these early impressions, yet they were for a great while a restraint upon me; they returned again and again, and it was very long before I could wholly shake them off; and when the Lord at length opened my eyes, I found a great benefit from the recollection of them." In the course of his subsequent wanderings, he picked up Shaftsbury's "Characteristics," "in a petty shop at Middleburg in Holland." "The title," says he, allured me to buy it, and the style and manner gave me great pleasure in reading. . . . . Thus with fine words and fair speeches, my simple heart was beguiled. . . . . No immediate effect followed; but it operated like a slow poison." Evil companionship finished what Shaftsbury began,—it confirmed him in blank infidelity. But when, at last, extreme suffering and danger brought him to cry to God for mercy, the sacred utterances with which his youthful mind had been stored unfolded their meaning to his heart; and that Word which he had taught himself to despise was now his best friend, the companion of his leisure hours, and the source of those holy lessons which, as a preacher, he afterwards gave out to his flock, and with which, as a hymnist, he enriched his undying hymns. Who can wonder that he sang of the Book thus?—

> Precious Bible! what a treasure
> Does the Word of God afford?
> All I want for life or pleasure,
> Food and med'cine, shield and sword:
> Let the world account me poor,
> Having this I need no more.
>
> Food to which the world's a stranger,
> Here my hungry soul enjoys;
> Of excess there is no danger,
> Tho' it fills, it never cloys:
> On a dying Christ I feed,
> He is meat and drink indeed!
>
> When my faith is faint and sickly,
> Or when Satan wounds my mind,
> Cordials to revive me quickly,
> Healing med'cines here I find:
> To the promises I flee,
> Each affords a remedy.

In the hour of dark temptation
　Satan cannot make me yield;
For the word of consolation
　Is to me the mighty shield:
While the Scripture truths are sure,
From his malice I'm secure.

Vain his threats to overcome me,
　When I take the Spirit's sword;
Then with ease I drive him from me,
　Satan trembles at the Word:
'Tis a sword for conquest made,
Keen the edge and strong the blade.

Shall I envy then the miser,
　Doting on his golden store?
Sure I am or should be wiser,
　I am rich, 'tis he is poor:
Jesus gives me in His Word,
Food and med'cine, shield and sword.

Charles Lamb once resolved, if possible, to check a young friend who was rather too ready to abandon himself to dependence on a literary profession, and he wrote to him, saying, "Throw yourself on the world, without any rational plan of support beyond what the chance employ of booksellers would afford you! Throw yourself rather, my dear sir, from the steep Tarpeian rock, slap-dash headlong upon iron spikes. If you have but five consolatory minutes between the desk and the bed, make much of them, and live a century in them, rather than turn slave to the booksellers. They are Turks and Tartars when they have poor authors at their beck. Hitherto you have been at arm's length from them—come not within their grasp. I have known many authors want for bread—some repining, others enjoying the blessed security of a counting-house—all agreeing they had rather have been tailors, weavers, what not? rather than the things they were. I have known some starved, some go mad, one dear friend literally dying in a workhouse. Oh, you know not—may you never know—the miseries of subsisting by authorship!" This strong preventive was effectual; and Bernard Barton stuck to his banking establishment at Woodbridge in Suffolk. Lamb knew his man and gave wise counsel. Happy was it for Barton that he listened to a true friend. His were not the talents for the general literary market. In 1820 he published a volume of miscellaneous poems, remarkable for their simple elegance, chasteness of style, and purity of feeling. The pieces will always be agreeable to those who love quiet English scenery pictured with gentle feeling; or meditative verses breathing tenderness and devotion, always soothing and always happy. There is little that would strike, little that would seem original; yet Bernard Barton is always welcome to the cultivated taste. He was a hymnist, and one hymn is about "the Book" and full of sweetness. With all his distinctive notions as a Quaker about "inward light," he had a deep reverence for the written Word, and a childlike trust in the certainty of its guidance; and expresses his love for inspired truth, and his faith in its lessons, in the hymn founded on Psalm cxix. 105—"Thy word is a lamp unto my feet"—

> Lamp of our feet, whereby we trace
> Our path when wont to stray,
> Stream from the fount of heavenly grace,
> Brook by the traveller's way.
>
> Bread of our souls whereon we feed,
> True manna from on high:
> Our guide and chart, wherein we read
> Of realms beyond the sky:
>
> Pillar of fire through watches dark,
> And radiant cloud by day;
> When waves would whelm our tossing bark,
> Our anchor and our stay:
>
> Word of the everlasting God,
> Will of His glorious Son;
> Without thee how could earth be trod,
> Or heaven itself be won?
>
> Lord, grant us all aright to learn
> The wisdom it imparts;
> And to its heavenly teaching turn,
> With simple, childlike hearts.

But pleasant as it is to sing these later hymns about the Book, the older songs must not be forgotten. Who can forget George Herbert's hymn on "the Holy Scriptures"? More antique it is, more quaint, less adapted to popular music than some others; yet how full of deep thought—too full, perhaps, for most thinkers now-a-days—and how richly it is coloured by the living breath of inspired truth itself! Nobody would expect anything but hymns and songs about truth and love from him. Whether at home or abroad, in the church or in the household, the author of the "Country Parson" was always, in appearance, manner, and spirit, the holy parson. "He was," says his venerable biographer, "for his person, of a stature inclining towards tallness; his body was very straight; and so far from being cumbered with too much flesh, that he was lean to an extremity. His aspect was cheerful, and his speech and motion did both declare him a gentleman; for they were all so meek and obliging, that they purchased love and respect from all that knew him." He entered, in his thirty-sixth year, on his parsonage at Bemerton, saying, "I beseech God that my humble and charitable life may so win upon others, as to bring glory to my Jesus, whom I have this day taken to be my Master and Governor; and I am so proud of His service, that I will always observe, and obey, and do His will, and always call Him Jesus my Master." And Herbert's life answered to his prayer. It was "so full of charity, humility, and all Christian virtues," says a friend, "that it deserves the eloquence of St. Chrysostom to commend and declare it!—a life that, if it were related by a pen like his, there would then be no need for this age to look back into times past for the examples of primitive piety, for they might be all found in the life of George Herbert." Alas! his holy career was short, though full. Dr. Humphrey Henchman, afterwards Bishop of London, who was present at his ordination to the priesthood, plaintively says, "I laid my hand on Mr. Herbert's head, and, alas! within less than three years, lent my shoulder to carry my dear friend to his grave." But "he, being dead, yet speaketh;" and speaketh in rich, glowing praise of the blessed Book from whose commands, doctrines, and promises he gathered the secret of his holy character and life.

> Oh Book! infinite sweetness! let my heart
> Suck every letter, and a honey gain,
> Precious for any grief in any part,
> To clear the breast, to mollify all pain.

Thou art all health, health thriving, till it make
  A full eternity: thou art a mass
Of strange delights, where we may wish and take.
  Ladies, look here; this is the thankful glass,

That mends the looker's eyes: this is the well
  That washes what it shows. Who can endear
Thy praise too much? Thou art heaven's lieger here,
  Working against the states of death and hell.

Thou art joy's handsel: heaven lies flat in thee,
Subject to every mounter's bended knee.

Oh that I knew how all thy lights combine,
  And the configurations of their glory!
Seeing not only how each verse doth shine,
  But all the constellations of the story.

This verse marks that, and both do make a motion
  Unto a third, that ten leaves off doth lie;
Then as dispersed herbs do watch a potion,
  These three make up some Christian's destiny.

Such are thy secrets, which my life makes good,
  And comments on thee; for in everything
Thy words do find me out, and parallels bring,
  And in another make me understood.

Stars are poor books, and oftentimes do miss:
This Book of stars lights to eternal bliss.

Would young men improve their taste, their thinking powers, and, above all, the tone of their piety? Let them make George Herbert their companion and study, until they lose sight of all in him that at first appears rugged, grotesque, and quaint in their deep enjoyment of his fragrant thoughts, poetic glow, and heavenly feeling; and when they wish for an occasional change to the more simple style of psalmody, they may turn to Watts's hymn on "Instruction from Scripture," founded on parts of Psalm cxix. :—

> How shall the young secure their hearts,
>   And guard their lives from sin?
> Thy Word the choicest rule imparts,
>   To keep the conscience clean.
>
> When once it enters to the mind,
>   It spreads such light abroad,
> The meanest souls instruction find,
>   And raise their thoughts to God.

'Tis like the sun, a heavenly light,
  That guides us all the day;
And through the dangers of the night,
  A lamp to lead our way.

The men that keep Thy law with care,
  And meditate Thy Word,
Grow wiser than their teachers are,
  And better know the Lord.

Thy precepts make me truly wise;
  I hate the sinner's road;
I hate my own vain thoughts that rise,
  But love Thy love, my God.

The starry heavens Thy rule obey,
  The earth maintains her place;
And these Thy servants night and day
  Thy skill and power express.

But still Thy law and gospel, Lord,
  Have lessons more divine:
Not earth stands firmer than Thy Word,
  Nor stars so nobly shine.

Thy Word is everlasting truth,
  How pure is ev'ry page;
That holy Book shall guide our youth,
  And well support our age.

CHAPTER XIV.

HYMNS OF THE SABBATH.

"How still the morning of the hallowed day!
Mute is the voice of rural labour, . . .
While from yon lowly roof, whose curling smoke
O'ermounts the mist, is heard, at intervals,
The voice of psalms, the simple song of praise."

"How certainly the outside world sometimes answers to the condition of our inner life! The face of creation seems troubled when our souls are uneasy. Signs of sorrow appear around us when our hearts are distressed. All music is discord when we ourselves are out of tune; and all forms are rugged, all outlines harsh, when irregularities and unlovely tempers are taking unholy shapes in our own inward selves. But all forms of creation become lines of beauty, all shapes make themselves agreeable, all sounds harmonize, and all influences are calm, when our souls are conformed to God's will, when we enjoy the repose of a spiritual Sabbath." These were the thoughts of a pilgrim who had lived and journeyed till he had seen all the companions of his earlier course drop off from the road, and who had learned to turn with tremulous delight towards anything in nature that seemed to wear an expression of sympathy with him in his loneliness. Hills, rocks, valleys, and waters, flowers, and all tiny forms of beauty, he had become happily familiar with; and friendship with nature, in his case, was so akin to friendship with "the God of all grace," that they seemed to blend their influences for his pleasure, and to act by turns as a sort of brotherhood on his behalf. He was sometimes far away from the Sabbath assemblies of God's people; but everything in the outer world, at such times, tendered its sympathies, and offered its ministrations, and joined him in the celebration of his Sunday service. So it was, one Sunday morning, as he went quietly, but with buoyant footsteps, over the soft, turfy undulations which, like the waves of a quietly-subsiding sea, sank from the hills of the coast down to the low cliff, and formed the marshy, lawn-like approach to a lone cottage which looked out upon the waters of the Atlantic. Every step brought up fragrance from the crushed camomile or the wild thyme. No breeze disturbed the sea. There was something solemnly calm in the very sunlight. "Nature feels her Sabbath," said he to himself, "and is still; but my undertoned music will only deepen her stillness;" and then, as he went, his steps kept tune with his low chant, as he sang a charming hymn, which in that day was just beginning to float about in a few private circles of religious life:—

> Hail, thou bright and sacred morn,
>   Risen with gladness in thy beams!
> Light, which not of earth is born,
>   From thy dawn in glory streams:
> Airs of heaven are breathed around,
> And each place is holy ground.
>
> Sad and weary were our way,
>   Fainting oft beneath our load,
> But for thee, thou blessed day,
>   Resting-place on life's rough road!
> Here flow forth the streams of grace,
> Strengthened hence we run the race.
>
> Great Creator, who this day
>   From Thy perfect work didst rest,
> By the souls that own Thy sway,
>   Hallow'd be its hours, and blest;
> Cares of earth aside be thrown,
> This day given to heaven alone!
>
> Saviour! who this day didst break
>   The dark prison of the tomb;
> Bid my slumbering soul awake,
>   Shine through all its sin and gloom:
> Let me, from my bonds set free,
> Rise from sin, and live to Thee!
>
> Blessed Spirit! Comforter!
>   Sent this day from Christ on high;

Lord, on me Thy gifts confer,
  Cleanse, illumine, sanctify:
All Thine influence shed abroad,
Lead me to the truth of God!

Soon, too soon, the sweet repose
  Of this day of God will cease;
Soon this glimpse of heaven will close,
  Vanish soon the hours of peace,
Soon return the toil, the strife,
All the weariness of life.

But the rest which yet remains
  For Thy people, Lord, above,
Knows nor change, nor fears, nor pains,
  Endless as their Saviour's love:
Oh, may every Sabbath here
Bring us to that rest more near!

The last line still lingered on his lips as he entered the cottage.

"Ah! you were singing," said a young woman who was lying on a couch, so placed that she could look out upon the ocean; "you were singing. Well, I do not wonder at that, for who could help singing on a morning like this? Does not all nature seem to feel its Sabbath hush and its Sabbath joy?"

"That was the very thought which moved me to sing," was the reply; "and I was indulging in that sort of inward murmur of which the psalmist speaks as of one of his devotional pleasures. I was murmuring the praise which seemed to rise with a kind of naturalness from my quiet heart, and Mrs. Lyte's beautiful hymn appeared to be my best form of expression."

"That is rather remarkable," said the young sufferer, with a smile that told the whole story of her long discipline of affliction, and the peaceful submission and patience which she had learnt in the process of her trial. "Just before you came in I was humming to myself that sweet Sabbath hymn by Bishop Heber. How often some of his hymns rise within my soul, as if the hand of my Redeemer had touched all the musical chords within me! I sing them to myself, while the sea is whispering and roaring by turns on the beach; and then I look on the waters as I lie here, and love to think of that cultivated and gifted man crossing the deep under the constraining power of his Redeemer's love, and gladly sacrificing all the comforts and honours of his native island for the joy of proclaiming peace to the multitudes of India. I think of him, gentleman, poet, scholar, theologian, as he was, going out to live and die amidst the idolatrous millions of that vast old country, that he might, as he said, 'in some degree, however small, be enabled to conduce to the spiritual advantage of creatures so goodly, so gentle, and now so misled and blinded.' How I love to follow him in his travels! Everything that he describes lives before me. How I like to watch him as the tear trembles in his eye at hearing one of his own blessed hymns sung far up in India, at Meerut, and sung, as he says, 'better than he had ever heard it sung before.' Then to go with him from Delhi to Bombay, from Bombay to Ceylon, where he seems to have caught the inspiration for his missionary hymn:—

> What though the spicy breezes
>   Blow soft o'er Ceylon's isle;
> Though every prospect pleases,
>   And only man is vile:
> In vain with lavish kindness
>   The gifts of God are strown,
> The heathen in his blindness
>   Bows down to wood and stone.
>
> Can we, whose souls are lighted
>   With wisdom from on high,
> Can we to men benighted
>   The lamp of life deny?
> Salvation! oh, salvation!
>   The joyful sound proclaim,
> Till each remotest nation
>   Has learnt Messiah's name.

And then to follow him to the south, the scene of his last charge, and his mysterious call to his reward. Oh that last kind, loving, truly Christian address, at Trichinopoly! How often I have read it. 'And now,' says he, 'depart in the faith and favour of the Lord; and if what you have learned and heard this day has been so far blessed as to produce a serious and lasting effect on you, let me entreat you to remember sometimes in your prayers those ministers of Christ who have laboured for your instruction, that we who have preached to you may not ourselves be cast away, but that it may be given to us also to walk in this present life according to the words of the gospel which we have received of the Lord, and to rejoice hereafter with you, the children of our care, in that land where the weary shall find repose, and the wicked cease from troubling; where we shall behold God as He is, and be ourselves made like unto God in innocence, and happiness, and immortality.' Blessed man! he soon found his rest after he had uttered these words. How touching it is, that story of his end! Alone in his last moment, and his happy spirit suddenly departing, and leaving his body in the waters of the bath in which he had sought refreshment after his Sabbath toils. I wonder where he wrote that beautiful Sabbath hymn. I have often pictured him lying yonder, sick and weary, under the pressure of a tropical climate, still bent on his holy mission, but feeling the lack of England's Sabbath pleasures, and looking upwards in hope—

>   Longing, gasping after home;

and then I seem to have pleasant sympathy with him; and his Lord's-day song comes with deeper pathos and richer music upon my soul as I sing it:—

> Thousands, O Lord of Hosts, to-day,
>   Within Thy temple meet;
> And tens of thousands throng to pay
>   Their homage at Thy feet.
>
> They see Thy power and glory there,
>   Where I have seen Thee too;
> They read, they hear, they join in prayer,
>   As I was wont to do.
>
> They sing Thy deeds as I have sung,
>   In sweet and solemn lays;
> Were I among them, my glad tongue
>   Might learn new themes of praise.
>
> For Thou art in the midst to teach,
>   While they look up to Thee;
> And Thou hast blessings, Lord, for each,
>   And blessings, too, for me.
>
> Behold Thy prisoner, loose my bands,
>   If 'tis Thy gracious will;
> If not, contented in Thy hands,
>   Only be with me still.

> I may not to Thy courts repair,
>   Yet here Thou surely art;
> Oh give me here a house of prayer,
>   Here Sabbath joys impart!
>
> To faith reveal the things unseen,
>   To hope the joys unfold;
> Let love, without a veil between,
>   Thy glory now behold."

The closing prayer of her hymn was answered. There was an ethereal light on her face as from the unfolding visions of faith. Her eyes seemed to reflect the smile of her loving Saviour. An air of deeper stillness pervaded the little chamber, and for a time the two remained in silence—silence that was full of Sabbath peace and joy. The poor girl had been long a sufferer. A spinal affection kept her to her couch; but she was contented and happy in daily companionship with Jesus. A little table-like bracket had been fixed on the wall by her bed-side, so that she could at any time take a book from it, or regale herself with the perfume of the flowers with which she was daily supplied. On that Sunday morning her visitor saw Herbert's poems near her; she had been using it, he thought, and taking it up, he said, "Do you like Herbert?"

"Oh, yes," said she, "I like him, for he makes me think, while I am enjoying the old-fashion music of his verses. There is that rich old hymn for 'Sunday'; it always sends my thoughts back to the time when, in my childhood, I used to keep my eyes on the glorious old painted window that was over against me in the church, and, while they were singing the anthem, used to fancy that the music and the coloured light were like one another somehow. I wish I could sing that hymn; but I am never tired of saying it over to myself. Read it to me, will you?"

The hymn was read; and how full of thought and Sabbath feeling it is—

> O day most calm, most bright,
> The fruit of this, the next world's bud,
> Th' indorsement of supreme delight,
> Writ by a friend, and with His blood;
> The couch of time, care's balm and bay,
> The week were dark but for thy light:
>   Thy torch doth show the way.

The other days and thou
Make up one man, whose face thou art,
Knocking at heaven with thy brow:
The working days are the back part;
The burden of the week lies there,
Making the whole to stoop and bow,
   Till thy release appear.

Man had straight forward gone
To endless death; but thou dost pull
And turn us round to look on One
Whom, if we were not very dull,
We could not choose but look on still:
Since there is no place so alone
   The which He doth not fill.

Sundays the pillars are
On which heaven's palace arched lies:
The other days fill up the spare
And hollow room with vanities;
They are the fruitful beds and borders
In God's rich garden: that is bare
   Which parts their ranks and orders.

The Sundays of man's life,
Threaded together on time's string,
Make bracelets to adorn the wife
Of the eternal glorious King.
On Sunday heaven's gate stands ope;
Blessings are plentiful and rife,
   More plentiful than hope.

This day my Saviour rose,
And did enclose this light for His:
That, as each beast his manger knows,
Man might not of his fodder miss.
Christ has took in this piece of ground,
And made a garden there for those
   Who want herbs for their wound.

The rest of our creation
Our great Redeemer did remove
With the same shake, which at His passion
Did th' earth and all things with it move,
As Samson bore the doors away,
Christ's hands, though nailed, wrought our salvation,
   And did unhinge that day.

The brightness of that day
We sullied by our foul offence:
Wherefore that robe we cast away,
Having a new at His expense,

> Whose drops of blood paid the full price,
> That was required to make us gay,
>   And fit for paradise.
>
> Thou art a day of mirth:
> And where the week-day trails on ground,
> Thy flight is higher, as thy birth:
> Oh let me take thee at the bound,
> Leaping with thee from seven to seven,
> Till that we both being tossed from earth,
>   Fly hand in hand to heaven.

"Thank you," said the smiling sufferer. "How often have I repeated that hymn to myself; and then I have gone off into pleasant dream-like thoughts about 'Holy George Herbert.' I have pictured Montgomery Castle where he was born, and I have imagined that birth-day, April 3, 1593, to be a Sunday; and then I have seen that blessed pious mother of his watching her boy with that look of 'cheerful gravity' which those who knew her wit and kindness and piety so admired; and then I have listened to that evening music from the pious boy's chamber at college, the music with which he cheered himself and guarded his own soul against outward mischiefs. Then comes up the image of Jane Danvers, who fell in love with him before she saw his face, and who became his wife three days after their first interview; and I think of what happy old Isaak Walton says about the wedded pair, 'The eternal lover of mankind made them happy in each other's mutual and equal affections and compliance, indeed so happy that there never was any opposition betwixt them, unless it were a contest which should most incline to a compliance with the other's desires. And though this begat, and continued in them, such a mutual love, and joy, and content, as was no way defective; yet this mutual content, and love, and joy did receive a daily augmentation by such daily obligingness to each other, as still added such new influences to the former fulness of these divine souls, as was only improvable in heaven, where they now enjoy it.' I think, too, of Bemerton, and long to visit it, to see the scene of that holy man's life as a parish priest, happy in his home and happy amidst his flock, happy in the church, and happy in the homes which he visited. I try to picture him on the ground before the altar in silent prayer on the day of his entrance on his charge; then going with his wife and household twice a day to prayers in the church; then practising psalmody with

> The sound of glory ringing in his ears;

then walking twice a week into Salisbury Cathedral, where he used, as he said, 'to find heaven on earth;' and then I see him on his last bed, worn to a shadow, but all soul and all heavenly devotion, glowing with hope and love. And oh! that last Sunday scene before he fled to his rest! when he rose from his bed, seized his favourite instrument, and sang as he played—

> My God, my God,
> My music shall find Thee,
> And every string
> Shall have his attribute to sing!

Finishing with part of that very hymn for 'Sunday,' which was just now read; thus at the very last, as Walton says, 'singing on earth such hymns and anthems as the angels, and he and Mr. Ferrar are now singing in heaven.' Blessed to me is the memory of George Herbert, were it only for that Sunday hymn. How pleasant it is to be here so quiet, and so near to Jesus, listening to such hymns! Do you know any others? Please to let me hear them. These spiritual songs so refresh me."

"Well," said the pilgrim, "there are Mason's 'Spiritual Songs;' have you any knowledge of them?"

"No; who was he? Tell me something about him; and then I shall be glad to hear some of his songs."

"I will try to meet your wishes. I am sure you would like some of his hymns. Richard Baxter says that Mason was 'the glory of the Church of England;' that 'the frame of his spirit was so heavenly, his deportment so humble and obliging, his discourse of spiritual things, and little else could we hear from him, so weighty, with such apt words and delightful air, that it charmed all that had any spiritual relish, and was not burdensome to others, as discourses of that nature have been from other ministers.'"

"Mr. Mason was a minister, then?"

"Yes; he was brought up in Northamptonshire, and

began his ministry in the same county, as curate of Isham, after he had gone through his course at Cambridge. In October, 1668, he became vicar of Stanton-Bury, and in January, 1674, rector of Water-Stratford, in Buckinghamshire, where he spent his holy and useful life, and finished his course in the year 1694. Like many other good men, he fell into some rather wild notions in his latter days. Among these notions some would class his persuasion that he had seen the Lord. In that, however, he was not more peculiar than very many highly spiritual Christians whose faith sometimes brightens into something very like open vision. He was wild in his notions about Christ's personal reign upon the earth; and, like many others who mistake fulfilled for unfulfilled prophecy, he led his neighbours astray into the fervent expectation that Christ would appear in His glory at Water-Stratford. But his mistakes were not inconsistent with perfect love, and he left the scene of mortality and human mistakes exclaiming, 'I am full of the loving-kindness of the Lord!' One who followed him in the parish of Stanton-Bury says, 'My acquaintance with Mr. Mason I have esteemed one of the greatest mercies I ever received. His affections were so fervent, and his zeal so great, that as they were the comfort, so they were the admiration of those who feared God and lived near him.' His hymns still live, to testify to his personal holiness, and to keep alive the fruits of his hallowed genius. His songs seem to have been relished by Pope, and Watts, and the Wesleys, who now and then garnished their own verses with choice bits from his hymns. James Montgomery was of opinion that 'his style is a middle tint between the raw colouring of Quarles and the daylight clearness of Watts,' that 'his talent is equally poised between both, having more vigour, but less versatility, than that of either his forerunner or his successor.' That is probably correct. But you would like to hear some of his verses. He has two Sabbath hymns. One of them would rather remind one of Herbert's hymns about which we have talked; this is it:—

> Blest day of God, most calm, most bright,
>   The first and best of days;
> The lab'rer's rest, the saint's delight,
>   A day of mirth and praise:

My Saviour's face did make thee shine,
 His rising did thee raise:
This made thee heavenly and divine
 Beyond the common days.

The first-fruits do a blessing prove
 To all the sheaves behind;
And they that do a Sabbath love,
 An happy week shall find:
My Lord on thee His name did fix,
 Which makes thee rich and gay;
Amidst His golden candlesticks
 My Saviour walks this day.

He walks in 's robes, His face shines bright,
 The stars are in His hand;
Out of His mouth, that place of might,
 A two-edged sword doth stand.
Graced with our Lord's appearance thus,
 As well as with His name,
Thou may'st demand respect from us
 Upon a double claim.

This day doth God His vessels broach,
 His conduits run with wine:
He that loves not this day's approach,
 Scorns heaven, and Saviour's shine.
What slaves are those who slav'ry choose,
 And garlick for their feast,
Whilst milk and honey they refuse,
 And the Almighty's rest?

This market day doth saints enrich,
 And smiles upon them all;
It is their Pentecost, on which
 The Holy Ghost doth fall.
Oh day of wonders! mercies' pawn,
 The weary soul's recruit,
The Christian's Goshen, heaven's dawn,
 The bud of endless fruit.

Oh could I love as I have loved
 Thy watches heretofore:
As England's glory thou hast proved,
 May'st thou be so yet more.
This day I must for God appear;
 For, Lord, the day is Thine:
Oh, let me spend it in Thy fear!
 Then shall the day be mine.

Throughout the day cease work and play,
 That I to God may rest;
Now let me talk with God, and walk
 With God, and I am blest."

"Do you not think," said the young listener, as the pilgrim finished, "do you not think that Mason must have seen Herbert's hymns? He has those happy expressions of Herbert's in his first line—

>Most calm, most bright.

Perhaps Herbert's hymn touched his chords of psalmody, and gave him the first note."

"Perhaps so; but he has another 'song of praise for the Lord's-day,' which is generally thought to be the better hymn; and it has original power and beauty enough to show that, though he might for once have caught a keynote from his predecessor, he had native talent distinctive enough to mark him as Herbert's brother hymnist. Listen to this:—

>My Lord, my Love was crucified,
>>He all the pains did bear;
>
>But in the sweetness of His rest
>>He makes His servants share.
>
>How sweetly rest Thy saints above,
>>Which in Thy bosom lie;
>
>The Church below doth rest in hope
>>Of that felicity.
>
>Thou, Lord, who daily feed'st Thy sheep,
>>Mak'st them a weekly feast:
>
>Thy flocks meet in their several folds
>>Upon this day of rest.
>
>Welcome and dear unto my soul
>>Are these sweet feasts of love;
>
>But what a Sabbath shall I keep
>>When I shall rest above.
>
>I bless Thy wise and wondrous love,
>>Which binds us to be free;
>
>Which makes us leave our earthly snares,
>>That we may come to Thee.
>
>I come, I wait, I hear, I pray:
>>Thy footsteps, Lord, I trace:
>
>I sing to think this is the way
>>Unto my Saviour's face.
>
>These are my preparation days:
>>And when my soul is drest,
>
>The Sabbaths shall deliver me,
>>To mine eternal rest."

"Yes, I like that," said the happy-looking girl,

> "What a Sabbath shall I keep,
> When I shall rest above!

Some of these old hymns have undying vigour and beauty. I have sometimes thought how much I should like to see and feel all the music and Christian life of the still older Latin hymns. I have one here in a translation, which I am very fond of, and I try to sing it sometimes on a Sunday morning, realizing, as far as I can, the thought that I am singing the very hymn which many, many sincere Christians have sung on Sunday mornings for more than a thousand years, it may be. This is the hymn I mean:—

> On this first day, when heaven and earth
> Rose at the Triune's word to birth;
> The day when He, who gave us breath,
> Revived our souls and vanquish'd death;
>
> Why close in sleep your languid eyes?
> Shake off dull slumber, wake, arise;
> And, mindful of the prophet's voice,
> Right early in our God rejoice.
>
> That He may hear the ascending cry;
> That He may stretch His hand from high;
> That He may cleanse and make us meet
> To join Him in that heavenly seat:
>
> That, while each consecrated hour
> We praise and sing His glorious power,
> The offerings of this day of rest
> May with His choicest gifts be blest.
>
> Paternal Glory, Sire of all,
> Thee with o'erflowing hearts we call,
> That we this day may serve Thee, freed
> From guilty thought and sinful deed:
>
> That no foul passion's lawless flame
> May injure this corporeal frame,
> Nor the unhallow'd heart's desire
> Plunge us in flames of fiercer fire.
>
> Saviour of men, whose blood alone
> Can for a ruin'd world atone,
> Cleanse Thou our hearts, and upward lift
> To share in Thy perennial gift.
>
> To Thee, most Holy Sire; to Thee,
> Co-equal, only Son, we flee:
> With Him, the union to complete,
> The Spirit best, the Paraclete."

"That hymn is very old," said the pilgrim. "It has been sung for ages, as you say, in its original form; but this is a translation by Bishop Mant, who was always happier in translating old hymns, and in emulating the ancients in hymns of his own, than he was in fencing with the Methodists in his Bampton Lectures, though his lectures did more than his hymns, it may be, in opening his way to a bishopric. It is always happier to move oneself to devotion by aiding the devotions of others, than to be offering battle to our neighbours about notions which those neighbours never held. It is more gracious to 'admonish one another in psalms, and hymns, and spiritual songs,' than to array ourselves against foes who do not exist, and to 'fight as one that beateth the air.' I say again, Mant was happy as a hymnist; some of his hymns will long outlive his lectures, and one of his best original hymns is 'commemorative of the Day of Holy Rest.' Let me repeat it—

>Blest day, by God in mercy given
> To soothe, refresh, and cheer,
>We greet the blest of all the seven,
> And hold thee doubly dear.
>
>We prize thee as the day of rest,
> Which toil nor travail knows;
>The Sabbath-day, when man and beast
> From week-day works repose.
>
>We prize thee as the day design'd
> From worldly studies freed,
>The Holy Day, to train the mind
> To holy thought and deed.
>
>We prize thee as God's living sign
> Join'd with His faithful Word,
>How man was form'd by power Divine,
> By power Divine restored.
>
>Blest day, by God's commandment made
> The goodliest of the seven,
>Type of the heavenly rest, our aid
> In journeying to heaven:
>
>May holy thoughts and holy rites
> Thy peaceful hours employ,
>Till we, through love of such delights,
> God's endless rest enjoy!

> There hymn, amid His heavenly host,
>   The praise on earth begun,
> Of Father, Son, and Holy Ghost,
>   The uncreated One!"

"Do you know that hymn, 'on the joys and blessings of the Sabbath,' which begins with—

> Dear is the hallowed morn to me?"

"No; whose is it?"

"It is said to be Allan Cunningham's, and I like it all tho better. I like hymns that come gushing from the heart of a man of original and uncultured genius in his devotional moments,—they are so fresh; and this one of Cunningham's is like the clear, tuneful rivulet of his native hills, that flows and sparkles with pure, joyful life,

> Adown by the greenwood side.

The author was a diligent, earnest man, whose life, from 1784 to 1842, was well filled, every nook, and corner, and chink of it. His work as the superintendent in Sir Francis Chantrey's studio would have been enough for any ordinary man; but, over and above all that, he has immortalized his name as the biographer of eminent British painters, sculptors, and architects, and has adorned his own memory with many a beautiful song. He has helped us to catch the spirit of the old Covenanters' love-songs and hill-side psalmody, and one enjoys his effusions the more entirely because he never prostituted his genius to the claims of vice. It cannot be said of him, as it is alleged of a more popular Scotch songster, that his unpublished songs have left a moral taint upon the social life of the neighbourhood in which they were circulated and sung. But let me sing to you his Sunday song, and then I must say good-bye. Try to sing with me:—

> Dear is the hallowed morn to me,
>   When village bells awake the day;
> And, by their sacred minstrelsy,
>   Call me from earthly cares away.
>
> And dear to me the winged hour,
>   Spent in Thy holy courts, O Lord!
> To feel devotion's soothing power,
>   And catch the manna of Thy Word.

And dear to me the loud Amen,
   Which echoes through the blest abode;
Which swells and sinks, and swells again,
   Dies on the walls, but lives to God.

And dear the rustic harmony,
   Sung with the pomp of village art;
That holy, heavenly melody,
   The music of a thankful heart.

In secret I have often prayed,
   And still the anxious tear would fall;
But, on Thy sacred altar laid,
   The fire descends, and dries them all.

Oft when the world, with iron hands,
   Has bound me in its six-days' chain,
This bursts them, like the strong man's bands,
   And lets my spirit loose again.

Then dear to me the Sabbath morn,
   The village bells, the shepherd's voice!
These oft have found my heart forlorn,
   And always bid that heart rejoice.

Go, man of pleasure, strike the lyre,
   Of broken Sabbaths sing the charms;
Ours be the prophet's car of fire,
   Which bears us to a Father's arms.

CHAPTER XV.

HYMNS BY THE WAY.

"Yea, they sing in the ways of the Lord."

How often has some sweet singer cheered his own way through the changes of life's journey with snatches of song! Some pretty peep, some quiet nook, or happy turn, or unfolding prospect, or storied way-mark, or remarkable adventure, or impressive event, has touched his soul, and awakened a tuneful tribute or suggested an immortal hymn. And in how many cases such hymns have helped to beguile the journey of other travellers, or furnished the means of lightening the steps of pilgrims of other days on their daily march. No hymnist was ever more open to wayside inspiration than Charles Wesley. His eye was always open to beauty and goodness. His ear was ever delicately alive to kindred harmonies, and his heart was never out of tune, never indisposed to entertain the tuneful thought that touched it. Hymns came welling up from his soul amidst the changes and activities of his evangelizing course, and the habit of wayside composition became so fixed, that in his last days, when he had gone beyond his "three score years and ten," and growing infirmity obliged him to perform his street journeys in London on a little pony, he always kept a supply of small cards in his pocket, and as he jogged along, he might be seen now and then jotting down a stanza; and then on arriving at City Road House, he was out of the saddle, and might be heard hurriedly calling for pen and ink that he might fix the results of his street inspirations. To him the saddle was the seat of ease and quiet, and had peculiar charms, as a place of poetic study. "Near Ripley," says he, with a spice of that sportive humour which is so often showing itself in his and in his brother's journals, "my horse threw and fell upon me. My companion thought I had broken my neck; but my leg only was bruised, my hand sprained, and my head stunned, which spoiled my making hymns till the next day." His journals afford many instructive illustrations of the manner in which his hymns were brought out of real life and passing circumstances. He goes to the Newcastle colliers with his message of salvation, and the fires amidst which he found them labouring awakened thoughts about divine flames, and brought from his kindling soul that stirring hymn—

> See how great a flame aspires,
>   Kindled by a spark of grace!
> Jesu's love the nations fires,
>   Sets the kingdoms on a blaze;
> To bring fire on earth He came;
>   Kindled in some hearts it is;
> Oh that all might catch the flame,
>   All partake the glorious bliss!

Touched, too, at the sight of needy and eager multitudes crowding around him to hear his proclamation of the Sinner's Friend, he utters his feelings in that outburst of beautiful song—

> Who are these that come from far,
>   Swifter than a flying cloud?
> Thick as flocking doves they are,
>   Eager in pursuit of God:
> Trembling as the storm draws nigh,
>   Hastening to the place of rest,
> See them to the windows fly,
>   To the ark of Jesu's breast!
>
> Who are these, but sinners poor,
>   Conscious of their lost estate;
> Sin-sick souls who for their cure
>   On the good Physician wait;
> Fallen, who bewail their fall,
>   Proffer'd mercy who embrace,
> Listening to the gospel call
>   Longing to be saved by grace?
>
> For his mate the turtle moans,
>   For his God the sinner sighs;
> Hark, the music of their groans,
>   Humble groans that pierce the skies!

> Surely God their sorrow hears,
>   Every accent, every look,
> Treasures up their gracious tears,
>   Notes their sufferings in His book.
>
> He who hath their cure begun,
>   Will He now despise their pain?
> Can He leave His work undone,
>   Bring them to the birth in vain?
> No; we all who seek shall find,
>   We who ask shall all receive,
> Be to Christ in spirit join'd,
>   Free from sin for ever live.

At another time he is found at Portland. He is on a missionary tour; like his brother John, going first to those who wanted him most. The uncultured and uncared for quarrymen, and their households, had drawn his zealous steps towards their rude and isolated scenes of life. Those to whom every passing glance at St. Paul's Cathedral yields fresh pleasure would think it worth while to visit Portland, as the source from which Wren drew his materials for giving reality to the conceptions of his genius. And all who love to listen to the "testimony of the rocks" would be drawn to Portland by the mysterious voices from the buried forests of its wonderful "dirt bed." But Charles Wesley, though free from sympathy with those who, like one of his preaching followers, "never go a step out of their way to see a curiosity or a wonder," yet kept his main object before him—the salvation of his perishing countrymen. On June 4th, 1746, we find him about nine o'clock at night, after a wearisome journey, arriving at William Nelson's quaint-looking old stone-house in the village of Fortune's Well. There, on the following Friday, he says, in true Wesley style, "I preached to a houseful of staring, loving people, from Jer. i. 20. Some wept, but most looked quite unawakened. At noon and night I preached on a hill in the midst of the island. Most of the inhabitants came to hear, but few as yet feel the burden of sin, or the want of a Saviour."

"Sunday, June 8th.—After evening service we had all the islanders that were able to come. I asked, 'Is it nothing to you, all ye that pass by?' About half a dozen answered, 'It is nothing to us,' by turning their backs, but the rest hearkened with greater signs of emotion than I had before observed. I found faith that our labour would not be in vain.

"Monday, June 9th.—At Southwell, the farthest village, I expounded the Song of Simeon. Some very old men attended. I distributed a few books among them, rode round 'the island, and returned by noon to preach on the hill, and by night at my lodgings. Now the power and blessing came. My mouth and their hearts were opened. The rocks were broken in pieces, and melted into tears on every side." And now the inspiration came on the hymnist as well as the preacher; and with the sound of the Portland hammers in his ears, and the sight of broken hearts before him, he cries—

>Come, O Thou all victorious Lord,
> Thy power to us make known:
>Strike with the hammer of Thy Word,
> And break these hearts of stone!
>
>Oh that we all might now begin
> Our foolishness to mourn;
>And turn at once from every sin,
> And to our Saviour turn!
>
>Give us ourselves and Thee to know,
> In this our gracious day;
>Repentance unto life bestow,
> And take our sins away.
>
>Conclude us first in unbelief,
> And freely then release;
>Fill every soul with sacred grief,
> And then with sacred peace.
>
>Impoverish, Lord, and then relieve,
> And then enrich the poor;
>The knowledge of our sickness give;
> The knowledge of our cure.
>
>That blessed sense of guilt impart,
> And then remove the load;
>Trouble, and wash the troubled heart
> In the atoning blood.
>
>Our desperate state through sin declare,
> And speak our sins forgiven;
>By perfect holiness prepare,
> And take us up to heaven.

The poetic pilgrim finds his way, by and by, into Cornwall, still in search of those who were most in want of truth; and here he finds himself in scenes and circumstances equally, and even more exciting, than all he had witnessed at Portland or in Newcastle. He found poets in Cornwall who could lustily sing their own verses, and serenade him under his window with

> Charles Wesley is come to town,
> To try to pull the churches down!

This, however, was a mistaken fancy on the part of the gifted mob; he was come not to pull down, but to gather and to build. Nor was he without success, as his journal testifies. A modern Romish tourist, who has gone over the line of Wesley's journey, says that "a curious spot in the parish of Gwennap may deserve a visit. An antiquary, stumbling upon it by chance, would be apt to fancy that he had lighted upon a Roman circus in a wonderful state of preservation. It is, however, a pit—so called—of modern formation, with circular seats of turf rising one above the other, precisely after the fashion of ancient amphitheatres, from the area of which the great apostle of Methodism used to preach to assembled thousands." Here Charles, as well as John, Wesley seems to have had the joy of seeing the fields "white unto the harvest." "On Sunday, August 10th, 1746," he tells us, "at Gwennap, nine or ten thousand, by computation, listened with all eagerness, while I commended them to God, and to the Word of His grace. For near two hours I was enabled to preach repentance towards God, and faith in Jesus Christ. I broke out again and again in prayer and exhortation. I believed not one word would return empty. Seventy years' sufferings were overpaid by one such opportunity. . . . . Never had we so large an effusion of the Spirit as in the society. . . . . I expressed the gratitude of my heart in the following thanksgiving:—

> All thanks be to God,
> Who scatters abroad,
> Throughout every place,
> By the least of His servants, His savour of grace.
> Who the victory gave,
> The praise let Him have,
> For the work He hath done:
> All honour and glory to Jesus alone.

  Our conquering Lord
  Hath prospered His Word,
  Hath made it prevail,
And mightily shaken the kingdom of hell.
  His arm He hath bared,
  And a people prepared
  His glory to show,
And witness the power of His passion below.

  He hath opened a door
  To the penitent poor,
  And rescued from sin,
And admitted the harlots and publicans in.
  They have heard the glad sound,
  They have liberty found
  Through the blood of the Lamb,
And plentiful pardon in Jesus' name.

  And shall we not sing
  Our Saviour and King?
  Thy witnesses, we
With rapture ascribe our salvation to Thee!
  Thou, Jesus, hast bless'd,
  And believers increased,
  Who thankfully own
We are freely forgiven through mercy alone.

  His Spirit revives
  His work in our lives,
  His wonders of grace,
So mightily wrought in the primitive days.
  Oh that all men might know
  His token below,
  Our Saviour confess,
And embrace the glad tidings of pardon and peace!

  Then Saviour of all,
  Effectually call
  The sinners that stray;
And, oh, let a nation be born in a day!
  Thy sign let them see,
  And flow unto Thee,
  For the oil and the wine,
For the blissful assurance of favour Divine.

  Our heathenish land,
  Beneath Thy command,
  In mercy receive;
And make us a pattern to all that believe:
  Then, then let it spread,
  Thy knowledge and dread,
  Till the earth is o'erflow'd,
And the universe filled with the glory of God."

He who could be thus jubilant over the work of the blessed Spirit upon the souls of sinful multitudes, was not, like some spiritual zealots, blind and heartless towards the beauties and grandeurs of the natural world. He must needs enjoy a visit to the "Land's End." And who would not? "Such a panorama of lonely grandeur as the Land's End affords to one fond of contemplating nature under her most sublime aspects, will not be readily forgotten," says a tasteful stranger, who once saw it; "a gentle green slope conducts the traveller to the edge of the cliff so designated. Here the scenery is at once of a sublime and awful character. From the rocks that guard the extremity of the promontory, he looks down perpendicularly upon a raging sea, the Atlantic Ocean bringing the full force of its mighty waves to bear against the iron-bound basement of the coast. All around are vast gigantic masses of granite, in every variety of grotesque form and situation; some hanging overhead, and seeming about to topple from their frail fastenings, and overwhelm the pigmy lords of creation in their fall. It would be difficult amidst this grand scenery not to recognise the striking handiwork of Divine foresight in the barrier which the wonderful cliffs of this tremendous coast oppose to the billows of the wide ocean, which perpetually thunder against their shores." Amidst these grandeurs Charles Wesley once stood; and there, it is said, feeling himself tremulous between the mysterious past and the boundless future, he gave utterance to the hymn which always impresses one with a sense of solemn awfulness—

> Thou God of glorious majesty,
> To Thee, against myself, to Thee,
>   A worm of earth I cry;
> A half-awakened child of man;
> An heir of endless bliss or pain;
>   A sinner born to die!
>
> Lo, on a narrow neck of land,
> 'Twixt two unbounded seas I stand,
>   Secure, insensible;
> A point of time, a moment's space,
> Removes me to that heavenly place,
>   Or shuts me up in hell.

The conception of this hymn rising from such a scene is

confessedly very fine; nor, perhaps, is the full sublimity of the hymn itself felt until one tries to sing it on that "awful neck of land." The tradition may be cherished. But Wesley himself says, "Tuesday, July, 29, 1753.—We rode to Zunning, and took up our lodgings at a hospitable farmer's. I walked with our brother Shepherd to the Land's End, and sang on the extremest point of the rocks—

> Come, Divine Immanuel, come,
> Take possession of Thy home;
> Now Thy mercy's wings expand,
> Stretch throughout the happy land.
>
> Carry on Thy victory,
> Spread Thy rule from sea to sea;
> Re-convert the ransomed race;
> Save us, save us, Lord, by grace.
>
> Take the purchase of Thy blood,
> Bring us to a pardoning God;
> Give us eyes to see our day,
> Hearts the glorious truth t' obey,
>
> Ears to hear the gospel sound,
> Grace doth more than sin abound;
> God appeased, and man forgiven,
> Peace on earth and joy in heaven.
>
> Oh that every soul might be
> Suddenly subdued to Thee!
> Oh that all in Thee might know
> Everlasting life below!
>
> Now Thy mercy's wings expand,
> Stretch throughout the happy land,
> Take possession of Thy home,
> Come, Divine Immanuel, come."

His thought seems to have turned on Isaiah's expression (chap. viii. 8), "And the stretching out of his wings shall fill the breadth of thy land, O Immanuel." At all events his heart was set upon his Saviour's glory, and his hopes upon the fulfilment of the promise, "He shall have dominion also from sea to sea." Everything he met with on his way must be turned to account in the pursuit of his great object. He could make the sublimities and beauties of nature pay tribute to his Divine Master; but he had tact and genius enough to turn the freaks and follies of men also into means of blessing and praise.

"Come here," said an old Cornishman, as he took the arm of a visitor in one of our south-western seaports, "come here and look at this house. This is the house in which I was born and reared; and here," he continued, leading his companion up a narrow passage, to an old-fashioned heavy door, with a ponderous iron knocker, "look at these pits and dents in the door, these were made once by the mob as they were trying to break in upon Mr. Wesley, who had taken refuge there. My father used to tell me the story, and put me to feel the marks in the door. Well, the people kept beating the door until they burst it open, and rushing in, they found that the dear little man was in a small room divided from the hall by a wooden partition. They were trying to force the door of the parlour, when up came some sailors from a ship-of-war; and as Jack is always ready for sport or mischief, they forced their way in, crying, 'Avast, boys!' and putting their shoulders to the door, in it went, and in they leaped. There was Mr. Wesley at the upper end of the room, calmly waiting the result. When the sailors got in, he quietly looked at them, and said, 'Who wants me?' They, quite as ready now to befriend the persecuted as they had been ignorantly to aid the persecutors, surrounded the Methodist, and violently clearing the way, and defying any one to touch him, they led him out in triumph, and conducted him to a boat as the safest mode of conveyance from the town."

"Well done, Jack Tars!" said the old Cornishman's companion; "well done! But I have a story about an adventure of Charles Wesley and some sailors, somewhere in these parts, I believe."

"Oh yes," was the reply; "my father knew all about that, too. Mr. C. Wesley had just begun a hymn in the open air, intending to preach to the gathering crowd, when some jolly fellows, 'half seas over,' as they say, came and struck up a favourite song. Between the hymn and their song it was but sorry music; but the preacher's ear was quick enough to catch the metre of their song, and to master their tune there and then. He challenged them to come again by and by, when he would be there, and sing a song to their tune. They came, and he gave out a new hymn made for the occasion; the new tune was started, and the merry tars very soon found themselves beaten, and giving up the contest, seemed to enjoy the hymn more than their old song. The hymn was this:—

> Listed into the cause of sin,
>   Why should a good be evil?
> Music, alas! too long has been
>   Prest to obey the devil.
> Drunken, or lewd, or light the lay,
>   Flowed to the soul's undoing;
> Widened and strewed with flowers the way
>   Down to eternal ruin.
>
> Who on the part of God will rise,
>   *Innocent sound* recover;
> Fly on the prey and take the prize,
>   Plunder the carnal lover;
> Strip him of every moving strain,
>   Every melting measure;
> Music in virtue's cause retain,
>   Rescue the holy pleasure?
>
> Come, let us try if Jesu's love
>   Will not as well inspire us;
> This is the theme of those above,
>   This upon earth shall fire us.
> Say, if your hearts are tuned to sing,
>   Is there a subject greater?
> Harmony all its strains may bring,
>   Jesu's name is sweeter.
>
> Jesus the soul of music is,
>   His is the noblest passion;
> Jesu's name is joy and peace,
>   Happiness and salvation.
> Jesu's name the dead can raise,
>   Show us our sins forgiven,
> Fill us with all the light of grace,
>   Carry us up to heaven.
>
> Who hath a right like us to sing—
>   Us whom His mercy raises?
> Merry our hearts, for Christ is King,
>   Cheerful are all our faces.
> Who of His love doth once partake,
>   He evermore rejoices;
> Melody in our hearts we make,
>   Melody with our voices.
>
> He that a sprinkled conscience hath,
>   He that in God is merry;
> Let him sing Psalms, the Spirit saith,
>   Joyful and never weary.

> Offer the sacrifice of praise,
>   Hearty and never ceasing;
> Spiritual songs and anthems raise,
>   Honour, and thanks, and blessing.
>
> Then let us in His praises join,
>   Triumph in His salvation;
> Glory ascribe to love Divine,
>   Worship and adoration.
>
> Heaven already is begun,
>   Opened in each believer;
> Only believe, and still go on,
>   Heaven is ours for ever!

"That's the hymn," said the old Cornishman, "and the tune was 'Nancy Dawson;' and a cheery thing it was to hear my father sing it, just as the old folks, he said, used to sing it. Yes, and I used to sing it with him, and love to sing it now, though he is gone, and my voice is not what it used to be. He and I shall join again, by and by, and then we shall sing as we never could sing in this world—

> Heaven is ours for ever!"

It has occurred to some, that one of Charles Wesley's most glorious hymns may have sprung into life under the influence of circumstances distinctive of some remarkable point on his personal way through life. That being supposed, the hymn may be classed with hymns by the way. The hymn in question is the one of which Watts, with great nobility of spirit, said, "That single poem, 'Wrestling Jacob,' is worth all the verses which I have ever written."

"I used often to read that hymn to my family," said a man whose face showed deep lines of sorrow overlying a calm expression of peacefulness, "and often have I called their attention to its wonderful combination of majesty and tenderness, beauty and power, rich music, deep feeling, graphic life, and lofty devotion. But when I used to read it to myself, I felt as if there were something in it as an expression of Christian experience which I could not make my own. Not that I ever adopted the opinion of a critic who thinks that it is a fault in a hymn to be 'in a too elevated strain of Christian experience;' no, Christians are prone enough to grovel. They often need elevated strains to keep them to the height of their calling. But I seemed to lack the power of singing that hymn with a full relish of its meaning and spirit. Were any peculiar circumstances needed to put me in a condition to adopt it as the felt utterance of my own heart? I prayed that I might understand its full power. Little, however, did I think that my prayer would be answered as it was. I was called to a journey with my household. On the way the hand of the Lord arrested us. The shadow of that hand grew dark, and yet darker. One child I watched as he passed from among us. Another was soon gone; and yet another. Then, last of all, the mother, the wife of my youth, and the light of my home! I was left alone in desolation! What a night was that! I wandered out into the darkness, and, friendless in my woe, paced the margin of a stream. I thought of Jacob, alone with God. Verily I had seen all that was dear to me on earth pass over the brook before me. Was I kept behind to meet with Jacob's God? I raised my eyes upward in silent prayer, and then it seemed as if my soul were seized with the spirit of agonizing prayer. A sense of the Divine power was upon me; and as I tried to fasten my soul upon the truth and love of God, now my only helper, it appeared as if some holy prompter were rehearsing my favourite hymn within me. My spirit seemed to pass through all the deep processes which that hymn records; and now it came gushing from an understanding heart :—

> Come, O Thou Traveller unknown,
>   Whom still I hold, but cannot see,
> My company before is gone,
>   And I am left alone with Thee;
> With Thee all night I mean to stay,
> And wrestle till the break of day.
>
> I need not tell Thee who I am,
>   My misery or sin declare;
> Thyself hast called me by my name;
>   Look on Thy hands, and read it there!
> But who, I ask Thee, who art Thou?
> Tell me Thy name, and tell me now.
>
> In vain Thou strugglest to get free,
>   I never will unloose my hold;
> Art Thou the Man that died for me?
>   The secret of Thy love unfold.
> Wrestling I will not let Thee go,
> Till I Thy name, Thy nature know.

Wilt Thou not yet to me reveal
  Thy new, unutterable name?
Tell me. I still beseech Thee, tell:
  To know it now resolved I am:
Wrestling I will not let Thee go,
Till I Thy name, Thy nature know.

'Tis all in vain to hold Thy tongue,
  Or touch the hollow of my thigh;
Though every sinew be unstrung,
  Out of my arms Thou shalt not fly:
Wrestling I will not let Thee go,
Till I Thy name, Thy nature know.

What though my shrinking flesh complain,
  And murmur to contend so long?
I rise superior to my pain;
  When I am weak then I am strong:
And when my all of strength shall fail,
I shall with the God-Man prevail.

My strength is gone; my nature dies;
  I sink beneath Thy weighty hand,
Faint to revive, and fall to rise;
  I fall, and yet by faith I stand:
I stand, and will not let Thee go,
Till I Thy name, Thy nature know.

Yield to me now, for I am weak,
  But confident in self-despair;
Speak to my heart, in blessings speak,
  Be conquer'd by my instant prayer;
Speak, or Thou never hence shalt move,
And tell me if Thy name is Love?

'Tis Love! 'tis Love! Thou diedst for me!
  I hear Thy whisper in my heart!
The morning breaks, the shadows flee;
  Pure universal Love Thou art!
To me, to all Thy bowels move;
Thy nature and Thy name is Love!

My prayer hath power with God; the grace
  Unspeakable I now receive;
Through faith I see Thee face to face,
  I see Thee face to face, and live:
In vain I have not wept and strove;
Thy nature and Thy name is Love.

I know Thee, Saviour, who Thou art:
  Jesus, the feeble sinner's Friend!
Nor wilt Thou with the night depart,
  But stay, and love me to the end!
Thy mercies never shall remove,
Thy nature and Thy name is Love.

The Sun of Righteousness on me
  Hath rose with healing in His wings;
Wither'd my nature's strength, from Thee
  My soul its life and succour brings;
My help is all laid up above;
Thy nature and Thy name is Love.

Contented now, upon my thigh
  I halt till life's short journey end;
All helplessness, all weakness, I
  On Thee alone for strength depend;
Nor have I power from Thee to move;
Thy nature and Thy name is Love.

Lame as I am, I take the prey,
  Hell, earth, and sin with ease o'ercome;
I leap for joy, pursue my way,
  And as a bounding hart fly home!
Through all eternity to prove,
Thy nature and Thy name is Love."

The author of this hymn came to the end of his journey at last. His toils, and wrestlings, and hymnings by the way were over; but, true to his calling up to the latest step, even when his feet were "dipped in the brim of the Jordan," he gave forth, as his final hymn by the way, his parting song—

In age and feebleness extreme,
Who shall a sinful worm redeem?
Jesus, my only hope Thou art,
Strength of my failing flesh and heart;
Oh, could I catch one smile from Thee,
And drop into eternity!

His prayer was answered. He caught that smile, and now it may be said of him, that the principles and feelings with which he began his course as a hymnist were his principles and feelings up to the end; they were holy and pure. "From the first day until the day of Christ" dawned on him, he had been "steadfast, unmovable, always abounding in the work of the Lord." This is more than can be recorded of some whose hymns still give pleasure to every Christian who knows and sings them. There is a touching and instructive tradition about one in particular, showing that hymns once given out from a simple loving Christian heart may serve to beguile the journey of many a pious wayfarer, while they now and then, in after days, spring up in the path of their authors to reprove them for denying and forsaking that Saviour of whom and to whom they once so sweetly sang. It used to be more easy to beguile the way with chat in the old coaching days than it is now amidst the hurry, rattle, and screech of our iron roads. It was more possible then to get an occasional bit of agreeable reading too, and, among inside passengers especially, there was, at times, a sort of Old English freedom in the mutual enjoyment of a book. It is said that one day, on one of the well-known roads, a lady had been for some time engaged over one page of a little book, which, in the course of the journey, she had occasionally consulted. Turning, at length, to her companion in travel, a gentleman from whose appearance she gathered that an appeal on such a question would not be disagreeable, she held the open page towards him, and said, "May I ask your attention to this hymn, and ask you to favour me with your opinion of it? Do you know it?" It was—

> Come, Thou Fount of every blessing,
> Tune my heart to sing Thy grace:
> Streams of mercy, never ceasing,
> Call for songs of loudest praise.
> Teach me some celestial measure,
> Sung by ransomed hosts above;
> Oh, the vast, the boundless treasure
> Of my Lord's unchanging love!
>
> Here I raise my Ebenezer;
> Hither, by Thy help I'm come;
> And I hope, by Thy good pleasure,
> Safely to arrive at home.
> Jesus sought me when a stranger,
> Wandering from the fold of God;
> He, to save my soul from danger,
> Interposed His precious blood.
>
> Oh! to grace how great a debtor,
> Daily I'm constrained to be;
> Let that grace, Lord, like a fetter,
> Bind my wandering soul to Thee.
> Prone to wander; Lord, I feel it;
> Prone to leave the God I love;
> Here's my heart, Lord, take and seal it,
> Seal it from Thy courts above.

Her companion glanced down the page, and made an

attempt to excuse himself from conversation on the merits of the hymn; but the lady ventured on another appeal.

"That hymn has given me so much pleasure," she said; "its sentiments so touch me; indeed, I cannot tell you how much good it has done me. Don't you think it very good?"

"Madam!" said the stranger, bursting into tears, "I am the poor unhappy man who wrote that hymn many years ago, and I would give a thousand worlds, if I had them, to enjoy the feelings I then had."

Poor Robinson! it was he, the victim of eccentricity, love of change, and self-conceit; it was he of whom Robert Hall said, "He had a musical voice, and was master of all its intonations; he had wonderful self-passion, and could say *what* he pleased, *when* he pleased, and *how* he pleased." Like many other men of popular and versatile talents, however, he ran a zigzag course. Now, one of Whitefield's converts, and a student at "the Tabernacle" as a Calvinistic Methodist; now, an Independent minister; now, a Baptist, translating Saurin's sermons, dealing in coals and corn, writing a history of baptism, in which all the jumbled powers and oddities of his character seem to be reflected; and, at last, a Socinian, groping his way downward into the cheerless gloom, to realize the awful meaning of an inspired utterance, "He that despised Moses' law died without mercy under two or three witnesses: of how much sorer punishment, suppose ye, shall he be thought worthy who hath trodden under foot the Son of God, and hath counted the blood of the covenant, wherewith he was sanctified, an unholy thing, and hath done despite unto the Spirit of grace?"

CHAPTER XVI.

HYMNS ON THE WATERS.

"Hast thou heard of a shell on the margin of ocean,
    Whose pearly recesses the echoes still keep,
Of the music it caught when, with tremulous motion,
    It joined in the concert poured forth by the deep?

"And fables have told us when far inland carried,
    To the waste sandy desert and dark ivied cave,
In its musical chambers some murmurs have tarried,
    It learnt long before of the wind and the wave."

JUST at the opening of the seventeenth century, a clergyman in Hull was stepping into a boat with a young couple, whom he was going to marry in Lincolnshire. The weather was calm, and there was the promise of a bright voyage to the scene of the wedding; but a mysterious sense of coming danger pressed upon the good parson's heart, and throwing his cane on shore as the boat went off, he cried, "Ho, for heaven!" The shout was prophetic; neither he, nor bridegroom, nor bride returned. They never reached the altar. They sank together. It was indeed, "Ho, for heaven!" The son of that prophetic pastor lived to give us one of the best boat songs that ever floated over the waters, or charmed a pilgrim on the ocean. This was Andrew Marvel, the friend of Milton, and his associate as private secretary to Cromwell. A man who was faithful to his principles, and held his integrity though tempted in the hour of need by offers of a royal bribe; one whose ability and honourable bearing secured his election as Member of Parliament for his native city; and whose genius, talent, honour, and wit were always engaged for goodness and truth against corruption, falsehood, and wrong. Did you ever read his whimsical reflections on Holland? They prove that Dutchmen were not his favourites. Their politics were not his. And his lines serve, too, to show the power which he could wield as a satirist :—

> Holland, that scarce deserves the name of land,
> As but th' offscouring of the British sand;
> And so much earth as was contributed
> By English pilots when they heave the lead,
> Or what by th' ocean's slow alluvion fell
> Of shipwreck'd cockle and the mussel shell—
> This undigested vomit of the sea
> Fell to the Dutch by just propriety.

This is enough as evidence that his memory justly inherits the distinction of great humour and satirical genius. But he was a good man. Nor was he, as a poet, less capable of tenderness and reverent beauty, when they were called for, than for logical and acute philippic. Of course, he would deeply sympathize with the emigrants who in his day fled their country to avoid the oppression to which they were subject for their religious and ecclesiastical principles; and for those of them who found their way to the Bermudas he wrote a hymn which lives to give pleasure to the devout taste of every following generation :—

> Where the remote Bermudas ride
> In ocean's bosom unespied,
> From a small boat that row'd along,
> The listening winds received their song.
>
> "What should we do but sing His praise
> That led us through the watery maze,
> Unto an isle so long unknown,
> And yet far kinder than our own!
>
> "Where He the huge sea-monsters racks,
> That lift the deep upon their backs;
> He lands us on a grassy stage,
> Safe from the storm's and tyrant's rage.
>
> "He gave us this eternal spring
> Which here enamels everything,
> And sends the fowls to us in care,
> On daily visits through the air.
>
> "He hangs in shades the orange bright,
> Like golden lamps in a green night,
> And in these rocks for us did frame,
> A temple where to sound His name.

> "Oh! let our voice His praise exalt
> Till it arrive at heaven's vault,
> Which then perhaps rebounding may
> Echo beyond the Mexique bay."
>
> Thus sang they in the English boat
> A holy and a cheerful note,
> And all the way to guide their chime,
> With falling oars they kept the time.

None but a kind heart, and a good one, too, would provide hymns like this for those who toil at the oar, and it is a happy thing for human life that such kind hearts do not fail. One follows another, as men need songs on the waters. Marvel sang for emigrant boatmen on the island shores of the west; Wordsworth has furnished us with hymn music from the boatmen on the Neckar. Those who have wandered on the Rhine, and have allowed themselves to be drawn aside by the charms which surround some of its tributaries, will remember the beauties that cluster about Heidelberg, and allow many of its river scenes to enrich the imagery of their dreams in after-life. It would not be difficult to picture one wanderer there; a wanderer in whose witching company many of us have sauntered on an "Excursion" among the highlands of Scotland, the English Lakes, and on the banks of the Wye and the Wharfe; a Cumberland man, tall, though scarcely of dignified carriage; evidently used to travel, notwithstanding his "narrowness and drop about the shoulders"; with a face, however, telling of deep thoughts and beautiful daydreams, and eyes that seemed like windows opening into some pure spiritual world, and emitting "the light that never was on land or sea." Who would not know William Wordsworth? and who would not enjoy to watch him, on the river bank or near the rapids, catching the spirit of the boatmen's chant, and helping us to sympathize with them in danger, and to join them in their hymn?—

> Jesu! bless our slender boat,
>   By the current swept along;
> Loud its threatenings—let them not
>   Drown the music of a song
> Breathed Thy mercy to implore,
> Where these troubled waters roar.
>
> Saviour, for our warning, seen
>   Bleeding on that precious rood;

If while through the meadows green
   Gently wound the peaceful flood,
We forgot Thee, do not Thou
Disregard Thy suppliants now!

Hither, like yon ancient tower
   Watching o'er the river's bed,
Fling the shadow of Thy power,
   Else we sleep among the dead;
Thou who trod'st the billowy sea,
Shield us in our jeopardy.

Guide our bark among the waves;
   Through the rocks our passage smooth;
Where the whirlpool frets and raves,
   Let Thy love its anger soothe;
All our hope is placed in Thee;
Miserere Domine!

No one can think of Wordsworth and the English lakes without having Coleridge and Southey before him. Nor could he fail to see that plain-looking house a little way out of Keswick, standing on a gentle eminence over the river Greta, near the old bridge. Greta Hall would be interesting to all who love songs on the waters; for there it was that Caroline Bowles appeared as Mrs. Southey a few years before the poet's death; and there she ministered to the paralysed man who had so widely influenced the literature of his times; and there, like his guardian spirit, she watched and soothed him through the dimness and depression of his closing hours. She would be thought of with deep respect as the second wife of Southey, but she has for ever established her claim on our admiration and esteem by such touching appeals to our best feelings as we have in her Mariner's Hymn:—

      Launch thy bark, mariner!
         Christian, God speed thee!
      Let loose the rudder-bands—
         Good angels lead thee!
      Set thy sails warily,
         Tempests will come;
      Steer thy course steadily;
         Christian, steer home!

      Look to the weather bow,
         Breakers are round thee;
      Let fall the plummet now,
         Shallows may ground thee.

Reef in the foresail, there!
　Hold the helm fast!
So—let the vessel wear—
　There swept the blast.

"What of the night, watchman?
　What of the night?"
"Cloudy—all quiet—
　No land yet—all's right."
Be wakeful, be vigilant—
　Danger may be
At an hour when all seemeth
　Securest to thee.

How! gains the leak so fast?
　Clean out the hold—
Hoist up thy merchandise,
　Heave out thy gold;
There—let the ingots go—
　Now the ship rights;
Hurra! the harbour's near—
　Lo! the red lights!

Slacken not sail yet
　At inlet or island;
Straight for the beacon steer,
　Straight for the high land;
Crowd all thy canvas on,
　Cut through the foam—
Christian, cast anchor now—
　Heaven is thy home!

Hymns on the waters come with their richer and deeper music to the heart when they are sung to us by gifted spirits, who have themselves gone "down to the sea in ships, to do business in great waters, to see the works of the Lord and His wonders in the deep;" or who, on missions of mercy, have been "in the deep," "in perils of waters, and in perils in the sea." Among these Charles Wesley is a remarkable example, combining as he does, in his ocean songs, the recollections of an experienced observer, fine poetic power, a jubilant faith, and devout feeling. There is a record in the journal which he kept on his voyage back from America, in 1736, which helps to open the secret of his success in his hymns for mariners: "Thursday, Oct. 28th," says he, "the captain warned me of a storm approaching. In the evening, at eight, it came, and rose higher and higher. Often I thought it must have come to its strength, for I did not lose a moment of it, being obliged by bodily suffering to rise frequently. At last the long-wished-for morning came, but brought no abatement of the storm. There was so prodigious a sea, that it quickly washed away our sheep, and half our hogs, and drowned most of our fowls. The ship had been new caulked at Boston, how carefully it now appeared; for, being deeply laden, the sea streamed in at all sides so plentifully, that it was so much as four men could do, by continual pumping, to keep her above water. I rose and lay down by turns, I it could remain in no posture long; strove vehemently to pray, but in vain; persisted in striving, yet still without effect. I prayed for power to pray, for faith in Jesus Christ, continually repeating His name, till I felt the virtue of it at last, and knew that I abode under the shadow of the Almighty. It was now about three in the afternoon, and the storm at the height. I endeavoured to encourage poor Mr. Brig and Cutler, who were in the utmost agony of fear. I prayed with them and for them till four, at which time the ship made so much water, that the captain, finding it impossible otherwise to save her from sinking, cut down the mizen mast. In this dreadful moment, I bless God, I found the comfort of hope, and such joy in finding I could hope as the world can neither give nor take away. I had that conviction of the power of God present with me, overruling my strongest passion, fear, and raising me above what I am by nature, as surpassed all rational evidence, and gave me a taste of the Divine goodness. At the same time I found myself constrained in spirit to bear witness to the truth." With scenes like these pictured in his soul, who can wonder that his hallowed genius found expression in such hymns as this:—

> O Thou who didst prepare
> The ocean's caverned cell,
> And teach the gathering waters there
> To meet and dwell;
> Toss'd in our reeling bark
> Upon this briny sea,
> Thy wondrous ways, O Lord, we mark,
> And sing to Thee.
>
> That glorious hand of Thine
> Which fills the fount of day,

And gives the lunar orb to shine
　　With silv'ry ray,
Which hangeth forth on high
　　The clustering dews of night,
Can point beneath a beamless sky
　　Our course aright.

Borne on the dark'ning wave,
　　In measured sweep we go,
Nor dread th' unfathomable grave
　　Which yawns below;
For He is nigh who trod
　　Amid the foaming spray,
Whose billows own'd th' Incarnate God,
　　And died away.

How terrible art Thou
　　In all Thy wonders shown;
Though veiled in Thine eternal brow,
　　Thy steps unknown!
Invisible to sight,
　　But oh! to faith how near;
Beneath the gloomiest cloud of night
　　Thou beamest here.

To peaceful rest we go,
　　And close our tranquil eyes;
Though deep beneath the waters flow,
　　And circling rise.
Though swells the flowing tide,
　　And threatens far above,
We know in Whom our souls confide
　　With fearless love.

Snatch'd from a darker deep,
　　And waves of wilder foam,
Thou, Lord, our trusting souls wilt keep.
　　And waft them home—
Home, where no storm can sound,
　　Nor angry waters roar,
Nor troublous billows heave around
　　That peaceful shore.

The journal continues, "Towards morning, the sea heard and obeyed the Divine voice, 'Peace, be still!' The calm day that now broke on the weather-beaten men was Sunday; and," says the hymnist, "my first business to-day—may it be the business of all my days!—was to offer up the sacrifice of praise and thanksgiving. Then we all joined in thanks for our deliverance." And how he could render thanks for such deliverances we know from the echo of his song. It is repeated to this day.

All praise to the Lord,
Who rules with a word
Th' untractable sea,
And limits its rage by His steadfast decree;
Whose providence binds
Or releases the winds,
And compels them again,
At His beck to put on the invisible chain.

Oh that all men would raise
A tribute of praise,
His goodness declare,
And thankful confess His fatherly care!
With joy we embrace
This pledge of His grace,
And wait to outfly
These storms of affliction, and land in the sky

It is natural that one who had known the mingled pleasures, discomforts, and dangers of a sea voyage, should look with kind sympathy on those who are just embarking; and, where a kind heart and ready muse are agreed, that sympathy would prompt a tuneful prayer for the use of all who look for God's blessing when "going on shipboard." Charles Wesley, always in tune for such service, has cheered tremulous hearts on many a deck with his hymn—

Lord, whom winds and waves obey,
Guide us through the watery way;
In the hollow of Thy hand,
Hide and bring us safe to land.

Jesus, let our faithful mind
Rest, on Thee alone reclined;
Every anxious thought repress,
Keep our souls in perfect peace.

Keep the souls whom now we leave,
Bid them to each other cleave;
Bid them walk on life's rough sea;
Bid them come by faith to Thee.

Save, till all these tempests end,
All who on Thy love depend;
Waft our happy spirits o'er;
Land us on the heavenly shore.

About a hundred and twenty years ago, on a low sandy island, almost covered with palm trees, a few leagues south-east from Sierra Leone, on the western coast of

Africa, a wretched-looking young Englishman might be seen toiling in a plantation of lemon trees. He was barely covered with an old trousers and shirt, a yard or two of cotton wrapped about his shoulders, and an old handkerchief around his head. There he worked, without shelter from the sun, or the gales and torrents of the rainy season, half-starved, craving unwholesome roots to allay his hunger. Like another prodigal, "no man gave unto him"—no, nor woman either. Slaves shunned him; and the only woman who noticed him was a sinful black tyrant, who, in vicious association with his master, sported with his miseries, and answered his appeals for mercy by aggravating his woe. He had brought himself into this condition by his reckless profligacy. He was but twenty; but his few years had been filled to overflowing with ungodliness in its most blasphemous forms. Born of a pious mother, his childhood hallowed by her instruction, and blessed in youth with fair prospects, he nevertheless took to the sea in early life in a manner which disappointed his friends; cut himself off from one good after another; was pressed into the naval service, degraded from his first honours; passed into the African trade on the slave coast; was now a castaway, and had become all but the hopeless slave of a man who engaged him in the meanest drudgery of his meanest traffic. This woe-begone prodigal was John Newton, afterwards known as the reverend rector of St. Woolnoth, London, the friend of Cowper, the compiler of the "Olney Hymns," and the hymnist whose songs have so often quickened failing hearts into cheerful worship both on land and at sea. His adventures on sea and land may be called romantic. On escaping from his degradation on the African coast, he was still a rover, but at last on a homeward voyage, Divine mercy arrested him. A terrible storm fell on them. Death raged around the sinking ship; and then it was, as he says, "I began to pray. . . . . I could not utter the prayer of faith; I could not draw near to a reconciled God, and call Him Father. My prayer was like the cry of the ravens, which yet the Lord does not disdain to hear." The Lord heard his cry. The storm was hushed; but then came on the horrible thought of slow death upon the deep from the failure of provisions, and the lack of means to hasten the shattered vessel toward the land. "I had a New Testament," he tells us, "I was struck with several passages, but particularly the 'Prodigal,' a case, I thought, that had never been so nearly exemplified as by myself; and then, the goodness of the father in receiving, say, in running to meet such a son, and this intended to illustrate the Lord's goodness to returning sinners. This gained upon me. I continued much in prayer; I saw that the Lord had interposed *so far* to save me, and I hoped he would do more. The outward circumstances helped in this place to make me still more serious and earnest in crying to Him who alone could relieve. I saw that, by the way pointed out in the gospel, God might declare, not His mercy only, but His justice also, in the pardon of sin on the account of the obedience and sufferings of Jesus Christ. . . . Thus, to all appearance, I was a new man." In this return to his heavenly Father, amidst the terrors of an ocean storm there was, it may be, the first kindling of that hallowed genius which afterwards recorded the penitent mourner's feelings thus:—

> I hear the tempest's awful sound,
> I feel the vessel's quick rebound;
> And fear might now my bosom fill,
> But Jesus tells me, "Peace! Be still!"
>
> More and more loud the billows roar,
> Far distant is the friendly shore;
> But even storms obey H will,
> And He can tell them, "Peace! Be still!"
>
> In this dread hour I cling to Thee,
> My Saviour crucified for me.
> If that I perish be Thy will,
> In death, Lord, whisper, "Peace! Be still!"
>
> My soul, I charge thee not to fear:
> Jesus is nigh, my prayer to hear;
> His promise He can now fulfil,
> And to the waves say, "Peace! Be still!"
>
> Hark! He has listen'd while I prayed,
> Slowly the tempest's rage is stayed;
> The yielding waves obey His will,
> Jesus hath bid them, "Peace! Be still!"
>
> Lord, I adore Thy sovereign power!
> My Rescuer from danger's hour;
> Oh, when dark fears my bosom fill,
> Whisper me ever, "Peace! Be still!"

Newton returned to his native land a new man, not, as he modestly said, "to all appearance" merely, but truly so in heart and life. His circumstances improved as his Christian character brightened; and although his peculiar habits, contracted under uncommon circumstances, kept him in almost a secret enjoyment of inward religion for several years, his light could not be hid. His Christian life was not interrupted even by the associations around him in the slave trade, which, like many good men of his day, he continued to share in. While yet a lad, he had conceived a pure and warm affection for a young girl, the daughter of his departed mother's nearest friends; and that affection which, like a cord of heaven's weaving, kept his heart in gentle bondage all through his seven years of wild, uneasy departure from God, now drew him into a happy marriage with the woman who was still the choice of his soul. And now his peaceful life was spent between quiet scenes at home and voyaging and travelling abroad. While in the country at home, "Some hours every day," he writes, "I passed in retirement, when the weather was fair; sometimes in the thickest woods, sometimes on the highest hills, where almost every step varied the prospect. There it was my custom for many years to perform my devotions. These rural scenes have a tendency both to refresh and compose my spirits. A beautiful diversified prospect gladdens my heart. I consider myself as in the great temple which 'the Lord has built for His own honour." He was now in easy circumstances; and what a change! What a hush was come upon him! and how the world even had altered its aspect towards him! "I remember," says he, "that on some of those mournful days which I spent on that African island, I was busied in planting lemon trees. The plants I put into the ground were no larger than a young gooseberry bush; my master and his black mistress, passing by my place, stopped awhile to look at me; at last, 'Who knows,' says he, 'who knows but by the time these trees grow up and bear, you may go home to England, obtain the command of a ship, and return to reap the fruit of your labours? we see strange things sometimes happen.' This, as he intended it, was a cutting sarcasm. I believe he thought it full as probable that I should live to be the king of Poland. Yet it proved a prediction, and they (one of them at least) lived to see me return from England, in the capacity he had mentioned, and pluck some of the first limes from those very trees." Yes, his life was a life of wondrous change and romantic interest. His course of life as a sea-captain was equally remarkable with his adventures as a young outcast. On his voyages, he rubbed up his Latin, until his classic reading was respectable. He mastered the Greek of the New Testament and the Septuagint, so far as to enjoy the sacred text. He learnt to read the Hebrew Pentateuch and Psalms without the aid of a lexicon; did something in Syriac; gained French enough to transact business in foreign parts, and read much of the best English divinity. What an interest gathers round the seafaring student! "To be at sea," he remarks, "withdrawn out of the reach of innumerable temptations, with opportunity and a turn of mind disposed to observe the wonders of God in the great deep, with the two noblest objects of sight, the expanded *heaven* and the expanded *ocean*, continually in view; and when evident interpositions of Divine Providence, in answer to prayer, occur almost every day;—these are helps to quicken and confirm the life of faith, which in a good measure supply to a religious sailor the want of those advantages which can be enjoyed only upon the shore. I never knew sweeter or more frequent hours of divine communion than in my last two voyages to Guinea, when I was either almost secluded from society on shipboard, or when on shore amongst the natives. I have wandered through the woods, reflecting on the singular goodness of the Lord to me, in a place where perhaps there was not a person that knew Him for some thousand miles around me. Many a time, upon these occasions, I have restored the beautiful lines of Propertius to their right owner; lines full of blasphemy and madness when addressed to a creature, but full of comfort and propriety in the mouth of a believer :—

Sic ego desertis passim bene vivere sylvis, etc., etc.

paraphrased—

In desert woods with Thee, my God,
Where human footsteps never trod,
How happy could I be :

> Thou my repose from care, my light
> Amidst the darkness of the night,
>   In solitude my company."

How instructive is it to watch this future pastor and hymnist through the processes of his preparation for the usefulness of his life's eventide. How the beauty of some of his hymns brightens, and how much more deeply they touch us, when they are read and sung with the scenes in which he learnt to sing vividly before us. Who can follow the studious, prayerful, and poetic sea-captain over the waters of his changeful life without having a richer relish for that sea-going hymn of his on Paul's voyage?—

> If Paul in Cæsar's court must stand,
>   He need not fear the sea;
> Secured from harm on every hand
>   By the Divine decree.
>
> Although the ship in which he sailed
>   By dreadful storms was tossed;
> The promise over all prevailed,
>   And not a life was lost.
>
> Jesus, the God whom Paul adored,
>   Who saves in time of need,
> Was then confessed by all on board,
>   A present help indeed.
>
> Though neither sun nor stars were seen,
>   Paul knew the Lord was near;
> And faith preserved his soul serene,
>   When others shook for fear.
>
> Believers thus are tossed about
>   On life's tempestuous main;
> But grace assures beyond a doubt
>   They shall their port attain.
>
> They must, they shall, appear one day
>   Before their Saviour's throne;
> The storms they meet with by the way
>   But make His power known.
>
> Their passage lies across the brink
>   Of many a threatening wave;
> The world expects to see them sink,
>   But Jesus lives to save.
>
> Lord, though we are but feeble worms,
>   Yet since Thy word is passed,
> We'll venture through a thousand storms,
>   To see Thy face at last.

Others besides old sailors, however, can sometimes give us hymns on the waters. Quiet, home-keeping spirits, like Toplady or Kelly, when they have felt the breath of that Spirit who " moved upon the face of the waters," have given out utterances which have been caught "afar off upon the sea," and have fallen upon the tremulous half-engulphed soul with hushing and reviving power, akin to the voice " which stilleth the noise of the seas, the noise of the waves, and the tumult of the people." " I was once on my way to the Antipodes," said a voyager, who had gone around the world several times. " The vessel was a transport; and we had a large number of troops on board. So multitudinous a companionship was not exactly to my taste on the high seas; but one must make the best of circumstances; and, on the whole, my cabin life was as pleasant as could be in such a case. All went on very safely till one night, the horrors of which will live to play discords on my nerves as long as nerves are a part of my inheritance. I had got into my berth, and was fast asleep; when about the middle of the night, I was startled by a shock, and then alarmed by a strange hubbub of creaking timbers, shuffling feet, and hoarse voices, striving with the whistling roaring wind, and then, my senses were scarcely clear from sleep, when there came a thundering crash; down went the vessel on her beam-ends, and down came the rushing sea, all but filling the cabins, and at once putting out the lights. There was an awful hush for a moment, and then the first voice that broke it came from an officer who leaped out of an adjoining berth, with imprecations that made my blood run chill, and cried, 'This is like hell when the fire is put out!' One felt for an instant as if he were engulphed in hell itself, but just then some gentle spirit seemed to touch my tremulous heart; there came a sweet calm over my soul. I quietly lay in my berth, and felt as if voices from the better land were singing to me that beautiful hymn—

> Why those fears? Behold, 'tis Jesus
> Holds the helm and guides the ship;
> Spread the sails and catch the breezes,
> Sent to waft us through the deep,
> To the regions
> Where the mourners cease to weep.

> Led by Him, we brave the ocean;
> Led by Him, the storm defy;
> Calm amidst tumultuous motion,
> Knowing that our Lord is nigh.
> Waves obey Him,
> And the storms before Him fly.
>
> Safe in His most sure protection,
> We shall pass the watery waste;
> Trusting to His wise direction,
> We shall gain the port at last;
> And, with wonder,
> Think on toils and dangers past.
>
> Oh, what pleasures there await us!
> There the tempests cease to roar;
> There it is, that they who hate us
> Shall molest our peace no more:
> Trouble ceases
> On that tranquil, happy shore!

We lived to outride the storm, but as long as I live I shall feel that the experience of that night for ever hallowed to me the memory of Thomas Kelly. His long life (from 1769 to 1855, began and ended in Dublin) was not spent in vain, if that hymn alone had been all its fruit. One thinks with pleasure of his sixty years of Christian usefulness; but, oh, that hymn! on that night! Blessings on his name!" As a hymnist, verily, Kelly's ever-living influence will illustrate his own happy saying. Lord Plunket, an old school-fellow of his, met him one day in later life, and said, "You will live to a great age, Mr. Kelly!" "Yes," was his reply, "I am confident I shall, as I expect never to die!"

The circumstances under which Kelly's charming verses came with such soothing music to the voyager amidst the horrors of the midnight squall, naturally send the thoughts to a scene in "the last days of Bishop Heber." Archdeacon Robinson states that, when sailing to Madras, they had a detachment of invalid troops on board. The good bishop's heart was engaged in their behalf, and he claimed the privilege of acting as their pastor. "I have too little in my situation," he said, "of those pastoral duties, which are as useful to the minister as to his people; and I am delighted at the opportunity thus unexpectedly afforded me." And so, with his Prayer-book in his hand, he went below from time to time, to minister to the sufferers. Nor was it in vain;

their hearts were touched. "Only think," they said, "of such a great man as the bishop coming between decks to pray with such poor fellows as we are." One poor mother on board had lost her infant; the bishop committed the little one to the deep, and then visited the mourner in her cabin, and ministered consolation to her heart. "At intervals," says a witness, "I hear him weeping and praying for her in his own cabin. I have never seen such tenderness, never such humble exercise of Christian love. Alas! how his spirit shames us all! I thank God that I have seen his tears, that I heard his prayers, his conversation with the afflicted mother, and his own private reflections upon it. It has made me love him more, and has given me a lesson of tenderness, in visiting the afflicted, that I trust will not be in vain." Happy was it for the transport ship in which Heber had a berth. Not that even his gracious presence could secure her from squalls, but his loving zeal could minister life to the souls on board; and when squalls came, his sanctified genius could teach his companions in danger to chant the disciples' prayer, "Save, Lord, or we perish!"

When through the torn sail
  The wild tempest is streaming,
When o'er the dark wave
  The red lightning is gleaming,
Nor hope lends a ray
  The poor seaman to cherish,
We fly to our Maker—
  "Save, Lord! or we perish!"

O Jesus! once toss'd
  On the breast of the billow,
Aroused by the shriek
  Of despair from Thy pillow,
High now in Thy glory
  Still the mariner cherish,
Who cries, in his anguish,
  "Save, Lord! or we perish!"

And oh, when the storm
  Of wild passion is raging,
When sin in our hearts
  Its fierce warfare is waging,
Arise in Thy strength,
  Thy redeemed to cherish,
Rebuke the destroyer—
  "Save, Lord! or we perish!"

CHAPTER XVII.

SONGS OF THE MORNING.

"But I will sing of Thy power: yea, I will sing aloud of Thy mercy in the morning."

IT is pleasant to sit in the oriel window of an old grammar-school library, with the many-coloured light falling on the open folio as it lies on the ponderous reading-desk, and to hear, amidst one's musings, the music of the boys' voices as their morning hymn comes floating up along the gallery, gently touching the soul with its mellow harmony. How many a time since the fourteenth century, when William of Wykeham opened his Winchester School, has such morning music charmed the old college of that storied city. Bishop Mant used to think with pleasure of the morning hymn which the boys used to sing in that school in his days. It was the simple, beautiful, and devout old song, "*Jam lucis orto sidere,*" etc., and nothing could be more happily chosen as a morning song for the young scholars. Mant threw his whole soul into his translation of it:—

> Brightly shines the morning star:
>   Pray we God His grace to give,
> That from sin and danger far
>   We the coming day may live.
>
> That the tongue by Him withheld,
>   May from sounds of strife refrain;
> That the eye, from roving quelled,
>   Seek not sights corrupt or vain;
>
> That the heart, with pureness fraught,
>   May from folly turn aside;
> And the flesh, by temperance taught,
>   Calm its lusts and veil its pride.

> That, when the day shall close,
>   And the night successive bring,
> We, triumphant o'er our foes,
>   May our hymn of glory sing;
>
> Glory, Sire of all, to Thee;
>   And to Thee, co-equal Son,
> With the Spirit glory be;
>   One in Three, and Three in One.

Between one and two hundred years before Mant's time, that same hymn was sung in that same school, and among the rest of the voices then swelling the devout music there was Ken's; and how far the style, and manner, and spirit of that ancient hymn served to form that habit of tuneful expression which afterwards distinguished the good bishop, who can tell? Should we ever have had his inimitable morning hymn but for that early Winchester exercise? Probably, when in after-life he used to chant his own morning and evening hymns to the music of his lute, his soul was giving forth the echoes of the old melody which had so deeply touched his poetic soul while yet a boy. To think of morning songs is always to think of Bishop Ken, and, whether the morning be bright or dull, his hymn is always fresh:—

> Awake, my soul, and with the sun
> Thy daily stage of duty run;
> Shake off dull sloth, and joyful rise
> To pay thy morning sacrifice.
>
> Thy precious time misspent redeem;
> Each present day thy last esteem;
> Improve thy talent with due care;
> For the great day thyself prepare.
>
> In conversation be sincere;
> Keep conscience as the noontide clear;
> Think how all-seeing God thy ways
> And all thy secret thoughts surveys.
>
> By influence of the light divine,
> Let thy own light to others shine;
> Reflect all heav'n's propitious rays,
> In ardent love and cheerful praise.
>
> Wake and lift up thyself, my heart,
> And with the angels bear thy part,
> Who all night long unwearied sing
> High praise to the Eternal King.

Awake! awake! ye heavenly choir,
May your devotion me inspire,
That I, like you, my age may spend,
Like you, may on my God attend.

May I, like you, in God delight,
Have all day long my God in sight,
Perform like you my Maker's will!
Oh may I never more do ill!

Had I your wings, to heaven I'd fly;
But God shall that defect supply;
And my soul, wing'd with warm desire,
Shall all day long to heaven aspire.

All praise to Thee, who safe has kept,
And hast refreshed me while I slept!
Grant, Lord, when I from death shall wake,
I may of endless light partake!

I would not wake nor rise again,
Ev'n heaven itself I would disdain,
Wert Thou not there to be enjoy'd
And I in hymns to be employ'd.

Heav'n is, dear Lord, where'er Thou art;
Oh never then from me depart!
For, to my soul, 'tis hell to be
But for one moment void of Thee.

Lord, I my vows to Thee renew;
Disperse my sins as morning dew,
Guard my first springs of thought and will,
And with Thyself my spirit fill.

Direct, control, suggest, this day,
All I design, or do, or say;
That all my powers, with all their might,
In Thy sole glory may unite.

Praise God, from whom all blessings flow!
Praise Him, all creatures here below!
Praise Him above, ye heavenly host!
Praise Father, Son, and Holy Ghost.

The best of men are never entirely independent of circumstances. Our religious feelings and expressions often take their tone from the atmosphere about us, and especially from the present physical condition of the outer man. Thought flows freely, or lags in heaviness, just as the subtle influences around us quicken or oppress. And though no mere circumstances can entirely quench the fire of genius, or prevent the Christian poet from uttering his inspirations, yet his hymns and songs will often be sprightly or plaintive as outward changes pass over him, or as the condition of his physical life is shadowy or bright. Each morning seems to bring its own inspiration to every pious hymnist. The morning song should be sprightly; but sometimes even the morning has shadows which give a kind of holy melancholy to the tone of praise. The praise that should wing its way upward, now and then lingers in the form of plaintive reflection or humble appeal. So in one of Toplady's songs of the morning. Not far from a spot in his Devonshire parish, where Cluniac monks used to sing such morning songs as came from their brother, Bernard of Morlaix, and others, his kindred hymnists, Toplady learnt to wear his weak body down by nightly study, until his morning songs became rather sombre or languid at times, so that they touch our human sympathy, while they give a subdued tone of feeling to our worship. Nevertheless, that day is well begun which opens with a song from the author of "Rock of Ages." His "Hymn for the Morning" runs thus:—

> Jesus, by whose grace I live,
>   From the fear of evil kept,
> Thou hast lengthen'd my reprieve,
>   Held in being while I slept;
> With the day my heart renew;
> Let me wake Thy will to do.
>
> Since the last revolving dawn
>   Scattered the nocturnal cloud,
> Oh, how many souls have gone,
>   Unprepared to meet their God!
> Yet Thou dost prolong my breath,
> Hast not seal'd my eyes in death.
>
> Oh, that I may keep Thy word,
>   Taught by Thee to watch and pray
> To Thy service, dearest Lord,
>   Sanctify th' ensuing day;
> Swift its fleeting moments haste;
> Doom'd, perhaps, to be my last.
>
> Crucified to all below,
>   Earth shall never be my care:
> Wealth and honour I forego;
>   This my only wish and care,
> Thine in life and death to be,
> Now and to eternity.

There was another hymnist of Toplady's time, of a merrier constitution than he—more disposed to look at the bright side of things, and having somewhat broader and more pleasant sympathy with the human multitude. His religious notions would, perhaps, have a brighter influence on his character and utterances than those of Toplady; while one at least of his fixed principles, as a Christian minister, would give a more lively and agreeable effect to his ministrations both in prose and verse. While Toplady was spending his energies in fruitless controversy, his contemporary, not, perhaps, less learned, but more practical, was acting on his own advice given to a younger man, " Look simply unto Jesus for preaching food, and what is wanted will be given, and what is given will be blessed, whether it be barley or a wheaten loaf, a crust or a crumb. When your heart is right, meek, and simple, Jesus will make an orator of you; when you grow lofty and are pleased with your prattle, Jesus will make a fool of you. Your mouth will be a flowing stream, or a fountain sealed, according as your heart is. Avoid all controversy in preaching, talking, or writing; preach nothing down but the devil, and nothing up but Jesus Christ." A man of such views, such principles, and such diction, when gifted with poetic genius, and a faculty for writing hymns, would surely give out pleasant songs for the common people—songs always loved, too, by the cultured lover of pure Saxon, strong sense, playful fancy, pith, point, and tender feeling. Such songs sometimes come from the heart and life of the amusing and lovable man who has bequeathed to us a morning hymn. His mornings were always bright, it would seem, and his hymn shows how his cheerful sense of renewed vigour was in harmony with his reverent reliance on his God.

> Through Jesu's watchful care
>   I safely pass the night;
> His providential arm was near,
>   And kept off every fright.
>
> No pains upon my bed
>   Prevented my repose;
> But laying down my weary head,
>   Refresh'd with sleep I rose.
>
> And here I stand possest
>   Of strength and vigour new;

And with my limbs and senses blest,
  Another morn I view.

From Thee my mercies flow,
  In pearly drops they fall;
But give a thankful bosom too,
  The sweetest pearl of all.

Be Thou my guide to-day,
  My arm whereon to rest,
My sun to cheer me on the way,
  My shield to guard my breast.

From Satan's fiery dart,
  And men of purpose base,
And from the plague within my heart,
  Defend me by Thy grace.

There is an amusing story told of the author of this hymn. He was one of those clergymen of his day who sometimes turned out from their parishes as occasional itinerant preachers, going up and down proclaiming the gospel to the neglected masses. He had come, it is said, to a village in the North of England on a Saturday evening. He must needs stay there over the Sabbath. But always ready for work, he requested his host at the inn to go to the parson of the parish and state that a clergyman was stopping at his house who would be glad to assist the vicar at the service to-morrow. The vicar was cautious. "We must be careful," said he, "for you know there are many of these wandering Methodist preachers about. What sort of a man is he?" "Oh, it is all right, sir," was the reply; "just see his nose, sir, that will tell you he is no Methodist." "Well, ask him to call on me in the morning," said the parson, "and I shall judge for myself."

The call was made, and the waggish and somewhat rubicund nose was a sufficient introduction to the pulpit. The morning came. The congregation gathered. The vicar read prayers, and then the stranger mounted the pulpit. It must be all right, the vicar may have thought; for there seemed to be waggish thoughts playing around the corners of the preacher's mouth, and there was that remarkable peaked and kindling nose which threatened to provoke a laugh among his hearers. Nor would his first address belie his features. It seemed to be pleasant talk from the pulpit. The preacher is rather homely and blunt.

But everybody listens, for everybody thinks and feels that the parson is speaking to him. By and by, however, his home-thrusts at the conscience make his hearers somewhat uneasy; but ere they are prepared for defence, the sharp piercing sentences come in such rapid succession that both vicar and flock find themselves arrested as sinners before God—

> And fools, who came to scoff, remained to pray.
> The service past, around the pious man,
> With steady zeal, each honest rustic ran;
> E'en children follow'd with endearing wile,
> And pluck'd his gown, to share the good man's smile.

The "good man's smile" was always ready for those who sought it, and his loving, mirthful heart was always open to those who wanted to know more about his Divine Lord and Master. The gifted itinerant was no other than the humorous but holy and eminently useful John Berridge, vicar of Everton, in Bedfordshire. His racy letters, brimful of wit; his "Christian World Unmasked," with its union of drollery and seriousness; the floating traditions about his active and holy life; and the still accumulating fruits of his preaching;—all serve to keep alive and fresh the memory of this early Methodist clergyman; this eccentric but sanctified genius, who, with Wesley and others, worked in the pulpit, with his pen, at home and abroad for the religious renovation of his country. He wrote his hymns as he preached his sermons, for those who needed them most; and he never failed to engage the hearts as well as the taste and understanding of those to whom he preached, and for whom he wrote. What child of God who has learnt his "Labourer's Morning Hymn," will ever cease to love the name of the man who has helped him to sing of a morning :—

> I thank my Lord for kindly rest
>   Afforded in the night;
> Refresh'd and with new vigour blest,
>   I wake to view the light.
>
> What need I grieve to earn my bread,
>   When Jesus did the same?
> If in my Master's steps I tread,
>   No harm I get, or shame.

Oh let me bless with thankful mind,
   My Saviour's love and care,
That I am neither sick, nor blind,
   Nor lame as others are!

A trusty workman I would be,
   And well my task pursue;
Work when my master does not see,
   And work with vigour too.

And whilst I ply the busy foot,
   Or heave the labouring arm,
Do Thou my withering strength recruit,
   And guard me well from harm.

To sweeten labour let my Lord
   Look on, and cast a smile;
For Jesus can such looks afford,
   As well the hours beguile.

Berridge was ready for all work, and for work among all classes, for his Master's sake; but in all his works, and among all classes, he was the same honest, transparent, loving spirit, acting and speaking with the most earnest purity amidst all the sparkle and play of his humorous genius; always, and to all, expressing himself in the purest, clearest, most pithy, racy, and proverb-like style of his native tongue. Now, as in his "Christian World Unmasked," he says, "Gentle reader, lend me a chair, and I will sit down and talk a little with you. Give me leave to feel your pulse. Sick, indeed, sir, very sick, of a mortal disease, which infects your whole mass of blood. . . . , Let me step into your closet, sir, and peep upon its furniture. My hands are pretty honest, you may trust me; and nothing will be found, I fear, to tempt a man to be a thief. Well, to be sure, what a filthy place is here! never swept for certain since you were christened! and what a fat idol stands skulking in the corner!—a darling sin, I warrant it! How it simpers, and seems as pleasant as a right eye! Can you find a will to part with it, or strength to pluck it out? And supposing you a match for the self-denial, can you so command your heart as to hate the sin you do forsake? This is certainly required; truth is called for in the inward parts." At another time he is writing to his dear Rowly (young Rowland Hill), "When I began to itinerate, a multitude of dangers seemed ready to engulph me. My friends were up in arms, my college was provoked, my bishop incensed, the clergy on fire, and the church canons were pointing their ghastly mouths at me; my first diocesan told me that I should soon be either in Bedlam or in jail. But, through the good blessing of my God, I am yet in the possession of my senses, my tithes, and my liberty; and He who has hitherto delivered, I trust will yet deliver me from ecclesiastical fires, and the paw of worldly bears. I have suffered from nothing except from lapidations and pillory treats, which yet have proved more frightful than hurtful. If you are invited to go out, and feel yourself inclined to do so, take a lover's leap, neck or nothing, and commend yourself to Jesus. Ask no man's leave to preach Christ; that is unevangelical and shameful. Seek not much advice about it; that is dangerous. Such advice, I find, generally comes the wrong way—heels uppermost. Most preachers love a snug church and a whole skin, and what they love they will prescribe. If you are determined to be evangelically regular, that is, secularly irregular, then expect, wherever you go, a storm will follow you, which may fright you, but will bring no real harm. Make the Lord your whole trust, and all will be well." And then again, from such stirring correspondence with clerical friends, we find him turning to give lessons in psalmody to such as do not often catch the attention of educated poets—the domestic servant. He teaches her to sing, as she begins her morning work :—

> To Jesus, my dear Lord, I owe
>   The rest I had this night;
> By Him preserved from every woe,
>   I wake to view the light.
>
> Accept, O Lord, my early praise,
>   It is Thy tribute due;
> And let the morning song I raise,
>   Rise with affection too.
>
> My dear Redeemer, while on earth,
>   A servant was to all;
> With ready foot He steppèd forth,
>   Attentive to each call.
>
> If unto labour I am bred,
>   My Saviour was the same;
> Why then should I a service dread,
>   Or count it any shame?

> Yet, Lord, I need a patient mind,
>   And beg a ready will,
> To pay my master service kind,
>   And every task fulfil.
>
> No saucy language I would use,
>   Nor act a treacherous part,
> But serve him with the purest views,
>   And work with freest heart.

Many labourers and many servants thank thee for thy verses, happy, plain-spoken, kind "old Berridge," and we hope to see thy face some bright morning when the Sabbath sun rises never to set again! There is something about "old Berridge" which reminds one of George Wither—the sympathy with all classes, with human nature under all circumstances, the hearty readiness to employ the whole soul for the good of all, and the wonderful facility for adapting forms of hymnic expression to the taste and heart of those for whom their good feeling is engaged. Wither has his morning hymn, too; and it is one of his finest; less rugged, and more free from those quaint conceits and uncouth modes of expression which suited the ear of his times better than our own. It was his way, and a good way it was, freely to give a "reason" not merely for "the hope within" him, but for all the utterances of his thought and feeling which he put forth to the world. "Many dangers hang over us all the day," he says, "therefore, before we venture forth to follow our affairs, we might be more safe if we were first charmed by such invocations as these:—

> Since Thou hast added now, O God!
> Unto my life another day,
> And giv'st me leave to walk abroad,
> And labour in my lawful way;
>   My walks and works with me begin;
>   Conduct me forth, and bring me in.
>
> In ev'ry power my soul enjoys
> Internal virtues to improve;
> In ev'ry sense that she employs
> In her external works to move,
>   Bless her, O God, and keep me sound,
>   From outward harm and inward wound.

Let sin nor Satan's fraud prevail,
To make my eye of reason blind;
Or faith, or hope, or love to fail,
Or any virtues of the mind;
 But more and more let them increase,
 And bring me to my end in peace.

Lewd courses let my feet forbear,
Keep Thou my hands from doing wrong;
Let not ill counsel pierce my ear,
Nor wicked words defile my tongue;
 And keep the windows of each eye,
 That no strange lusts climb in thereby.

But guard Thou safe my heart in chief,
That neither hate, revenge, or fear,
Nor vain desire, vain joy, or grief,
Obtain command or dwelling there.
 And, Lord, with ev'ry saving grace,
 Still true to Thee maintain that place.

From open wrongs, from secret hates,
Preserve me likewise, Lord, this day;
From slanderous tongues, from wicked mates,
From ev'ry danger in my way.
 My goods to me, secure Thou too,
 And prosper all the works I do.

So till the evening of this morn,
My time shall then so well be spent,
That when the twilight shall return,
I may enjoy it with content;
 And to Thy praise and honour say,
 That this has proved a happy day."

But who, in the course of his morning devotions, can omit a song which so associates the first kindlings of praise and thanksgiving with balmy thought about gracious example, as the hymn which comes to us from the reverend, gentle, elegant, and glowing Bishop Heber? His eye falls, it may be, on David's anthem of thanksgiving, "Blessed be the Lord, who daily loadeth us with benefits," and his devout and tuneful spirit sings:—

 What secret hand at morning light,
  By stealth unseals mine eye;
 Draws back the curtain of the night,
  And opens earth and sky?

 'Tis Thine, my God!—the same which kept
  My resting hours from harm;
 No ill came nigh me, for I slept,
  Beneath th' Almighty's arm.

'Tis Thine my daily bread which brings
　　Like manna scattered round;
And clothes me as the lily springs
　　In beauty from the ground.

This is the hand which saved my frame,
　　And gave my pulse to beat;
Which bare me oft through flood and flame,
　　Through tempest cold, and heat.

In death's dark valley though I stray,
　　'Twould there my steps attend;
Guide with the staff my lonely way,
　　And with the rod defend.

May that dear Hand uphold me still,
　　Through life's uncertain race,
To bring me to Thy holy hill,
　　And to Thy dwelling-place.

Have you learnt to sing within yourself a hymn like this as each morning opens on you? If not, enter on the practice and pursue it, until it becomes your morning habit, and you will realize the habitual enjoyment of a poor, but religiously intelligent man, whose very appearance and manners were beautifully illustrative of a peaceful, happy religion. It was thought that the secret of his inward but evident repose would be touched by one question; he was asked, "I suppose your first work of a morning is to pray?"

"No."

"No! What then is it?"

"Praise," said he. "Praise is my first act; and when the day begins with praise, prayer and every good thing comes in its turn; for you soon learn the happy art of turning the bright side of things towards yourself, of looking at God's goodness until it always cheers you, of marking the blessings of each hour as the hour passes, and of communing with a happy future until you find it possible to 'rejoice evermore, pray without ceasing, and in everything give thanks.' Thus 'joy in Christ Jesus' passes into prayer, and prayer into thanks, and thanksgiving brings the happy soul back again to the blessed Saviour; and so the day passes, and from hour to hour the heart keeps up its music like a sweet peal of bells; yes, and the Holy

Spirit Himself seems to be ringing the changes in my soul of praise and prayer, love and joy, gratitude and peace."

"Thank you," said the old man's friend, "thank you for your lesson on morning music. God gives you the grace of praise 'new every morning'; you must have some favourite morning hymns."

"Oh yes, many, many a hymn and psalm come springing up, and sometimes I wonder how they come, for I do not know that I ever took very great pains to learn them. Among them all I have my favourite verses, and they are always fresh; and it strikes me that they bring their own tunes with them, for the verses no sooner come to my mind, than some suitable tune flows from my tongue. Scarcely a morning opens but these verses are forthcoming from my heart and lips:—

> Christ, whose glory fills the skies,
>   Christ, the true, the only light,
> Sun of Righteousness, arise,
>   Triumph o'er the shades of night.
> Day-spring from on high, be near,
> Day-star in my heart appear.
>
> Oh disclose Thy lovely face,
>   Quicken all my drooping powers;
> Gasps my fainting soul for grace,
>   As a thirsty land for showers.
> Haste, my Lord, no more delay,
> Come, my Saviour, come away.
>
> Dark and cheerless is the morn,
>   Unaccompanied by Thee;
> Joyless is the day's return,
>   Till Thy mercy's beams I see.
> Till Thou inward light impart,
> Glad my eyes and cheer my heart.
>
> Visit, then, this soul of mine,
>   Pierce the gloom of sin and grief;
> Fill me, Radiancy Divine,
>   Scatter all my unbelief;
> More and more Thyself display,
> Shining to the perfect day."

"Whose verses are these?"

"Whose? Why, Charles Wesley's; and they are so like him. Prayer and praise are always so cheerfully intermingling in his hymns. He must have been a cheerful Christian; and I like cheerful Christians, they are so consistent with their profession. If the New Testament teaches anything, it is that the disciples of Jesus are to be happy; and Charles Wesley's spiritual songs appear to breathe that lively, happy spirit which is so sweetly in tune with the promises of the new covenant. There is another morning hymn of his that I am fond of singing. It tells out one's sense of weakness and dependence so sweetly, and yet gives the longing soul new fire, and makes it feel that while it kindles into warmer desires after God, everything within, and everything without, brightens with spiritual joy. This is the hymn:—

> Jesus, the all-restoring word,
>   My fallen spirit's hope,
> After Thy lovely likeness, Lord,
>   Ah, when shall I wake up?
>
> Thou, O my God! Thou only art
>   The Life, the Truth, the Way;
> Quicken my soul, instruct my heart,
>   My sinking footsteps stay.
>
> Of all Thou hast in earth below,
>   In heaven above to give,
> Give me Thy only love to know,
>   In Thee to walk and live.
>
> Fill me with all the life of love;
>   In mystic union join
> Me to Thyself, and let me prove
>   The fellowship divine.
>
> Open the intercourse between
>   My longing soul and Thee,
> Never to be broke off again
>   To all eternity."

CHAPTER XVIII.

SONGS IN THE NIGHT.

"Ye shall have a song, as in the night when a holy solemnity is kept."

"THOUGHTS at night are deepest," said the heavenly-minded Leighton. And perhaps some who are more used to night watchings than to "night thoughts" will be disposed to take up his style, and pronounce that music at night is sweetest. At all events, many of those who have known the weariness of night watches will have some pleasant recollections of times when their spirits have been cheered by a night carol, or when some pipe or flute, or horn, has given them a strain, plaintive or merry, touching their jaded soul pleasantly as it has come floating upon the calm air of night. It has seemed doubly sweet in the dark and dreary hour; and has brought its own welcome to the watcher. For some reason or other, night music seems to have a more mellow richness and sweeter melting touch for the soul when we listen to it by the seaside. On the wild precipitous coast of Northern Cornwall, there are the remains of an ancient castle. Tradition says it was the birth-place of the British King Arthur. More certain records show that as early as 1245, Richard, Earl of Cornwall, gave shelter there to the rebellious David, Prince of Wales; that, after witnessing many changes, it became a state prison under Richard II.; that in 1385, John Northampton, Lord Mayor of London, for his "unruly mayoralty was condemned thither as a perpetual penitentiary;" and that about ten years later it held as a prisoner Thomas, Earl of Warwick. About the middle of the sixteenth century, the first and last "antiquary royal" of England, John Leland, visited the spot, and

R

says, "This castelle hath bene a marvelus strong and notable forteris, and almost *situ loci* inexpugnabile, especially for the dungeon, that is on a great high terrible cragge, environed with the se, but having a draw-bridge from the residew of the castelle into it. Shepe now fede within the dungeon. The residew of the buildings of the castelle be sore wether-beten and yn ruine, but it hath beene a large thinge."

A somewhat later chronicler describes it in his day—"Half of the buildings were raised on the continent, and the other half on an iland, continued together (within man's remembrance) by a drawe bridge, but now divorced by the down-faln steepe cliffes, on the farther side, which, though it shut out the sea from his wonted recourse, hath yet more strengthened the iland; for in passing thither you must first descend with a dangerous declyning, and then make a worse ascent, by a path, through his stickleness occasioning, and through his steepnesse threatening, the ruin of your life, with the falling of your foote. At the top, two other terrifying steps give you an entrance to the hill, which supplieth pasture for sheep and cowyes; upon the same I saw a decayed chappelle. Under the iland runs a cove, throw which you may rowe at ful sea, but not without a kind of horrour at the uncouthnesse of the place." A tourist who saw it in the reign of James I., says:—"By a very narrow rockye and wyndinge waye up the steepe sea cliffe, under which the sea waves wallow, and so assayle the foundation of the ile, as may astonish an unstable brayne to consider the perill, for the least slipp of the foote sendes the whole bodye into the devouringe sea; and the worste of all is higheste of all, nere the gate of entraunce into the hill, where the offensive stones so exposed hang over the head, as while a man respecteth his footinge he endaungers his head; and lookinge to save the head, endaungers the footinge, according to the old proverb, *Incidit in Scyllam qui vult vitare Charybdim*—He must have his eyes that will scale Tyntagelle."

Not quite thirty years ago, an enthusiastic band of pedestrians reached this romantic scene. It was about twelve o'clock at night; and the young moon was throwing a faint light over the sea, gently touching the ruined walls, and half revealing the mysteries of the "great high terrible cragge." All the dangers which the old chroniclers had felt were threatening still; but they were braved, and the green sward within the old bounds of the "dungeon" was gained. There the band gathered. It was a still night. The sea far below was whispering among the caves and rocks. But the hush was broken by the sudden swell of a night song. The voices of the devout travellers were as harmonious as their souls while they sang:—

> Join all ye ransomed sons of grace,
> The holy joy prolong,
> And shout to the Redeemer's praise
> A solemn midnight song.
>
> Blessing, and thanks, and love, and might
> Be to our Jesus given,
> Who turns our darkness into light,
> Who turns our hell to heaven.
>
> Thither our faithful souls He leads,
> Thither He bids us rise
> With crowns of joy upon our heads,
> To meet Him in the skies.

This was the first time probably that old Tintagel had heard a midnight song like this. It was one of Charles Wesley's "watch-night" hymns. And what holy associations gather around those finely-adapted "Songs of the Night Season!" The primitive martyr churches were in "watchings often." Theirs were nights of prayers, interwoven with psalms and hymns; vigils, sometimes in fear and sometimes jubilant. And who can chant the hymns that have come down to us from the night services of early childlike generations of Christian households, without catching a little of their holy, watchful spirit! The first "watch-night" among the Methodists was held in London on the 9th of April, 1742. "The custom," says a Methodist chronicler, "was begun at Kingswood by the colliers there, who, before their conversion, used to spend every Saturday night at the ale-house." "We commonly chose," says Wesley himself, "for this solemn service, the Friday night nearest the full moon, either before or after, that those of the congregation who live at a distance may have light to their several houses. The service begins half an hour past eight, and continues till a little after midnight. We have often found a peculiar blessing at these seasons. There is generally a deep awe upon the congregation; perhaps, in some measure, owing to the silence of night—particularly in singing the hymn with which we commonly conclude:"—

> Hearken to the solemn voice,
>   The awful midnight cry!
> Waiting souls, rejoice, rejoice,
>   And see the Bridegroom nigh:
> Lo! He comes to keep His word,
>   Light and joy His looks impart:
> Go ye forth to meet your Lord,
>   And meet Him in your heart.
>
> Ye who faint beneath the load
>   Of sin, your heads lift up;
> See your great redeeming God,
>   He comes and bids you hope:
> In the midnight of your grief,
>   Jesus doth His mourners cheer;
> Lo! He brings you sure relief;
>   Believe, and feel Him here.
>
> Ye whose loins are girt, stand forth,
>   Whose lamps are burning bright;
> Worthy, in your Saviour's worth,
>   To walk with Him in white:
> Jesus bids your hearts be clean;
>   Bids you all His promise prove;
> Jesus comes to cast out sin,
>   And perfect you in love.
>
> Wait we all in patient hope,
>   Till Christ, the Judge, shall come;
> We shall soon be all caught up
>   To meet the general doom:
> In an hour to us unknown,
>   As a thief in deepest night,
> Christ shall suddenly come down
>   With all His saints in light.
>
> Happy he whom Christ shall find
>   Watching to see Him come;
> Him, the Judge of all mankind
>   Shall bear triumphant home.
> Who can answer to His word?
>   Which of you dares meet His day?
> "Rise, and come to judgment!" Lord,
>   We rise, and come away.

A watch-night of great solemnity is always observed by the Methodists on New Year's Eve. A sermon is preached, suitable addresses are given, and the intervals are spent in singing and prayer; all kneel, and spend some minutes, immediately before and after the stroke of midnight, in silent prayer, broken at length by the hymn with which they enter on the New Year.

Between thirty and forty years ago, there was an English missionary and his wife stationed on the island of Zante, "the flower of the Levant," in the Ionian Sea. The mission was a quiet one, and, like most quiet things, it had some lasting fruit; but like English rule, in more cases than one, its duration proved to be limited. The missionary came back alone; God had taken from him the wife of his youth. There is one now living who remembers how the tears crept down his cheeks as he listened to that missionary's plaintive and touching story. "My wife and I," said he, "entered on our work in hope; but we soon felt that we were pilgrims indeed in a strange land. We had sympathy from few; none joined us in our distinctive religious services; but we kept at our work. New Year's Eve came round, and my dear wife and I observed the watch-night by ourselves. We could sing, both of us, and our voices were as one; and we prayed by turns, and sang together, as midnight approached, some verses of Charles Wesley's:—

> We will not close our wakeful eyes,
>   We will not let our eyelids sleep,
> But humbly lift them to the skies,
>   And all a solemn vigil keep:
> So many years on sin bestow'd,
> Can we not watch one night for God?
>
> We can, O Jesus, for Thy sake
>   Devote our every hour to Thee:
> Speak but the word, our souls shall wake,
>   And sing with cheerful melody;
> Thy praise shall our glad tongues employ,
> And every heart shall dance for joy.
>
> Oh may we all triumphant rise,
>   With joy upon our heads return,
> And far above these nether skies,
>   By Thee on eagles' wings upborne,
> Through all yon radiant circles move,
> And gain the highest heaven of love!

"The next New Year's Eve came, for years roll along amidst all human changes, but, ah! my wife was gone! I had watched her across the Jordan, and I was alone. What could I do? It was the watch-night. I had to watch alone with God. Where could I watch but by my Mary's grave-side? There I went; there I wept; there I prayed. I had no soul to commune with or to speak to; but surely, I thought, my Mary is here; and better even than that, my Jesus is here. I tried to sing again what we sang together the year before, but tears choked my utterance till the midnight hour struck, and then there was a hush in my soul; I knelt by my Mary's grave, renewed my covenant with Christ, gave myself once more to His will; and, feeling as if I were not without blessed company—yea, as if I heard one beloved voice in harmony with mine—I raised the old New Year's song, and sang as in company with the glorified—

> Come, let us anew our journey pursue,
>   Roll round with the year,
> And never stand still till the Master appear.
>
> His adorable will let us gladly fulfil,
>   And our talents improve,
> By the patience of hope and the labour of love.
>
> Our life is a dream: our time, as a stream,
>   Glides swiftly away;
> And the fugitive moment refuses to stay.
>
> The arrow is flown; the moment is gone;
>   The millennial year
> Rushes on to our view, and eternity's here.
>
> Oh that each in the day of his coming may say,
>   'I have fought my way through;
> I have finished the work Thou didst give me to do.'
>
> Oh that each from his Lord may receive the glad word,
>   'Well, and faithfully done;
> Enter into my joy, and sit down on my throne.'

This was my last watch-night hymn in the Ionian Sea; and 'I call to remembrance my song in the night,' and now calmly await the call unto that world where

> Death, and grief, and pain,
> And parting are no more."

The lone missionary had his call from above at last. He and his Mary join their voices again now, not in night songs, but in hymns of gratitude to Him who once gave them "songs in the night" in the house of their pilgrimage. There is one happy spirit with whom they are now associated, to whom thousands are indebted for happy means of beguiling the wearisome hours of wakeful nights in sickness and languor. He learnt to extract devout music from the hours of suffering which passed over him; and thus solacing his own soul, he has left consolation for all true lovers of sweet and soothing hymns at night.

"What, in tears again, my dear doctor!" Lady Huntingdon said, more than once of a morning, as she entered the room where a very impersonation of meekness, resignation, and love, was reclining, with a tremulous tear on his cheek.

"Yes," was the reply; "but they are tears of joy, my dear lady."

These tears of joy were upon the placid countenance of Philip Doddridge. His outward man was perishing, but "the inward man was renewed day by day." Yes, and night by night, for he had caught the spirit of Wesley's night song:—

> O Thou jealous God! come down,
>   God of spotless purity;
> Claim, and seize me for Thine own,
>   Consecrate my heart to Thee:
> Under Thy protection take;
>   Songs in the right season give;
> Let me sleep to Thee, and wake;
>   Let me die to Thee, and live.
>
> Only tell me I am Thine,
>   And Thou wilt not quit Thy right;
> Answer me in dreams divine,
>   Dreams and visions of the night;
> Bid me even in sleep go on
>   Restlessly, my God desire;
> Mourn for God in every groan,
>   God in every thought require.
>
> Loose me from the chains of sense,
>   Set me from the body free;
> Draw with stronger influence
>   My unfetter'd soul to Thee:

> In me, Lord, Thyself reveal;
>   Fill me with a sweet surprise;
> Let me, Thee, when waking feel,
>   Let me in Thy image rise.

It was not in vain that he had sought to hallow his writings by using his pen in private companionship with his Saviour. It was not in vain that the first Monday in every month was spent in meditation, intercession, and prayer, in that consecrated vestry of his meeting-house in Northampton. He had become so holily familiar with truth and love, that his days of decline were blessed with tears of heavenly joy, and his wakeful nights became fruitful with hymns and psalms. How the grateful calmness, the spiritual repose, the Christian submission, and the heavenly glow of the saintly hymnist's spirit continues to breathe on us as we chant with him on the return of night:—

> Interval of grateful shade,
> Welcome to my weary head;
> Welcome slumber to my eyes,
> Tired with glaring vanities.
>
> My great Master still allows
> Needful periods of repose;
> By my heavenly Father blest,
> Thus I give my powers to rest.
>
> Heavenly Father! gracious name!
> Night and day His love the same!
> Far be each suspicious thought,
> Every anxious care forgot.
>
> Thou, my ever-bounteous God,
> Crown'st my days with various good
> Thy kind eye, that cannot sleep,
> These defenceless hours shall keep.
>
> What though downy slumbers flee,
> Strangers to my couch and me?
> Sleepless, well I know to rest,
> Lodged within my Father's breast.
>
> While the empress of the night
> Scatters mild her silver light;
> While the vivid planets stray,
> Various through their mystic way;
>
> While the stars unnumbered roll
> Round the ever constant pole,
> Far above these spangled skies
> All my soul to God shall rise.

'Mid the silence of the night,
Mingling with those angels bright,
Whose harmonious voices raise,
Ceaseless love and ceaseless praise.

Through the throng His gentle ear
Shall my tuneless accents hear;
From on high doth He impart
Secret comfort to my heart.

He in these serenest hours
Guides my intellectual powers,
And His Spirit doth diffuse
Sweeter far than midnight dews,

Lifting all my thoughts above,
On the wings of faith and love:
Blest alternative to me,
Thus to sleep, or wake with Thee.

What if death my sleep invade?
Should I be of death afraid?
Whilst encircled by Thy arm,
Death may strike, but cannot harm.

What if beams of opening day
Shine around my breathless clay?
Brighter visions from on high
Shall regale my mental eye.

Tender friends awhile may mourn
Me from their embraces torn;
Dearer, better friends I have
In the realms beyond the grave.

See the guardian angels nigh,
Wait to waft my soul on high!
See the golden gates displayed;
See the crown to grace my head;

See a flood of sacred light,
Which no more shall yield to night.
Transitory world, farewell!
Jesus calls, with Him to dwell!

With Thy heavenly presence blest,
Death is life, and labour rest;
Welcome sleep or death to me,
Still secure, for still with Thee.

Doddridge's hymns, and some of his most useful prose treatises, were produced in stray moments, or what have been called loose intervals of time. They came richly oozing through the crevices of the day or the night, the overflowings of a mind full of goodness for all who needed blessing. So when harder work had wearied his thinking head, and all but exhausted his spirits, his tuneful genius breathed forth its life for his own refreshment in his hymn for the night; and so his prose chapters on "The Rise and Progress of Religion in the Soul" were penned now and then as the happy thoughts' occurred, and welled up during moments of comparative leisure. And it is beyond our power to say which has instilled its saving unction into the greater number of human souls—his midnight hymn, or his "prayers" for the seeker of "religion in the soul." Will those who have gathered life from the daily study of his prose pages outnumber the sufferers whose night watches have been brightened by the Divine music of his hymn? Who can tell? The fruit of both is ever living, and is ever accumulating its harvest joys. And the fruit of the one is ever mixing with the kindred fruit of the other. The holy work of a few well-improved fragments of time gives out a virtue which, like well-directed electrical influence, conveys gracious and quickening power to hearts far away in space, and at the most distant points of time. Baxter filled up his remnants of hours by writing his "Saint's Everlasting Rest;" that book touched the soul of Doddridge, and gave it life. Doddridge, in turn, employed his leisure moments in throwing off his pages on "Religion in the Soul;" those pages touched the heart of Wilberforce, and engaged his intellect for Christ. He filled up spare hours by writing his "Practical View of Christianity;" that volume touched the mighty mind and heart of Chalmers: and whose mind and heart has not been, and will not be, touched by the works of Chalmers?

"I used to read a great many books in my young days," said a languid sufferer to one who sat by him, "but of all I ever read, nothing did me so much good, and so helped me to see my way clear to Christ, as Doddridge's 'Rise and Progress of Religion in the Soul.' I was then feeling after God, and a young friend lent me the book; and oh, how thankful I shall always be for it! The prayers at the ends of the chapters were such gracious helps to me. I used to pray them over on my knees, with many tears; and then I learnt the happy art of throwing the soul into a suitable form of prayer. Indeed, these forms of prayer taught me to pray. And the answers have been coming upon me ever since. Here I am, often half the night sleepless and uneasy; but if anything hushes me, it is going over those pages, and then in turn humming a hymn to myself."

"What is your favourite hymn? Do you use Doddridge's beautiful hymn 'for the night'?"

"No, I did not know that he had written one. Had I known it, I should have chosen that above all; I love Doddridge so much. I wish I had known his hymn. But my favourite has been the good old hymn for midnight, by Bishop Ken."

Well did the sufferer call that hymn, "the good old hymn." It is good, and will always be good; it is as fresh now as when it was first sung. The saintly old bishop, put out of his bishopric for conscience' sake, had gone from his residence at Longleat, in Wiltshire, on a visit to his nephew, so dear to those who love good biography, Isaac Walton, then Prebendary of Salisbury. That great storm which swept over the island, in 1703, touched the old city rather roughly as it passed, and blew down a stack of chimneys, which fell cutting through the bed-room in which Ken was lodged, without touching his person; but rushing on upon Wells, it hurled another stack through the chamber of the bishop who had supplanted Ken, and killed him on the spot. Strange thoughts would perplex some minds as to the meaning of this variety of action by the same storm; but whatever we may think, it may be that we owe much of the spirit and power of Ken's midnight hymn to the effects of that preserving presence which was manifest in his case. With what swelling feeling would he ever after sing in his night-watch:—

> My God, now I from sleep awake,
> The sole possession of me take;
> From midnight terrors me secure,
> And guard my heart from thoughts impure!
>
> Bless'd angels, while we silent lie,
> Your hallelujahs sing on high;
> You joyful hymn the Ever-blest,
> Before the throne, and never rest.

I, with your choir celestial join
In offering up a hymn divine;
With you in heaven I hope to dwell,
And bid the night and world farewell.

My soul, when I shake off this dust,
Lord, in Thy arms I will entrust:
Oh make me Thy peculiar care;
Some mansion for my soul prepare!

Give me a place at Thy saints' feet,
Or some fall'n angel's vacant seat;
I'll strive to sing as loud as they
Who sit above in brighter day.

Oh may I always ready stand,
With my lamp burning in my hand;
May I in sight of heaven rejoice
Whene'er I hear the Bridegroom's voice!

All praise to Thee, in light arrayed,
Who light Thy dwelling-place hast made;
A boundless ocean of bright beams
From Thy all-glorious Godhead streams.

The sun in its meridian height
Is very darkness in Thy sight;
My soul, oh, lighten and inflame
With thought and love of Thy great name.

Bless'd Jesu, Thou, on heaven intent,
Whole nights hast in devotion spent;
But I, frail creature, soon am tired,
And all my zeal is soon expired.

My soul, how canst thou weary grow
Of antedating bliss below?
In sacred hymns, and heavenly love,
Which will eternal be above?

Shine on me, Lord, new life impart,
Fresh ardours kindle in my heart;
One ray of Thy all-quickening light
Dispels the sloth and clouds of night.

Lord, lest the tempter me surprise,
Watch over Thine own sacrifice;
All loose, all idle thoughts cast out,
And make my very dreams devout.

Praise God, from whom all blessings flow;
Praise Him, all creatures here below;
Praise Him above, ye heavenly host;
Praise Father, Son, and Holy Ghost.

Heaven has watched over many a night-watcher besides Bishop Ken. It is now nearly a hundred years ago that a poor girl in Ipswich lost her father, and her mother being left with a large family unprovided for, she, at the age of sixteen, went out into domestic service. There, however, she was seized with a complicated disorder, which baffled all medical skill, and shut her up to a life of suffering. But her affliction was hallowed to her. Christ revealed Himself as her Saviour, and became her Divine companion. She taught herself to write, and then solaced herself during the weary days and nights of languishing by composing hymns and psalms. Her songs were worthy of notice, and were published by her friends as "Songs in the Night." Her genius and piety, spirit and expression, are fairly given in an acrostic which reveals her name :—

S hall I presume to tell the world my name?
U p to this hour I glory in my shame:
S o great my weakness, that I boast of might,
A fool in knowledge, yet in wisdom right;
N o life, and yet I live; I'm sick, and well;
N ot far from heaven, though on the brink of hell,
A nd words and oaths, and blood, delight me well.
H ow strange! I'm deaf, and dumb, and lame, and blind,
A nd hear, and see, and walk, and talk, you find.
R obbed by my dearest friend, I'm truly poor,
R iches immense I always have in store.
I 'm fed by mortals; but let mortals know
S uch is my food, no mortal can bestow.
O h, how I long to die, and wish to live!
N ow, if you can, explain th' account I give.

Her songs are appropriately entitled "Songs in the Night." Mere circumstances were all dark around her; but there was undying light in her soul, and her hymns breathe a reverent cheerfulness, a placid resignation, and a comfortable hope. Her genius was uncultured, but in sentiment, diction, and musical tone, many of her hymns are worthy of being closet companions with the night songs of hymnists bearing far more distinguished names. The poor sufferer used to sing as night came on:—

God of my days, God of my nights,
Source of my soul's supreme delights,
Come, manifest Thy love to me,
And let me close this day with Thee.

Nearness to Christ I fain would find,
Oh let not distance vex my mind;
I long to know my sins forgiven,
To converse with the God of heaven.

Send, Source of Light, some cheering ray,
To turn my darkness into day;
I mourn, and think Thy absence long,
Oh listen to my evening song.

Command my blindness to depart,
Still keep me from a careless heart;
Lord, captivate each vain desire,
And raise these vile affections higher.

Oh let the mercies of this day
Teach me to praise as well as pray:
Now take, my soul, on Jesu's breast,
Thy sweetest, safest, surest rest!

In her last hours she was truly "compassed about with songs of deliverance." "I have not sung for some time," she said. "Sing with me; it will not hurt me. Sing Dr. Watts's hymn:—

How sweet and awful is the place,
   With Christ within the doors;
While everlasting love displays
   The choicest of her stores."

The hymn was softly sung by her friends; and then she added, "Let us sing again":—

Come, let us join our cheerful songs
   With angels round the throne;
Ten thousand thousand are their tongues,
   But all their joys are one.

Worthy the Lamb that died, they cry,
   To be exalted thus;
Worthy the Lamb, our lips reply,
   For He was slain for us.

Jesus is worthy to receive
   Honour and power divine;
And blessings more than we can give,
   Be, Lord, for ever Thine.

Nobody seemed able to sing with her. Her voice was like something more than human, and she waved her arm exultingly, as she sang. "You do not sing with me," she said; "well, I cannot forbear." Then she continued nearly the whole night warbling softly, though at times apparently dying. Her last night was full of song; and just before she took her upward flight, she pointed heavenward, and said, "I cannot talk, but I shall soon sing *there.*"

CHAPTER XIX.

MARRIAGE SONGS AND BIRTHDAY HYMNS.

"And both Jesus was called, and his disciples, to the marriage."

It is said of Solomon that "his songs were a thousand and five." One of this number occupies a distinguished place in the sacred canon, and is called "The Song of Songs, which is Solomon's," or "the most beautiful or excellent of his songs." It was written a thousand years before Christ—long before the earliest profane poets whose works are extant; but the freshness of its unrivalled beauty has remained through all the changes of time and manners, while its charms continue to exert their power under all the disadvantages of incompetent translation. It may be called a pastoral, in which two leading characters are represented as speaking and acting throughout the poem. The one is a king called Shelomoh, "The peaceful, or Prince of Peace," the other a female, who from being a rustic shepherdess becomes his queen; she bears the name of Shelomith, which is simply the feminine form of Shelomoh. Whether this poem was written by Solomon on the occasion of his own marriage or not, it seems to stand among the oracles of inspiration as a seal of divine approbation on the institution of marriage, or as the fixed light of God's smile upon the fervid but modest and delicate affection of conjugal life. Both ancients and moderns, Jews and Christians, have agreed that under its face of poetic beauty an allegorical meaning is hid, for the instruction and solace of the teachable, chaste, and believing soul. Indeed, we cannot conceive that Ezra, a man under divine inspiration, and the members of the great synagogue, or those who assisted in collecting the sacred writings, would have admitted this song into the sacred canon if they had not a full conviction that under its mysterious and luxuriant imagery there lay concealed some great truths bearing on the interests of God's kingdom and people. It is an Oriental book, written by a highly poetical Eastern monarch, intended, in the first place, for an Oriental people such as seven-eighths of the human race have been, and such as form one-half of the present population of the earth. The book should therefore be interpreted in accordance with Eastern manners and rules of composition. It has always been the universal custom in the East to represent spiritual things under such figures as are beautifully sketched in the Song of Solomon. Numerous examples might be quoted from mere heathen authorities; but the Bible is full of them. David, Isaiah, Jeremiah, the evangelists, apostles, and our Lord Himself, all speak of the intercourse of the divine and the human under the imagery of marriage feasts and conjugal communion. And in this light the Song of Solomon has always been viewed, both by Jews and Christians. The Jews explained it as a song of Jehovah's love for the synagogue; the Christians, as celebrating the union of Christ and His Church. Both have agreed, however, that the spirit and design of the book can be realized by none but the chaste and devotional mind. The Jews denied it to the weak and the profane, as too strong for the one, and too holy for the other. They have always guarded and honoured it not only as holy, but as they say, "the Holy of holies"; and have ever used it as an incentive to holy thought and intense devotion. While the Christians, who have consulted it as the expression of Christ's love to the community of the faithful, have ever found in it a refreshing sweetness and power, leading them, as it does, to meditate on the mutual affection of the Redeemer and His people, associated with trials and vicissitudes in this life, but promising perfect fruition and repose in the world to come. This may be illustrated by one passage from a personal history.

"Ah! my dear friend, is that you?" said a kind-hearted and intelligent Polish Jew, as he affectionately took the hand of a Methodist preacher, who had taken his seat by the side of his sick-bed. The two had known each other in earlier life, and had learnt to "love one another," distinct as they were in creed as well as by birth. After some years of separation, the Gentile had found out his Jewish brother and first Hebrew teacher, in his affliction; and now once more they were heart to heart, and entered into communion about the sacred text which they had at one time so lovingly studied together. The Jew was gentle, tender, and open as a child, and freely told out his hope in the mercy of that God who had been pleased, as he said, "to put the innocent for the uninnocent, that the sinner, who was penitent over the sacrifice, and trusted there, might be saved." And then he talked about divine love, how it begat love in us; what a comfort it was to him; how it helped him in his sickness; and how it disposed him to love everybody around him. The holy texts from his Hebrew Bible "came bubbling up in his mind," he said, "and there were no words which seemed to speak the feelings of his heart so happily as some of the words in Solomon's Song."

"Somebody said to me, the other day," he remarked, 'What is the use of Solomon's Song? I cannot understand it; I think it had better be left out of the book!' Oh, I was grieved; and I said, that is wicked. No! you do not see the use of that blessed book! how can you? You do not understand it. How should you? Those who do not love the truth cannot see the use of it, or understand it. You are not a spiritual man; and you do not see. There now is my box, poor looking box to you. What is the use of it? you may say, it might as well be thrown away. Ah! it is locked! you do not see what is in it! nor can you tell what is the value or the beauty of the jewels that are there. But if I give you the key, and you open it, then you may be able to talk about the box, for you will see and know all that is in it. So you have no key to Solomon's Song; none but spiritual men have a key to it!"

And so the afflicted Hebrew talked. He might have communed, one would think, with that disciple of Gamaliel who says, "The natural man receiveth not the things of the Spirit of God, for they are foolishness to him; neither can he know them, because they are spiritually discerned. But he that is spiritual judgeth all things." Nor could his Methodist friend help thinking, at the moment, of Charles Wesley's metrical introduction to Solomon's Song. There was something so remarkably akin in the pure simplicity of the poor Hebrew's thoughts and those of the Methodist poet. Wesley expresses what the Jew thought and felt, with becoming purity and spirit, and in a pleasant hymnic form, thus:—

> Hence, ye profane; far off remove,
> Ye strangers to redeeming love;
> Sinners, whom Jesus never knew,
> The Song of Songs is not for you!
> Away, ye worldly goats and swine,
> Who trample on this pearl divine,
> Which only wisdom's sons esteem,
> While fools and infidels blaspheme.
>
> With deepest shame, with humblest fear,
> I to Thine oracle draw near,
> To meet Thee in the holiest place,
> To learn the secret of Thy grace.
> Now, Lord, explain the mystery,
> Display Thy precious self to me,
> And when Thou dost the veil remove,
> My heart shall sing the song of love.
>
> Thou heavenly Solomon divine,
> To teach the Song of Songs is Thine;
> Thy Spirit alone the depth reveals,
> Opens the book, and breaks the seals:
> Oh might I find the bar removed,
> And love the Lord as I am loved,
> This moment gain my heart's desire,
> The next within Thine arms expire!

The Jew kindled with his theme, and with that charming intonation which is natural to the children of the synagogue, he gave voice to his loving heart in a succession of stanzas from the "Song of Songs." He repeated again and again with growing warmth, and with a music of expression that seemed like the voice of love itself, "Tell me, O Thou whom my soul loveth, where Thou feedest, where Thou makest Thy flock to rest at noon!" The afflicted child of Abraham had wandered long among strangers, and was now longing for rest with the Great Shepherd to whom his fathers had been gathered. By a Methodist, such as his friend and visitor was, Charles Wesley was, of course, thought of again, and that tender, glowing paraphrase of Solomon's stanza came, as the Jew who had quoted it said, "bubbling up in the mind":—

> Thou Shepherd of Israel and mine,
>   The joy and desire of my heart,
> For closer communion I pine,
>   I long to reside where Thou art:
> The pasture I languish to find,
>   Where all, who their Shepherd obey,
> Are fed on Thy bosom reclined,
>   And screen'd from the heat of the day.
>
> Ah! show me that happiest place,
>   The place of Thy people's abode,
> Where saints in an ecstasy gaze,
>   And hang on a crucified God.
> Thy love for a sinner declare,
>   Thy passion and death on the tree:
> My spirit to Calvary bear,
>   To suffer and triumph with Thee.
>
> 'Tis there, with the lambs of Thy flock,
>   There only I covet to rest,
> To lie at the foot of the rock,
>   Or rise to lie hid in Thy breast:
> 'Tis there I would always abide,
>   And never a moment depart;
> Conceal'd in the cleft of Thy side,
>   Eternally held in Thy heart.

"Do you think that the 'Song of Songs' was written by Solomon on the occasion of his own marriage?" said the Gentile visitor to the Jewish patient.

"Yes, that is my opinion. I think God has given it to us as a marriage song, to show that marriage is His own arrangement and ordinance for our comfort, and the purity and happiness of the world. But it means something more than that; it is a song of love between the Messiah and His people. Ah! that is a mysterious love; but it is sweet, and he only who enjoys it deeply can sing Solomon's Song as it was intended to be sung."

In hearing this from a Jew, who would not think of one, in earlier times, who was trained a Pharisee, but becoming, like the suffering Polish wanderer, a truly spiritual man, uttered kindred thoughts? "Husbands, love your wives, even as Christ also loved the Church, and gave Himself for it; that He might sanctify and cleanse it with the washing of water by the Word, that He might present it to Himself a glorious Church, not having spot, or wrinkle, or any such thing; but that it should be holy and without blemish. So ought men to love their wives as their own bodies. He that loveth his wife loveth himself. For no man ever yet hated his own flesh; but nourisheth and cherisheth it, even as the Lord the Church; for we are members of His body, of His flesh, and of His bones. For this cause shall a man leave his father and mother, and shall be joined unto his wife, and they two shall be one flesh. This a great mystery: but I speak concerning Christ and the Church."

If, then, Solomon's Song is an inspired marriage song, having under its beautiful surface a spiritual allusion to a still deeper mystery of love, marriage songs are not unacceptable to God, nor can they be out of place at a wedding-feast. They should, however, emulate the spirit and tone of the inspired exemplar; and the hymnist who so happily introduces Solomon's divine pastoral, and who has left us so many sweet little hymnic paraphrases of favourite passages from the "Song of Songs," has furnished an appropriate song for the bridal morn. One who so deeply enjoyed the chaste pleasures of conjugal life, and whose soul was so full of hymn and song, would certainly aid the newly-married pair with forms of devout expression. Here is one of his marriage hymns:—

> Thou God of truth and love,
>   We seek Thy perfect way,
> Ready Thy choice to approve,
>   Thy Providence to obey;
> Enter into Thy wise design,
> And sweetly lose our will in Thine.
>
> Why hast Thou cast our lot
>   In the same age and place?
> And why together brought
>   To see each other's face?
> To join with softest sympathy,
> And mix our friendly souls with Thee?
>
> Didst Thou not make us one,
>   That we might one remain,
> Together travel on,
>   And bear each other's pain;
> Till all Thy utmost goodness prove,
> And rise renew'd in perfect love?

Surely Thou didst unite
  Our kindred spirits here,
That all hereafter might
  Before Thy throne appear;
Meet at the marriage of the Lamb,
And all Thy glorious love proclaim.

Then let us ever bear
  The blessed end in view,
And join, with mutual care,
  To fight our passage through;
And kindly help each other on,
Till all receive the starry crown.

Oh may the Spirit seal
  Our souls unto that day,
With all Thy fulness fill,
  And then transport away!
Away to our eternal rest,
Away to our Redeemer's breast!

Old George Withers would make marriage songs as a matter of course; for he made songs and hymns about everything, for all times, all conditions, and all circumstances. His "Halleluiah" is full of psalms for days of every name and shade, and for every part of every day; for nights starry and nights dark, for sea and for land, for storm and for calm, for battle and for peace. He has hymns for all seasons; for workers, for idlers, for kinsfolk, for strangers, for the bond and the free, for plenty and for famine, for kings and for people, for pastors and for flocks, for seed-time and for harvest, for saints and for sinners, for young and for old, for every place, for every calling, for all the world, and for "himself." His marriage song must have a choir in advance and a choir in the rear. He teaches us to hymn it over a marriage-contract. "This hymn," says he, "is tendered to those who purpose a contract of marriage, in hope it may so remember them to consider what they intend that it shall keep them from proceeding farther than they lawful may, and from professing more than they mean. Sing this," he adds, "as *Te Deum*":—

Lord! in Thy name, and in Thy fear
  Our faith we plighted have;
And that our meanings are sincere,
  Thy witness now we crave.

We come not only to repeat
  Our vows before Thy face,
But that we may likewise entreat
  Thy favour and Thy grace.

For mutual helpers while we live,
  According to our might;
Ourselves we to each other give,
  So far as we have right;
And we profess that free we are,
  For aught that we do know,
To be each other's wedded pair,
  If Thou permit it so.

We see no contradicting cause,
  But that we may be joined,
Without infringement of the laws
  Whereby we are confined.
Nor any such infirmity
  In us do we suspect
As that our marriage bond thereby
  Shall prove of no effect.

We have no guileful dealings used,
  Our purpose to acquire,
Nor one another's trust abused,
  To gain what we desire.
But our affections are sincere,
  And as they have been true,
Upright those courses likewise are,
  By which we them pursue.

If both have now, O Lord, professed
  What may not be denied;
Let our affections so be blest
  That nothing us divide.
Let not by beauty, wit, or wealth,
  By high or low degree,
By want of riches or of health
  Our hearts estrangèd be.

But if that either of us now
  Hath trod a faithless way,
Or shall infringe this holy vow
  Before our wedding day:
Lord! let the party innocent,
  From blame and guilt be free;
For truth a contract never meant,
  Where naught but falsehoods be.

Then out of his full soul the quaint but musical and happy hymnist pours forth a song for the marriage, telling us that "God is hereby besought to bless the marriage solemnized to all there present, and so to prosper the bridegroom and bride in their desires and affections, that the waters of their carnal contentment may be turned into the wine of spiritual delights":—

> To grace, O Lord! a marriage feast
>   In Cana, long ago,
> It pleased Thee to be a guest,
>   And there Thy power to show;
> For by a miracle divine,
>   When they their wine had spent,
> Thou changedst water into wine,
>   Which did their want prevent.
>
> Lord! let the brightness of Thy face
>   Among us now appear;
> So let the bounties of Thy grace
>   Be manifested here:
> That neither bridegroom, bride, nor guest,
>   In body or in mind,
> Of less content may be possess'd,
>   Than they have hope to find.
>
> All joys which in a married life,
>   Well matchèd couples know,
> On this new wedded man and wife
>   Vouchsafe Thou to bestow;
> Fulfil their hopes, prevent their fears,
>   Grant them their just desires;
> Increase that love which keeps off cares,
>   And warms with lawful fires.
>
> To wine those heartless waters turn
>   Which in their vessels be;
> To give them comfort when they mourn,
>   And make them glad in Thee.
> And though the pleasures of their love
>   Have yet a pleasing taste,
> Yet let them daily sweeter prove,
>   And best of all at last.

The dear old hymnist seems to have had contentment in marriage, and is willing that all who are blessed with like satisfaction in matrimonial life should never lack the means of expressing their settled pleasure in devout and cheerful psalmody; and he introduces his hymn "for one contentedly married" by insinuating some very salutary lessons to parties concerned. "The intent of this ode," he says, "is to show that our natural affections are never fully satisfied in the choice of our helpers, until God bring man and wife together by, as it were, making the one out of the other through a frequent conversing together, and by observing and approving each other's condition, which is never done till those passions are cast into a sleep which make them dote on wealth, honour, beauty, and such unfit marriage makers":—

> Since they in singing take delight
>   Who in their love unhappy be,
> Why should not I in song delight
>   Who from their sorrow now are free?
> That such as can believe may know
> What comforts are on earth below,
> And prove what blessings may be won
> By loving so as I have done.
>
> When first affection warmed my blood,
>   Which was ere wit could ripen'd be,
> And ere I fully understood
>   What fire it was that warmed me;
> My youthful heat a love begat,
> That love did love I know not what;
> But this I know, I felt more pains
> Than many a broken heart sustains.
>
> When years informed me how to see
>   What had such wandering passions wrought,
> The more my knowledge grew to be,
>   The greater torments still it brought;
> Then sought I means to cure love's wound,
> The more I sought, less ease I found;
> And milder pangs than I have had,
> Make many lovers sick and mad.
>
> I have a deep-indented heart,
>   Which no content would let me find,
> Until her proper counterpart
>   Should thereunto be firmly joined;
> Ere far I sought or searched much,
> I many found who seemed such,
> But them when I did nearly view
> Not one in heart was fully true.
>
> Alas! thought I, to what I seek
>   Why should so many draw so near,
> And at the last prove nothing like
>   To what at first they did appear?
> So much why do so many please,
> Since I was made for none of these?
> And why in show have I been one,
> Beloved much, yet loved of none?

Could wealth have bought my marriage bed,
  Or honour brought me true delight,
I could these ways have better sped
  Than many do believe I might;
Nay, beauty, though none loves it more,
Nor proffer'd loves though I had store,
Could make me think now found is she
That proves a helper fit for me.

Nor ease nor pleasure could I find
  In beauty, honour, love, or pelf;
Nor means to gain a settled mind,
  Till I had found my second self;
Thus till our grand-dame Eve was made,
No helper our first parent had;
Which proves a wife in value more
Than all the creatures made before.

Half tired in seeking what I sought
  I fell into a sleep at last;
And God for me my wishes wrought,
  When hope of them were almost past;
With Adam I this favour had,
That out of me my wife was made,
And when I waked I espied
That God for me had found a bride.

How He this riddle brought to pass,
  This curious world shall never hear!
A secret work of His it was,
  Nor fit for ev'ry vulgar ear:
Out of each other formed were we,
Within a third our beings be;
And our well-being was begun,
By being in ourselves undone.

I have the height of my desire,
  In secret no dislike I find;
Love warms me with a kindly fire,
  No jealous pangs torment my mind:
I breathe no sigh, I make no moan,
As others do, and I have done;
Nor do I mark, nor do I care,
How fair or lovely others are.

My heart at quiet lets me lie,
  And moves no passion in my breast;
Nor tempting tongue, nor speaking eye,
  Nor smiling lip, can break my rest;
The peer I sought by me is found,
My earthly hopes by thee are crown'd;
And I in one all pleasures find,
That may be found in womankind.

> Each hath of other like esteem,
>   And what that is we need not tell;
> For we are one though two we seem,
>   And in each other's hearts we dwell:
> There dwells He two embracing thus
> By whom we were endeared thus;
> He makes us rich, though seeming poor,
> And when we want will give us more.
>
> Lord! let our love in Thee begun,
>   In Thee, likewise, continuance have;
> And if Thy will may so be done,
>   Together lodge us in one grave;
> Then on the Lamb's great wedding-day
> Raise us together from the clay;
> And where the Bridegroom doth remain
> Let us both live and love again.

Another of this prolific poet's songs is "a hymn for house-warming." "The ancient and laudable use of house-warmings is here insinuated," as he says, "for in this hymn the friends assembled are taught to beseech God Almighty to make that habitation prosperous and comfortable to them and theirs, who are newly come thither to dwell":—

> Among those points of neighbourhood
>   Which our forefathers did allow,
> That custom in esteem hath stood
>   Which we do put in practice now.
> For when their friends new dwellings had,
> Them thus they welcome thither made;
> That they the sooner might be free
> From strangeness, where they strangers be.
>
> To this good end we partly came,
>   And partly friendship to augment;
> But if we fail not in the same,
>   This is the prime of our intent.
> We come with holy charms to bless
> The house our friends do now possess;
> In hope that God amen will say,
> To that for which we now shall pray.
>
> Lord! keep this place, we Thee desire,
>   To these new comers ever free,
> From raging winds, from harmful fire,
>   From waters that offensive be;
> From graceless child, from servants ill,
> From neighbours bearing no good will:
> And from the chiefest plague of life,
> A husband false, a faithless wife.

Let neither thieves that rove by night,
   Nor those that sneak about by day,
Have power their persons to affright,
   Or to purloin their goods away.
Let nothing here be seen or heard
To make by day or night afear'd;
No sudden cries, no fearful noise,
No vision grim nor dreadful voice.

Let on this house no curse remain,
   If any on the same is laid;
Let no imposture power obtain
   To make the meanest wit afraid.
Let here nor Zim nor Dim be seen,
The fabled fairy king or queen;
Nor such delusions as are said
To make the former age afraid.

Keep also, Lord, we pray, from hence
   As much as frailty will allow;
The guiltiness of each offence,
   Which to a crying sin may grow.
Let no more want, wealth, hope, or fear,
Nor greater griefs nor joys be here;
Thou may still keep them in Thy grace,
Who shall be dwellers in this place.

But that just measure let them have
   Of every means which may acquire,
The blessedness which they most crave,
   Who to the truest bliss aspire.
And if well-wishers absent be,
Who better wish them can than we,
To make this blessing up entire,
We thereto add what they desire.

The composition of verses on cheerful themes has not unfrequently afforded refreshment to afflicted genius. It was so with a hymn-writer of the last century. "Ill health," says he, in a preface to a collection of hymns, "some years past, having kept me from travelling or preaching, I took up the trade of hymn-making, a handicraft much followed of late, but a business I was not born or bred to, and undertaken chiefly to keep a long sickness from preying on my spirit, and to make tedious nights pass over more smoothly. Some tinkling employment was wanted, which might amuse and not fatigue me." Merry old Berridge! even he, at times, needed "some tinkling employment" to keep his spirits up; and even he had seasons of reaction from cheerful excitement, during which the good fruit of his recreation was in danger of being consigned to oblivion. "These hymns," he writes, "were composed in a six months' illness, and have since laid neglected by me; often threatened with the fire, but have escaped that martyrdom. Fatherly mercy prevented that literary death, for authors can seldom prove cruel to their own offspring, however deformed; but they came into the world naked, neither clothed with recommendation or correction of any friend. Such as they are, I offer them to the reader, and suppose he may find in them the common lot of human productions, some things to blame and some to commend. Some of the hymns have occasionally rambled into magazines, under the signature of '*Old Everton*' and are now finding their way home again." Among these returning ramblers there is his hymn on "a Christian wedding," and those who wish to enter on married life with the holy songs of a hallowed wedding-day in their hearts will be thankful for the fruit of "Old Everton's" "tinkling employment," and learn to sing with him:—

> Our Jesus freely did appear
> To grace a marriage feast;
> And, Lord, we ask Thy presence here,
> To make a wedding guest.
>
> Upon the bridal pair look down,
> Who now have plighted hands;
> Their union with Thy favour crown,
> And bless the nuptial bands.
>
> With gifts of grace their hearts endow,
> Of all rich dowries best!
> Their substance bless, and peace bestow,
> To sweeten all the rest.
>
> In purest love their souls unite,
> And link'd in kindly care,
> To render family burdens light,
> By taking mutual share;
>
> True helpers may they prove indeed
> In prayer, and faith, and hope;
> And see with joy a godly seed
> To build the household up.
>
> As Isaac and Rebecca, give
> A pattern chaste and kind;
> So may this new-met couple live
> In faithful friendship joined.

The joys and contentment of matrimony should never interfere with the pleasures of commemorating one's birthday. The birth-day of wife or husband, of son or daughter, affords an opportunity of cheerful congratulation and devout thanksgiving. Nor can we forget to hang another wreath about our memorial of the man who has done so much to brighten the changes of domestic life with his sprightly and instructive hymns. "They who observe their birth-days," says the poet who taught us to sing at a "house-warming," "which many anciently have done, and some yet do, may by this hymn be remembered of such meditations as are pertinent to their anniversary, and God may be thereby the more often praised for our temporal being:—

> Lord, on this day Thou didst bestow
>   A breathing life on me;
> This day an actor here below,
>   I first began to be;
> And but few rounds the sun hath made
>   Since I that now am here,
> No portion of an essence had
>   Except in Thee it were.
>
> But now there is a part of me—
>   And, Lord, from Thee it springs—
> That shall both named and numbered be
>   With everlasting things.
> And that which time doth wear away,
>   Time's ruin will restore,
> To be rejoined thereto for aye,
>   When time shall be no more.
>
> We now are Thy probationers,
>   And as we run this race,
> The life which is to come prefers
>   To honour or disgrace.
> And they which here the pathway miss
>   That unto virtue tends,
> Shall find no means nor hope of bliss
>   When this brief lifetime ends.
>
> Another year is now begun,
>   And yet I do not see
> How far the time which forth has run,
>   I can account to Thee.
> For I confess I have misspent—
>   My longings to fulfil—
> The times which unto me were but
>   To execute Thy will.

And in the days which are behind,
  Behind if any be,
What profit may I hope to find,
  What will they pleasure me?
Since, though time past I might redeem,
  So much that work will cost,
As, first or last, my time will seem
  In hazard to be lost.

Lord, let this day of my first birth,
  Occasion yearly give,
To keep me mindful why on earth
  My being I receive;
And of my second birth, likewise,
  So mind Thou me thereby,
That I to life may not arise,
  A second death to die.

But let this day, and all the days,
  Which I hereafter view,
Employèd be to give Thee praise,
  To whom all praise is due.
And thus let no man say of me,
  When I to dust return,
Oh, well with him now would it be,
  If he had ne'er been born.

Charles Wesley never allowed a birth-day to pass without some cheerful hymn. Like Withers, he knew how to extract sweets from every passing hour, and never failed to engage the inspiration which touched him as times and seasons went along in brightening with songs every token of our mortal state. No one whom he teaches to sing on his birth-day can forget that hymn which closes with so fine an allusion to the beautiful old Jewish tradition that God drew the soul of Moses out of his body with a kiss; a tradition founded on Deut. xxxiv. 5, "He died according to the word of the Lord," or literally, "at the mouth of Jehovah." The sprightly verses run thus:—

God of my life, to Thee
  My cheerful soul I raise;
Thy goodness bade me be,
  And still prolongs my days.
I see my natal hour return,
And bless the day that I was born.

A clod of living earth,
  Oh glorify Thy name,

> For whom alone my birth,
>   And all my blessings came;
> Creating and preserving grace,
> Let all that is within me praise!
>
> Long as I live beneath,
>   To Thee, O let me live;
> To Thee my every breath
>   In thanks and praises give.
> Whate'er I have, whate'er I am,
> Shall magnify my Maker's name.
>
> My soul, and all its powers,
>   Thine, wholly Thine, shall be:
> All, all my happy hours
>   I consecrate to Thee.
> Me to Thine image now restore,
> And I shall praise Thee evermore.
>
> I wait Thy will to do,
>   As angels do in heaven;
> In Christ a creature new,
>   Most graciously forgiven.
> I wait Thy perfect will to prove,
> All sanctified by spotless love.
>
> Then, when the work is done—
>   The work of faith with power—
> Receive Thy favoured son,
>   In death's triumphant hour,
> Like Moses to Thyself convey,
> And kiss my raptured soul away.

George Withers and Charles Wesley have helped to deck many a bridal service with wreaths of song, and to hallow the merriment of many a grateful birth-day; but there is a name which will ever be balmy to those who devoutly hail the light of a wedding-day. The tender simplicity and quiet devotion of Keble's hymn on "Holy Matrimony" will always be welcome to those who wish to have their nuptial joys happily interwoven with prayer and praise:—

> The voice that breathed o'er Eden,
>   The earliest wedding-day,
> The primal marriage blessing,
>   It hath not passed away.
>
> Still in the pure espousal
>   Of Christian man and maid,
> The Holy Three are with us,
>   The threefold grace is said:

For dower of blessed children,
  For love and faith's sweet sake,
For high mysterious union,
  Which nought on earth may break.

Be present, awful Father,
  To give away this bride,
As Eve Thou gav'st to Adam,
  Out of his own pierced side.

Be present, Son of Mary,
  To join their loving hands,
As Thou didst bind two natures
  In Thine eternal bands.

Be present, holiest Spirit,
  To bless them as they kneel;
As Thou, for Christ, the Bridegroom,
  The heavenly spouse doth seal.

Oh spread Thy pure wing o'er them,
  Let no ill power find place,
When onward to Thine altar,
  The hallow'd path they trace.

To cast their crowns before Thee,
  In perfect sacrifice,
Till to the home of gladness,
  With Christ's own bride they rise.

CHAPTER XX.

HYMNS FROM BENEATH THE CLOUD.

"When gathering clouds around I view,
And days are dark, and friends are few,
On Him I lean, who not in vain
Experienced every human pain;
He sees my wants, allays my fears,
And counts and treasures up my tears."

THE "mercy-seat" of old was sometimes covered with a mysterious cloud, whose shade graciously qualified the lustre of Divine majesty, and from whose depths were evolved the most cheering tokens of God's favour. From that cloud Aaron had seen the fire of wrath shoot forth to consume his unholy sons, and to him it was now like the shadow of death, the fearful symbol of his bitterest trial as a parent and as a priest. But God, by the mouth of Moses, encouraged him to approach, even to that cloud, with the blood of a sin-offering in his hand, giving him the promise, "I will appear in the cloud upon the mercy-seat." The believing Christian, like Aaron, has access to the mercy-seat of his reconciled God, but sometimes finds a cloud on it. His heavenly Father occasionally permits dark mysterious trials to overshadow his way to the propitiatory; trials which, though they appear inscrutable, are blessings in disguise, dispensations of mercy in the form of mysterious trial. He is assured, however, that while he comes by faith in the sacrifice of Christ, those very trials will afford some of the most satisfactory revelations of God's character and will, "I will appear as a cloud upon the mercy-seat." And when our clouds are around the mercy-seat, in gracious association with the purposes of mercy, and the Divine wisdom and power, goodness, holiness, and love, are opened upon the soul from the very clouds which overshadow it, our sorrows are turned into joy, rather than followed by it, and our hearts are comforted with hymns and "songs of deliverance." About forty years ago, Wilson, in his "Noctes Ambrosianæ," says, "Have you seen a little volume entitled 'Tales in Verse, by the Rev. H. F. Lyte,' which seems to have reached a second edition? Now that is the right kind of religious poetry. Mr. Lyte shows how the sins and sorrows of men flow from irreligion, in simple yet strong domestic narrations, told in a style and spirit reminding one sometimes of Goldsmith and sometimes of Crabbe. A volume so humble in its appearance and pretensions runs the risk of being jostled off the highway into by-paths; and, indeed, no harm if it should, for in such retired places it will be pleasant reading—pensive in the shade, and cheerful in the sunshine. Mr. Lyte has reaped

> The harvest of a quiet eye
> That broods and sleeps on its own heart,

and his Christian tales will be read with interest and instruction by many a fireside. 'The Brothers' is exceedingly beautiful. *He ought to give us another volume.*" The gentle and unpretending man, whose volume was so beautiful a reflection of his own character, did "give us another volume," under the title of "Poems, Chiefly Religious." Some of his poems were, indeed, hymns from under the cloud. Though comparatively young, he had often found clouds "upon the mercy-seat." But God had appeared to him, inspiring and hallowing his genius, and calling up songs from his heart, that have been peacefully and resignedly sung by many a tried, but happy Christian. Here is one springing from "thoughts in weakness," and entitled "Submission"—

> Yet think not, O my soul, to keep
>   Thy progress on to God,
> By any road less rough and steep
>   Than that thy fathers trod.
> In tears and trials thou must sow
>   To reap in joy and love;
> We cannot find our home below,
>   And hope for one above.

No; here we labour, watch, and pray,
  Our rest and peace are there;
God will not take the thorn away,
  But give us strength to bear.
The holiest, greatest, best, have thus
  In wisdom learnt to grow;
Yea, He that gave Himself for us
  Was perfected by woe.

Thou—Man of Sorrows—Thou didst not
  The bitter cup decline,
Why should I claim a better lot,
  A smoother path than Thine?
Thou sought'st no treasure here on earth,
  No glory 'neath the skies;
And what Thou dream'dst so little worth,
  Shall I so highly prize?

Did not reproach and wrong rain down
  Upon Thy hallowed head?
Didst Thou not strip off glory's crown
  To wear the thorns instead?
When foes reviled, didst Thou reply,
  Or render ill for ill?
Didst Thou for man bleed, faint, and die,
  And shall I falter still?

In early life to Thee I was
  Consigned by solemn vow,
Enlisted 'neath Thy holy cross,
  Shall I desert it now?
I then 'gainst ev'ry hostile power
  Engaged to follow Thee;
And shall I, at the trying hour,
  Be found the first to flee?

Thou didst not flee, O King of love,
  When Thou wert sorely tried;
When all men fled, and God above
  Appeared His face to hide,
Intent that guiltless blood to shed,
  That should for guilt atone,
The mighty winepress Thou didst tread,
  Unshrinking, though alone.

And shall I murmur or repine
  At aught Thy hand may send?
To whom should I my cause resign,
  If not to such a friend?
Where love and wisdom deign to choose,
  Shall I the choice condemn,
Or dare the medicine to refuse
  That is prescribed by them?

Oh, small the gain when men aspire
  Their Maker to control;
He gives, perhaps, their hearts' desire,
  And leanness to their soul.
Not His to quench the smoking flax,
  Or break the bruised reed;
Or with one pang our patience tax,
  But what He knows we need.

Yet must our steadfastness be tried—
  Yet must our graces grow
By holy warfare. What beside
  Did we expect below?
Is not the way to heavenly gain
  Through earthly grief and loss?
Rest must be won by toil and pain—
  The crown repays the cross.

As woods, when shaken by the breeze,
  Take deeper, firmer root;
As winter's frosts but make the trees
  Abound in summer fruit;
So every heaven-sent pang and throe
  That Christian firmness tries,
But nerves us for our work below,
  And forms us for the skies.

He who sang like this had all the qualifications of a sweet pensive hymnist; but his intellect and heart must have had long chastening. The cloudy shadows were often upon him. Though of somewhat gentle blood, coming into the world at Kelso, in June, 1793, and having all the early advantage of a much-beloved mother's gentle influence and holy lessons, he was soon made to feel the misery of narrow resources, and had to struggle hard for the benefit of a liberal education. His superior and versatile talent, in happy association with firm integrity and amiable temper, opened his way to academical honour, and at last to a "dreary" Irish curacy. While tenderly and faithfully watching a brother clergyman in his last moments, his own heart was made free by the truth which sustained the dying Christian. But watchings by the sick, and subsequent labours on behalf of the bereaved widow and her children, overtaxed his system, and he sank into that consumptive tendency which brought frequent clouds over him all through his remaining life. He travelled on the Continent; and on his return, after trying the climate of

Bristol, and, "after being jostled about from one curacy to another," he settled for a time as lecturer, in the quiet little town of Marazion, on the shore of the beautiful bay of Mount St. Michael, in Cornwall. Here he married. Then, he is found at Lymington, writing poems and the tales that so charmed Professor Wilson. Then on the banks of the Dart, in South Devon. Those who have had the joy of gliding on the waters of that lovely river well remember its strange twists and turns—especially at one point, where it turns back on its course, and where, in following it, we seem now to be plunging into a depth of oaken woods, and now are suddenly amidst an open amphitheatre of leafy heights rising one above another, and opening here and there into bright green lawns and forny slopes. Around a point, and there, under the shelter of hills crowned with billowy foliage, her line of rustic roofs just peeping above the many masses of copse and garden verdure, in dreamy stillness, and in simple and homely beauty, is the village of Dittisham. There the wandering curate nestled in a cottage; going out now and then to officiate at Lower Brixham. Brixham was at last his parish; and there, for twenty years, he toiled in his pastorate under many a cloud—clouds of personal suffering, clouds of pastoral difficulty and discouragement. To his tender, sensitive nature, the peculiar condition of his flock must frequently have been a source of trial. His charge was the busy, shrewd, somewhat rough, but warm-hearted population of a fishing coast and sea-faring district, which had been subjected to all the corrupting influences peculiar to the neighbourhood of naval and military forces during the French war. The social character of his flock had been rendered still more difficult to deal with by the religious prejudices which had sprung up amidst the doctrinal strife between the disciples of such teachers as Dr. Hawker of Plymouth, and their Arminian opponents. The form and face of one old Arminian is still remembered at Brixham—one who was always apt at argument, but who was inexhaustible, too, in the use of sarcasm where argument seemed to be pointless. He was seen one Sunday morning, just outside the door of the Calvinist chapel, bending over the margin of a filthy pool. As the congregation came out, he was in the act of stirring up the stagnant water with a long stick. "What are you looking for?" said his theological antagonists, as they gathered around him. "I am searching," said he, without looking up, but still stirring up the mud, "I am searching for the 'eternal decrees'!" Among a people capable of such modes of religious strife, and with characters so complicated, and under the sway of so many influences, Mr. Lyte would have many a cloud passing over his spirits during his course of pastoral labour. But he never shrank from work. His heart never quailed in suffering. But he solaced himself, and frequently softened and subdued the hard natures around him with hymns from under the cloud. He made hymns for his little ones, and hymns for his hardy fishermen, and hymns for sufferers like himself. How many a cloudy day was cheered by a song like this!—

> My spirit on Thy care,
>   Blest Saviour, I recline;
> Thou wilt not leave me to despair,
>   For Thou art love Divine.
>
> In Thee I place my trust,
>   On Thee I calmly rest;
> I know Thee good, I know Thee just,
>   And count Thy choice the best.
>
> Whate'er events betide,
>   Thy will they all perform;
> Safe in Thy breast my head I hide,
>   Nor fear the coming storm.
>
> Let good or ill befal,
>   It must be good for me;
> Secure of having Thee in all,
>   Of having all in Thee.

The Brixham hymnist's days were numbered. His strength gradually failed. The climate of Italy was several times tried; and his life was spun out for a little while. But the end must come. The autumn of 1847 was approaching, and he must needs take his last journey to the genial south. It was always hard to leave his dear Berry Head. "They tell me," says he, "that the sea is injurious to me. I hope not; for I know of no divorce I should more deprecate than from the lordly ocean. From childhood it has been my friend and playmate, and never have I been weary of gazing on its glorious face. Besides, if I cannot live by tho sea, adieu to poor Berry Head—adieu to the wild birds, and wild flowers, and all the objects that have made my old residence so attractive." But by-and-by he adds, "I am meditating flight again to the south. The little faithful robin is every morning at my window, sweetly warning me that autumnal hours are at hand. The swallows are preparing for flight, and inviting me to accompany them; and yet, alas! while I talk of flying, I am just able to crawl, and ask myself whether I shall be able to leave England at all." He did go, never to return. Before he went, he wished once more to preach to his people. His family was alarmed at the thought; but he gently replied, "It is better to *wear* out than to *rust* out." He felt equal to this last effort, and had no fear. He preached. It was on the "Holy Communion," and it was solemnly significant to hear him say, "Oh, brethren, I can speak feelingly, experimentally, on this point; and I stand here among you seasonably to-day, as alive from the dead, if I may hope to impress it upon you, and induce you to prepare for that solemn hour, which must come to all, by a timely acquaintance with, appreciation of, dependence on, the death of Christ." This was his last appeal. And for the last time he dispensed the sacred elements to his sorrowing flock; and then, exhausted with his effort, he retired with a soul in sweet repose on that Christ whom he had preached with his dying breath. And as the evening drew on he handed to a near and dear relative those undying verses, and his own adapted music for the hymn:—

> Abide with me! Fast falls the eventide;
> The darkness deepens; Lord, with me abide!
> When other helpers fail, and comforts flee,
> Help of the helpless, oh, abide with me!
>
> Swift to its close ebbs out life's little day;
> Earth's joys grow dim; its glories pass away;
> Change and decay in all around I see;
> O Thou, who changest not, abide with me!
>
> Not a brief glance I beg, a passing word,
> But as Thou dwell'st with Thy disciples, Lord,
> Familiar, condescending, patient, free,
> Come, not to sojourn, but abide with me!

Come not in terrors, as the King of kings,
But kind and good, with healing in Thy wings:
Tears for all woes, a heart for every plea,
Come, Friend of sinners, and thus bide with me!

Thou on my head in early youth didst smile,
And, though rebellious and perverse meanwhile,
Thou hast not left me, oft as I left Thee,
On to the close, O Lord, abide with me!

I need Thy presence every passing hour,
What but Thy grace can foil the tempter's power?
Who like Thyself my guide and stay can be,
Through cloud and sunshine, oh, abide with me!

I fear no foe with Thee at hand to bless:
Ills have no weight, and tears no bitterness.
Where is death's sting? where, grave, thy victory?
I triumph still, if Thou abide with me.

Hold, then, Thy cross before my closing eyes;
Shine through the gloom, and point me to the skies;
Heaven's morning breaks, and earth's vain shadows flee,
In life and death, O Lord, abide with me!

This was his last hymn upon earth. He reached Nice, and there his spirit entered into rest. He pointed upwards in passing, and murmured softly, "peace," "joy!" while his face brightened into smiles as the shadow of his last cloud melted before the "Light of Life."

Lyte was not the first pastor and preacher who was used to sing hymns under the cloud. The complex opinions and tempers of society around him in his parish, often perplexing his soul, and making it less easy to keep up his spirits under personal affliction, might remind us of the strange varieties of religious and social life which distinguished the times of Richard Baxter; and probably aggravated that good pastor's sufferings in his own person. No student of curiosities in human life and character could possibly desire a more rare and comprehensive collection of religious party freaks, fancies, and monstrous delusions, than clustered within the range of Richard Baxter's observation. With multiform battalions of Presbyterians, Independents, and Anabaptists, there were Familists begotten in the hotbeds of America, Seekers, Ranters, Quakers, and the stunned and astonished admirers of Jacob Behmen—all pressing their bewildering claims upon his notice. How many a trial of faith and patience must he have had amidst his opportunities of insight into party complications! If we may judge from the tone of his remarks on parties at court, some of his heaviest trials from without must have come upon him in his intercourse with Cromwell. He had several interviews with the Protector; and he speaks of being "wearied" with his speeches, and says, "I told him a little of my judgment; and when two of his company had spun out a great deal more of the time in such tedious but mere ignorant speeches, some four or five hours being spent, I told him that if he would be at the labour to read it, I could tell him more of my mind in writing on two sheets than in that way of speaking in many days. . . . He received my paper, but I scarce believe that he ever read it; for I saw that what he learned must be from himself, being more disposed to speak many hours than to hear one; and little heeding what another said when he had spoken himself." Who would not like to have had the privilege of a quiet glance or two, first at one and then at the other of those two great antagonist faces, during the grave performance of this comical act? Who can pretend to a conception of the style in which the political chief kept up appearances? Baxter's visage would of course be true to its mission. A remakable visage was that of his; never to be forgotten if once seen. Long it was, but decided. Hard, some would say, but telling with fearful eloquence how bravely his righteous soul maintained a life struggle against the acrid humours of a diseased body; how superhuman labours for the world's health had been continued amidst losses of blood and daily sweats, brought upon him, he tells us, by "the acrimonious medicaments" of stupid doctors who thought to save him from the effects of a youthful taste for sour apples, by over-doses of "scurvy grass," wormwood-beer, horse-radish, and mustard! He looked, indeed, like one who, as a last remedy for a depressing affliction, had literally swallowed a "gold bullet of thirty shillings' weight," and, having taken it, "knew not how to be delivered of it again!" With all this, the marks of a confessor were traceable on the good man's countenance. He had been driven from place to place. Now, in prison for preaching at Acton; now, kept out of his pulpit by a military guard; now, seized again, and his goods and books sold to pay the fine for preaching five sermons—he being so ill that he could not be imprisoned without danger of death; and now again, in the King's Bench under a warrant from the villanous Jeffreys, for writing a paraphrase on the New Testament. His later life was often "in peril" for Christ's sake; and there must have been something deeply touching in that impress of dignified sorrow which brought tears into the eyes of Judge Hale when he saw the persecuted man standing before the Bench. His presence must have been felt wherever he appeared. Everybody who knew him acknowledged his mental and moral grandeur. And yet there was a maziness about the action of his versatile powers which seems to be for ever hindering us from completing our estimate of his character. Here, he is seen searching for some mode of effecting a comprehension of religious parties; there, he seems to be pushing and poking in every direction, just by way of keeping things around him alive; ever and anon, however, stopping to make distinctions, or stumbling upon some difficulties which keep him back from his object. Now, he is thundering in the pulpit; now, catechising children; now, lecturing "the powers that be"; now, acting the pastor in true plodding style; now, smelling out heresies, or scenting disguised papists and infidels; and now, making reformed liturgies for all scrupulous souls. How wondrous is the action of his pen! To-day, we see it sketching scenes of "everlasting rest," as if it were an ethereal plume; to-morrow, it is waving to call up terrors from beneath upon the consciences of sinners. Then again, he wields it as a polemical lance, with all the sharpness and unsparing dexterity of a Saracen knight-errant; and then, as if instinct with hopeful submission, it gives birth to a hymn from beneath clouds of trial and suffering, thus:—

> Now, it belongs not to my care
>   Whether I die or live;
> To love and serve Thee is my share,
>   And this Thy grace must give.
>
> If death shall bruise this springing seed
>   Before it comes to fruit,
> The will with Thee goes for the deed,
>   Thy life was in the root.

Would I long bear my heavy load,
  And keep my sorrows long?
Would I long sin against my God,
  And His dear mercy wrong?

How much is sinful flesh my foe,
  That doth my soul pervert
To linger here in sin and woe,
  And steals from God my heart!

Christ leads me through no darker rooms
  Than He went through before;
He that unto God's kingdom comes
  Must enter by this door.

Come, Lord, when grace hath made me meet
  Thy blessed face to see;
For if Thy work on earth be sweet,
  What will Thy glory be?

Then I shall end my sad complaints,
  And weary, sinful days,
And join with the triumphant saints
  That sing Jehovah's praise.

My knowledge of that life is small;
  The eye of faith is dim;
But it's enough that Christ knows all,
  And I shall be with Him.

This is among the ever-living fruits of Richard Baxter's trials. He lived to toil and sing amidst clouds of all variety in weight and shade. But one cloud of more mysterious depth and more awful darkness came at intervals, in a later period, upon a gentler spirit than Baxter, one who seemed far less prepared to rejoice in tribulation. What morbid horrors sometimes wrapped the soul of Cowper! and yet he sang. His hymns arose even from his depth of depression; nor was there ever a sweeter, more simple, and trustful hymn from beneath a cloud than this:—

O Lord, my best desire fulfil,
  And help me to resign
Life, health, and comfort to Thy will,
  And make Thy pleasure mine.

Why should I shrink from Thy command,
  Whose love forbids my fears?
Or tremble at the gracious hand
  That wipes away my tears?

> No, rather let me freely yield
>   What most I prize to Thee,
> Who never hast a good withheld,
>   Or wilt withhold from me.
>
> Thy favour, all my journey through,
>   Thou art engaged to grant;
> What else I want, or think I do,
>   'Tis better still to want.
>
> But ah! my inward spirit cries,
>   Still bend me to Thy sway!
> Else the next cloud that veils the skies
>   Drives all those thoughts away.

Like Cowper, "Theodosia," or Anne Steele, spent her life in quiet retirement, suffering the mysterious will of God alone, or in a retreat to which but few kindred spirits had access. Her rural home, under the shelter of the Hampshire Downs, was to her ceaselessly overshadowed by affliction. She was ever bending beneath infirmities which limited her sphere of physical activity; but she exemplified the inspired truth that, though "no chastening for the present seemeth to be joyous, but grievous, nevertheless afterward it yieldeth the peaceable fruits of righteousness unto them which are exercised thereby." The fruit in her case, as in many others, was to be perpetually renewing itself. Many of her best hymns were the fruit of hallowed affliction, and they live to bring forth "the peaceable fruits of righteousness" in the souls of chastened Christians from generation to generation. How many a heart "desiring resignation and thankfulness" she has taught to sing:—

> When I survey life's varied scene,
>   Amid the darkest hours,
> Sweet rays of comfort shine between,
>   And thorns are mix'd with flowers.
>
> Lord, teach me to adore Thy hand,
>   From whence my comforts flow;
> And let me in this desert land,
>   A glimpse of Canaan know.
>
> Is health and ease my happy share?
>   Oh, may I bless my God;
> Thy kindness let my songs declare,
>   And spread Thy praise abroad.

While such delightful gifts as these
    Are kindly dealt to me,
Be all my hours of health and ease
    Devoted, Lord, to Thee.

In griefs and pains Thy sacred word
    (Dear solace of my soul!)
Celestial comforts can afford,
    And all their power control.

When present sufferings pain my heart,
    Or future terrors rise,
And light and hope almost depart
    From these dejected eyes:

Thy powerful word supports my hope,
    Sweet cordial of the mind;
And bears my fainting spirit up,
    And bids me wait resign'd.

And oh, whate'er of earthly bliss
    Thy sovereign hand denies,
Accepted at Thy throne of grace,
    Let this petition rise:

" Give me a calm, a thankful heart,
    From every murmur free;
The blessings of Thy grace impart,
    And let me live to Thee.

" Let the sweet hope that Thou art mine,
    My path of life attend;
Thy presence through my journey shine,
    And bless its happy end."

These childlike expressions of Anne Steele's calm resignation and heavenly desires will, perhaps, bring up in many a heart a feeling of gratitude for the songs of many other devout but suffering women. Who has not been melted into more perfect resignation, amidst the sorrows of daily life, while singing, in harmony with the family group of an evening, Charlotte Elliott's well-known verses, " Thy will be done!"

My God and Father, while I stray
Far from my home on life's rough way,
Oh teach me from my heart to say,
    Thy will be done!

Though dark my path and sad my lot,
Let me be still, and murmur not,
Or breathe the prayer divinely taught,
    Thy will be done!

What though in lonely grief I sigh
For friends beloved, no longer nigh,
Submissive still would I reply,
    Thy will be done!

Though Thou hast called me to resign
What most I prized, it ne'er was mine,
I have but yielded what was Thine;
    Thy will be done!

Should grief or sickness waste away
My life in premature decay,
My Father! still I strive to say,
    Thy will be done!

Let but my fainting heart be blest
With Thy sweet Spirit for its guest,
My God, to Thee I leave the rest;
    Thy will be done!

Renew my will from day to day;
Blend it with Thine; and take away
All that now makes it hard to say,
    Thy will be done!

Then, when on earth I breathe no more,
The prayer, oft mix'd with tears before,
I'll sing upon a happier shore,
    Thy will be done!

How this hushes the tremulous heart! and how gently the touches of its music persuade the soul into repose beneath the "cloud upon the mercy-seat"! Charles Wesley's hymns, entitled, "Believer's Suffering," are of another class. They lack, in most cases, that tender, soothing grace which has distinguished the songs of more retired and less observed sufferers; but of all hymns beneath clouds of trial, they approach nearest, it may be, to that triumphant faith, unquenchable joy, and boastful reliance on God, which St. Paul exemplifies and sets forth in his teaching. So in those fine verses of his:—

Peace! doubting heart; my God's I am!
  Who form'd me man, forbids my fear:
The Lord hath call'd me by my name;
  The Lord protects, for ever near;
His blood for me did once atone,
And still He loves and guards His own.

When passing through the watery deep,
  I ask in faith His promised aid,

The waves in awful distance keep,
　And shrink from my devoted head;
Fearless their violence I dare,
They cannot harm, for God is there.

To Him mine eye of faith I turn,
　And through the fire pursue my way;
The fire forgets its power to burn,
　The lambent flames around me play;
I own His power, accept the sign,
And shout to prove the Saviour mine.

Still nigh me, O my Saviour, stand!
　And guard in fierce temptation's hour;
Hide in the hollow of Thy hand;
　Show forth in me thy Saviour's power;
Still be Thy arms my sure defence:
Nor earth nor hell shall pluck me thence.

Since Thou hast bid me come to Thee,
　(Good as Thou art, and strong to save;)
I'll walk o'er life's tempestuous sea,
　Upborne by the unyielding wave,
Dauntless, though rocks of pride be near,
And yawning whirlpools of despair.

When darkness intercepts the skies,
　And sorrow's waves around us roll,
When high the storms of passion rise,
　And half o'erwhelm my sinking soul,
My soul a sudden calm shall feel,
And hear a whisper, "Peace, be still!"

Though in affliction's furnace tried,
　Unhurt on snares and death I'll tread,
Though sin assail, and hell, thrown wide,
　Pour all its horrors on my head;
Like Moses' bush, I'll mount the higher,
And flourish unconsumed in fire.

No Christian sufferer can sing this without having St. Paul's utterances amidst tribulation sounding in his ear and in his heart, "We rejoice in hope of the glory of God; and not only so, but we glory in tribulation also, knowing that tribulation worketh patience; and patience, experience; and experience, hope; and hope maketh not ashamed, because the love of God is shed abroad in our hearts by the Holy Ghost which is given unto us. . . . . I am exceeding joyful in all our tribulations. . . . . Who shall separate us from the love of Christ? shall tribulation, or distress, or persecution, or famine, or peril, or sword? Nay, in all these things we are more than conquerors through Him that loved us. For I am persuaded, that neither death, nor life, nor angels, nor principalities, nor powers, nor things present, nor things to come, nor height, nor depth, nor any other creature, shall be able to separate us from the love of God, which is in Christ Jesus our Lord."

CHAPTER XXI.

HYMNS OF GETHSEMANE AND THE CROSS.

"God forbid that I should glory, save in the cross of our Lord Jesus Christ."

THERE are some doctrines of Christianity which all true believers acknowledge as peculiarly sacred — doctrines whose proper place in the Christian system is far removed from the inquisitive touch of mere reason; so that they stand confessedly exempt from the test of human controversy. Such doctrines seem to be the "heavenly things" which answer to the most hallowed types of former ages. Like the consecrated symbols of the "holiest place," they are designed neither to gratify the eye of vain curiosity, nor to furnish the disputer with materials for strife. No, they are never to be approached but for purposes of devotion. Among these inviolable truths is the doctrine of the cross. This excites the highest devotion of the glorified; while it is viewed with the deepest veneration by "the holy church throughout all the world." What the ark or the altar was to the ancient Jew, the cross is to the true Christian, his holiest thing. While he comes to it as his guide to the mercy-seat, it is his joy, his glory, his life; but when he carries it into the battle-field, he loses his Shekinah, and that in which he gloried is profaned by the aliens of Askalon and Gath. While he comes to the altar of the cross with his hands washed in innocency, he receives the blessings of a propitiation; but when he ventures to mutilate the altar that he may secure weapons for theological combat, he is in danger of being scathed by the fire which but now had kindled his sacrifice. Hence there is nothing which revelation so carefully guards as the cross of Jesus Christ. Around this the angels make their circles, with holy desire to look into its mysteries. By this, Moses and the prophets take their stand, and pour around it the jasper light of visions and the glory of prophetic oracles. Here are trains of typical priests, attended by the prefigurations of bleeding victims and sacrificial patterns. By the scene of agony and the cross, apostles and martyrs bear witness, and watch, and pray. Of the cross they write and speak; for the cross they toil, and suffer, and die. The cross is their only altar, their highest boast, their strength in life, their hope in death, their song in heaven. What a mysterious hush comes over the soul at the mention of Gethsemane! What a holy charm is there in the cross! How deeply the heart, in its best moments, responds to the name of Christ crucified!—

> Is it not strange, the darkest hour
>   That ever dawn'd on sinful earth
> Should touch the heart with softer power
>   For comfort, than an angel's mirth?
> That to the cross the mourner's eye should turn,
> Sooner than where the stars of Christmas burn?
>
> Yet so it is: for duly there
>   The bitter herbs of earth are set,
> Till temper'd by the Saviour's prayer,
>   And with the Saviour's life-blood wet,
> They turn to sweetness, and drop holy balm,
> Soft as imprison'd martyr's death-bed calm.

But those only know this "sweetness" who have felt the bitterness of sin, and have come to Calvary hopeless of healing balm from every other source. Nor has any human psalmist ever breathed the spirit of Gethsemane or the cross until his own heart has been agonized by a sense of its sinfulness, and, by virtue of the Redeemer's blood, has been melted into loving sympathy with his suffering Lord. No mere genius can worthily sing of the "agony and bloody sweat." No unhallowed poetic intellect has ever produced a hymn replete with the Divine life and saving power of the cross. Those hymns of Gethsemane and the cross which are most precious to saintly hearts, and which will be sung with deeper and deeper feeling by every coming generation of English Christians, are from the pens of those whose will and affections have been most profoundly hallowed in fellowship with Him whose soul, for our sakes, was "exceeding sorrowful, even unto death." One of these has said, "The week before Easter, 1757, I had such an amazing view of the agony of Christ in the garden, as I know not well how to describe. I was lost in wonder and adoration; and the impression was too deep, I believe, ever to be obliterated. I shall say no more of this; but only remark, that, notwithstanding all that is talked about the sufferings of Jesus, none can know anything of them, but by the Holy Ghost; and I believe, that he that knows most knows but very little. It was then I made the first part of my hymn 'On the Passion.'" That hymn remains, thus:—

> Come, all ye chosen saints of God
> That long to feel the cleansing blood,
> In pensive pleasures join with me
> To sing of sad Gethsemane.
>
> Gethsemane, the olive press!
> (And why so call'd let Christians guess,)
> Fit name, fit place, where vengeance strove,
> And grip'd and grappled hard with love.
>
> 'Twas here the Lord of life appeared,
> And sigh'd, and groan'd, and pray'd, and fear'd!
> Bore all Incarnate God could bear,
> With strength enough, and none to spare.
>
> The powers of hell united pressed,
> And squeezed His heart, and bruised His breast.
> What dreadful conflicts raged within,
> When sweat and blood forced through the skin!
>
> Despatched from heaven an angel stood,
> Amazed to find Him bathed in blood;
> Adored by angels, and obeyed;
> But lower now than angels made!
>
> He stood to strengthen, not to fight:
> Justice exacts its utmost mite.
> This Victim vengeance will pursue:
> He undertook, and must go through.
>
> Three favoured servants, left not far,
> Were bid to wait and watch the war;
> But Christ withdrawn, what watch we keep
> To shun the sight, they sank in sleep.
>
> Backwards and forwards thrice He ran,
> As if He sought some help from man:
> Or wished, at least, they would condole
> ('Twas all they could) His tortured soul.

Whate'er He sought for, there was none:
Our Captain fought the field alone.
Soon as the Chief to battle led,
That moment every soldier fled.

Mysterious conflict! dark disguise!
Hid from all creatures' peering eyes.
Angels astonish'd view'd the scene,
And wonder yet what all could mean.

O Mount of Olives, sacred grove!
O garden, scene of tragic love!
What bitter herbs thy beds produce!
How rank their scent, how harsh their juice!

Rare virtues now these herbs contain;
The Saviour suck'd out all their bane.
My mouth with those if conscience cram,
I'll eat them with the Paschal Lamb.

O Kedron, gloomy brook, how foul
Thy black, polluted waters roll!
No tongue can tell, but some can taste,
The filth that into thee was cast.

In Eden's garden there was food
Of every kind for man while good;
But banish'd hence, we flee to thee,
O garden of Gethsemane!

The hymnist who thus so deeply sympathized with his agonizing Lord was Joseph Hart, who, from 1760 to 1768, was the earnest, eloquent, and much-beloved minister of the congregation which met in the old wooden meeting-house in Jewin Street, built in 1672 for the well-known William Jenkyn. Born in London, about the year 1712, and brought up by pious parents, he began, when entering on manhood, to be deeply anxious about his personal salvation. For seven years his life was, as he tells us, "an uneasy, restless round of sinning and repenting, working and dreading. At length the Lord was pleased to comfort me a little by enabling me to appropriate, in some measure, the merits of the Saviour to my own soul. In this blessed state my continuance was but short, for, rushing impetuously into notions beyond my experience, I hasted to make myself a Christian by mere doctrine, adopting other men's opinions before I had tried them; and set up for a great light in religion, disregarding the internal work of grace began in my soul by the Holy Ghost. This liberty, assumed by myself and not given by Christ, soon grew to libertinism, in which I took large progressive strides, and advanced to a dreadful height, both in principle and practice. In a word, I ran such dangerous lengths both of carnal and spiritual wickedness, that I even outwent professed infidels, and shocked the irreligious and profane with my horrid blasphemies and monstrous impieties. . . In this abominable state I continued for more than ten years. . . . Then I began by degrees to reform a little, and to live in a more soberly and orderly manner. . . . For several years I went on in this easy, cool, smooth, and indolent manner, with a lukewarm, insipid kind of religion. . . . But the fountains of the great deeps of my sinful nature were not broken up. . . . Nor was the blood of Christ effectually applied to my soul. I looked on His death, indeed, as the grand sacrifice for sin, but I did not see the inestimable value of His blood and righteousness clearly enough to make me abhor myself, and count all things but dung and dross. On the contrary, when I used to read the Scriptures (which I now did constantly, both in English and the original languages), though my mind was often affected, and my understanding illuminated by many passages that treated of the Saviour, yet I was so far from seeing or owning that there was such a necessity for His death, and that it could be of such infinite value as is represented, that I have often resolved—oh, the horrible depth of man's fall, and the desperate wickedness of the human heart!—that I never would believe it. After a time, I fell into a deep despondency of mind, and, shunning all company, I went about alone, bewailing my sad and dark condition. . . . This suffering was aggravated by physical infirmity and pain, and in this sad state I went moping about till Whit Sunday, 1757, when I happened to go in the afternoon to the Moravian Chapel in Fetter Lane. The minister preached from Rev. iii. 10. I was much impressed. I thought of hastening to Tottenham Court Chapel, but presently altered my mind, and returned to my own house. I was hardly got home, when I felt myself melting away into a strange softness of affection which made me fling myself on my knees before God. My horrors were immediately expelled, and such light and comfort flowed into my heart as no words can paint. The Lord, by His Spirit of love, came not in a visionary manner into my brain, but with such Divine power and energy into my soul that I was lost in blissful amazement. I cried out, 'What, me, Lord?' His Spirit answered in me, 'Yes, thee!' I objected, 'But I have been so unspeakably vile and wicked!' The answer was, 'I pardon thee freely and fully!' The alteration I then felt in my soul was as sudden and palpable as that which is experienced by a person staggering and almost sinking under a burden when it is immediately taken from his shoulders. Tears ran in streams from my eyes for a considerable while, and I was so swallowed up in joy and thankfulness that I hardly knew where I was. I threw myself willingly into my Saviour's hands; lay weeping at His feet, wholly resigned to His will, and only begging that I might, if He were graciously pleased to permit it, be of some service to His Church and people. . . . Jesus Christ and Him crucified is now the only thing I desire to know. All things to me are rich only when they are enriched with the blood of the Lamb." In this remarkable course of soul discipline, and this deep experience of Divine mercy through the sufferings and death of the Saviour whom he had blasphemed, is to be found the secret of that spiritual freshness and touching power of his hymn on the "passion and the cross." None but a heart like his could have uttered his hymn on Good Friday:—

> Oh! what a sad and doleful night
>   Preceded that day's morn,
> When darkness seized the Lord of light,
>   And sin by Christ was borne!
>
> When our intolerable load
>   Upon His soul was laid,
> And the vindictive wrath of God
>   Flamed furious on His head!
>
> We in our Conqueror well may boast:
>   For none but God alone
> Can know how dear the victory cost,
>   How hardly it was won.
>
> Forth from the garden fully tried,
>   Our bruised Champion came,
> To suffer what remain'd beside
>   Of pain, and grief, and shame.

Mock'd, spat upon, and crown'd with thorns,
  A spectacle He stood;
His back with scourges lashed and torn,
  A victim bathed in blood.

Nail'd to the cross through hands and feet,
  He hung in open view;
To make His sorrows quite complete,
  By God deserted too!

Through nature's works the woes He felt
  With soft infection ran;
The hardest things could break or melt,
  Except the heart of man!

This day before Thee, Lord, we come,
  Oh, melt our hearts, or break;
For, should we now continue dumb,
  The very stones would speak!

True, Thou hast paid the heavy debt,
  And made believers clean;
But he knows nothing of it yet
  Who is not grieved at sin.

A faithful friend of grief partakes;
  But union can be none
Betwixt a heart like melting wax
  And hearts as hard as stone;

Betwixt a Head diffusing blood,
  And members sound and whole;
Betwixt an agonizing God,
  And an unfeeling soul.

Lord, my long'd happiness is full,
  When I can go with Thee
To Golgotha: the place of skull
  Is heav'n on earth to me!

With a soul thus finding its heaven at the foot of the cross, and overflowing with the love of Christ, and pity and compassion for those whose sins were laid upon Jesus, and to whom his Divine Master was saying, "Come unto me," Mr. Hart had his way opened to the pulpit in Jewin Street, where, for eight years, he zealously and affectionately pressed the invitations of his Lord upon the hearts of his fellow-men. Nor can the spirit of his ministry be better expressed than in his simple, warm, and persuasive hymn, entitled, "Come, and welcome, to Jesus Christ:"—

Come, ye sinners, poor and wretched,
　Weak and wounded, sick, and sore;
Jesus ready stands to save you,
　Full of pity, joined with power,
　　He is able,
　He is willing; doubt no more.

Ho! ye needy, come, and welcome,
　God's free bounty glorify;
True belief, and true repentance,
　Ev'ry grace that brings us nigh,
　　Without money,
　Come to Jesus Christ and buy.

Let not conscience make you linger,
　Nor of fitness fondly dream;
All the fitness He requireth,
　Is to feel your need of Him.
　　This He gives you;
　'Tis the Spirit's rising beam.

Come, ye weary, heavy-laden,
　Bruised and mangled by the fall;
If you tarry till you're better,
　You will never come at all.
　　Not the righteous,
　Sinners Jesus came to call.

View Him grov'lling in the garden,
　Lo! your Maker prostrate lies;
On the bloody tree behold Him!
　Hear Him cry before He dies,
　　" It is finish'd!"
　Sinner, will not this suffice?

Lo! th' incarnate God ascended
　Pleads the merits of His blood;
Venture on Him, venture wholly,
　Let no other trust intrude.
　　None but Jesus
　Can do helpless sinners good.

Saints and angels, join'd in concert,
　Sing the praises of the Lamb;
While the blissful seats of heaven
　Sweetly echo with His name.
　　Halleluiah!
　Sinners here may sing the same.

All who are familiar with hymns of the cross will always associate the names of two hymnists in loving companionship at the Saviour's feet, the names of two men of different training and different temper, in some things alike, and yet unlike—Newton and Cowper—more happy in their union as hymnists than in the fruit of their spiritual fellowship. There was Newton on the banks of the Ouse, with his iron frame still unbroken by the hardships, changes, and excesses of an ungodly life, spent in hostile climates and on shipboard, now giving his redeemed energies to Christ, and pouring forth the peace, and joy, and hope, and love of his regenerated nature from the pulpit, and in his Olney hymns. Ever alive to the virtue of the atonement, he touchingly records the story of his own conversion in the hymn which he teaches us to sing while " looking at the cross " :—

> In evil long I took delight,
>   Unawed by shame or fear,
> Till a new object struck my sight,
>   And stopp'd my wild career.
>
> I saw One hanging on the tree,
>   In agonies and blood,
> Who fixed His languid eyes on me,
>   As near His cross I stood.
>
> Sure never till my latest breath
>   Can I forget that look;
> It seem'd to charge me with His death,
>   Though not a word He spoke.
>
> My conscience felt and own'd the guilt,
>   And plunged me in despair;
> I saw my sins His blood had spilt,
>   And help'd to nail Him there.
>
> Alas! I knew not what I did,
>   But now my tears are vain;
> Where shall my trembling soul be hid?
>   For I the Lord have slain.
>
> A second look He gave, which said
>   " I freely all forgive;
> The blood is for thy ransom paid,
>   I die that thou may'st live."
>
> Thus, while His death my sin displays
>   In all its blackest hue,
> (Such is the mystery of grace),
>   It seals my pardon too.

> With pleasing grief, and mournful joy,
>   My spirit now is fill'd,
> That I should such a life destroy,
>   Yet live by Him I kill'd.

There, too, was the timid, gentle Cowper, ever tremulous as he thought of eternal woe. There, on the banks of the same quiet Ouse, brooding over the inward horrors of his diseased imagination, yet ever proving to those around him the goodness of his heart, and out of his gracious treasures preparing blessings for the future generations of those who love purity, beauty, and truth. Unhappy, and yet happy Cowper! Who does not weep over his sorrows? Who does not bless heaven for his genius, his devotion, and his works? Who does not, as he speeds past on the rail, look with a sigh and a smile upon his quiet birth-place, Berkhampstead, still reposing in its verdant hollow? And few, perhaps, as the old tower of his father's church is lost to sight, will fail to indulge in pensive thoughts about the pensive man, who, after a youth-tide spent "from morning to night in giggling and making giggle," was found shattered and broken in spirits, victimized by morbid melancholy, living, as he tells us, like one descending a ladder which dipped into the infernal regions, until he hung on the last frail step, only needing a touch to send him for ever into the fiery abyss. Now at Huntingdon, now at Olney, and then at Weston. Ministered to, as by angels, by his Mary, Mrs. Unwin, Lady Austen, and Lady Hesketh; tormented ever and anon by dark fiendish thoughts about himself, he writes for amusement or for relief; and with a fancy ever fresh, a poetic genius as pure and clear as the morning, and, amidst all his dreadful fears, with a heart most tenderly alive to good, and most warmly devoted to his Redeemer, he graced his friend Newton's Olney Hymn-book with many a precious gem, and taught all who have followed him to the cross to sing of the Blessed One in whose Divine presence he and the kind companions of his fitful life are now for ever at rest. He now realizes the hopes which in one of his happier moments on earth he uttered in that immortal hymn of "Praise for the Fountain Opened;" that hymn that will always be on some happy lips:—

There is a fountain fill'd with blood,
  Drawn from Emmanuel's veins,
And sinners plunged beneath that flood,
  Lose all their guilty stains.

The dying thief rejoiced to see
  That fountain in his day;
And there have I, as vile as he,
  Wash'd all my sins away.

Dear dying Lamb, Thy precious blood
  Shall never lose its power,
Till all the ransom'd Church of God
  Be saved to sin no more.

E'er since by faith I saw the stream
  Thy flowing wounds supply,
Redeeming love has been my theme,
  And shall be till I die.

Then in a nobler, sweeter song,
  I'll sing Thy power to save,
When this poor lisping, stamm'ring tongue
  Lies silent in the grave.

Lord, I believe Thou hast prepared
  (Unworthy though I be)
For me a blood-bought free reward,
  A golden harp for me!

'Tis strung, and tuned, for endless years,
  And formed by power Divine,
To sound in God the Father's ears
  No other name but Thine.

Many consecrated singers gather around the cross; generation after generation they press upward to the holy scene; and each brings its tributary hymns. The devoted genius is of all variety; the manner of the music changes as the hymnists follow each other; but amidst all changes of time, all variations of circumstance, rhythm, rhyme, metre, and tone, the theme is the same, ever fresh, never exhausted—the holy, the mysterious, the life-giving cross. Greek choristers may pass away, Latin hymnists may leave the world—a Wesley, a Toplady, a Hart, a Newton, and a Cowper may cease their mortal psalmody, but voices come on still; the hymning does not cease. Witness this strain that floated across the Irish Channel a few years ago from one who still lives to sing on a "Good Friday." "And it was about the sixth hour, and there was darkness all over the land until the ninth hour":—

Dark and dim the daylight rose,
Destined with Thy life to close;
With the life Thou didst assume
As Thy passport through the tomb;
But a drop in the great sea,
Lord, of Thine eternity.

On the tree accursèd dying,
Death and hell beneath Thee lying,
There their doom long look'd for meet,
Crush'd beneath Thy bruisèd feet;
Bitter scorn and cruel pain
Do their worst with Thee in vain,
For Thou answerest not again!

Prayers for them are Thy replies
To Thy taunting enemies;
From Thy piercèd side doth flow
Medicine for all our woe.

Thy dear arms outstretch'd we see,
Drawing the whole world to Thee;
And that head so meekly bow'd
'Neath the momentary cloud,
Breathes, with its departing breath,
Life accomplishèd in death.

Lo! the veil is rent asunder,
Darkness over head, and under;
Graves are open'd, earth doth quake,
And the very dead awake.

Angels who beside Thee kept
Watch, and o'er Thy passion wept,
Now before Thee, at the gate
Of Thy paradise, do wait;
Hymns celestial round Thee pouring,
As they bend, the might adoring
Of Thy Godhead laid to rest
In the regions of the blest.

Saviour of Thy people! Now,
With Thy wounded hands and brow,
Gone to plead beside the Throne,
Thy redemption for Thine own,
Grace to seek in large supplies,
Even for Thine enemies;

Hear us when to Thee we cry,
Make us feel that Thou art nigh,
Help us when in time of need,
We Thy great deliv'rance plead;
Cleanse us with Thy precious blood,
O Thou gentle Lamb of God!

By Thy cross and passion save us;
By the hope those suff'rings gave us;
By Thine agony and sweat;
By Thy prayers on Olivet;
By Thy sighs and by Thy tears;
By Thy people's hopes and fears;
By the peace vouchsafed to Thee
When in dark Gethsemane!

By the sacramental tide
Gushing from Thy wounded side;
By the load of others' sin,
That oppress'd Thy soul within;
By the wondrous love Thou bore us,
That by death Thou shouldst restore us;
By that mercy and that love,
Hear us, Lord, in heav'n above!

In the midnight of our sadness,
In the noontide of our gladness,
Through each changing scene of life,
Calm and sunshine, storm and strife;
At the last dread parting hour,
In Thy judgment's might and power—

Lord, deliver and defend us,
Let Thy Spirit still attend us;
Be Thine eye our leading star,
Guiding upward from afar;
Here,—the surety Thou art nigh,
There,—the blest reality!

This fine help to our devotion on the anniversary of the Holy Cross is from the "Parish Musings" of John S. B. Monsell, now the vicar of Egham, in Surrey. And every heart that has learnt to utter a daily litany, and with holy fervour to cry, "By Thine agony and bloody sweat; By Thy cross and passion, Good Lord deliver us!" will ever think of the reverend hymnist as one whose "Musings" have kindled holy fire in many, many a heart beside his own. Nor can our gratitude ever equal the blessing which comes upon England in answer to the metrical prayers of her pious laymen; laymen whose simple and earnest piety adorns many a lordly home of the land; laymen, who wear their knightly honours in humble dependence on their Saviour; and who, like Sir Robert Grant, have mind and heart enough to lead the devotions of the multitudes around them, in solemn litanies like this:—

Saviour, when in dust to Thee
Low we bend the adoring knee ;
When repentant to the skies
Scarce we lift our weeping eyes ;
Oh ! by all the pains and woe
Suffer'd once for man below,
Bending from Thy throne on high,
Hear our solemn Litany !

By Thy helpless infant years ;
By Thy life of want and tears ;
By Thy days of sore distress
In the savage wilderness ;
By the dread mysterious hour
Of th' insulting tempter's power :
Turn, oh, turn a favouring eye,
Hear our solemn Litany !

By the sacred griefs that wept
O'er the grave where Lazarus slept ;
By the boding tears that flowed
Over Salem's loved abode ;
By the anguish'd sigh that told
Treachery lurk'd within Thy fold ;
From Thy seat above the sky,
Hear our solemn Litany !

By Thine hour of dire despair ;
By Thine agony of prayer ;
By the cross, the nail, the thorn,
Piercing spear, and torturing scorn ;
By the gloom that veil'd the skies
O'er the dreadful sacrifice !
Listen to our humble cry,
Hear our solemn Litany !

By Thy deep expiring groan ;
By the sad sepulchral stone ;
By the vault, whose dark abode
Held in vain the rising God ;
Oh ! from earth to heaven restored,
Mighty re-ascended Lord,
Listen, listen to the cry
Of our solemn Litany !

Calvary was a scene of mournful attraction to the "women which followed Jesus from Galilee, ministering unto Him. Among which was Mary Magdalene, and Mary the mother of James and Joses, and the mother of Zebedee's children." Blessed women ! To them it was a dark day indeed. That cross was to them a bitter cross ;

for it was the cross of their beloved Master. But they found life in that very cross; and out of that deep darkness came the light of life, healing for ever their broken hearts. Women have never ceased to surround the cross. They come from age to age, not from Galilee merely, but from far off among the Gentiles. Theirs has been the deepest homage; theirs the warmest devotion; theirs the profoundest sympathy; theirs the sweetest songs. Among the women, the English women, who have loved the cross, and sung of its salvation, Caroline Bowles, afterwards Mrs. Southey, has left one touching proof of her own living, happy interest in her Saviour's death. It comes to us in a hymn which devoutly records her own heart's experience on Calvary; while it affords the secret of that Christian tenderness which she exemplified as the gentle and pious helpmeet of the declining and departing Southey. Her hymn beautifully shows the harmony between reverent peacefulness and holy joy in all true devotion to the cross: thus:—

> Down from the willow bough
>   My slumbering harp I'll take,
> And bid its silent strings
>   To heavenly themes awake;
> Peaceful let its breathings be
> When I sing of Calvary.
>
> Love, love divine I sing;
>   Oh for a seraph's lyre,
> Bathed in Siloa's stream,
>   And touch'd with living fire;
> Lofty, pure the strain should be
> When I sing of Calvary.
>
> Love, love on earth appears,
>   The wretched throng His way;
> He beareth all their griefs,
>   He wipes their tears away!
> Soft and sweet the strain should be,
> Saviour, when I sing of Thee.
>
> He saw me as He passed,
>   In hopeless sorrow lie,
> Condemned and doomed to death,
>   And no salvation nigh;
> Loud and long the strain should be,
> When I sing His love to me.

"I die for thee," He said—
 Behold the cross arise;
And lo, He bows His head—
 He bows His head and dies.
Soft, my harp, thy breathing be,
Let me weep on Calvary.

He lives! again He lives!
 I hear the voice of love,
He comes to soothe my fears,
 And draw my soul above;
Joyful now the strain should be,
When I sing of Calvary.

CHAPTER XXII.

FUNERAL HYMNS.

"So when even was come, the Lord of the vineyard saith unto his steward, Call the labourers, and give them their hire."

Who has not gone to the grave-side often enough, even during a short life, to become mournfully familiar with the solemn magnificence of our English Burial Service? It can scarcely be said which is the more deeply impressive, the holy fervour, reverent submission, soaring faith, and heavenward swell of the prayers, or the simple grandeur of the anthems, awing and melting us by turns. Now the soul kindles, and now it softens into tears; and now again its death-song becomes intense with prayerful feeling, as the utterances rise:—

> In the midst of life we are in death:
> Of whom may we seek for succour
> But of Thee, O Lord!
> Who for our sins art justly displeased.
> Yet, O Lord God most holy,
> O Lord most mighty,
> O holy and most merciful Saviour,
> Deliver us not into the bitter pains
> Of eternal death!
> Thou knowest, Lord, the secrets of our hearts;
> Shut not Thy merciful ears to our prayer;
> But spare us, Lord most holy,
> O God most mighty,
> O holy and merciful Saviour,
> Thou most worthy Judge eternal,
> Suffer us not at our last hour,
> For any pains of death,
> To fall from Thee!

This is an ancient hymn. It comes to us borne along from generation to generation by the voices of nearly a thousand years. Just about the beginning of the tenth century, there was a Swiss monk in the celebrated monastery of St. Gall, whose name was Notker. If not " slow of speech," he lisped, and was, therefore, nicknamed by his brethren, Balbulus. His defect of speech, however, as in the case of many a deep thinker and bright genius, was no check upon his thoughts; he was a quiet thinker. Nor did it prevent the play of his somewhat hallowed imagination. As he watched the samphire-gatherers fearfully pendant over the brink of death, as they pursued their perilous calling on the precipices around St. Gall, he caught the suggestion of "death in the midst of life;" and when he saw the bridge-builders at Martinsbruck exposing themselves every moment to death, in order to secure for the living a safe passage over danger, the suggestion ripened into a fruitful form; and his monastery was taught to sing or chant the anthem which soon became common to entire Christendom. Notker himself died, and was buried in 912; but his funeral hymn will never die while any European Christians live to bury their dead amidst the solemnities of the ancient service for the grave-side. Notker's hymn long formed a part of the funeral service in Germany; and Luther's translation of it is still with us, rendered into English thus—

> In the midst of life, behold
>   Death hath girt us round,
> Whom for help then shall we pray,
>   Where shall grace be found?
> In Thee, O Lord, alone!
> We rue the evil we have done,
> That Thy wrath on us hath drawn.
>   Holy Lord and God!
>   Strong and holy God!
> Merciful and holy Saviour,
>   Eternal God!
> Leave us not to sink beneath
> Those dark pains of bitter death,
>   Kyrie eleison.
>
> In the midst of death, the jaws
>   Of hell against us gape.
> Who from peril dire as this
>   Openeth us escape?

'Tis Thou, O Lord, alone!
Our bitter suffering and our sin
Pity from Thy mercy win,
    Holy Lord and God!
    Strong and holy God!
Merciful and holy Saviour!
    Eternal God!
Let not dread our souls o'erwhelm,
Of the dark and burning realm,
    Kyrie eleison.

In the midst of hell would sin
    Drive us to despair;
Whither shall we flee away?
    Where is refuge, where?
With Thee, Lord Christ, alone!
For Thou hast shed Thy precious blood,
All our sins Thou makest good.
    Holy Lord and God!
    Strong and holy God!
Merciful and holy Saviour!
    Eternal God,
Leave us not to fall on death,
From the hope of Thy true faith,
    Kyrie eleison!

In the year 1768, as the month of May was closing, there was a great gathering in the burial ground of Bunhill Fields. The crowd was densely packed around an open grave, by the side of which stood the Rev. Andrew Kinsman, of Plymouth. He was delivering a funeral oration, in the course of which he said of the departed:—"I had the pleasure of knowing, and, I will say, the honour, too, of preaching the Gospel to his aged parents, who both died in the faith. I knew him to be the son of many prayers years ago; and from this knowledge, as soon as I had read his 'Experience' and hymns (believing his tender parents' earnest addresses to the throne of grace for him were in some measure answered), I found my heart warmed with the relation, and my soul knit to the writer. This love led me eagerly to seek after a personal interview, and, from the year 1759, a religious and literary correspondence ensued. Oh, how full were his epistles of sound experience! How sweetly did he write of Jesus and His great salvation! Since that we have loved as brethren and servants of the same Master." The address was ended, and then the multitude lifted up their voices and sang:—

Sons of God by bless'd adoption,
 View the dead with steady eyes;
What is sown thus in corruption
 Shall in incorruption rise.
What is sown in death's dishonour
 Shall revive to glory's light;
What is sown in this weak manner
 Shall be raised in matchless might.

Earthly cavern, to thy keeping
 We commit our brother's dust;
Keep it safely, softly sleeping,
 Till our Lord demand thy trust.
Sweetly sleep, dear saint, in Jesus:
 Thou with us shalt wake from death;
Hold he cannot, though he seize us;
 We his power defy by faith.

Jesus, Thy rich consolations
 To Thy mourning people send;
May we all, with faith and patience,
 Wait for our approaching end.
Keep from courage, vain or vaunted;
 For our change our hearts prepare:
Give us confidence undaunted,
 Cheerful hope and godly fear.

The funeral hymn had been written by the one whose dust was now covered. The grave was closed, and the stone which was laid upon it is still there; and those who visit the spot should linger awhile, and think of the youthful errors and sins, the dark conflicts, the bitter tears, the spiritual struggles, the sound conversion, the consecrated talents, the faithful ministry, and the fresh and fruitful hymns of Joseph Hart; and when they have caught the fragrance of his memory, and hear the songs of those who still thank God for his ministry in the old meeting-house of Jewin Street, they may be ready to chant the soothing and assuring hymn which arose, in some solemn moments, nearly fifty years ago, from the heart of Henry Hart Milman, whose venerable form is now fast bending towards the sepulchre of his fathers, as if in token that the hymn will soon serve as his own requiem:—

Brother, thou art gone before us, and thy saintly soul is flown
Where tears are wiped from every eye, and sorrow is unknown;
From the burden of the flesh, and from care and fear released,
Where the wicked cease from troubling, and the weary are at rest.

The toilsome way thou'st travelled o'er, and borne the heavy load;
But Christ has taught thy weary feet to reach His blest abode:
Thou'rt sleeping now, like Lazarus, upon his Father's breast,
Where the wicked cease from troubling, and the weary are at rest.

Sin can never taint thee now, nor doubt thy faith assail;
Nor thy meek trust in Jesus Christ and the Holy Spirit fail:
And then thou'rt sure to meet the good, whom on earth thou lovedst best,
Where the wicked cease from troubling, and the weary are at rest.

Earth to earth, and dust to dust, the solemn priest hath said;
So we lay the turf above thee now, and we seal thy narrow bed;
But thy spirit, brother, soars away among the faithful blest,
Where the wicked cease from troubling, and the weary are at rest.

And when the Lord shall summon us, whom thou hast left behind,
May we, untainted by the world, as sure a welcome find!
May each, like thee, depart in peace, to be a glorious guest,
Where the wicked cease from troubling, and the weary are at rest.

In the same hallowed burial-ground with Joseph Hart lies the body of Susanna Wesley, the mother of John Wesley and Charles, the Methodist hymnist. She finished her course in a chamber at the very top of the old building at Moorfields. That chamber, during her parting moments, was the scene of intense devotion; all the saintly woman's daughters sat on her bedside, and sang a requiem, to her parting soul—such a requiem, it may be, as her own son has given us:—

> Happy soul, thy days are ended,
>   All thy mourning days below;
> Go, by angel guards attended,
>   To the sight of Jesus go!
>
> Waiting to receive thy spirit,
>   Lo, the Saviour stands above,
> Shows the purchase of His merit,
>   Reaches out the crown of love!
>
> Struggle through thy latest passion,
>   To thy dear Redeemer's breast,
> To His uttermost salvation,
>   To His everlasting rest.
>
> For the joy He sets before thee,
>   Bear a momentary pain,
> Die to live the life of glory;
>   Suffer, with thy Lord to reign!

Her children's tremulous song ceased, and then, says her own son John, "She continued in just the same way as my father was, struggling and gasping for life, though, as I could judge by several signs, perfectly sensible, till near four o'clock. I was then going to drink a dish of tea, being faint and weary, when one called me again to the bedside. It was just four o'clock. She opened her eyes wide, and fixed them upward for a moment. Then the lids dropped, and the soul was set at liberty, without one struggle, or groan, or sigh. We stood around the bed, and fulfilled her last request, uttered a little before she lost her speech, 'Children, as soon as I am released, sing a song of praise to God.'" What psalm they sang is not yet recorded; but that triumphant death-scene would ever live in the souls of those who formed that family choir around the corpse of their gifted, loving, sainted mother. And in the deep, solemn joys of that hour may be found the secret of the inspiration to which we owe several of Charles Wesley's unrivalled hymns. The "psalm of praise to God" which was sung by the bereaved family around the bed of their widowed mother may have given those touches to the hymnist's chastened heart which brought out his Hymn on the Death of a Widow—a hymn which may be supposed to express the triumphant faith which for the moment subdued the more tender feelings of Susanna Wesley's children, and which has many, many a time since then gone swelling upwards from the scene of Christian victory, until the voices of resigned and reliant orphans have mingled with the songs of the reunited parents before God:—

> Give glory to Jesus our Head,
>   With all that encompass His throne;
> A widow, a widow indeed,
>   A mother in Israel is gone!
> The winter of trouble is past;
>   The storms of affliction are o'er;
> Her struggle is ended at last,
>   And sorrow and death are no more.
>
> The soul hath o'ertaken her mate,
>   And caught him again in the sky!
> Advanced to her happy estate,
>   And pleasure that never shall die!

When glorified spirits, by sight,
    Converse in their holy abode,
As stars in the firmament bright,
    And pure as the angels of God.

O Heaven! what a triumph is there!
    Where all in His praises agree;
His beautiful character bear,
    And shine with the glory they see:
The glory of God and the Lamb
    (While all in the ecstasy join)
Darts into their spiritual frame,
    And gives the enjoyment Divine.

In loud hallelujahs they sing,
    And harmony echoes His praise;
When, lo! the Celestial King
    Pours out the full light of His face:
The joy neither angel nor saint
    Can bear, so ineffably great;
But, lo! the whole company faint,
    And heaven is found—at His feet.

It is probable, too, that his mother's last words, "Sing as soon as I am released," suggested to the son the hymn which so harmonizes with the thoughts and feelings which hallowed her final hour:—

Blessing, honour, thanks, and praise,
    Pay we, gracious God, to Thee:
Thou, in Thine abundant grace,
    Givest us the victory:
True and faithful to Thy word,
    Thou hast glorified Thy Son,
Jesus Christ, our dying Lord,
    He for us the fight hath won.

Lo! the prisoner is released,
    Lighten'd of his fleshly load;
Where the weary are at rest,
    He is gather'd unto God.
Lo! the pain of life is past;
    All his warfare now is o'er;
Death and hell behind are cast,
    Grief and suffering are no more.

Yes, the Christian's course is run,
    Ended is the glorious strife;
Fought the fight, the work is done,
    Death is swallow'd up of life!

> Borne by angels on their wings,
>   Far from earth the spirit flies,
> Finds his God, and sits, and sings,
>   Triumphing in Paradise.
>
> Join we then with one accord
>   In the new, the joyful song:
> Absent from our loving Lord
>   We shall not continue long.
> We shall quit the house of clay,
>   We a better lot shall share;
> We shall see the realms of day,
>   Meet our happy brother there.
>
> Let the world bewail their dead,
>   Fondly of their loss complain;
> Brother, friend, by Jesus freed,
>   Death to Thee, to us is gain:
> Thou art enter'd into joy:
>   Let the unbelievers mourn;
> We in songs our lives employ,
>   Till we all to God return.

There are no funeral hymns equal, on the whole, to Charles Wesley's; none which so fully express that sublime union of solemn awe, victorious faith, and overflowing joy, which is embodied in the writings and examples of inspired men and primitive saints. With a few exceptions, they are lacking in soft plaintiveness, but in energy and grandeur they are matchless. None but the soul who enjoys a clear and deep interest in eternal life, and has a realizing impression of the nearness of the heavenly world, can sing them with the spirit in which they were written. To be felt in the fulness of their power, they should be heard as they have sometimes been sung by a devout crowd of Cornish miners at the burial of a departed comrade. As a class, or race, Cornish miners seem to be distinguished by a sort of religious instinct or taste. A kind of devotional feeling appears to sway them. At all events, their minds soon take a pious turn under the influence of truth, when suitably administered, especially in some of its forms. They are not to be touched by anything religiously cold in spirit, or entirely bald in devotion. To them naked logic is equally powerless with mere figurative swell or wordy show. They must have a union of the sensuous and the practical. Their hearts are to be reached and moved most easily through the understanding. To call their intellect into pleasurable exercise about religion is most fully to engage their affections on its behalf. They are, indeed, religiously intelligent in a high degree; and Mrs. Schimmelpenninck showed that her discrimination as an observer was quite equal to her power of literary expression, when she said that "the Cornishman who seeks religion, seeks it not to inspire him in conversation, but to support him in adversity, or accidents of the most appalling nature, and at the hour of death. Hence, his religion is a religion not of cant, but of spirit and truth." Then, they love music, too, especially sacred music; and, for the most part, have voices which seem to give out the fine tone of their Christian character. No people have been more benefited by the labours of the Wesleys; no men, as a class, are better prepared to appreciate Charles Wesley's funeral hymns; and none have ever given them more worthy expression.

Those who have rambled among the remarkable variations of Cornish scenery will remember the picturesque hill of Carnbræ. The wild romantic scramble up among its scattered masses of granite, which lie in heaps among the furze and heath, the venerable fragment of a castle on the top, the curious piles of weather-beaten rocks, looking as if they had been familiar with the lights and shadows of the world's childhood, and the glorious prospect of hill, and plain, and sea, which opens around one—all contribute to give a sense of enlargement and exhilaration, strangely associated with feelings of awe, which can never be entirely lost. Amidst the exciting varieties of the more distant prospect, there is something touching in the appearance of a lonely old grey tower at the foot of the hill, speaking to the soul, as it does so plaintively, in memory of a former race of Cornish saints. It is the parish steeple of Redruth. Some few years ago, of a summer's evening, a long crowd was seen passing down the church path from the town, pressing around a bier as if they would affectionately guard it in front, and flank, and rear, and singing as they moved. The strain was measured like their steps, and it was in the minor key, although it seemed at times more like a triumphant shout than a wail of sorrow. They were keeping up the beautiful custom of their fathers, the evening funeral, and the burial hymn from the house of bereavement to the grave. They were singing one of their grandest tunes to one of Charles Wesley's grandest hymns:—

> Rejoice for a brother deceased,
>   Our loss is his infinite gain;
> A soul out of prison released,
>   And free from its bodily chain;
> With songs let us follow his flight
>   And mount with his spirit above,
> Escaped to the mansions of light,
>   And lodged in the Eden of love.
>
> Our brother the haven hath gain'd,
>   Out-flying the tempest and wind;
> His rest he hath sooner obtained,
>   And left his companions behind,
> Still toss'd on a sea of distress,
>   Hard toiling to make the blest shore,
> Where all is assurance and peace,
>   And sorrow and sin are no more.

As the music of the last line melted away, there was the quiet swell of a calm but majestic voice—"I am the resurrection and the life, saith the Lord."—The bier and the train passed into the ancient sanctuary, by and by again to appear, moving towards the grave. The benediction had scarcely closed the funeral service before the devout multitude once more lifted up its voice—it was a full, a mighty voice—and pressing around the open grave, they uttered, in thrilling tones, that glowing and impassioned hymn that seems to melt the earthly and the heavenly into one:—

> Come, let us join our friends above,
>   That have obtained the prize,
> And on the eagle wings of love
>   To joys celestial rise.
> Let all the saints terrestrial sing
>   With those to glory gone,
> For all the servants of our King
>   In earth and heaven are one.
>
> One family, we dwell in Him,
>   One church, above, beneath,
> Though now divided by the stream,
>   The narrow stream of death.

One army of the living God,
  To His command we bow;
Part of His host hath cross'd the flood,
  And part is crossing now.

Ten thousand to their endless home
  This solemn moment fly:
And we are to the margin come,
  And we expect to die;
His militant embodied host
  With wishful looks we stand;
And long to see that happy coast,
  And reach that heavenly land.

Our old companions in distress
  We haste again to see,
And eager long for our release
  And full felicity:
Even now by faith we join our hands
  With those that went before,
And greet the blood-besprinkled bands
  On the eternal shore.

Our spirits too shall quickly join,
  Like theirs with glory crown'd,
And shout to see our Captain's sign,
  To hear His trumpet sound.
Oh! that we now might grasp our Guide!
  Oh! that the word were given!
Come, Lord of Hosts! the waves divide,
  And land us all in heaven!

The swell of the closing appeal was thrilling. The men's voices were not to be surpassed. Their bass tones were distinctive of their class. It might be supposed that the inimitable deep round fulness, the organ-like tone of a Cornish miner's bass voice had some subtle relation to the peculiar atmospheric influences to which his lungs are subject; so that the music of his voice would seem like an unearthly remembrancer of the fact that a great proportion of Cornwall's subterranean workmen are doomed to an early death. Among the singers at that funeral there was one young man who appeared to be rapt while he sang. It seemed as if his music were that of pure spirit. How he kindled as he poured forth some of the last notes! There was something in his voice, something in his expression, something in the flow of light from his eye, which might be thought to mark him as the next to whom a summons from above would come. "Yes," thought one who looked at him that evening under the calm light of the setting sun, "you are singing your own requiem, young man!" And so it was. The one who noted the unmistakable token of his nearness to the land of his fathers, shortly found him on his deathbed. But he had not lost the spirit of that triumphant hymn. "I am going!" said he, "I am going! going early; but God has brightened my short life into a full one! Oh, those hymns! they have taught me to live in the light of the future! They have been 'my songs in the house of my pilgrimage'! How often when I have sung them down deep in the mine has the darkness been light about me! Never, since I learnt to praise God from my heart, have I begun to work in the rock for blasting, without stopping a moment to ask myself, 'Now, if the hole should go off about me, am I ready for heaven?' Sometimes, sir, there has been a little shrinking and some doubt, and then I have dropped on my knees, and asked God to bless me before I gave one stroke; and never did I pray in vain; my prayer has always passed into praise. And those blessed hymns have come bursting from my heart and lips as I have toiled at the point of death! Oh, sir! do you remember our singing at the last funeral?" "Yes," it was replied, "and some thought then, that you would never sing again;" "Never sing again, sir! why I shall sing for ever! Oh that glorious hymn, let us sing it now!" And he began:—

> Oh! that we now might grasp our Guide!
> Oh! that the word were given!
> Come, Lord of Hosts! the waves divide,
> And land us....land....*me*....now in——

"Heaven!" he would have sung, but he was gone! He had joined another choir!

Such uses and such fruits of funeral psalmody might have suggested the lines which a grandson of good Dr. Hawker, of Plymouth, Wesley's contemporary, inscribed on the grave-stone of one of his young parishioners in the quiet burial-place of Morwenstow, on the Cornish coast. The memorial verses are not unworthy of their author, nor of their title, "A Cornish Death-Song:"—

Sing! from the chamber to the grave,
  Thus did the dead man say:
A sound of melody I crave
  Upon my burial day!

Bring forth some tuneful instrument,
  And let your voices rise;
My spirit listen'd as it went
  To music of the skies!

Sing sweetly as you travel on,
  And keep the funeral show:
The angels sing where I am gone,
  And you should sing below!

Sing from the threshold to the porch,
  Until you hear the bell;
And sing you loudly in the church
  The psalms I love so well.

Then bear me gently to the grave;
  And as you pass along,
Remember 'twas my wish to have
  A pleasant funeral song!

So earth to earth—and dust to dust—
  And though my bones decay,
My soul shall sing among the just,
  Until the judgment day!

CHAPTER XXIII.

JUDGMENT HYMNS.

" And after these things I heard a voice of much people in heaven, saying, Alleluia; salvation, and glory, and honour, and power, unto the Lord our God: for true and righteous are His judgments."

FROM age to age the Christian Church has been listening in solemn awe to her Divine Master's utterance, "When the Son of Man shall come in His glory, and all the holy angels with Him, then shall He sit upon the throne of His glory; and before Him shall be gathered all nations." Nor at any period since the time when the glory of the descending Judge filled the visions of apostles, has the Church entirely lost her sense of the Bridegroom's approach; there have been seasons of slumber, and many have fallen asleep; but watchful virgins have always kept their lamps trimmed and burning, with oil in their vessels, while their watchful hours have been kept vocal with successive songs of holy confidence and patient joyful hope. Scarcely have the tones of one hymn died away before another has been grandly swelling upon the ear of Christendom. In the fourteenth century the music of the Church was becoming faint. Truth was sending out its messages, but in undertones. Spiritual religion was keeping up its struggling existence within narrow retreats. But even then, as in every crisis of Christian history, there came awakening voices, such as those of Francis of Assissi, and his friend and biographer, Thomas of Celano; one, the great father of itinerant preaching friars; the other, that hymnist whose one judgment hymn roused the slumbering choirs of Europe, and still sends forth its deep and solemn music, making sinners' ears tingle, and thrilling the heart of every

Christian generation. The hymn is the natural voice of the times which gave it birth. It is the voice of bondage rather than of freedom, of fearfulness rather than of joy. It is the language of a prodigal deprecating his Father's wrath, rather than the utterance of a son jubilant in anticipation of his inheritance. Its tone is one of deeper humiliation than that of apostolic days; it is not equal to that "full assurance of hope" which the hymns of later times express. But it has doubtless helped many a heart to prepare for judgment, and brought timely comfort to many departing souls by its solemn and unearthly music. It has gathered deeper interest in the affections of many from its association with the last moments of Sir Walter Scott. He requested, as he neared the end, that a dear relative would read to him. "What book shall I read?" it was asked. "What book?" said he; "there is but one!" Blessed book! that alone could show him his way; but after hearing God's voice, his soul fell back upon ancient songs. Some of the magnificent old hymns in which he had delighted were now murmured by the dying poet. Those who were gathered around him say, "We have often heard distinctly the cadence of the 'Dies Iræ,' Thomas of Celano's grand and immortal Song of Judgment. Scott had himself translated it in part. No translation, however, among the scores which have been issued, can be called fully adequate in all respects. The spirit and tone have been faithfully and powerfully rendered thus:—

>Lo, the day of wrath, the day,
>Earth and heaven melt away,
>David and the Sybil say.
>
>Stoutest heart with fear shall quiver,
>When to Him that erreth never,
>All must strict account deliver.
>
>Lo! the trumpet's wondrous pealing,
>Rung through each sepulchral dwelling,
>All before the throne compelling!
>
>Nature shrinks appall'd, and death,
>When the dead regain their breath,
>To the Judge each answereth.
>
>Then the Written Book is set,
>All things are contained in it,
>Then each learns his sentence meet.

When the Judge appears again,
Hidden things shall be made plain,
Nothing unavenged remain.

What shall I, unworthy, plead?
Who for me will intercede,
When the just will mercy need?

King of dreadful majesty,
Who sav'st the saved of mercy free,
Fount of pity, save Thou me!

Think of me, good Lord, I pray,
Who trodd'st for me the bitter way,
Nor forsake me in that day.

Weary sat'st Thou, seeking me,
Diedst redeeming on the tree;
Not in vain such toil can be!

Judge avenging, let me win
Free remission of my sin,
Ere that dreadful day begin.

Sinful, o'er my sins I groan,
Guilt my crimson'd face must own,
Spare, O God, Thy suppliant one.

Mary was by Thee forgiven,
To the thief Thou open'dst heaven,
Hope to me, too, Thou hast given.

All unworthy is my prayer;
Gracious One, be gracious there;
From that quenchless fire, oh spare.

Place Thou me at Thy right hand,
'Mongst Thy sheep, oh make me stand,
Far from the convicted band.

When the accursed condemn'd shall be
Doom'd to keenest flames by Thee,
'Midst the blessed call Thou me.

Contrite, suppliant, I pray,
Ashes on my heart I lay,
Care Thou for me in that day.

To write a judgment hymn with that spirit, and power, and majesty which become the theme, requires a glowing intellect under the full command of inspired truth; a genius in deep sympathy with Divine revelations; a soul devoutly familiar with spiritual unseen things, capable, by strong faith, of realizing the presence of the Judge, and of expressing its sense of that presence so as to make others see and feel much of what it sees and feels itself; one indeed who lives in frequent visions of the unearthly and the divine. Hymnists of this class have sometimes sprung up where, by most people, they would not be looked for. On the morning of October 24th, 1753, a somewhat remarkable figure was seen walking out from the town of Bradford, in Wiltshire. He had on a long, heavy great-coat, covering a dress of dark blue, of primitive cut, rather after the style of the ordinary dress of a modern English bishop. He wore heavy riding-boots, however, and had saddle-bags filled with books and linen slung across his shoulder. His face would arrest attention; the open, well-formed, manly features, and the ever-kindling eye giving expression to a rare combination of acute perception, deep thoughtfulness, logical power, happy temper, quiet humour, and bold imagination. It was one of Mr. Wesley's itinerant preachers, on his way to Cornwall, afoot. After many curious adventures on the road, he entered on his perilous "round" among the then rude masses of the extreme west. His own rare bit of autobiography helps us to follow his steps. "As to trials," says he, "I do not remember that I had any in these parts which deserve the name. Indeed, in one place the high constable came to press me for a soldier while I was preaching. He said, 'As you preach so well, you are very fit to serve his Majesty. I therefore desire you will get ready to go with me to a magistrate to-morrow morning.' I answered, 'Why not to-night? I am ready to go with you now.' He then said, 'Well, you may first finish your sermon.' Accordingly, I began again where I had left off, and the constable and his companion stayed to hear me, and then went quietly away. The next morning I waited for his return, but he never came; so that, in all probability, what he heard was a means, at least, of cooling his courage."

The man who could act and write like this was no common man. He was a dreamer, at all events; for he tells us:—"When I was in this neighbourhood, I dreamed one night that Christ was come in the clouds to judge the world, and also that He looked exceeding black at me. When I awoke I was much alarmed. I therefore humbled myself exceedingly, with fastings and prayer, and was determined never to give over till my evidence of the love of Christ was made quite clear. One day, as I was at prayer in my room, with my eyes shut, the Lord, as it were, appeared, to the eye of my mind, as standing just before me, while ten thousand small streams of blood seemed to issue from every part of His body. This sight was so unexpected, and at the same time so seasonable, that, for once, I wept aloud; yea, and almost fainted away. I now more fully believed His love to me, and that, if He was then to come to judgment, He would not frown, but rather smile on me; therefore I loved and praised Him with all my heart. Some years after, I had a dream of a quite different sort; I dreamed that I was talking with two women concerning the day of judgment. Among other things, I thought I told them I was certain it was very near. On hearing this, I thought they burst into laughter, and rejected all I said. Being much grieved at this, I told them, 'I will go and see if it is not as I said.' Accordingly I went to the door, and, on looking up southward, thought I saw the heavens open, and a stream of fire, as large as a small river, issuing forth. On seeing this, I thought I ran back to the women, and said, 'You would not believe me; but come to the door, and you will see with your own eyes that the day is come.' On hearing this, I thought they were much alarmed, and ran with me to the door. By the time we were got thither, I thought the whole concave, southward, was filled with an exceedingly thick, fiery mist, which swiftly moved northward in a huge body, filling the whole space between the heaven and the earth as it came along. As it drew near, I thought, 'The day is come of which I have so often told the world, and now, in a few moments, I shall see how it will be with me to all eternity.' And for a moment I seemed to feel myself in a state of awful suspense. When the fire was come close to me, I was going to shrink back, but thought, 'This is all in vain, as there is now no place of shelter left.' I then pushed myself forward into it, and found that the fire had no power to hurt me, for I stood as easy in the midst of it as ever I did in the open air. The joy I felt, on being able to stand unhurt and undismayed amidst this awful burning, cannot be described. Even so shall it be with all who are careful to enter in at the strait gate, and to walk closely and steadily in the narrow way all the days of their life. All these shall

> Stand secure, and smile,
> Amidst the jarring elements,
> The wreck of matter and the crash of worlds!"

This dream might remind us of Charles Wesley's grand hymn:—

> Stand th' omnipotent decree:
> Jehovah's will be done!
> Nature's end we wait to see,
> And hear her final groan;
> Let this earth dissolve, and blend
> In death the wicked and the just;
> Let those ponderous orbs descend,
> And grind us into dust.
>
> Rests secure the righteous man,
> At his Redeemer's beck,
> Sure to emerge, and rise again,
> And mount above the wreck;
> Lo, the heavenly spirit towers,
> Like flame, o'er nature's funeral pyre,
> Triumphs in immortal powers,
> And claps his wings of fire!
>
> Nothing hath the just to lose
> By worlds on worlds destroyed,
> Far beneath his feet he views
> With smiles the flaming void;
> Sees the universe renew'd,
> The grand millennial reign begun,
> Shouts, with all the sons of God,
> Around the eternal throne!
>
> Resting in this glorious hope
> To be at last restored,
> Yield we now our bodies up
> To earthquake, plague, or sword.
> Listening for the call Divine,
> The latest trumpet of the seven;
> Soon our souls and dust shall join,
> And both fly up to heaven.

The dreamer may have had this hymn in his mind; at all events, the visions of judgment, the awful scenes of the consummation entranced him. And whether his dreams arose from the cherished imaginations of his soul in its daily communion with the future, or whether the dream which he records gave to his consecrated genius the inspiring touches which kindled it into song, the story of his dreams will ever be associated with his immortal judgment hymn:—

>Come, immortal King of Glory!
> Now with all Thy saints appear;
>While astonish'd worlds adore Thee,
> And the dead Thy clarions hear.
>   Shine refulgent,
> And Thy deity maintain.
>
>Hail! the world's adored Creator!
> In Thy radiant vesture seen.
>Hail! the Lord of life and nature!
> Hail! the Almighty Nazarene!
>   They who pierced Him,
> Every eye shall see Him come.
>
>But, how diverse the sensation!
> Saints with joy and rapture fill'd,
>Glow with holy exultation,
> To redemption's glory seal'd:
>   While the wicked
> Wail His coming's dread design.
>
>Lo! He comes with clouds descending:
> Hark! the trump of God is blown:
>And th' archangel's voice attending,
> Make the high procession known.
>   Sons of *Adam*,
> Rise and stand before your God!
>
>Crowns and sceptres fall before Him,
> Kings and conquerors own His sway,
>Haughtiest monarchs now adore Him,
> While they see His lightnings play.
>   How triumphant
> Is the world's Redeemer now.
>
>Light primeval in its lustre
> Doth in Jesu's aspect shine;
>Blazing comets are not fiercer
> Than His eyes of flame Divine.
>   Oh, how dreadful
> Doth the Crucified appear!
>
>Hear His voice as mighty thunder,
> Sounding in eternal roar,
>While its echo rends in sunder
> Rocks and mountains, sea and shore.
>   Hark, His accents
> Thro' th' unfathom'd deep resound!

See His throne of jasper whiteness;
　Throne of justice and of grace;
See Jehovah's equal brightness
　Shining in Emmanuel's face.
　　Saints exulting
Shout with joy th' accomplish'd prayer.

"Come, Lord Jesus, oh come quickly:"
　Oft has pray'd the mourning bride.
Lo! He answers, "I come quickly,"
　Who Thy coming may abide?
　　All who loved Him,
All who long'd to see His day.

See the awful expectation!
　See the heavens themselves on fire!
Melting in the conflagration,
　See the elements expire!
　　While the trumpet
Blows around, "Ye dead, arise!"

Lo! the dead arise, and standing
　At their great Creator's bar:
While the Judge of all commanding,
　Cries, "To meet your God prepare."
　　All whose judgments
And His ways are equal found!

Now the dreadful volumes opening,
　Scenes of various deeds disclose,
While the Judge proclaims the sentence,
　Righteous sentence on His foes:
　　Wrath to sinners;
To His saints the crown of life!

Gather ye His saints together,
　Now with Him in judgment sit;
See the vile as stubble wither,
　Ashes now beneath your feet!
　　While His vengeance
Seals their everlasting doom.

Hark! the universal groaning;
　Hark! the cries of guilt and fear;
Hear them each his fate bemoaning,
　Each the cause bemoaning hear.
　　God no longer
Patient, merciful or kind.

"Come, ye mountains, and fall on us,
　Come, ye rocks, our heads conceal,
For the day is come upon us,
　Day of wrath that burns to hell;
　　Where the gnawing
Worm of conscience never dies.

Where no more for them remaining,
  Hope no more awaits their call;
But in iron bonds detaining,
  Heav'ns high justice binds up all.
    While His mercy
  To remorseless judgment turns.

Lo! the God of all contending,
  Calls the heavens from afar,
Bids, O earth, thy sons attending,
  Hear Him, for Himself declare
    All His wisdom,
  And His righteous acts unfold.

Stopt for ever all complaining;
  Stopt the mouth of murmuring pride;
Fools no more their God disdaining,
  Atheists now no more deride,
    But with trembling
  Wait His judgment's last award.

"Go from Me," He saith, "ye cursed,"
  Ye for whom I bled in vain,
Who My utmost grace resisted;
  Go ye to unending pain.
    Lord Almighty,
  True and righteous are Thy ways!

"Come," He saith, "ye heirs of glory,"
  Come, ye purchase of my blood,
Claim the kingdom now before you,
  Rise, and fill the mount of God:
    Fix'd for ever,
  Where the Lamb on Sion stands.

See ten thousand burning seraphs
  From their thrones as lightnings fly:
Take, they cry, your seats above us,
  Nearest Him that rules the sky,
    Patient sufferers,
  How rewarded are ye now!

Ransom'd victors, see His ensign,
  Waving high in purple air!
Jesus, with His ancients reigning,
  Shall to each His conquest share:
    He who made them
  More than conquerors thro' His blood.

Now their trials all are ended,
  Now the dubious warfare's o'er;
Joy no more with sorrow blended;
  They shall sigh and weep no more:
    God for ever
  Wipes the tear from every eye.

Thro' His passion, all victorious;
　Now they drink immortal wine:
In Emmanuel's likeness, glorious
　As the firmament they shine:
　　Shine for ever
　With the bright and morning star.

Where His sceptre's sway extending,
　Jesus high His right maintains;
Heaven, and earth, and hell commanding,
　God omnipotent He reigns:
　　Prince of princes!
　King of kings, and Lord of lords!

Shining in His bright expansion,
　King of saints behold Him sit!
Joy of each adoring mansion,
　Sunk for ever at His feet.
　　Lord of Glory!
　And His kingdom without end!

Shout aloud, ye ethereal choirs,
　Triumph in Jehovah's praise,
Kindle all your heavenly fires,
　All your palms of vict'ry raise:
　　Shout His conquests,
　Shout, "Salvation to the Lamb."

See in sacred pomp ascending,
　Jesus and His glorious train:
Countless myriads now attending
　Hail the empyrean plain.
　　"Hallelujah,"
　First and last and Lord of all!

In full triumph see them marching,
　Through the gates of massy light:
While the city walls are sparkling
　With meridian glory bright.
　　Oh how lovely
　Are the dwellings of the Lamb!

See His beauty all resplendent:
　See in Him the Godhead shine:
See Him above all transcendent,
　Full of Deity Divine.
　　Hail! eternal!
　Sov'reign Lord of worlds unknown!

On His throne of sapphired azure,
　High above all height He reigns:
Reigns the fount of endless pleasure;
　Self-subsistent He remains.
　　How diffusive
　Shines the uncreated blaze!

Hosts angelic all adore Him,
  Circling round His orient seat,
Elders cast their crowns before Him,
  Fall and worship at His feet.
    Oh how "holy,
  "And how reverend is Thy name!"

Shout aloud the new creation,
  All ye heavenly arches ring,
Echo to the Lord—salvation,
  "Glory to th' eternal king!"
    Dread Jehovah!
  "God with God! and Son of man!"

I am Alpha and Omega,
  I the first and last am He:
He who was and is to come—who
  Am and will for ever be:
    Jah, Jehovah,
  Jah, Jehovah, is my name.

Hail! Thou Alpha and Omega!
  First and last of all alone!
He that is, and was, and shall be,
  And beside whom there is none,
    Take the glory,
  Great eternal Three in One!

Praise be to the Father given:
  Praise to the co-eval Son:
Praise the Spirit, one and seven:
  Praise the mystic Three in One,
    Hallelujah!
  Everlasting praise be Thine.

The dreamer will be known from his hymn. He was no other than Thomas Olivers, the wandering Methodist preacher, Wesley's companion, and Toplady's theological antagonist. Thomas Olivers was born at Tregonan, in Montgomeryshire, in 1725. His father died four years after his birth; in three months his mother's heart was broken by her loss; and he, with a younger brother, were left to the care of his mother's friends. Placed at a neighbouring school, he "received such learning as was thought necessary"; but proved a more apt scholar in vice than in virtue. At eighteen he was apprenticed to a shoemaker, and entered on a course of youthful profligacy in which he soon outstripped most of his compeers; and was obliged at length to fly from the scene of his wickedness, in order to escape public indignation. As a wanderer from place to place, he exemplified the misery of those who plunge deeper and deeper into sin, vainly striving to shake off, or alleviate the terrors of an evil conscience. Reduced at last to beggary, and extreme wretchedness of mind and body, he found his way to hear Whitefield preach at Bristol. The preacher's text was, "Is not this a brand plucked out of the fire?" It was a word in season. Olivers became a new man, and on the first Sunday after, "I went," he says, "to the cathedral at six in the morning. When the *Te Deum* was read, I felt as if I had done with earth and was praising God before His throne. No words can set forth the joy, the rapture, the awe and reverence I felt." His course was altered. He joined the Methodists. All his debts were gradually paid. He began to preach; was at length sent into Cornwall by Mr. Wesley; and having run a useful, happy, and honourable course, he suddenly departed in March, 1799, leaving his dust to be deposited in Wesley's own tomb. He has bequeathed to us one of the grandest judgment hymns that ever the Church sang, or that ever brought the sound of the Judge's approach to the ears of the world. It is remarkable that Charles Wesley and he should have the same line in the two hymns that so strikingly rival each other in magnificence. Each sings:

Lo! He comes with clouds descending.

Whether Wesley caught the key-note from Olivers, or Olivers from Wesley, they evidently breathed the same inspiration. Each hymnist has the same vivid realization of the overwhelming majesty of the final scene; and neither of the two hymns can be devoutly sung without an ever-deepening feeling of solemn awe and reverent hope. How striking and sublime is Wesley's third verse, in which the Judge appears still bearing the tokens of His passion, thus exciting the holy rapture of those who have been redeemed by His agony and death:—

> The dear tokens of His passion
> Still His dazzling body bears;
> Cause of endless exultation
> To His ransom'd worshippers:
> With what rapture
> Gaze we on those glorious scars!

Most of Charles Wesley's judgment hymns are of the highest class. Several of them were written in December, 1755, just when the public mind was agitated by the fearful news of the Lisbon earthquake; and while the nation was in tremulous suspense, awaiting the threatened French invasion. Some of these have special allusion to the distinguishing circumstances of the times; but others may be on the lips and hearts of all, in all ages, who prayerfully look for the day of account. No hymn can more graciously dispose the subjects of future judicial inspection for the holiest and safest posture of readiness for the trumpet's voice than this:—

> Thou Judge of quick and dead,
>   Before whose bar severe,
> With holy joy or guilty dread,
>   We all shall soon appear;
> Our caution'd souls prepare
>   For that tremendous day;
> And fill us now with watchful care,
>   And stir us up to pray—
>
> To pray and wait the hour,
>   That awful hour unknown;
> When, robed in majesty and power,
>   Thou shalt from heaven come down,
> The immortal Son of man,
>   To judge the human race,
> With all Thy Father's dazzling train,
>   With all Thy glorious grace.
>
> To damp our earthly joys,
>   To increase our gracious fears,
> For ever let the Archangel's voice
>   Be sounding in our ears;
> The solemn midnight cry,
>   "Ye dead, the Judge is come;
> Arise and meet Him in the sky,
>   And meet your instant doom!"
>
> Oh, may we thus be found
>   Obedient to His word;
> Attentive to the trumpet's sound,
>   And looking for our Lord!
> Oh, may we thus ensure
>   A lot among the blest;
> And watch a moment to secure
>   An everlasting rest!

But among the many judgment hymns which must be ever precious to those who "look for their Lord," who can forget one that rose from Oxford, about forty years ago, kindling afresh the faith of English Christians, and awakening the Church to brighter and holier anticipations of its Lord's descent. Henry Hart Milman will always be reverenced by the lovers of high class Church history, and be thought of with admiration and thankfulness by all who enjoy the Christian hymn when it rises into impressive grandeur. Dean Milman, now a venerable man bending under the weight of years, is the son of Sir Francis Milman, physician to George III. Born in 1791; educated at Eton and Oxford, he was advanced in 1817 to the vicarage of St. Mary's, Reading; and four years after was installed as University Professor of Poetry at Oxford; and while filling that chair, he gave forth his hymn on "The Last Day":—

> The chariot, the chariot! its wheels roll on fire,
> As the Lord cometh down in the pomp of His ire;
> Self-moving, it drives on its pathway of cloud,
> And the heavens with the burthen of Godhead are bowed.
>
> The glory, the glory! around Him are poured,
> The myriads of angels that wait on the Lord;
> And the glorified saints, and the martyrs are there,
> And all who the palm-wreath of victory wear.
>
> The trumpet, the trumpet! the dead have all heard,
> Lo! the depths of the stone-covered charnel are stirred;
> From the ocean and earth, from the south and the north,
> Lo! the vast generations of ages come forth!
>
> The judgment, the judgment! the thrones are all set,
> Where the Lamb and the white-vested elders are met;
> All flesh is at once in the sight of the Lord,
> And the doom of eternity hangs on His word.
>
> Oh mercy, oh mercy! look down from above,
> Redeemer, on us Thy sad children, with love.
> When beneath, to their darkness the wicked are driven,
> May our sanctified souls find a mansion in heaven.

CHAPTER XXIV.

SONGS OF GLORY.

"And the ransomed of the Lord shall return, and come to Sion with songs and everlasting joy upon their heads."

THERE are many who look wishfully for immortal pleasures in heaven, while they withhold themselves from preparatory religious pleasures upon earth. And some, too, who with a sort of instinctive yearning for repose in the future, sing of eternal rest, though as yet they have not been fully submissive to Him who is the only source and giver of rest. There are moments in the life of human genius when divine and celestial realities assert their claims on the gifted soul, and call out from it songs and hymns, which have a music and a power for minds far more spiritual than the author's, a music and a power which the hymnist himself, perhaps, never so deeply felt. Thomas Moore, it may be, though expressing the aspiration of his own soul in one of its better moments, never knew with how deep a charm his verses touch the more fully sanctified spirit, who patiently longs for the moment of its upward spring into eternal life.

> The bird let loose in Eastern skies
>   When hastening fondly home,
> Ne'er stoops to earth his wing, nor flies
>   Where idle warblers roam;
> But high she shoots through air and light,
>   Above all low delay,
> Where nothing earthly bounds her flight,
>   Nor shadow dims her way.
>
> So grant me, God, from every care,
>   And stain of passion free,
> Aloft, through virtue's purer air,
>   To hold my course to Thee!

> No sin to cloud, no lure to stay
>   My soul as home she springs;
> Thy sunshine on her joyful way,
>   Thy freedom in her wings!

Many a heavenly-minded Christian, with whom Moore would have but little sympathy, will thank God for the pen of the man who has thus afforded him a tuneful form of expressing what he himself could never so express, while pluming his wings for a homeward flight. So, the same hymnist has furnished a song of glory which those whose heavenliness is a principle and habit, rather than a mere sentiment, will always sing with feelings richer probably, and holier, than the inspiration which gave it birth:—

> This world is all a fleeting show
>   For man's illusion given;
> The smiles of joy, the tears of woe,
> Deceitful shine, deceitful flow;
>   There's nothing true but Heaven!
>
> And false the light on glory's plume,
>   As fading hues of even;
> And love, and hope, and beauty's bloom
> Are blossoms gathered from the tomb;
>   There's nothing bright but Heaven!
>
> Poor wanderers of a stormy day,
>   From wave to wave we're driven;
> And fancy's flash, and reason's ray,
> Serve but to light the troubled way;
>   There's nothing calm but Heaven!

To those whose heavenly-mindedness is pure enough to long for the future without being embittered with the present, this hymn expresses a Christian's preference for heaven; a peaceful and holy superiority to the vanities of earth; but on other lips it may have another meaning: it may be the language of one who turns plaintively towards heaven in the crisis of bitter disappointment and vexation with the falsehoods of this world. Those who can sing from their hearts—

> Thou know'st in the spirit of prayer,
>   We long Thy appearing to see,
> Resign'd to the burden we bear,
>   But longing to triumph with Thee;
> 'Tis good at Thy word to be here,
>   'Tis better in Thee to be gone,
> And see Thee in glory appear,
>   And rise to a share in Thy throne;

those who in "patience possess their souls," while they linger in sweet suspense on the shadowy borders of time, love rather the quiet and submissive joyfulness of songs like Anne Steele's hymn on "The Promised Land." Peacefully looking out into the brightening distance from her chamber of sickness, or from her garden terrace, where her Saviour's strength was made perfect in her weakness, or from the avenue of fir-trees where whispers of mortal strife sometimes touched her ear, she used to sing:—

  Far from these narrow scenes of night
   Unbounded glories rise,
  And realms of infinite delight,
   Unknown to mortal eyes.

  Far distant land! could mortal eyes
   But half its joys explore,
  How would our spirits long to rise,
   And dwell on earth no more!

  There pain and sickness never come,
   And grief no more complains!
  Health triumphs in immortal bloom,
   And endless pleasure reigns!

  From discord free, and war's alarms,
   And want and pining care;
  Plenty and peace unite their charms,
   And smile unchanging there.

  There rich varieties of joy
   Continual feast the mind;
  Pleasures which fill, but never cloy,
   Immortal and refined!

  No factious strife, no envy there,
   The sons of peace molest;
  But harmony and love sincere
   Fill every happy breast.

  No cloud those blissful regions know,
   For ever bright and fair!
  For sin, the source of mortal woe,
   Can never enter there.

  There no alternate night is known,
   Nor sun's faint sickly ray;
  But glory from the sacred throne
   Spreads everlasting day.

  The glorious monarch there displays
   His beams of wondrous grace;
  His happy subjects sing His praise,
   And bow before His face.

> Oh may the heavenly prospect fire
> Our hearts with ardent love,
> Till ways of faith and strong desire
> Bear every thought above.
>
> Prepare us, Lord, by grace Divine,
> For Thy bright courts on high;
> Then bid our spirits rise and join
> The chorus of the sky.

Who can sing of Canaan without recalling some lovely scenes of southern England, and thinking of one whose harp was often strung in praise of—

> Sweet fields beyond the swelling flood?

In the year 1782, there was a deacon of the Independent church at Southampton, whose son, in his eighteenth year, felt, now and then, during the Sunday psalm or hymn, somewhat like a finely sensitive ear feels at the sound of a file sharpening a saw; and he complained that the old hymnists were sadly out of taste. "Give us something better, young man," was the reply. The young man did it; and the church was invited to close its evening service with a new hymn, thus:—

> Behold the glories of the Lamb
> Amidst His Father's throne;
> Prepare new honours for His name,
> And songs before unknown.
>
> Let elders worship at His feet,
> The church adore around,
> With vials full of odours sweet,
> And harps of sweeter sound.
>
> Those are the prayers of the saints,
> And those the hymns they raise:
> Jesus is kind to our complaints,
> He loves to hear our praise.
>
> Eternal Father, who shall look
> Into Thy secret will?
> Who but the Son shall take that book,
> And open every seal?
>
> He shall fulfil Thy great decrees,
> The Son deserves it well;
> Lo, in His hand the sov'reign keys
> Of heaven, and death, and hell!
>
> Now to the Lamb that once was slain,
> Be endless blessings paid;
> Salvation, glory, joy remain
> For ever on Thy head.

Thou hast redeem'd our souls with blood,
    Hast set the pris'ners free,
Hast made us kings and priests to God,
    And we shall reign with Thee.

The worlds of nature and of grace
    Are put beneath Thy power;
Then shorten these delaying days,
    And bring the promised hour!

This was Isaac Watts's first hymn; a new vein of song was opened; the little hymnist had struck a chord which gave birth to fresh harmonies in the church. Hymn followed hymn, until the young essayist published his first and successful edition of "Hymns and Spiritual Songs." Young poets are susceptible of love and beauty, and Isaac soon paid court to the accomplished and pious Elizabeth Singer, afterwards better known as Mrs. Rowe. She told her suitor that she loved the jewel, but could not admire the casket, and thus lost the honour of being Mrs. Watts; while she sent the grieved young Christian poet to his Saviour's feet, devoutly to consecrate himself for life to science, philosophy, literature, and the service of holy song. How sweetly his disappointment in the creature melts in devotion to his Lord:—

How vain are all things here below!
    How false, and yet how fair!
Each pleasure hath its poison too,
    And every sweet a snare.

The brightest things below the sky
    Give but a flatt'ring light;
We should suspect some danger nigh
    Where we possess delight.

Our dearest joys and nearest friends,
    The partners of our blood,
How they divide our wav'ring minds,
    And leave but half for God.

The fondness of a creature's love,
    How strong it strikes the sense!
Thither the warm affections move,
    Nor can we call them thence.

Dear Saviour! let Thy beauties be
    My soul's eternal food,
And grace command my heart away
    From all created good.

Thus driven back from the pursuit of conjugal pleasures, he turns to the future with more entire affection. Heaven brightens on him as earth withholds its smile; and sitting at his parlour window, looking out upon the waters of the Itchen, with the Isle of Wight in the distance, and the rich landscape opening its inviting beauties on the other side of the river, he thought of Canaan, and the Jordan, and the final passage, and the calm and immortal repose of the inheritance beyond; and then arose that soothing and cheering hymn which, as long as Christianity expresses its hopes in the English language, will pleasantly sustain its title in the hearts of God's children, and assure them that "a prospect of heaven makes death easy." How many souls have felt this prospect brightening as they sang :—

> There is a land of pure delight,
>   Where saints immortal reign;
> Infinite day excludes the night,
>   And pleasures banish pain.
>
> There everlasting spring abides,
>   And never-with'ring flowers;
> Death, like a narrow sea, divides
>   This heavenly land from ours.
>
> Sweet fields, beyond the swelling flood,
>   Stand dress'd in living green;
> So to the Jews old Canaan stood,
>   While Jordan rolled between.
>
> But tim'rous mortals start and shrink
>   To cross this narrow sea;
> And linger, shivering on the brink,
>   And fear to launch away.
>
> Oh! could we make our doubts remove,
>   Those gloomy doubts that rise,
> And see the Canaan that we love
>   With unbeclouded eyes!
>
> Could we but climb where Moses stood,
>   And view the landscape o'er,
> Not Jordan's stream, nor death's cold flood,
>   Should fright us from the shore.

Watts passed from the mortal shore, and happily crossed the river, in his seventy-fifth year, after a season of

> Calm decay and peace divine.

The beautiful retirement and holy friendships of Abney Park, the last retreat of Watts, would be associated in the mind who loves sweet songs of glory, with a picture once exhibited in the Royal Academy—a picture of George Herbert in his garden at Bemerton. That garden was the little earthly paradise where Herbert used to sing of a brighter land, and pour forth his warm desires for freedom to wing his way to rest. His paradise at Bemerton detained him but a little more than two years. Just before his soul ceased to be

> An entangled, hampered thing,

he put a small manuscript into a friend's hand, saying, "Sir, I pray deliver this little book to my dear brother Farrer, and tell him he shall find in it a picture of the many spiritual conflicts that have passed betwixt God and my soul before I would subject mine to the will of Jesus my Master, in whose service I have now found perfect freedom. Desire him to read it, and then, if he can think it may turn to the advantage of any dejected poor soul, let it be made public; if not, let him burn it, for I and it are less than the least of God's mercies." "Brother Farrer" did not burn it: it was too precious a legacy; and were there nothing else in it but his hymn of desire after God and his "Home," it would be truly "the precious life-blood of a master spirit, embalmed and treasured up on purpose to a life beyond life." The song has a quaintness, here and there, which scarcely suits the modern taste; there are little curious conceits and grotesque allusions, which to us do not appear as natural as they really were to the writer himself; but the exquisite fancy, the rich imagination, the pregnant thought, the spiritual music, and the intensely holy feeling which show themselves in "the Temple," all combine in his rhythmical prayer for the freedom of "Home," and invite us to chant:—

> Come, Lord, my head doth burn, my heart is sick,
>   While Thou dost ever, ever stay;
> Thy long deferrings wound me to the quick,
>   My spirit gaspeth night and day.
>   Oh show Thyself to me,
>   Or take me up to Thee!

Yet if Thou stayest still, why must I stay?
  My God, what is this world to me?
This world of woe? Hence, all ye clouds, away,
  Away, I must get up and see.
    Oh show Thyself to me,
    Or take me up to Thee!

What is this weary world, this meat and drink,
  That chains us by the teeth so fast?
What is this woman-kind, which I can wink
  Into a blackness and distaste?
    Oh show Thyself to me,
    Or take me up to Thee!

With one small sigh Thou gavest me th' other day
  I blasted all the joys about me;
And scowling on them as they pined away,
  Now come again, said I, and plant me.
    Oh show Thyself to me,
    Or take me up to Thee!

Nothing but drought and dearth, but bush and brake,
  Which way soe'er I look, I see.
Some may dream merrily, and when they wake,
  They dress themselves and come to Thee.
    Oh show Thyself to me,
    Or take me up to Thee!

We talk of harvests; there are no such things,
  But when we leave our corn and hay;
There is no fruitful year, but that which brings
  The last and loved, though dreadful day.
    Oh show Thyself to me,
    Or take me up to Thee!

Oh loose this frame, this knot of man untie,
  That my free soul may use her wing,
Which now is pinion'd with mortality,
  As an entangled, hampered thing.
    Oh show Thyself to me,
    Or take me up to Thee!

What have I left, that I should stay and groan?
  The most of me to heaven is fled;
My thoughts and joys are all pack'd up and gone,
  And for their old acquaintance plead.
    Oh show Thyself to me,
    Or take me up to Thee!

Come, dearest Lord, pass not this holy season,
  My flesh and bones and joints do pray;

And even my verse, when by the rhyme and reason
    The word is *stay*, says ever, *come*.
        Oh show Thyself to me,
        Or take me up to Thee!

Herbert's hymn found an echo from the parish of another country parson. John Mason may have heard the voice from Bemerton in his rectory at Water-Stratford. At all events he breathed the spirit of Herbert; his manner is somewhat akin, and his diction marks his brotherhood. Like his predecessor in quaint but hallowed song, the secret of Mason's sweetness and power in divine melody was found in his private devotion. Six times a day he went aside to wrestle with his Lord in prayer; and his character and life exemplified the saying, "When thou prayest, enter into thy closet, and when thou hast shut thy door, pray to thy Father which is in secret; and thy Father which seeth in secret shall reward thee openly." The reward came on Mason in his strength to labour, and his grace to sing; in the fruit of his happy toil among his parishioners, and in the joys which his songs of praise called up around him while he lived, and perpetuated in the heart of successive generations with whom, though dead, he yet sings. His voice is still in our ears in his "Song of Praise for the Hope of Glory:"—

>   I sojourn in a vale of tears,
>   Alas, how can I sing?
>   My harp doth on the willows hang,
>   Distuned in every string.
>   My music is a captive's chains,
>   Harsh sounds my ears do fill;
>   How shall I sing sweet Sion's song
>   On this side Sion's hill?
>
>   Yet lo! I hear a joyful sound,
>   Surely I quickly come;
>   Each word much sweetness doth distil,
>   Like a full honey-comb.
>   And dost Thou come, my dearest Lord?
>   And dost Thou surely come?
>   And dost Thou surely quickly come?
>   Methinks I am at home.
>
>   Come then, my dearest, dearest Lord,
>   My sweetest, surest Friend;
>   Come, for I loathe these Kedar tents,
>   The fiery chariots send.

What have I here? my thoughts and joys
  Are all pack'd up and gone;
My eager soul would follow them
  To Thine eternal throne.

What have I in this barren land?
  My Jesus is not here:
Mine eyes will ne'er be blest, until
  My Jesus doth appear.

My Jesus is gone up to heaven
  To get a place for me;
For 'tis His will that where He is,
  There should His servants be.

Canaan I view from Pisgah's top,
  Of Canaan's grapes I taste;
My Lord, who sends unto me here,
  Will send for me at last.

I have a God that changeth not,
  Why should I be perplext?
My God, that owns me in this world,
  Will own me in the next.

Go fearless, then, my soul, with God
  Into another room;
Thou, who hast walked with Him here,
  Go see thy God at home.

View death with a believing eye,
  It hath an angel's face;
And this kind angel will prefer
  Thee to an angel's place.

The grave is but a fining pot
  Unto believing eyes,
For there the flesh shall lose its dross,
  And like the sun shall rise.

The world, which I have known too well,
  Hath mocked me with its lies;
How gladly could I leave behind
  Its vexing vanities!

My dearest friends they dwell above,
  There will I go to see;
And all my friends in Christ below
  Will soon come after me.

Fear not the trump's earth-rending sound,
  Dread not the day of doom,
For He that is to be thy judge,
  Thy Saviour is become.

Blest be my God that gives me light,
  Who in the dark did grope;
Blest be my God, the God of love,
  Who causeth me to hope.

> Here's the Word's signet, comfort's staff,
>   And here is grace's chain;
> By these Thy pledges, Lord, I know
>   My hopes are not in vain.

There are some modern songs of glory which are in sweet harmony with Herbert's music about "Home," and with the echoes of that music from the soul of the saintly Mason. There are "Parish Musings," which, as the musing hymnist modestly says, claim no merit but this, "that they are practical, not theoretical; not the cold musings of the head of one at ease, but the warm gushings of the heart of one toiling himself, and striving to lead others amid the dust and conflict of the journey of life." Ears that are finely tuned may, even in the passing bell, hear the Master's voice, "Arise, let us go hence;" but the voice, though solemn, is happy, for it calls us towards "Home:"—

> Deep tolls the muffled bell
>   With its voice of woe;
> Bidding solemn, sad farewell
>   To all things below;
>   Home, home!
>   Come home!
>   Thus it seems to say—
>   Where rest
>   Awaits the blest,
>   In eternal day!
>
> Sweet sounds the Sabbath bell,
>   Summoning to prayer,
> Bidding cheerful, glad farewell
>   To all worldly care;
>   Oh! enter in,
>   And from sin,
>   Thus it seems to say—
>   Here rest,
>   Where the blest
>   Come to kneel and pray!
>
> Lord! so true to Thee alone,
>   Tune this discordant soul,
> That with the same soft Sabbath tone
>   Whenever it may toll;
>   That sweet bell
>   Of joy may tell,
>   And ever seem to say—
>   Home, home!
>   Come home!
>   Come to Christ away!

Do we cry, in childlike longing, "When, Lord?" and "How long?" the same sweet psalmist gives the answer, "Soon and for ever!" "Go thou thy way till the end be; for thou shalt rest, and stand in thy lot at the end of the days." Mr. Monsell brings a holy song out of "a dying Christian's last words," thus:—

> "Soon and for ever,"
>   Such promise our trust,
> Tho' ashes to ashes,
>   And dust unto dust:
> "Soon and for ever"
>   Our union shall be
> Made perfect, our glorious
>   Redeemer, in Thee;
> When the sins and the sorrows
>   Of time shall be o'er,
> Its pangs and its partings
>   Remembered no more;
> Where life cannot fail,
>   And where death cannot sever,
> Christians with Christ shall be
>   "Soon and for ever."
>
> "Soon and for ever,"
>   The breaking of day
> Shall drive all the night-clouds
>   Of sorrow away:
> "Soon and for ever,"
>   We'll see as we're seen,
> And learn the deep meaning
>   Of things that have been;
> When fightings without us,
>   And fears from within,
> Shall weary no more
>   In the warfare with sin;
> Where fears, and where tears,
>   And where death shall be never;
> Christians with Christ shall be
>   "Soon and for ever."
>
> "Soon and for ever,"
>   The work shall be done;
> The warfare accomplish'd,
>   The victory won:
> "Soon and for ever,"
>   The soldier lay down
> His sword for a harp,
>   And his cross for a crown.
> Then droop not in sorrow,
>   Despond not in fear;

> A glorious to-morrow
> Is brightening and near;
> When (blessed reward
> Of each faithful endeavour)
> Christians with Christ shall be
> "Soon and for ever."

Mr. Monsell is always sweet and pleasant, though his music has mostly a plaintive tone, even when he sings of heaven. To some spirits this tone is always welcome; to others the future is full of bright, cheerful, and exultant songs. In dispensing "psalms, and hymns, and spiritual songs," the inspiring Spirit deals with us according to our faith.

"I remember," said an old man, the other day, his face brightening with the recollections which he was calling up —"I remember, some years ago, a minister coming into our neighbourhood to preach. He was a good man, and a good preacher; but I can mind his singing much better than his sermons. He used to preach not far from where I lived; and when I saw the people flocking to the chapel, I used to go to hear the famous singer. Ah, he was a singer! And I believe one great secret of his music was, that his heart was in it. His voice was like an angel's, as they say, though I never heard an angel sing; but I can scarcely think that an angel, or any other singer, could beat that happy-looking preacher. He was a man with a long face, and a high, bald head. And his eyes used to sparkle as he sang, as if the hymns were coming up from his soul; and so they did. There was one hymn I always liked to hear him sing, he would sing it after the sermon; it was one of his own composing, and the tune was his, too. I learnt to sing it myself, and I taught my boy to sing it; and sometimes, long after that singing preacher was gone to his own 'Jerusalem divine,' my boy and I, and three or four more, used to get together of an evening, and sing it in full harmony. Oh, it was so rich; and it seemed to lift one towards heaven while we sang. This was the hymn:"—

> Jerusalem divine,
> When shall I call thee mine?
> And to thy holy hill attain,
> Where weary pilgrims rest,
> And in thy glories blest,
> With God Messiah ever reign?

> The saints and angels join
> In fellowship divine,
> And rapture swells the solemn lay:
> While all with one accord
> Adore their glorious Lord,
> And shout His praise in endless day.
>
> May I but find the grace
> To fill an humble place
> In that inheritance above;
> My tuneful voice I'll raise
> In songs of loudest praise,
> To spread Thy fame, Redeeming Love!
>
> Reign, true Messiah, reign!
> Thy kingdom shall remain
> When stars and sun no more shall shine,
> Mysterious Deity,
> Who ne'er began to be,
> To sound Thy endless praise be mine!

The musical preacher and hymnist left happy impressions upon very many souls, besides the old man who recorded his music. The preacher was Benjamin Rhodes, the son of a schoolmaster at Hexborough, in the West Riding of Yorkshire. He was born in the year 1743, and had the advantage of a pious training by godly parents. Before he was eleven years of age, his father took him to hear Mr. Whitefield; he was melted into tears, and received religious impressions which, though dimmed occasionally during his youthful course, finally led him to Christian decision and eminent devotedness to Christ. When about nineteen, his religious enjoyments were great. "In this happy season," he tells us, "my joy frequently prevented my sleep, while my soul was taken up with Him who is altogether lovely; and in ecstasies of joy, in the stillness of the night, I often sang my great Deliverer's praise." Thus his native musical powers, and his talent as a hymnist, were hallowed by religious delight. In the year 1766, he was employed by Mr. Wesley as an itinerant preacher, and was faithful and happy in that calling for about half a century. His end answered to the simplicity of his character and the integrity of his life; it was peace. He is now honoured as the author of that one hymn, the latter part of which the old man used to sing with such pleasure. Mr. Rhodes was not a rival of Charles Wesley, but his "Jerusalem divine" may be a companion hymn for Wesley's songs of glory, the songs which, probably, come nearest to the apostolic standard of Christian hope. One of them melted the judge and the entire court in Exeter Castle, about twelve or thirteen years ago. A good young woman had been set upon by a villain, on her way from the Sunday school, and was left for dead by the roadside. On being discovered, she was restored to consciousness so far as to identify the perpetrator of the crime; and then she died, singing one of Charles Wesley's triumphant anthems of hope:—

> How happy every child of grace,
>   Who knows his sins forgiven!
> This earth, he cries, is not my place,
>   I seek my place in heaven;
> A country far from mortal sight;—
>   Yet, oh! by faith I see
> The land of rest, the saints' delight,
>   The heaven prepared for me.
>
> A stranger in the world below,
>   I calmly sojourn here;
> Nor can its happiness or woe
>   Provoke my hope or fear:
> Its evils in a moment end,
>   Its joys as soon are past;
> But, oh! the bliss to which I tend
>   Eternally shall last.
>
> To that Jerusalem above
>   With singing I repair;
> While in the flesh my hope and love,
>   My heart and soul are there;
> There my exalted Saviour stands,
>   My merciful High Priest,
> And still extends His wounded hands
>   To take me to His breast.
>
> What is there here to court my stay,
>   Or hold me back from home,
> While angels beckon me away,
>   And Jesus bids me come?
> Shall I regret my parted friends
>   Still in the vale confined?
> Nay, but whene'er my soul ascends,
>   They will not stay behind.

> The race we all are running now;
>   And if I first attain,
> They too their willing head shall bow,
>   They too the prize shall gain.
> Now on the brink of death we stand;
>   And if I pass before,
> They all shall soon escape to land,
>   And hail me on the shore.
>
> Then let me suddenly remove,
>   That hidden life to share;
> I shall not lose my friends above,
>   But more enjoy them there.
> There we in Jesu's praise shall join,
>   His boundless love proclaim,
> And solemnize in songs divine
>   The marriage of the Lamb.
>
> Oh, what a blessed hope is ours!
>   While here on earth we stay,
> We more than taste the heavenly powers,
>   And antedate that day:
> We feel the resurrection near,
>   Our life in Christ conceal'd,
> And with His glorious presence here
>   Our earthen vessels fill'd.
>
> Oh, would He more of heaven bestow,
>   And let the vessel break,
> And let our ransom'd spirits go
>   To grasp the God we seek:
> In rapt'rous awe on Him to gaze
>   Who bought the sight for me;
> And shout, and wonder at His grace,
>   Through all eternity!

The counsel for the prosecution at the murderer's trial, in his appeal to the jury, described the death-scene, and rehearsed the hymn, a part of which the dying girl sang on her upward flight. The judge, the jury, all but the prisoner, wept. Who could help it? To hear, in that solemn court, the youthful martyr's song of glory! and such a song! Many hearts there on that day were ready to repeat the last song of the young murdered Christian:—

> Oh, would He more of heaven bestow,
>   And let the vessel break,
> And let our ransom'd spirits go
>   To grasp the God we seek!

THE END.

INDEX TO THE HYMNS.

		PAGE
A SURE stronghold our God is He	Luther	11
All praise to Thee, my God, this night	Ken	53
A hymn of glory let us sing	Bede	79
Away with our sorrow and fear	C. Wesley	155
Almighty Father! the rolling year is full of Thee	Thompson	178
All thanks be to God	C. Wesley	215
All praise to the Lord	C. Wesley	234
Awake, my soul, and with the sun	Ken	244
Among those points of neighbourhood	Wither	283
Abide with me! Fast falls the eventide	Henry F. Lyte	295
BEFORE Thy heavenly Word revealed	Mrs. Julius Collins	18
Bright the vision that delighted	Mant	31
Babe, the gift of God's sweet mercy	Ephrem Syrus	59
By cool Siloam's shady rill	Heber	62
Before the need-fare	Bede	78
Before Jehovah's awful throne	Watts	158
Blest day of God, most calm, most bright	Mason	204
Blest day by God in mercy given	Mant	208
Brightly shines the morning star	Translation by Mant	243
Brother, thou art gone before us	Milman	325
Blessing, honour, thanks and praise	C. Wesley	328
Behold the glories of the Lamb	Watts	352
CHRIST, Thou the champion of that war-worn host	Lowenstern	11
Christ, my God, I come to praise Thee	Gregory of Nazianzen	51
Christ, our day, our brightest light	St. Augustine's time	54

INDEX TO THE HYMNS.

		PAGE
Come, Holy Ghost, our souls inspire	Gregory I.	71
Can I my fate no more withstand	Queen Maria of Hungary	104
Come, then, Thou great Deliverer, come	C. Wesley	151
Come let us join our friends above	C. Wesley	155, 331
Come ye that love the Lord	Watts	157
Come, oh come! in pious lays	Wither	172
Come, Thou all victorious Lord	C. Wesley	214
Come, Divine Immanuel, come	C. Wesley	218
Come, O Thou traveller unknown	C. Wesley	222
Come, Thou fount of every blessing	Robinson	225
Come, let us anew our journey pursue	C. Wesley	262
Come, let us join our cheerful songs	Watts	270
Come, all ye chosen saints of God	Joseph Hart	308
Come, ye sinners poor and wretched	Joseph Hart	313
Come, immortal King of Glory	T. Olivers	341
Come, Lord, my head doth burn, my heart is sick	Herbert	355
Christ, whose glory fills the sky	C. Wesley	255
Dear is the hallowed morn to me	Allan Cunningham	209
Dark and dim the daylight rose	Monsell	317
Down from the willow bough	Caroline Bowles	320
Deep tolls the muffled bell	Monsell	359
From our midnight sleep uprising	Early Christian	32
Fix, oh fix each crimson wound	St. Bernard	90
Fear not, oh little flock, the foe	Altenburg	103
Father of mercies, in Thy Word	Anne Steele	182
Far from these narrow scenes of night	Anne Steele	351
Gentle Jesus, meek and mild	C. Wesley	68
God save our gracious Queen	Dr. John Bull	113
Glory, and honour, and praise	Theodulf of Orleans	117
Great God, here at ease	Madame Guion	123
God is a name my soul adores	Watts	165
God of my days, God of my nights	Susanna Harrison	269
God of my life, to Thee	C. Wesley	287
Give glory to Jesus our Head	C. Wesley	327
Here from afar the finished height	C. Wesley	46
Hear us now, O King eternal	Gregory of Nazianzen	49

INDEX TO THE HYMNS.

		PAGE
Holy art Thou, holy....*From the Saxon in the "Codex Exoniensis"*		75
Hence in Thy truth Thy Church delights..	*Mant*	83
High the angel choirs are raising	*Thomas à Kempis*	98
Holy Spirit, come, we pray	*King Robert of France*	101
Has David Christ to come foreshow'd	*Samuel Wesley, Jun.*	133
Hail to the Lord's Anointed	*James Montgomery*	138
He dies, the Friend of sinners dies	*Watts*	158
How happy is the pilgrim's lot	*John Wesley*	160
High in the heavens, eternal God	*Watts*	165
How shall the young secure their hearts	*Watts*	193
Hail, thou bright and sacred morn	*Mrs. Lyte*	196
Hearken to the solemn voice	*C. Wesley*	260
How sweet and awful is the place	*Watts*	270
Hence, ye profane, far off remove	*C. Wesley*	275
Happy soul, thy days are ended	*C. Wesley*	326
How vain are all things here below	*Watts*	353
How happy every child of grace	*C. Wesley*	363
I LOVE (and have some cause to love) the earth	*Quarles*	84
I, whom of late	*Wither*	128
If thy verse do bravely tower	*Wither*	129
Inspirer of the ancient seers	*C. Wesley*	186
In age and feebleness extreme	*C. Wesley*	224
I hear the tempest's awful sound	*Newton*	236
If Paul in Cæsar's court must stand	*Newton*	239
I thank my Lord for kindly rest	*Berridge*	249
Interval of grateful shade	*Doddridge*	264
Is it not strange, the darkest hour	*Keble*	307
In evil long I took delight	*Newton*	314
In the midst of life we are in death	*Notker*	322
In the midst of life, behold	*Luther*	323
I sojourn in a vale of tears	*Mason*	357
JUST as I am, without one plea	*Charlotte Elliott*	39
Jesus, my Lord, in Thy dear name unite	*Anne Steele*	42
Jesus, the only thought of Thee	*St. Bernard*	86
Jesus, my Redeemer, lives *Louisa Henrietta, Electress of Brandenburgh*		105
Jesus, lover of my soul	*C. Wesley*	152
Jesus, cast a look on me	*Berridge*	159

		PAGE
Jesu! bless our slender boat.............	*Wordsworth*.....	229
Jesus, by whose grace I live.............	*Toplady*	246
Jesus, the all-restoring Word	*C. Wesley*........	256
Join, all ye ransomed sons of grace	*C. Wesley*........	259
Jerusalem divine........................	*B. Rhodes*........	361
Jerusalem the golden	*Bernard of Morlaix*	95
Jerusalem, my happy home..............	*Francis Baker*....	118
LORD, Thou art God	*First Christians* ..	16
Long-suffering Jesus, precious Jesus	*Early Christian* ..	34
Lead, Holy One, lead...................	*Clement of Alexandria*	47
Lamb of God, I look to Thee	*C. Wesley*........	69
Let me true communion know............	*St. Bernard*......	93
Leave all to God	*Anthony Ulric, Duke of Brunswick*	107
Lord, Thy best blessings shed............	*Henry F. Lyte*....	115
Let earth and heaven agree..............	*C. Wesley*........	151
Lord, when my raptured thought surveys..	*Anne Steele*......	174
Lamp of our feet, whereby we trace......	*Bernard Barton* ..	191
Listed into the cause of sin	*C. Wesley*........	220
Launch thy bark, mariner	*Caroline Bowles* ..	230
Lord, whom winds and seas obey	*C. Wesley*........	234
Lord, in Thy name and in Thy fear	*Wither*..........	278
Lord, on this day Thou didst bestow......	*Wither*..........	286
Lo, the day of wrath, the day	*Thomas of Celano*	336
MY fatherland alone to me remains........	*Gregory of Nazianzen*	50
Maker of all, the Lord	*Ambrose of Milan*	54
My dearest Protector, see how they detain..	*Madame Guion* ..	125
My Shepherd will supply my need........	*Watts*	140
My Lord, my love was crucified	*Mason*	206
My God, now I from sleep awake	*Ken*	267
My spirit on Thy care	*Henry F. Lyte*....	295
My God and Father, while I stray	*Charlotte Elliott*..	302
Now it belongs not to my care	*Richard Baxter* ..	299
O KING of glory.......................	*Bede*............	78
O Thou, the first, the greatest friend	*Burns*	145
O Love Divine, how sweet thou art	*C. Wesley*........	154
Oh, what a gloomy, cheerless scene	*Monsell*..........	168
Oh book! infinite sweetness! let my heart	*Herbert*	192
Oh day most calm, most bright	*Herbert*	200

INDEX TO THE HYMNS.

		PAGE
On this first day, when heaven and earth *From Latin hymn, by Mant*		207
O Thou who didst prepare	*C. Wesley*	232
O Thou jealous God! come down	*C. Wesley*	263
Our Jesus freely did appear	*Berridge*	285
O Lord, my best desire fulfil	*Cowper*	300
Oh! what a sad and doleful night	*Joseph Hart*	311
PRAISED be Thy name for ever, O our King	*Synagogue Service*	17
Praise to God, immortal praise	*Letitia Barbauld*	177
Precious Bible! what a treasure	*Newton*	189
Peace! doubting heart; my God's I am!	*C. Wesley*	303
ROCK of Ages, cleft for me	*Toplady*	35
Redeemer of the nations, come	*Ephrem Syrus*	61
Raise the conquering martyr's song	*Bede*	80
Rejoice for a brother deceased	*C. Wesley*	331
SING unto the Lord!	*Ancient Israel*	2
Sweet hymns I attune	*Synagogue Hymn of Glory*	17
Sleep well, my dear; sleep safe and free	*Luther*	63
Sweet baby, sleep; what ails my dear?	*Wither*	64
See how great a flame aspires	*C. Wesley*	212
Since Thou hast added now, O God!	*Wither*	252
Since they in singing take delight	*Wither*	281
Sons of God by bless'd adoption	*Joseph Hart*	325
Sing from the chamber to the grave	*R. S. Hawker*	334
Stand th' omnipotent decree!	*C. Wesley*	340
Saviour, when in dust to Thee	*Robert Grant*	319
Soon and for ever	*Monsell*	360
THE God of Abraham praise	*T. Olivers*	24
The godly grief, the pleasing smart	*C. Wesley*	34
Thou lovely Source of true delight	*Anne Steele*	40
'Tis gone, that bright and orbed blaze	*Keble*	55
To Thee, O God, be praises	*Ephrem Syrus*	58
They say 'tis a sin to sorrow	*R. S. Hawker*	59
'Twas silence in Thy temple, Lord	*Keble*	72
This is joy, this is true pleasure	*Elizabeth, Queen of Bohemia*	110
The spacious firmament on high	*Addison*	137
Thee, O Lord, the good, the just	*C. Wesley*	142
The busy tribes of flesh and blood	*Watts*	146

		PAGE
The Lord is our refuge, the Lord is our guide	*Henry F. Lyte*	147
The royal ensigns onward go	*Venantius Fortunatus*	76
The great day of wrath is coming	*Early Judgment Hymn*	82
The world is old and sinful	*Bernard of Morlaix*	94
Thou art, O God, the life and light	*T. Moore*	167
There is a book who runs may read	*Keble*	171
The table of my heart prepare	*C. Wesley*	184
The Spirit breathes upon the word.......	*Cowper*	187
Thousands, O Lord of Hosts, to-day.....	*Heber*	199
Thou God of glorious majesty...........	*C. Wesley*	217
Through Jesu's watchful care	*Berridge*	247
To Jesus, my dear Lord, I owe	*Berridge*	251
Thou Shepherd of Israel and mine	*C. Wesley*	276
Thou God of truth and love	*C. Wesley*	277
To grace, O Lord, a marriage feast	*Wither*	280
The voice that breathed o'er Eden	*Keble*	288
There is a fountain fill'd with blood	*Cowper*	316
Thou Judge of quick and dead	*C. Wesley*	347
The chariot, the chariot! its wheels roll on fire.................................	*Milman*	348
The bird let loose in Eastern skies	*T. Moore*	349
This world is all a fleeting show..........	*T. Moore*	350
Thou know'st in the spirit of prayer.....	*C. Wesley*	350
There is a land of pure delight	*Watts*	354
We sat down and wept by the waters.....	*Byron*	20
When Israel of the Lord beloved	*Walter Scott*	23
We adore Thy pure image	*Early Christian* ..	33
Why should our garments, made to hide ..	*Watts*	66
When Jesus left His Father's throne.....	*James Montgomery*	70
When my dying hour must be...........	*St. Bernard*......	90
When ransom'd Israel came	*Samuel Wesley, Sen.*	134
What though the spicy breezes	*Heber*	198
Who are these that come from far	*C. Wesley*	212
Where the remote Bermudas ride	*Andrew Marvel* ..	228
Why those fears? behold, 'tis Jesus	*Kelly*	240
When through the torn sail..............	*Heber*	242
What secret hand at morning light	*Heber*	253
We will not close our wakeful eyes	*C. Wesley*	261
When I survey life's varied scene	*Anne Steele*	301
Yet think not, O my soul, to keep	*Henry F. Lyte*	291

GENERAL INDEX.

---o---

	PAGE
ANCIENT Israel's hymn	2
Africa's first love, and songs	10
Anonymous hymns in the early church	32
Augustine's recollections of early hymnology	60
Above the clouds, in the west of England	164
A noble and gifted widow	103
Addison's thoughts about Psalm cxiv.: his boyhood	135
Anne Steele's home in Hampshire	173
Albert the good: his last hymn	12
A happy pilgrim, hymning on his way	196
Allan Cunningham's songs and hymns	209
A poet's visit to Portland, and its results	213
Andrew Marvel: his character, satires, and hymns	227
A prodigal rescued in a storm	235
A Christian bishop on shipboard	241
Awful scene in a transport ship	240
Amusing story of a clerical hymnist	248
Antidote for daily dangers	252
An old Christian's account of his morning music	255
A calm and holy sunset to life	297
A great Puritan: his versatile powers	299
Apostolic style of singing under trial	303
Abney Park, Watts's last retreat	355
Assize Court in tears	364
Approach of the Bridegroom felt by the Church	335
BAXTER and his psalm-singing flock at Kidderminster	8
Byron, Scott, and Olivers, a trio	20
Byron at Falmouth, and the lesson he received	21

GENERAL INDEX.

	PAGE
Burgundy and its saintly hymnists	88
Bernard of Morlaix in his monastic home	93
Brunswick family and its hymnists	106
Brixham, an interesting scene in its parish church	113
Burns in his better time as a psalm-writer	144
Berridge's hymn on Psalm cxxxi. 2, spoiled	158
Broughton, and its pastor	176
Boat scene and bridal party at Hull in the olden time	227
Bishop Burnet's good advice to a graceless pastor	176
Barbauld, Anna Letitia: her character and pursuits	176
Beautiful and impressive passage in Wesley's experience	184
Bernard Barton: his character and poems	190
Bright and cheerful piety in a hymnist	247
Berridge's racy letters and essays	250
Beautiful finish to a suffering life	271
Baxter, and his complex times	297
Bunhill Fields, and a funeral oration in 1768	324
Bemerton, and Herbert's rich bequest	355
Benjamin Rhodes, preacher and hymnist	362
CHRISTIANITY cheerful in its nature	3
Cornish psalmody and religious life	9
Cobden's last hours	12
Collins, Mrs. Julius: her translations	18
Clement of Alexandria, and Wesley	46
Challenge for a new style of hymn	352
Cornish mother's lament	59
Chanting hymns of praise on a hill-side	172
Cowper and Newton, unlike and yet one	187
Charles Wesley's eye for beauties by the way	211
Charles Lamb's warning to Bernard Barton	190
Cornwall: one of its pits as seen by a Romish tourist	215
Cornish rhyme in honour of Charles Wesley	215
Christian genius in its last moments on earth	224
Caroline Bowles as Mrs. Southey at Keswick	230
Circumstances in their influence on a poet	245
Call from a waggish-looking parson, and its results	248
Chain of conversions	266
Classic divinity of England: its centre the Bible	180
Contentment in marriage	280
Clouds upon the mercy-seat	290
Cromwell and Richard Baxter face to face	298

GENERAL INDEX.

	PAGE
Cowper's sufferings and songs	300
Christian tenderness learnt on Calvary	319
Carnbræ, and its surrounding scenery	330
Cornish death-song	334
Christian sympathy with the beauties and harmonies of nature	170

DEVONIAN scenes,. poetic pilgrims	133
Danvers, Jane: her love for Herbert	202
Doddridge in tears, yet happy	263
Dreams suggestive of hymns	338
Dean Milman, family, and course	348
Disappointment of Watts, and its happy issue	353

EGYPT, her scenes and songsters	44
Evening songs, their succession in the Church	50
Elizabeth Singer's response to her poetic suitor	353
England's second birth-time	82
England's renovation in the seventeenth century	83
Easter reflections and feelings	307

FIRST Latin missionaries to England	74
F. B. P. in the Tower, and his long hymn	118
Foolish Dick, the happy pilgrim	161
Fragments of time well filled	266
Funeral hymns excelling in grandeur and power	329
Frequent prayer the secret of Mason's sweetness and grace	357

GERMANS, and their love of psalmody	10
Gregory of Nazianzen: scenes of his life and times	48
George Wither's portrait	65
Gregory the Great: his character and works	73
Germ of the "Dies Iræ"	82
Gustavus Adolphus: his character and victories	102
Guion, Madame: her conversion, trials, songs, and death	121
Grave-side anthems	322

HYMNIC style of early language	1
Hymns in their influence on the spiritual life of the Church	2
Hymns favourites with children	4
Hallelujah victories	7
Hugh Capet of France, and his son Robert	100

GENERAL INDEX.

	PAGE
Hymn-menders instructed and reproved	150
Hymn-books for all classes	150
Holy Scripture in its influence on great writers	183
Herbert: his person, short and full career	192
Henchman's plaintive record of Herbert's life	192
Heber: his last charge	198
Heaven in a little chamber of sickness	200
Hymn-composing in the saddle: its dangers and fruits	211
Hymnists gathering songs from the deep	231
Hebrew talk about the secrets of truth	274
Hymns for everybody, by George Wither	278
House-warming in old times	283
Hart the hymnist: his experience and ministry	309
Henry H. Milman in his decline	325
Heaven seen from the sick chamber	351
"Home," a summons from the muffled bell	359
ITINERANT life, and its adventures	338
Irish hymn-menders	153
"In the midst of life we are in death"	323
JAMES MONTGOMERY on the childhood of Jesus	70
John Bull the author of the National Anthem	113
John Wesley as a hymnist	159
Jewish consolation on a sick-bed	274
Joseph Hart's funeral	324
KEN: his trials and character	51
Keble, in harmony with the music of former ages	55
Kingly students and hymn-writers	100
Keble's beautiful interweaving of nature and grace	170
Kennicott's thirty years' labour on his Hebrew Bible: his gifted "help-meet," and how she helped him	181
Kelly and Lord Plunket, old school-fellow	241
Ken's recollections of Winchester	244
King Arthur's castle in North Cornwall	257
LASTING influence of hymns learnt in childhood	4
Lullabies, and their authors	63
Lichfield, private chat and public services	71
Lichfield, and its Cathedral Close	136

	PAGE
Louisa Henrietta of Brandenburgh, and her hushing song	105
Lady Aletta, St. Bernard's mother	89
Land's End: its grandeurs................................	217
Leighton's time for deepest thought	257
Loneliness on New Year's Eve	262
Lady Huntingdon and Dr. Doddridge	263
Lyte, Henry F.: his birthplace and beautiful career	293
Lyte: his preaching and hymns	113
Laymen's hallowed genius	318
Last words suggestive to consecrated genius	328
Last Sunday of a parson	203
Last words of a departing Christian	360
Last moments of a murdered Sunday-school teacher..........	363

MELANCHOLY Christians...................................	3
Mesopotamia: its psalmists and psalmody	57
Monkish monarchs and martial rulers......................	102
Maria of Hungary, and her hymn in bereavement	103
Marriages of princes by lot	108
Meditation about departed worthies	136
Montgomery's fine version of Psalm lxxii.	138
Mysteries in the history of old books	141
Moore's Irish Melodies, and his Wiltshire cottage............	167
Monsell, and his "Parish Musings"	169
Milton and John Bunyan, their obligation to the Bible........	183
Mason's character, by Richard Baxter	203
Mason and Herbert alike in piety and genius	206
Mant, as a translator of Latin hymns......................	207
Mant, ignorant of those about whom he lectured	208
Morning hymn in Mant's school days	243
Methodist clergyman of early times.......................	249
Missionary sorrows in the Island of Zante	261
Methodist preacher and Polish Jew in happy companionship ..	273
Medical skill in Baxter's times	298
Mystery and joy of the cross	306
Monsell, and his sanctified muse	318
Monica and St. Ambrose	61

NATIONAL character swayed by popular songs	6
National anthems and their power	7
Nature and grace in harmony.............................	168

GENERAL INDEX.

	PAGE
Newton's illustration of variety in Christian character and calling	188
Newton's eventful life	231
Night scenes in the Ionian Sea	261
Northampton, monthly devotion in its old meeting-house	264
Nuptial joys interwoven with praise and prayer	288
Notker, and his immortal hymn	323
OLD age melted and hallowed by renewal of early impressions	5
Our English Bible, and what is in it	181
"Old Everton" on a "Christian wedding"	285
Olivers the hymnist and companion of Wesley	345
Old hymnists out of taste	352
Old man's story about a tuneful preacher	361
PASTORAL recollections of first hymn lessons	5
Primitive Christian psalmody in relation to that of the Synagogue	16
Poetic gifts hallowed for the good of the Church	19
Pomeroy, Dr.: his interesting story about Armenian psalmody	35
Palm-Sunday at Mentz in the time of Louis Debonnaire	116
Psalm from a prison window	116
Patmos, and its songs	117
Psalms "done into metre"	132
Prolific hymnists and fast poets	140
Peace and joy in affliction	197
Piety associated with some false notions	204
Portland, and its people	213
Praise as the first act in the morning	254
Poverty, piety, and genius in a girl	269
Praise for the fountain opened, from a sufferer	315
Parish musings on Good Friday	316
Piety and taste in Cornwall	329
"QUEEN of Hearts:" her parentage, life, character, and hymn	108
ROBERT HALL, an incident in his history	31
Robinson of Cambridge: an adventure in a stage coach	225
Robert Hall's opinion of Robinson	226
Romantic adventures of a hymnist	235
"Rock of Ages:" its birthplace	246

	PAGE
Romantic scene in pilgrim life	258
"Rise and progress of Religion in the Soul"	266
Requiem by the bed-side of a departing saint	327
Redruth Churchyard, and its burial hymns	330
Remarkable traveller in 1753	338

Song of a persecuted girl in Cornwall	10
St. Paul's view of spiritual song	14
Synagogue hymns	17
Scott, Walter: his faithfulness to Byron	22
Scotch mothers, and the happy fruit of their psalmody	120
Saxon slaves in the Roman market	74
St. George and the Dragon	75
Saxon hymnology	75
St. Bernard's birthplace, parentage, character, and happy death	88
Sea Captain's death song	152
Scene from the top of an old tower	164
Songs above the storm	165
Songs from old Ireland	168
Scotland the birthplace of genius	178
Shaftesbury's "Characteristics:" their mischievous influence	189
Spmpathy of the soul with the outer world	195
Stories of other days, by an old Cornishman	219
Sabbath peace on the waters	233
Secret of happy and useful preaching	247
Suffering mingled with songs in the night	267
Solomon's Song: its claims and design	272
Sweets extracted from birthdays	287
Songs of suffering women	301
Susanna Wesley's last charge	327
Southampton psalmody in early times	352
Scene in Exeter Castle during the Assizes	363
Song of a murdered young Christian	364

Toplady and Olivers as controversialists and hymnists	27
"*Ter Sanctus*," "*Gloria in excelsis*," and the "*Te Deum*"	30
Toplady's parish: his life and character	36
"Theodosia:" her thoughts and hymns	43
Theodulph of Orleans	117
Tiverton Grammar School and its old master	133
"The spirit of the Psalms," by H. F. Lyte	146

	PAGE
Thomas à Kempis: his cloister life, his "Imitation of Christ," and his hymns	97
Thompson's character: his grand closing hymn	178
Talk in a sea-side cottage	197
Tintagel ruins by the sea	258
Tinkling employment for a merry old man	284
Tales in verse	291
The decrees, and where to find them: a queer story	295
The young miner singing his own requiem	333
Triumphant song with the last breath	333
Thomas of Celano's judgment hymn	336
Thomas Moore's better moments and upward looks	349
"*Veni Creator Spiritus:*" its author	73
Venantius Fortunatus: his character and friends	76
Venerable Bede at Wearmouth: his last hours, etc.	77
WINCHESTER School	52
Watts and Wesley: their comparative merits in children's hymns	67
Wither, George: his sympathy with prisoners	127
Wesley, Samuel, sen.: his version of psalms	134
Wesley, Charles, as a psalmist	141
Wesley's dictionary and the preface to his hymn-book	148
Wesley as a hymn-mender	156
Women's voices in songs of creation	173
Walton's beautiful sketch of Herbert's conjugal life	202
"Wrestling Jacob," by C. Wesley, remarkably illustrated	222
Wordsworth at Heidelberg and on the Neckar	229
William of Wykeham and his school	243
Watch-night services among old Methodists	259
Wilson and his "Noctes Ambrosianæ"	291
Women at the cross	319
Walter Scott's last breathings	336
Watts's first essay at hymn writing	353
Women devoted to song	38
YOUTHFUL suffering hushed by Bernard's hymn	95
Yearning for future repose	349

www.ingramcontent.com/pod-product-compliance
Lightning Source LLC
Chambersburg PA
CBHW031414230426
43668CB00007B/307